Transformed

Transformed

*A White Mississippi Pastor's Journey
into Civil Rights and Beyond*

❖   ❖   ❖

William G. McAtee

Foreword by William F. Winter

University Press of Mississippi / Jackson

Willie Morris Books in
Memoir and Biography

www.upress.state.ms.us

The University Press of Mississippi is a member of
the Association of American University Presses.

Access to back issues of the *Columbian-Progress*
courtesy of the Chancery Clerk's Office,
Marion County Court House, Columbia, MS.

Access to Mayor McLean's "Race Relations" file courtesy of
Marion County Historical Society Museum and Archives.

Access to Mississippi State Sovereignty
Commission collection courtesy of Mississippi
Department of Archives and History.

First printing 2011

∞

Library of Congress Cataloging-in-Publication Data

McAtee, William G.
Transformed : a white Mississippi pastor's journey into civil rights
and beyond / William G. McAtee ; foreword by William F. Winter.
p. cm. — (Willie Morris books in memoir and biography)
Includes bibliographical references and index.
ISBN 978-1-61703-115-1 (cloth : alk. paper) — ISBN 978-1-61703-116-8
(ebook) 1. McAtee, William G. 2. Civil rights workers—Mississippi—Columbia—Biography. 3. Presbyterian Church (U.S.A.)—
Clergy—Biography. 4. Columbia (Miss.)—Race relations. 5. Columbia (Miss.)—Politics and government—20th century. 6. Civil rights
movements—Mississippi—History—20th century. 7. African Americans—Civil rights—Mississippi—History—20th century. I. Title.
F349.C69M43 2011
323.092—dc22
[B]   2011011685

British Library Cataloging-in-Publication Data available

To
Amos Payton, Isaac Pittman, L. Z. Blankinship, N. A. Dickson,
Curtis Styles, W. J. McClenton, Ira Grupper,
and Earl D. "Buddy" McLean

*"Determined, ordinary individuals . . .
deemed what transpired far from obscure
and for the most part, life changing."*

Contents

Foreword

This is a chronicle that revives powerful memories for me, as it will for many of my fellow southerners who read it. I shared many experiences similar to those that Bill McAtee recounts in this memoir of his life in Mississippi as a Presbyterian minister in the 1960s. That is when our paths first crossed.

As a Presbyterian layman I was aware of his work in the church, but as a state public official at the time I also knew of his courageous leadership in the communities where he lived and served during that tumultuous period. No one is better equipped to write this volume than he is. As a fourth generation Mississippian, he had the credentials and the credibility to play a significant role in helping to tamp down the raw passions and mindless racial prejudice that threatened for a critical time to throw a whole state into chaos.

He came to this position well prepared. The Mississippi-born son of a Presbyterian minister, he understood from his own boyhood the complicated racial mores that marked the history of the Deep South, and he also was aware of how the issue of racial segregation dominated opinion in the market place, in education, in politics, and even (or maybe especially) in many churches. This background afforded him a historical perspective on the complex events that marked the transformation of a particular community and ultimately an entire region in the three decades after the end of World War II. He had, as a result, remarkable insight into the deep-seated and in some communities almost fanatical opposition with which any change in the pattern of racial segregation was viewed by most of the white South.

He understood how this way of life had developed in the desolate years following the South's defeat in the Civil War. It had been out of that chaotic time that a *de facto* and then a *de jure* system of racial segregation emerged under the mandate of the United States Supreme Court in the *Plessy v. Ferguson* case in 1896. The more than half century of court-sanctioned Jim Crow practices that followed that decision gave legal status to a totally segregated and, in practice, largely unequal society. This inequality was reflected in the denial of African Americans' right to vote and to use public facilities and services, including education and transportation, except on a segregated basis. Most white southerners embraced these arrangements, and it was not until the *Brown* decision of 1954 and subsequent passage by Congress of the Civil Rights Act of 1964 and the Voting Rights Act of 1965 that the reign of Jim Crow was finally ended.

In May 1964, exactly ten years after *Brown*, Bill McAtee, a young and largely untested minister, preached his first sermon in the Presbyterian Church in the small city of Columbia, deep in the Piney Woods of south Mississippi. Normally this would not have been regarded as a life-changing event in his ministerial career, but it occurred at the beginning of what soon came to be known as the "long hot summer of 1964." Only a few days after his arrival in Columbia an event occurred in Neshoba County, approximately one hundred miles to the northeast, which brought the righteous wrath of the nation down on the State of Mississippi. On a steamy Sunday night in June three young civil rights workers, two white and one black, were brutally murdered on a rural road outside the community of Philadelphia after they had attempted to help register black voters. Their battered bodies were found weeks later buried beneath an earthen dam. Already regarded in many circles as a pariah because of its history of racial violence, the state now faced a major crisis as many other student activists from across the country flooded into a number of its communities, including Columbia, to try to bring an end to segregation and to register black citizens to vote.

It was into this seething cauldron that McAtee stepped in the first days of his new ministry. He was already deeply troubled by the resistance of so many of his fellow southerners to any change in the racial status quo. Now he understood that he could not be a passive bystander in the face of the daunting challenges facing his new hometown. There were many southern communities where he would not, as a Presbyterian minister, have been able to take a public stand on behalf of ending segregation. As he was soon to learn, Columbia was not one of those resist-to-the-bitter-end places. It had a solid base of professional, business, and civic leadership and a wise and courageous mayor named Buddy McLean. The mayor, who was a member of McAtee's congregation, was determined that his community not be a scene of violence and reckless defiance of the law. He believed that a fair and even-handed approach had to be maintained as the townspeople worked out their deep-seated differences. While there were numerous provocations, in the form of threats and boycotts, the community largely

avoided the bitter confrontations that were the fate of many other southern towns and cities. In the end, the schools were peacefully integrated,
public facilities were opened to all, and a basic spirit of civility developed
that made Columbia an encouraging example for the state.

What is most valuable about this volume is the lesson that it holds out
for all of us Americans: that only by reaching out to each other in a spirit
of mutual respect and good will can we, in this racially diverse country,
achieve the unity that is essential to our national well being. But this book
is more than a commentary on civil rights and racial reconciliation. It is
also a bold exposition of the less obvious but related struggles that were
going on at that time in some of our religious denominations, including
the Southern Presbyterian Church of which Bill McAtee and I were a part.
The emotional cross currents that swept over every area of our society in
those volatile years challenged those of us who were confronted by these
issues to reexamine what we believed in and stood for.

With the retrospection that the passing years have given us, we now
recognize how ill served we were at that time by a dogmatic and misguided
adherence to social and political delusion and to sectarian rigidity. However, as Bill McAtee so candidly reminds us, we cannot rest comfortably
on the progress toward tolerance, equity and justice we have made. There
are still too many old wrongs to be righted, old wounds to be healed, old
barriers to be removed. These may represent the most difficult challenges
of all. A commitment to the unending work of reconciliation and forgiveness must be the legacy and charge that we hold and pass on to those who
follow us. A book like this helps provide us with the inspiration to move
on down that long, tortuous road toward a final embrace of our common
humanity.

—HON. WILLIAM F. WINTER, Governor of Mississippi, 1980–84

Preface

How I came to write this book is but a continuation of the story I wanted to tell. Back in early November 2008, shortly after this country elected its first African American president, I received a forwarded e-mail that was sent to Second Presbyterian Church, Lexington, Kentucky. It was from Chris Watts, Curator, Marion County Museum and Archives in Columbia, Mississippi.[1] Watts was "researching the town's history during the struggle for civil rights [in the 1960s] which is sketchy at best." He noted he "hit upon the name of William G. McAtee more than once, thinking he might be a civil rights worker in the area at the time." Some of the information he ran across indicated that I was "a religious leader of some type." Watts had no clue as to where I lived or whether I was a black or a white person until he found on Second Church's website a sermon I had preached there.

I responded, and that ignited a flurry of e-mail exchanges in which we established an acquaintance that soon generated evidence of mutual excitement for documenting and preserving a record of that critical time in the history of Columbia and Marion County. One day when Watts was straightening some things out he found a folder entitled "Race Relations," where he kept seeing my name. He said, "It nearly knocked the breath from me. I had NO clue that civil rights workers were as active as they were in Columbia." Later in the course of our conversations, I identified that folder as having been Mayor Earl D. "Buddy" McLean's personal file. His wife had sent it to me after his death but later requested that I send it to the museum.[2]

Watts continued to dig around in the archives and reported that, "[The] more I learned, the more I realized that this project is so much larger than a simple newspaper column. It *deserves* more than just a frivolous newspaper column." He noted that the Historical Society had published "The History of Marion County" in 1976, in which only a few pages indicated that some black schools were constructed and some reference to local black leaders was made. "Not one word was committed to paper that mentioned any of the social progress that came about from the struggles of

xiii

the mid-1960s." He urged me to follow up on my offer to share my memories of that time because, he said, I had "walked the streets of Columbia some forty-three years ago, you knew those men and women, you experienced it" and "time is running short." He promised to volunteer his personal spare time to do research on behalf of the project.

As our conversations continued, I became convinced that capturing this history was very important and that I wanted to write this book for several reasons. The primary reason was that it would give me an opportunity to draw on my memory of the time when leadership segments of the community, both black and white, came together over a relatively short period (1964–66) to face difficult challenges and prevent the community from being destroyed by violence and division, working together to make it a better place. An overwhelming sense of suspicious reluctance and residual fear was the immediate challenge that had to be overcome in those days. Only then could the inhumane and despicable injustice perpetuated by slavery and segregation be repudiated head on.

Through the years, when asked what it was like to be a pastor in Mississippi in the 1960s, I would sometimes respond, with a slightly sarcastic lilt in my voice, "Oh, it was a great time for a fourth generation Mississippian to be at home!"[3] I thought about that comment and realized that it required a more serious critique of my experience than that flip answer implied. How did being a multi-generation Mississippian shape the person I was? How did this background, along with the pursuit of my call to ministry, contribute to what I was becoming through transformation of my own attitudes and behavior regarding race during this brief period of my life? What moral imperatives were driving me to tell my story? Seeking more thoughtful answers to these questions became the second compelling reason for me to write this book as a personal accounting.

Capturing history can take many forms, ranging from formal academic research to informal storytelling. I never claimed to be professionally trained as a historian. If I have to have a label, I would simply say I am an "informal historian." My view of history is shaped by the fact that I do not want to live in the past but cannot separate myself from it. I fully understand who I am or am becoming by placing myself in relation to my family, my church, and my social, political, economic, and geographic contexts. These dynamic relationships and contexts shaped my perspective on life, giving it meaning, and taught me how to relate to others. Relationships, experiences, and reflections are at the heart of "story." Memories and relevant human relationships, cultural qualities long employed by

Mississippi storytellers, give remarkable power to story, in my estimation. Understanding "story as history" is essential to this book. In telling the story I become an informal historian of the front porch rocking chair variety, belonging to the genre of "oral culture," rather than "literate culture" as defined by Tex Sample.[4]

I also view myself as an amateur cultural anthropologist, curious about the world in which he lives, who occasionally records some meaning gleaned from his experiences. My approach to experiencing and observing life attempts to make connections between seemingly random and disparate events or phenomena. The connections are not always coherent or readily explained. Nonetheless there are connections. Serious attention to what has taken place is needed to sort out the relevant from the irrelevant. If there is some relevant meaning worth passing on to others, the story is simply told well, leaving interpretation to the hearer. Selectivity in capturing story as history is essential, for it would not be useful, even impossible, to recount every single event that took place within a day or week or month or year or decade to derive the meaning of that time. Analyzing discriminating slices of what took place in a particular time is often a sufficient means to gain a deeper insight into what was taking place in the larger context. I began to reach such understanding only after years had passed since the events that took place in Columbia during 1964–66.

As a participant in the events portrayed in this narrative, I had access to both primary and secondary information that might not be available to others. Other participants in the same events or outside observers may, based on their memory or perspectives or research, select different facts and events from which to make their own observations and draw conclusions. Their results may be very different and at times contradictory to mine. The line between perception and fact is often not clear. Both have their own form of power in shaping events. I had to treat both perception and fact with great care and clarity when chronicling my memories and what I learned about myself and the world around me, as well as the "So Whats?" for future generations.

❖ ❖ ❖

The setting for the story told in this book, from the perspective of one who was an active participant in these events, was Mississippi at the mid-point of the turbulent and watershed years of the 1960s. The primary discriminating slices on which this story was based took place between March 1,

1964 and October 17, 1966, although secondary events took place before and after that time.

Research for this project took on the excitement of an archeological dig. The prime dig sites for the relevant core of the story were Mayor McLean's "Race Relations" file, the musty "artifacts" in a folder I had kept for years, and images of that time seared into the recesses of my memory and very being. Among the fading letters and newspaper clippings in both files were bits and pieces of handwritten notes, some dated and some not. Some merely listed names, with check marks or stars scribbled beside them requiring speculation as to their meaning. As each shard-like artifact came to light, clues emerged leading to a few active participants who were still alive and who once viewed the same events from different sides of the street. Their different memories and different perceptions added texture to the collective story as the discriminating slices were reconstructed from my perspective.

As I began to write, I had in mind a format that would reflect how I experienced life in varying relationships and contexts. My primary focus was on the relevant core of the story: the mayor's leadership, who I was and became, what it will take to complete the story and convey "learnings" worth passing on. Interspersed among these primary experiences, to give wider cultural context to the core narrative, were vignettes concerning the daily life of family and friends; regional and national power struggles within the Presbyterian Church; exchanges between officials of national governmental agencies and local school officials pertaining to desegregation plans; and current events reported in newspaper articles depicting the violent atmosphere of the times and other whites' responses to the civil rights movement and desegregation.

Seemingly random placement of all these primary experiences and vignettes may contribute to a sense of incoherence in the story as spun and connections between them may not always be readily apparent. But this is precisely how I experienced the events of the story I am telling, which were often random and incoherent and unexplained. I hope the reader will get the flavor of some of my experiences. The challenge in writing the story was to select the most relevant vignettes and describe them as clearly as possible in words communicating my perception of what took place. I tried to do so without robbing the reader's own sense of the story or violating the integrity of the format.

The outline of the book is the framework that gives coherence to the core of the story. To set the stage for this narrative, Part I: Prelude

(Chapters 1–4) begins with my call to Columbia, including the history of the church and my connections with it that authenticated my candidacy; the historical background of Columbia that set the context in which the mayor's story unfolded; who I was growing up and how I saw myself during those days when I did little analysis of my views on race; my preparation for ministry and experiences of a first call pastorate; and the start-up in my second call in Columbia during Freedom Summer of 1964.

Central to the narrative, Part II: Engagement (Chapters 5–10), contains the chronological unfolding of the story surrounding the mayor's election and his leadership of the white power structure and community at large during 1965–66 in complying with the Civil Rights Act of 1964 and the Voting Rights Acts of 1965. The interaction of white moderates with their black cohorts is the primary focus of this part of the narrative, not the civil rights movement *per se* or the attitudes of the most ardent segregationists, though certainly these perspectives are integral to the story.

Analysis of the narrative in Part III: Reflections (Chapters 11–13), affords glimpses of the mayor's wisdom, wisdom that motivated his life and public service. This section of the book also includes a more in-depth exploration of my life's journey, my search for truth and understanding of how my views on race evolved. I discuss how seeing my great grandfather's "properties" listed on a computer screen prompted my exploration of apologies, reparations and impunity. Finally, I consider what learnings are worth passing on to current and future generations, including what it will take for others to complete the story.

The epilogue raises the question of what is required in the twenty-first century to determine the lasting importance of what took place in the mid-1960s regarding race relations. Recounting what happened after 1966 to the principals and other personages who appear in this narrative brings closure to the story.

Church historian Louis B. Weeks once wrote: "Narratives make the most readable histories, and I honestly think they tell the truest tale of the past."[5] So, let the telling begin.

PART I

Prelude

CHAPTER 1

Columbia Comes Calling

The first time I laid eyes on E. D. "Buddy" McLean, Jr., was on March 1, 1964. It was a Sunday afternoon, when he flew up to Amory, Mississippi, with part of the pulpit committee from the Columbia Presbyterian Church to see if I would consider becoming their pastor. I always thought that was a strange name for the committee, because I felt certain they had a pulpit but needed a preacher to fill it! In time it became known as a pastor search committee or pastor nominating committee.

One or two others were with Buddy McLean. I think Tinsley "T-Bone" Thrower might have been with him. "T-Bone" was married to Betty Johnson, and both were friends of Frank Brooks, a seminary classmate of mine who had given the committee my name for consideration. Brooks grew up in Lake, Mississippi, and graduated in 1956 from Mississippi State, where the preaching and example of Robert H. "Bob" Walkup at First Presbyterian Church, Starkville, tutored him. Betty Johnson Thrower's family was members of that congregation. Although I was not actively looking for a new call, I agreed to meet with the Columbia group in part as a courtesy to my friend, who wanted me to join him in South Mississippi Presbytery. Brooks over subsequent decades became one of my closest friends and colleagues.

It was an interesting afternoon, because we met in the Twin Beech airplane belonging to the Walker Stores, which were rapidly turning into Bill's Dollar Stores.[1] Its president was Bill Walker whose sister, Justina (better known as Tina) was Buddy's wife. I had had a few conversations with pulpit committees but none in a setting quite like this. At the time this version of the Beech H-18 had conventional landing gear consisting of two big primary wheels under the wings and a small wheel beneath the tail of the plane. When on the ground, this configuration caused the front of the plane to slant up sharply causing a slightly disorienting sensation for passengers until it got airborne. Later, after an unceremonious, yet safe, belly landing at the Columbia airport when the landing gear did not descend properly, the plane would be fitted with a tricycle undercarriage that allowed it to sit parallel to the ground creating a more comfortable orientation for the passengers.

On one side of the cabin, as I recall, two seats faced each other with a small table between them. Across the aisle were other seats facing forward. Buddy sat at the table with his back to the cockpit and I sat on the other side with my back to the tail of the plane. T-Bone sat across the aisle. This meant that, because of the slant of the plane, I was "looking up to Buddy" during the course of the conversation. Maybe this arrangement was to become a metaphor for our relationship, but at the time it was simply a matter of getting acquainted in an unusual setting—including an initial exploration of mutual interest to see if a "call" to the Columbia Church might be in the offing.

I do not recall the details of the conversation, partly because I was infatuated with the airplane and all it stood for, all so foreign to my experience. But what began as a routine discussion about calling a pastor turned into something we would discover had far-reaching implications, not only for us personally, but for the church and the community we were called to serve. We parted with a handshake and the sense that we all wanted to pursue the conversation at a later date.

That later date came much quicker than I anticipated. Within a few days I received word from Buddy that the committee wanted me to come to Columbia to meet with them. In that era, conventional Presbyterian wisdom suggested, for some unclear reason, that the most favorable length of stay in a pastorate was five years, especially in one's first call. But this rule was not mandatory and not always followed. After a pastor left, congregations would then spend an average of twelve to fifteen months with vacant pulpits while they regrouped and searched for a new pastor and the cycle would begin again. In later years, while assisting pastors and pastor nominating committees in the call process, I developed a program called "Healthy Beginnings" based largely on what I had learned from my own experience that gave new meaning to this five-year cycle.[2]

Although I was about to complete five years in my first call at Amory, consideration of another call was tempered by the fact that I had been granted a three-month sabbatical by the Amory church to go to Louisville Seminary to write the master's thesis I had been working on for a year or so. I had arranged for a summer intern to come from Columbia Seminary in Decatur, Georgia, to cover my pastoral duties at Amory while I was away. At the time of the interview, we were in the midst of preparations for a week of evangelistic services beginning on March 15. That was a big event for any congregation to engineer.

Despite these constraints, I agreed to drive to Columbia to meet with the committee on March 10. Ordinarily, Presbyterian ministers were no longer preaching trial sermons as such when considering a call. But they prevailed on me to conduct the mid-week prayer service, when I presented a sermon entitled "The 20-20 Vision of the Church." Forty-five members of the congregation were in attendance. After the service, I met with the committee for an extended period of time and shared with them my plans for the sabbatical study leave. As a condition for considering a call from the Columbia Church, I asked for a similar arrangement, permitting me to be in Louisville over the summer to write my master's thesis. Again, we parted with a growing understanding that we had a match in the making and the details could be worked out.

I was not the only candidate under consideration. Bill Walker, also a member of the committee, made a trip to Mobile, Alabama, in March during Mardi Gras to interview a prospective minister for the church. While there, a friend of his arranged for Bill to escort Gloria Merry to the King's Luncheon at the Mobile Country Club. Her first reaction was: "Who wants to meet a redneck from Mississippi who owns dime stores?" She said later that she "was surprised to see that he *was* good-looking . . . but *so* old!"[3] The long and short of the story was that the interview with the minister did not pan out, although the trip was not a complete loss. Less than a year later, on February 27, 1965, Bill and Gloria were married at St. Paul's Episcopal Church in Mobile, with the reception at the Mobile Country Club.[4]

In a week or so after my visit in Columbia with the committee, I received a call from Buddy saying they were prepared to recommend to the congregation that I be elected as its pastor and that the terms of call included hiring a seminary intern to cover the period when I was away working on my master's thesis. Dwain Epps, a seminary student at San Francisco Presbyterian Seminary, was available to fill the summer intern position. Epps had worked with Frank Brooks as a lay volunteer in the Westminster Presbyterian Church in Gulfport while stationed at Keesler Field in the Air Force before going to seminary.

After a time of prayer and serious consideration I agreed to have them go forward with their recommendation and would accept the call "if the way be clear." The congregational meeting was called and the vote was overwhelmingly in favor of the recommendation, but there were ten opposing votes. It was not clear exactly what the opposition was about, but Buddy assured me that this was a very supportive vote and I should not be concerned. Later I was led to believe that the reason for the opposing votes might have had to do with "my theology" or possibly my "views on race" or the commingling of the two, a common practice at the time. I never was sure, but the split vote hovered in the background the entire time I was there. I accepted the call and then proceeded to have the Session at Amory announce a congregational meeting for April 12 to ask the Presbytery of St. Andrew to dissolve the pastoral relation there so I could accept the call to Columbia.

This request was granted, and I preached my final sermon, "I'll Remember April," in Amory on April 26, 1964, with this text: "Forgetting what lies behind and straining forward to what lies ahead" (Phil. 3:13b RSV).[5] I could never forget the Amory church, for it was my place of "firsts." I celebrated life with the congregation there as we walked together in the throes of crises—in sorrow, in sickness, in death. We shared in the joys of marriage and birth, of watching children grow and learn. I would always remember them when April came again, for this pastorate was an important landmark in my life, the culmination of a joyous and fruitful ministry where both the congregants and I had grown and matured in our Christian faith. I told them I also celebrated the life that was before them, for their potential was so great. We had come far together in our common ministry. I knew from the beginning that one day "this lovely day w[ould] lengthen into evening," but I was content knowing I was loved "once in April."[6]

The movers from Stringer Moving and Storage Company of Columbia came the following week for us. We loaded our nine-month-old son William Neal in our 1962 Rambler Cross Country station wagon[7] and headed down Highway 45, south to our new home and my second call. Three of the women in the church sent their maids out to help us unpack, but this offer was a bit disconcerting because we were used to taking care of those things ourselves. One of the women in the church that operated the Coca-Cola plant treated us with a case of Cokes to welcome us. We managed to get through the first day and launched into a busy week getting settled.

Somewhere in the midst of all the interruptions and mounds of seeming trivia I kept remembering that Sunday was coming and I had no sermon. But in the back of my mind I kept asking, "What am I here for; what really matters; what really has priority; what is the anchor that will give our life and work here stability?" As I sorted through boxes of books to get my study set up, the first verse of Genesis gave the clue as to what ultimately comes first: "In the Beginning, God . . . ." Before I knew it, I had my first sermon about what comes first.

The first sermon I preached in Columbia on May 3 was "The Priority of God."[8] I raised the questions I had been mulling over and then concluded that sermon by saying, "I am convinced that God is still working his will in this old troubled world, whether we think so or not. God is working through imperfect vessels like you and me." So on this day of firsts, I humbly called upon each member of the congregation to cast aside all priorities established by his or her own standards. "All I ask is that we all rely completely upon the sovereignty of God as the foundation of all our undertakings here. . . . [If] we fail at any point, it will be because we have foolishly turned our backs on the priority of God and have clamored after our own selfish way." At the time, I had no inkling of what form our life together would take or how it would all play out, but I was hopeful. The following Sunday evening, May 10, the commission of South Mississippi Presbytery installed me as pastor of the Columbia Presbyterian Church.[9] My second venture at being pastor and church was officially under way.

The first priority had been proclaimed. Now the second priority was at hand. Building relations and making connections were so critical at the start of any pastorate. I knew I had only six weeks to begin to get to know the congregation before I left for the summer to write my master's thesis. I was determined to visit in as many households as possible in this time. I took the membership rolls and set up a chart of family units in five geographical zones in my ministerial log. Before the six weeks were up, I had visited in forty-four of the eighty-one households spread across the five zones. In the first three months after I returned in the fall, I visited most of those I missed on the first round. Many of those I saw on the first round, I visited a second time.

Those first six weeks were a busy time. In addition to the visitation program there were two services on Sunday, as well as a midweek prayer service, to prepare for. On Sunday evening, May 31, I was invited to preach at the Fifth Sunday union service at Methodist Church. This was the beginning of a very meaningful relationship between the pastor there, N. A. Dickson, and me. My ministerial log shows that I preached on the subject, "When it rains, it Pours," a take-off on a Morton's Salt advertisement of the day.[10] I intoned: "Salt ads flavor to life; it also defends against rottenness and corruption; it is a purifying force in the world," implying we are the salt of the earth. Was this a portent of things to come?

Dwain Epps, our summer intern, arrived during the first week of June and moved into the guest room at the manse with us. He was to spend the summer preaching on Sundays, leading prayer services one evening a week and devoting a considerable amount of time with the young people. His first Sunday in worship was June 7, when he participated in the first communion service I conducted. The next day he left to be a counselor in the Presbytery youth camp.

Before Epps and I came to Columbia, we both made personal commitments to be in the wedding of two of our good friends. Around noon on Friday I went by the presbytery camp and picked Epps up to go to Corinth, Mississippi, for the wedding of Frank Brooks to Jo Anne Biggers on Saturday, June 13. Epps and I, along with several other clergy friends, were in the wedding. We arrived in time for the rehearsal and dinner. After these festivities ended, we discovered we were housed at a motel next to the weight scales on the highway. We were blessed with the lights from the scales facility, which kept our rooms brightly lit, and our sleep was punctured by the penetrating voice from the loudspeaker announcing, "Aw 'ight," indicating to the truckers it was all right for them to move on!

To compound the discomfort, before I turned in I had tangled with one of those legendary Mississippi delights: a meringue. Those wise to such things know what heavy humidity can do: It turns meringues into something akin to crazy glue. The night was very humid when I first chomped down on one of the sweets. With my second bite I discovered to my dismay that one of my fillings had been relocated from a tooth to the meringue. At eight a.m. the day of the wedding I was in a Biggers cousin's dentist chair getting my filling replaced!

So here I was, the head usher with a numb mouth. In addition to overseeing the proper seating of all the guests and seeing that the bridal party processed at the proper time and order, one of my other duties was to roll out the white satin runner down the middle aisle right before Mr. Biggers escorted his daughter to the altar. The person who had arranged the details for the wedding had provided a large runner roll that was positioned at the steps of the chancel. On cue, Epps and I strode down the aisle; each took hold of one side of the roller handle and began to unfurl the runner in a dignified way to the back of the sanctuary. When we got to the vestibule we discovered that the roll had been only half expended, much to the dismay of the bride, who looked on trying to figure out how she was to step over the thing. So I ordered the outside doors opened wide and we proceeded down the front walk until it was all rolled out.

Later, a picture in the wedding album of the front of the church sanctuary made it look like a huge insect with its white tongue grotesquely protruding halfway to the street!

It was a great wedding. Years later Bob Walkup, who was one of the officiating ministers, described the occasion in a letter to Margo Reitz, who had roomed with Jo Anne when Margo was director of Christian education in Starkville with Bob: "It was some wedding with more ministers than some Presbyteries. I do wish you could have been there. Jo Anne was lovely and Frank was badly shaken. It was all Ed Wilson [the other officiating minister] and I could do to brace him up and send him forth."[11]

Epps and I drove well into Saturday night to get back to Columbia. This long automobile road trip, as so often is the case, gave us the opportunity to begin building a deep and long-lasting relationship. It also gave us uninterrupted time to explore the issues of the day. My sermon the next day for Sunday worship on June 14 was titled, "Forbid Them Not."[12] I baptized my first child, who according to my ministerial log "screamed the whole time!" I rounded out my first six weeks in Columbia by preaching on "Pigs and Pearls" at the evening worship service.[13] I do not recall the significance of this title. During the following week, my family and I left Columbia to go to Louisville, Kentucky, for my study leave, about three months short of my thirtieth birthday.

❖ ❖ ❖

Malcolm Gladwell wrote in *Outliers* that if one is to understand what happens in one particular moment in history "you have to go back into the past—and not just one or two generations. You have to go back two or three or four hundred years, to a country on the other side of the ocean, and look closely at what exactly the people in a very specific geographic area of that country did for a living."[14] It is not always possible to go back as far as Gladwell suggests, but going back several generations for a look into the roots of one's community or family heritage can give some clues as to what shapes a community or how one's personal identity is formed.

At the time I accepted the call to Columbia, I had not given much thought to—and neither did I actually know very much about—the life experiences and cultural legacies that were handed down to a new generation of blacks and whites from earlier generations. Such factors created the context for what was taking place in Columbia and Marion County at this particular moment in history. To understand the unprecedented challenges that the community had to confront in the mid-1960s, it was important for me as I began to construct this narrative.

I vaguely remember from the Mississippi history class dating from my school days at Brookhaven that the part of the state where I lived, including Columbia and Marion County, was situated in that vast section of land south of the Ohio River and east of the Mississippi River known as the Southwest Territory. It was organized as an incorporated territory of the United States in 1790. I also had learned that a narrow band of land, extending a hundred miles north of what now is the east-west Louisiana-Mississippi boundary and covering approximately the southern half of the present states of Alabama and Mississippi, was known as the Territory of Mississippi. This band of land was ceded to the United States from Spain in 1795. The Territory of Mississippi was organized on May 7, 1798, as an incorporated territory of the United States.[15]

What was missing from my early education and missing from its history books was any mention that much of the land, aside from the settlements and forts occupied there by migrants from the other U.S. territories, was still claimed by the Choctaw Indians. The Spanish government relinquished its claim to the Choctaw Indian lands in 1798, but land owned by the Choctaws was not finally ceded to the United States until the Treaty of Mount Dexter was ratified on November 16, 1805.[16] Included in the treaty was land in which Columbia and Marion County are now located. Not a word was said about their fate when white settlers occupied these lands. There was no mention of positive contributions made by Native American culture to the emerging culture of Columbia and Marion County introduced by white settlers coming from the east coast.[17]

Other experiences and legacies that helped shape the context of the 1960s in Columbia and Marion County originated in the Great Migration to the Mississippi Territory between 1798 and 1819.[18] In 1790, only 9.3 percent of the white population in the Southwest Territory (Tennessee, Alabama, Mississippi) owned slaves, while 34.3 percent of South Carolinians were slaveholders, and 17.8 percent of citizens U.S. overall were slaveholders. By 1850, 44.6 percent of Mississippi's population, 58.1 percent of South Carolina's, and 10.1 percent of the U.S. population were slaveholders.[19]

The first African slaves in Marion County came along with the first settlers to the Mississippi Territory. The 1816 Marion County census, taken one year before statehood, records that 61 percent of heads of families were slaveholders, with five of these men owning more than twenty slaves. The "peculiar institution" of slavery existed in Marion County until the conclusion of the Civil War, although some accounts suggest that freedom for some may have come earlier, during the war itself.[20]

Also missing from my schooling was anything about the positive cultural contributions and the suffering of the African slaves brought to Marion County as parts of the households of the white settlers. We know a great deal about half of Columbia's history, that of the dominant white population, but very little has been written from the perspective of the slaves or their descendents. What happened to them after the Emancipation Proclamation? What did they and their families bring to the events in this narrative about the civil rights struggle in Columbia during the mid-1960s?

Finding answers to these questions and those raised concerning the cultural contributions of Native Americans was beyond the scope of this account.[21] I sincerely hope this memoir will encourage more people who lived that side of the separate but unequal divide to complement my words with their own stories about their origins and how they experienced these events.

Religion, politics, and commerce also provided experiences and cultural legacies that helped shape the context of the 1960s in Columbia and Marion County. About 1806 or 1807, four Ford brothers migrated from South Carolina to what became the southern part of Marion County. Joseph settled on the east side of the Pearl River near the present Hub community. John, a Methodist minister, settled on the west side of the Pearl River near what is now Sandy Hook. He built a house of Spanish design with a perimeter stockade around it as protection from the hostile Indian tribes still roaming the area, earning it the name of "Ford's Fort." A friendly Indian named Tallapoosa warned the family of possible raids, and neighbors would gather there for safety. In John's family of seven children, all but one became Methodist ministers or married one.[22]

Early settlers migrating from South Carolina to the newly created Mississippi Territory from former Indian land traveled up the Pearl River to a spot accessible for landing, possibly where buffalo trails came down to the water, near the present site of Columbia. Marion County was founded in 1811 and named after a Revolutionary War hero named General Francis Marion, the "Swamp Fox." One Dougan M'Laughlin came to Marion County from a settlement of Scottish highlanders in North Carolina and established his home between Ball's Mill Creek and Hurricane Creek in the southern part of the county. He was a devout Presbyterian and later represented Marion County in the state legislature.[23]

Andrew Jackson was said to have visited Ford House in November 1814 on his way to New Orleans for the final battle of the War of 1812. Ford House became the focal point for both political and religious activities in this part of the Mississippi Territory. In 1816 the Pearl River Convention met there to draw up resolutions that Judge Toulmin carried to the U.S. Congress requesting statehood for the Mississippi Territory. The following year, in 1817, the Constitutional Convention met at Ford House, enacting the documents that led to Mississippi becoming the twentieth sovereign state in the Union on December 10, 1817. Two annual conferences of the Methodist Church convened here: one in 1814 and the other in 1818.[24]

Initially the settlement that became Columbia was known as Lott's Bluff, named after early settlers, John and William Lott, who had migrated from their home in Columbia, South Carolina. The thriving village near fertile lands was incorporated as the state's fourth municipality in 1819, not long after Mississippi achieved statehood. The new state's capitol was located in Columbia between November 1821 and early 1822. At that time the fifth session of the state legislature met in Columbia and inaugurated Governor Walter Leake as the third governor of Mississippi. Other important business transacted included the selection of LeFleur's Bluff, later named Jackson, as the permanent capitol.[25]

Events across the nation at the time that Mississippi became a fledgling state (1817) and Columbia was incorporated (1819) had a profound impact on these locales for decades and cannot be ignored. More in depth study of these events is beyond the scope of this narrative, but the key issues involved are mentioned here in passing to point out the complexity and magnitude of this part of the region's heritage. These events were fraught with a variety of loyalties that tugged the citizenry in divergent and opposing direction, the most prominent being the tension generated over the struggle for power between national and regional interests. National tariffs, growing concentration of unregulated power and influence in the hands of a few individuals and institutions; tension between interests of the centralized government and those of the states; attempts to translate states' rights opinion into the sentiment for nullification; Indian removal; consolidation and restriction of the power of the presidency were the critical issues facing the Union in the first thirty years of the nineteenth century.[26]

Finally, the overarching issue of slavery and its attendant racism, together with the violent intimidation and psychological insult of segregation following the Civil War, engulfed the Union in earnest in the last thirty years of the century and beyond. With the threat of slave rebellions, emancipation or civil rights legislation threatening the purity of the dominant white culture—especially at the lower end of the economic ladder—a recipe for violence was cooked up, producing vigilantes, Ku Klux Klans, White Citizens' Councils, and still later, the Mississippi State Sovereignty Commission.

From earliest days, commerce was key to the growth and prosperity of Columbia and Marion County. The ability to move commercial goods productively in and out of the region in the early years was attributed to the presence of the Pearl River and the proximity of Jackson's military road. The lands of the old Mississippi Territory were covered with a vast area of virgin forest of the finest long leaf yellow pine, some exceeding three feet in diameter. The export needs of the timber industry in the late nineteenth and early twentieth centuries led to the development of the regional railroad system that crisscrossed north to south and east to west through Columbia. These railroads provided ample access to northern and southern markets for rural south Mississippi.

As the virgin forest was depleted, new commercial opportunities were created to fill the economic gap created by the decline of the timber industry. In one such venture, Hugh L. White, in his second term as mayor of Columbia in 1929, developed "a scheme built on the tenets of New South boosterism, business progressivism, and a 'home-grown' rural propensity for 'making-do.' The result was the so-called Columbia Plan, the forerunner of the Balance Agriculture with Industry Program [BAWI]." White persuaded a wide spectrum of local citizens to take out small personal promissory notes to secure funding for construction of a building to house the Reliance Manufacturing Company, which he was trying to attract to the community. The plan worked, and before long the plant hired "more than twice the anticipated number of workers and contributed substantially to the economic revival."[27]

Later, the BAWI plan that succeeded in Columbia received mixed reviews when Governor White instituted the statewide program in his first term as governor. He showed little sympathy for labor. Although the plan provided some relief for the short-term economic crisis in the state, it did "undermine the old plantation paternalism that held so many in economic bondage," even though many blacks failed to benefit from the new jobs. The plan opened the door for women to economic opportunities beyond the farm, making a significant change in the gender equation and rearranging the social order in coming decades. Nonetheless, some observed,

"BAWI assured Mississippi of a more contentious social atmosphere in the decades following the Great Depression."[28]

What Marion County and Columbia became in the mid-twentieth century clearly indicated the degree to which the culture created here early on reflected the dominant Anglo-Saxon-Protestant, rural-agricultural society characteristic of the South. One positive legacy from this culture that helped shape the 1960s was the Mississippi Rural Center at Lampton in Marion County, which was inspired and supported by the Women's Division of Christian Service of the Methodist Church (white), through its Board of Missions. The center, the heart of the Lampton community in Marion County, was dedicated on February 9, 1949, a dream come true for many people, both black and white, who had worked hard to make it a reality. Its purpose was to "enrich the lives of the people in this largest black rural community in Mississippi." From the beginning, its cornerstone of faith was "faith in the potential of the black people whom the Center was originally designed to serve."[29]

The main building of the center consisted of an auditorium that seated twelve hundred people and also served as a gym. It contained clubrooms, a library, a kitchen, and restroom facilities and offices for the director and secretary. Spiritual, social, and educational experiences were provided to "develop desirable attitudes toward home and family life, home ownership, citizenship, health practices, worthy use of leisure time, and gainful employment." The health department was brought in "to conduct public health clinics; County and Home Agents assisted with 4-H clubs and home making activities, and local scout leaders helped with troops for both boys and girls." Year round recreation programs were available for all ages. The Rural Center had a profound effect, improving the welfare and enriching the lives of the largest black rural community in Mississippi in spite of limited resources.[30]

Finally, the experiences of the Presbyterian Church are critical to an understanding of the unprecedented challenges that had to be confronted in the mid-1960s. Since this was my province, I felt it necessary to reflect in detail on these experiences and legacies in three areas: The history of the church and my connections with it that authenticated my call; the relational web of the ecclesiastical culture of Mississippi Presbyterianism; and the shift in the power dynamics within the ecclesiastical structures of the Presbyterian Church in Mississippi, where theology and race were so inextricably entwined.

The origins of the Columbia Presbyterian Church are not clear, though it seems there was more than one organizing date. Some felt that there must have been some kind of Presbyterian church in Marion County during the nineteenth century. The earliest existing record shows a Commission of Meridian Presbytery was appointed to organize a church in Columbia, Mississippi, on April 24, 1910. It was enrolled as a member of Meridian Presbytery at a meeting on May 10, 1910. The boundaries between Meridian and Mississippi Presbyteries were altered on November 20, 1912, to transfer the counties of Marion and Lawrence from Meridian to Mississippi Presbytery. During the interval between 1910 and 1912 the Columbia church became dormant. In 1912 a contingent of Presbyterians migrated from McComb, Mississippi, when a lumber industry came to Columbia.[31] Included in that group was the J. J. White family, whose son Hugh L. White later served two terms as mayor of Columbia and two terms as governor of Mississippi.

In its meeting on April 16, 1913, Mississippi Presbytery received a report that the church in Columbia had been organized and that the services of R. A. Bolling, a theological student from Louisville Seminary, were secured for the summer. Bolling was born in Durant, Mississippi, in Holmes County. Bolling then served as the first pastor of the Columbia Church from 1914 to 1916. The White family contributed significantly to the construction of the original church house erected in 1914–1915 on the southeast corner of Church Street and Oak Avenue, site of the church's present location.[32]

W. H. Hill, chairman of the Home Missions Committee of the presbytery, directed the Columbia work during this time as part of the special mission of the First Presbyterian Church, Brookhaven, where Hill soon became pastor.[33] During the Second World War, when my daddy served the Brookhaven Church, Hill's son Billy was one of my wartime heroes and encouraged me to play the trombone like he did in the Navy band during the war—which we referred to as simply "WW II."

After leaving Columbia, Bolling eventually became pastor of the First Presbyterian Church, Cleveland, Mississippi. On January 20, 1935, he shared in the worship of the neighboring Presbyterian church at Shaw where my daddy was pastor. Daddy also served the Union Church at Benoit. Bolling baptized me that day!

From 1944 to 1964, the Columbia congregation experienced the "five-year filled pulpit" cycle in orderly fashion. This twenty-year period was a vibrant and active time in the church's life, reflecting the growth and energy typified by the early post-World War II years. Marsh M. Calloway,[34] a freewheeling, cigar chomping, Stetson wearing, Cadillac driving Texan was pastor from 1945 to 1950.

While my daddy was pastor at Brookhaven, I went with him to Columbia on the occasion of the installation of Calloway as pastor there in 1945. I remember distinctly having dinner up on Keys Hill at the home of Governor and Mrs. White. I was around eleven years old at the time. The dinner was served in a very formal manner in what I recall as an almost dark candlelit setting. That is about all I remember about the dinner or the installation service.

Calloway later was of the opinion that the dominant role played by the governor in the life of the congregation contributed to its stagnation and lack of growth. As happens in smaller congregations, one strong-willed person can take control of all aspects of its life, be it a matriarch or a man sometimes referred to as the "buck elder." One day Calloway allegedly confronted the governor with words to this effect: "The prayers of this congregation do not get through the cobwebs in the ceiling of the sanctuary because of you!" The governor forthwith moved his membership to the J. J. White Memorial Presbyterian Church in McComb, named in memory of his parents. I recall many a Sunday evening as an adolescent crouching under the dining room table in the manse at Brookhaven looking through the closed French doors to the living room, listening to Calloway pour out his heart over the situation he was facing in Columbia to my father, his colleague in ministry. The details of the conflict were never clear to me, but the deep anguish was certainly evident.

Calloway was a counselor at youth camps sponsored by the Presbytery of Mississippi at Percy Quinn State Park in the latter 1940s and early 1950s. He was also at the synod conferences held at Belhaven College in Jackson. He had a profound effect on the formative years of scores of us young people across the state. Because of those early camp and conference experiences with Calloway, I made friends with young people from Columbia like Dick Wolfe and Carolyn Pope. Carolyn and I developed a significant teenage relationship and exchanged letters during the year between camps. I saw her on occasions when we had district Presbyterian Youth rallies and when our high school football team went to play the Columbia team in the fall.

One other person who would later be part of the Columbia story was Bobby Buchanan. His dad was the pastor of the Presbyterian church in

Magnolia. I knew them both through youth work in the presbytery and through my dad. Mr. Buchanan became seriously ill and died on January 21, 1947. I lost track of Bobby and his sister Louise for a period until I came to Columbia as pastor. Bobby and Louise had come to live with their aunt and uncle, the Syd Armstrongs. Bobby worked at his uncle's store downtown. He later married and after a while started his own business importing artificial flowers.

A building fund was established in March of 1947 in spite of the turmoil Calloway experienced during this time.[35] But it was during the next five-year ministerial cycle begun in 1954 that the dream of a new building began to become a reality. Calloway left Columbia in 1950 to serve the churches of Rosedale, Benoit and Shaw. Virgil L. Bryant, Jr. became the next pastor in 1952. Bryant was born in Lexington, Mississippi, in Holmes County, where his father was pastor. The junior Bryant was a graduate of Southwestern at Memphis and Columbia Presbyterian Seminary. Bryant was in Southwestern with my sister. He was instrumental in initiating the first phase of the building program. The Educational Building opened for use on February 20, 1955. Two years later plans were submitted and construction was begun on the second phase, the sanctuary. Worship was held in a temporary chapel set up in the Fellowship Hall of the Educational Building.[36] Having gotten the construction under way, Bryant felt he had completed his ministry and in 1957 accepted a call to the Briarwood Presbyterian Church in Jackson, Mississippi. And thus another five-year pastorate was completed.

Construction continued during the vacancy part of the ministerial cycle before the third five-year pastorate began. In 1958, August Schmitt, Jr. was called to be the new pastor from his first pastorate at the Rosedale and Benoit Churches. Schmitt and I overlapped for a year as students at Southwestern. On April 6, 1958, Schmitt led the first service of worship in the newly completed sanctuary.

One more property issue was addressed during this pastorate. Since they came, the Schmitt family had not occupied the old manse on the southwest corner of Oak Avenue and Church Street across from the church. The manse had seen many years of service. Muriel Gear Hart, wife of "Mac" Hart, told me years later that she was born in Columbia and lived in that manse. Her father, Felix B. Gear, was pastor from 1928 to 1934. Evans Brown and his wife, Janie, years later after they came to Kentucky, told me stories about living there when he was pastor from 1934 to 1938. But now the manse was "neither adequate nor acceptable for the pastor's

home in its present condition." So on November 29, 1959, an opportunity
to obtain a house at 1609 Orchard Drive in Golden Acres became available
and the church again "showed its faith and courage and agreed to make
the purchase."[37] With the major building programs completed and most
of the indebtedness retired, Schmitt spent the rest of the third five-year
filled pulpit phase since 1945 preparing for the fiftieth anniversary celebration in 1960 of the founding of the congregation. He also concentrated on
new programs that utilized these new facilities. The 1959 records showed
progress made during the previous few years: "membership, 143; Sunday
School enrollment, 123; and a budget for 1960 of $19,000 for all causes with
prospects for growth and services as bright as the promises of God."[38] All
this added up to a productive pastorate for Schmitt.

Only recently did Schmitt tell me how his social views became a factor
during his time in Columbia. Although considering himself theologically
conservative, he was like many of us more open to changes in the separate
but unequal culture in which we had grown up. He said he was rather quiet
about these views, but on one occasion some in the community took issue
with them. Someone approached the session of the Columbia congregation, urging that Schmitt be dismissed because of his beliefs regarding
race. The session refused the request. This was the end of the matter—
other than a cross was burned in his yard. In 1963 Schmitt accepted a call
to First Presbyterian Church, Biloxi, leaving the congregation without an
installed pastor until Buddy's flight to Amory.

During the decade prior to my arrival in Columbia, storm clouds were
gathering on two fronts: in the Presbyterian Church, with the failed vote to
reunite the Northern and Southern Presbyterian Churches in 1954–55; and
in society in general, with the U.S. Supreme Court's decision in *Brown v.
Board of Education* (1954). These were not mutually exclusive forces bringing about radical change in my world and the world in which I was called
to serve. The Supreme Court decision resulted in radical changes in the
ways schools and other public institutions were segregated. In this tinder-
box context, Presbyterian reunion was considered and defeated. Reunion
was synonymous with integration for those who opposed it.

Historically, the Southern Presbyterians in Mississippi, who separated
from the national body of Presbyterians during the Civil War over slavery,
considered themselves to be classical Calvinists, very conventional and
traditional. In the Synod of Mississippi and in its presbyteries (the statewide and sub-regional ecclesial courts governing Presbyterians) theology
and race sometimes collided with great intensity. But somehow a delicate

equilibrium was maintained, holding the church together without massive division for almost one hundred years.

The scale was, however, weighted in favor of the segregationists. Rev. G. T. Gillespie, president emeritus of Belhaven, one of the Synod of Mississippi's institutions, made his famous "A Christian View of Segregation" speech before the synod on November 4, 1954. In it he said, "[T]he crux of this whole problem of racial relations . . . is essentially a choice between the Anglo-Saxon ideal of racial integrity maintained by the consistent applications of the principle of segregation, and the Communist goal of amalgamation, implemented by the wiping out of all distinctions and the fostering of the most intimate contact between the races in all relations of life." He backed up his position with scripture, as he interpreted it. Reprints of this speech became a cornerstone handout for the Citizens' Councils.[39]

During the 1950s, Belhaven College also began to attract more conservative ministers from other Presbyterian denominations beyond its own bounds. Some served as professors at the college, while other were placed through its influence in local congregations in strategic locations around the synod. Serious polarization began to creep into the life of the synod dividing these newcomers from those who considered themselves loyalists to the national denomination. This polarization would soon play a key role in the exodus from Mississippi of many loyalists, including me.

Some of us native sons were later convinced that these ecclesiastical carpetbaggers exploited the racial situation as a means of taking over church institutions to use for their own political purposes.[40] Race, often under the guise of theology, became the central battleground in the 1954–55 attempts at denominational reunion. The five presbyteries comprising the Synod of Mississippi did their part in soundly defeating the proposal in the General Assembly, the national governing body of Southern Presbyterians. With that decision behind the Synod, it still faced the issue of race. I was not yet directly involved in all this, because at the time I was fully engaged in my first three years of college life at Southwestern at Memphis. However, I would get the first taste of its aftermath during my senior year.

Following the defeat of denominational reunion in 1954–55, the session of the Brookhaven Presbyterian Church where my dad served his last call as pastor passed a resolution in November 1957 concerning the growing tension over desegregation being "forced upon us." The resolution took issue with our Presbyterian denominational agencies by questioning their authority to make "deliverances concerning social, political, and economic questions." Their opposition was based on the assertion that this attitude was contradictory to the Westminster Confession of Faith, the church's mission of saving souls, separation of church and state, and the right to private judgment in all secular matters. They also went "on record disapproving the belief that segregation is unchristian and further as disapproving [the belief] that segregation is discriminating." The vote of the session was unanimous.[41]

Four short months after this resolution was passed, my dad suffered a massive heart attack while attending a board of trustees meeting at Southwestern on March 18, 1958, and died within hours. By midnight Millye and I had packed our '56 Chevy and headed south on that long through-the-night drive to Brookhaven. This was a devastating blow to me in my "middler" year at Louisville Seminary. Dad and I had just exchanged the first letters in which we began to lay out our respective views on matters of faith and practice in the present context. Regretfully, that became an unfinished conversation for me. He had been one deeply respected and beloved statesman of the church in Mississippi and was a leader in efforts to maintain the delicate equilibrium holding the church together. He and his cohorts came of age in ministry around the close of the Great War and led the church through the Depression and the dark days of World War II. They were models of ministry for us in the post-war generation. We had never heard of the word "mentors," but that is what these men were for us. And now their terms of service were coming to an end and our time was yet to come.

Before Dad's untimely death I had this notion that I wanted to return home to Mississippi to begin my service in ministry by "replicating pastor and church" as inherited and experienced through my dad's generation of ministers, which I so deeply admired. I looked forward to leading in worship and in education programs; experiencing the high and holy events around Christmas and Easter; doing weddings and funerals; making pastoral calls in the hospitals and homes; conducting the sacraments and leading communicant classes; enjoying family night suppers and special events for kids going away to college; and arranging weeks of evangelistic services among other responsibilities. I was not too excited about the stewardship season and dealing with the annual budget, because the pastor's compensation usually was the first four items on it. But I knew that came with the territory. I wanted to be active in presbytery life, especially in the camps and conferences that had meant so much to me as a young person. This is what I looked forward to in replicating pastor and church after I completed my seminary studies, and Mississippi was where I wanted to serve.

It was where my faith journey began and where I wanted it to continue to grow. Struggles with race and social issues were not yet high on my list of priorities, though they soon would be.

Although the turmoil in society in general was still somewhat abstract to me, turmoil in the church was not. A subtle but growing resentment was creeping into my life over those "outside clerics" that were coming into my home and threatening church as I had known it. Not long after my dad's funeral service, those represented by the more conservative ministers that had come to Mississippi from other Presbyterian denominations began to plan how they could engineer a call to one of their persuasion to become the new minister in the Brookhaven church. By year's end they had succeeded. This turn of events added insult to injury, for it struck me as a rather opportunistic way to shift the balance of ecclesiastical power at a time of great personal and congregational loss.

Little did we know at the time the Columbia congregation called me as its pastor that what seemed like a new, routine pastorate in the "five-year filled pulpit" cycle would be broken this time around. Nonetheless, what began with seemingly limited connections between the church and me proved otherwise. The web that prepared me for this call and wove this match together was rather extensive, although not evident to me until later. The significance of the connecting fibers of names and places and churches that continued to crop up in the narrative may seem to the casual observer to be a stretch, but in the ecclesiastical culture of Mississippi Presbyterianism and the local culture in general, such interrelatedness is plausible. This was the context in which I learned the meaning of pastor and church as I had experienced it growing up under the influence of my dad's generation of ministers. It was the stuff out of which identity is formed and doors are opened. This ecclesiastical relational web no doubt played a significant role in authenticating my call, though it was hardly spoken of at the time. It was a silent and sanctified version of the Mississippi standard conversation opener, "Who was your Daddy and where are you from?"

My call to Columbia was in actuality far from ordinary. The personal loss I experienced from my dad's death created deep inside me a new urgency to my seeking a call in Mississippi. I was coming home in order to take up the fallen leader's mantle and take his place—or so I thought. I got as far as northeast Mississippi in my first call in 1959. My second call got me to south Mississippi in 1964, closer to where I grew up and one more stop before I was through.

But I am ahead of my story.

CHAPTER 2

Where You From?

"Hey, Boy, where you from anyway?"

"Well, I was born up in Bolivar County at Shaw, Mississippi. I'm a fourth generation Mississippian."

"Hell, Boy, that makes it worse!"

I was a bit shocked at what the man said but not really surprised, even though I had hoped for a different response. Somehow I had wished, in true Mississippi fashion, to demonstrate I was "one of us" and not "one of them" (them being "outside troublemakers") by establishing my ancestry. This conversation took place sometime in south Mississippi in the mid-1960s, when Hattiesburg to the east, McComb to the west, and Bogalusa to the south were all going up in flames, both literally and figuratively. And there, right in the middle, sat Columbia, Mississippi, in Marion County, trying to figure out what was in store for it. I do not remember my interrogator or the circumstances, but it was obvious there was a serious discrepancy in our views as to what attitude or stance our city and county should take in the face of the social changes that were overtaking us.

True, I was a newcomer to the community, but I did not consider myself an outsider. Somehow, I guess I had the mistaken idea that a fourth generation Mississippian would count for something. Maybe that assumption was naïve or too rational in the face of such overheated emotions. After all, I had come to be pastor to a congregation of important persons in the community. That role, I assumed, gave me entree into the good graces of the community. To pastor was my call. I never did nor have since considered myself a social activist in the popular sense that stirred up such contempt among those committed to resistance to change in the 1960s. I never held dreams of crusading for some cause that would change the world. I never marched in the streets and led protests against some real or perceived injustice.

The "Hell, Boy, that makes it worse!" comment was tantamount to saying I was worse than the outside troublemakers because I was a turncoat traitor to "our cause." "You, of all people, should know better." This sort of suspicion only added to my feelings of ambiguity in deciding the right thing to do, because it heightened the fear and mistrust that was so pervasive in that time. It was not until years later that I began to delve into what was working in my life that led me to do the things I did, and into the views I held way back in the 1960s. I am not sure I have yet come to a definitive conclusion in the matter, but only gathered some hints along the way. I was not the first or the last Mississippian to go down this path, trying to untangle the circuitous route that leads us to derive meaning from our life. Sometimes the reasons become clear, while at other times the riddle is never solved to one's satisfaction.

❖ ❖ ❖

Back in March of 1982, Charlie Stanford and I were in a church governing body meeting in Nashville, Tennessee. Charlie grew up in Laurel, Mississippi, graduated from Mississippi State and Louisville Presbyterian Seminary, and found his way back to Mississippi. In 1959 he became pastor of the Jones Memorial Presbyterian Church in Meridian, after a short swing through Vidalia, Louisiana, the year before. Somewhere along the way he had crossed paths with Will Campbell, the legendary "bootleg" Baptist preacher as he called himself. Campbell was iconoclastic in the manner in which he lived out his Christian convictions of "loving God and your neighbor as yourself, including your enemies." This lifestyle ran the gamut from playing ping-pong with a black man while campus minister at Ole Miss in the 1950s, to Campbell's visit with jailed KKKers later on—both of which episodes drew considerable ire from his detractors on both sides of the fence. Charlie and I decided that since we had an afternoon off from our meeting it was time to make our pilgrimage to visit Campbell out at nearby Mt. Juliet.

Charlie made the arrangements, and we drove out to meet Will at the appointed time at his place. He took us out in the yard near the main house into his little log cabin studio where he did his writing. We questioned each other about our respective journeys, looking for places where our backgrounds might have intersected. Charlie and Will relived some of their mutual experiences. Our conversation was immersed in the droning sounds of a power mower doing its thing outside. Will noted with a wry smile that his wife just loved to cut the yard on her riding mower!

I told Will that I had roamed around Brookhaven in my mind, trying to locate places he had mentioned in his book, *Brother to A Dragon Fly*. He experienced his first call to preach as guest minister for the chaplain at the CCC installation there. I was particularly interested in trying to locate to no avail the "tourist home" of some "questionable repute," where the chaplain arranged lodging for him as "a cynical prank intended to further embarrass the green and inexperienced preacher boy who had gotten in his way . . . and ruined his own plans for the evening." Campbell acknowledged that he "had spent my first night as a circuit riding preacher in a whorehouse."[1]

Eventually Will pointed to a sheet of paper in the old standard typewriter on a stand near his desk and said that he was working on his new book, *Providence*. He soon launched into the story of how in the 1930s large landowners in Mississippi had evicted from the land-poor black and white sharecroppers who had supported the Southern Tenant Farmers' Union. This organization had challenged the sharecropper system, and for a time it looked as if it might change the power structure of the South. The union led efforts to better the lot of the tenants. The power structure took umbrage, to put it mildly, with these efforts, viewing them as a threat to the status quo. Tenants lived in a situation where "hunger was a reality, starvation a likelihood, mass murder an abiding threat." When manipulation of racial fears was exhausted, "many large landowners turned to other measures, violent measures. Local legal apparatus were [*sic*] as much a part of the system as were gin belts, shotguns, and lynch ropes."[2]

Will said that this volatile dynamic was at play when some students and friends of Reinhold Niebuhr came into Bolivar County in 1936 and bought two thousand acres to form the Delta Cooperative Farm, an experimental cooperative designed to alleviate the suffering of the tenants. They called the place Roshdale. Labeling anything a "cooperative" was tantamount to waving a red flag in the face of the powerful. Two years later the cooperators moved their portion of the operation to Holmes County, Section Thirteen, Township Sixteen, Range One East, and named it Providence Farm.[3]

Will skipped over a lot of the history of Providence Farm, which he was chronicling in his new book. He did tell us about some of his activities in recent years, when efforts were made to dispose of the property that had fallen into disuse. This included a deal with the Nature Conservancy, a national organization dedicated to reclaiming wilderness land for the preservation of endangered species. Many proposals had been made as to whom the most likely recipient should be.

Will told how he had cooked up what was to some a crazy idea. He proposed that the board overseeing the Providence Farm property, on which he served, should give the land to the Choctaw Indians over at Philadelphia so they could come to Holmes County and create some form of economic development project that would benefit the poor blacks and whites in the area. After all, this had been part of the Choctaws' ancestral home before the Treaty of Dancing Rabbit Creek relocated them to Arkansas and Oklahoma. In the end, Will said the property that had lain fallow for years went to the Department of Interior as a National Wildlife Refuge.[4] Later when reading his book *Providence*, my thoughts lingered over how the Delta Cooperative Farm came to Bolivar County two years after I was born there, and I had never heard a word about it until now. However, Dancing Rabbit Creek was familiar to me.

Finally, as our conversation about the legacy and fate of Providence Farm was beginning to wind down, I said, "Will, I am curious about something. How is it that you and your cousin, Jerry Clower, drank from that same well growing up on Route Four, Liberty, Mississippi (Amite County), and your views on life there turned out so diametrically different?" In later years Clower became a well-known fertilizer salesman turned comedian whose act reflected the popular humor of the times. Will studied the question for a bit and finally admitted, "I have absolutely no idea why." He went on to say that Jerry finally was coming around, though twenty-five years too late, now that he was trying to integrate his church up there in Yazoo City!

Somehow this conversation got me to thinking about what it meant to be a fourth generation Mississippian, "where I was from"—at least from my father's side—and how that shaped who I am and what I came to do. One of my great-grandfathers, William Jefferson Fatheree, was killed defending the Confederacy on the first or second day of the final siege of Vicksburg in the spring of 1863. His death was emblematic of the devastating loss of a whole generation during the Civil War. The leadership loss was particularly devastating to the State of Mississippi, owing to the exceptionally high death rate among males of this generation.

Fatheree had migrated from Mississippi to a farm near St. Francisville, Louisiana, on the Mississippi River above Baton Rogue. When the war broke out, he moved his wife and four children (three daughters and one son) back to the Ebenezer Community in Holmes County, Mississippi to be with his wife's family. His wife, Mary Elizabeth Williamson, was the daughter of Rev. Humphrey and Rebecca Thompson Williamson, my great-great-grandparents. He was a prominent Methodist "bishop" in the area.[5] It is my understanding that the term "bishop" did not carry the same connotation it does today, but was similar to the title "reverend," and referred to the function of "circuit rider."

On December 24, 1862, Fatheree wrote what was to be his last letter to "My Dear Wife" and mailed it to Ebenezer. The women of our family ceremoniously passed down that letter from one generation to the next with great care.[6] In the letter Fatheree expressed his desperate yearning for peace and his affection for his wife and his family. He gave her some advice on how to conduct their domestic affairs and care for the children until he returned from war. Special attention was given to their baby girl, Emma, who was cutting teeth. Miss Emma grew up and became my paternal grandmother.

After the war was over Fatheree's widow Eliza was a live-in tutor for the children of the Hart family in a small community named Hart Town near Ebenezer. She reportedly taught school at the nearby Little Red School House in Holmes County before she married William Henry Meek, a doctor, and moved to the Mississippi Gulf Coast. Four daughters were born to this union.

My other great-grandfather, William McAtee (I), was born in Washington County, Kentucky, on January 9, 1801. His life extended a decade beyond the crisis of the Civil War. It is not clear who his parents were, but it is suspected that his family may have been part of a large group of Roman Catholic families that migrated in 1785 from St. Mary's County, Maryland, to the Cartwright Creek Settlement in Nelson County, Kentucky, part of which later became Washington County. This first William McAtee, according to family lore, was a "Kaintuck," a member of an adventurous and daring group of entrepreneurs who rode the high waterways in flatboats to a wider world far beyond their wildest dreams.

A book titled *Early Times in Washington County Kentucky* tells the story of the fifty-foot long flatboats called "Orleans boats." It notes that Parker Warehouse, on Big Beech Fork, where Cartwright's Creek enters it, was one of the locations where the Orleans boat were loaded with all sorts of produce: sometimes 250 barrels of whiskey (8,500 gallons), flour, hemp, tobacco, meats, and so on. They would wait there until spring high water and then launch out for a precarious trip down the Beech Fork to the Rolling Fork to the Salt to the Ohio at West Point, then on to New Orleans via the Ohio and Mississippi Rivers.[7] It is possible that this was the launching point for McAtee's wild ride south. The adventurers, having delivered their goods, would then make their way back to Kentucky by way of the Natchez Trace.

The family speculated that William may have gotten tired at some point of traveling back up the Trace and decided to stay in Mississippi. A more plausible explanation is that new opportunities opened up in Mississippi in an unexpected way. He began to take possession of land in Beat Four of Attala County in 1840, some ten years after Andrew Jackson signed the Treaty of Dancing Rabbit Creek with Greenwood Leflore. Over time, he accumulated several parcels of land that amounted to around two thousand acres that were cleared and farmed by the slaves he owned. The western boundary of my great-grandfather's plantation in Attala County along the Seneasha tributary of the Big Black River was also near the treaty line.

He was almost fifty years old when he married Sarah Meek, twenty-seven years his junior and the daughter of Rev. James W. and Mary (Polly) Wyche Meek, my other great-great-grandparents. Meek was another Methodist "bishop" who came to Mississippi as a missionary to the Choctaw Indians. The bishop was also a physician and taught at a seminary in Alabama before coming to the Harmonia and Joseph communities a short distance north of the McAtee Plantation at Seneasha. Their son, William Henry Meek, was the doctor who married Mary Eliza Williamson Fatheree.

Sarah had long red hair that, according to family lore, the slaves vied to brush out. Oftentimes Sarah was called out to attend the sick, a skill she must have learned from her father and brother doctors. William built a big house with columns and wide-board floors for his growing family of four sons and a daughter. He stocked it with some fine marble-top pieces and other furnishings from as far away as France. He maintained an impressive library for his family's edification and provided a tutor for his children.

But this way of life was not sustainable, and he suffered great economic losses due to the outcome of the Civil War, as did other owners of large landholdings. He did maintain some of the land before passing it on to his wife and children after he died, but they did not live in the manner to which they had been accustomed. The big house was eventually stripped down and its columns removed. What remained of the house, before it finally burned to the ground years later, was salvaged to construct nondescript tenant houses nearby. I remember as a child walking up to one of those tenant houses and seeing fifteen or so inch-wide boards, with decorative grooves running the length of each side, used as outside vertical siding. And I remember being told, "These came from the big house."

While this plantation was at the height of its glory, the next William McAtee (II), my grandfather, was born there on May 27, 1857. War was only a few years away. In later years, he told how he loved playing around the slave quarters. Growing up he took advantage of the family library and was introduced to a wider world of knowledge under the guidance of the tutor provided by his father.

This William married Emma Fatheree on December 22, 1882, and they began their family. Lifford, their first son, was born in 1883, but lived only a year. Three sons and three daughters were born between 1884 and 1904 and lived to adulthood: Albert (Bunk), Euna, William Harvey, Claude, Doris and Hallie.

In February 1889, William (II) inherited a red clay hill farm that belonged to his mother's family. It was located in the southeast corner of Beat Four, Attala County, near Bolatusha on the Leake County line, some distance from the plantation where he grew up. It became known as Lone Hill Farm. The "Old Place," as it was known, turned out to be poor land for farming. William's brother, Junious, inherited the adjacent bottomland at the foot of the hill, which was better suited to agriculture, and he was the prosperous one for a while. William's son Bunk took a bride, and his daughter Euna took a husband. Both built houses on the Old Place and began to raise families of their own.

Grandpa was not cut out to be a farmer. He did manage to raise some cotton, corn, and livestock. And he was a perfectionist about raising sugarcane and making molasses. He insisted that the end product be not sorghum molasses but blue ribbon cane syrup. He figured out a way to extend the cooking pan from the standard fifteen feet to eighteen feet, so that he could control the raw sugarcane liquid as it flowed without interruption through the pan. It would come out perfectly at the end of the pan. He said it cooked too fast in the fifteen-foot pan, making it burn and requiring one to throw raw liquid in it at different points to maintain the right temperature, but this process ruined the taste. This was his secret to perfecting the flavor that gained him the reputation of producing the best sugarcane syrup in the surrounding area.

In later years my Aunt Doris spoke of Grandpa McAtee as a dreamer who liked to study the stars and his astronomy books. She thought that probably in another time—other than Reconstruction—he would have been better educated and had work that better fit his intellectual abilities. But she said he was a loving father and a gentle man. On one occasion his soft-spoken gentleness forsook him. There are a couple of versions of how this happened. One said he was driving his team of mules to the wagon when he rounded a curve and was run off the road by a fast-moving, oncoming team driven by one of the deacons of the Primitive Methodist Church he attended. As they passed, Grandpa cussed the deacon for his recklessness. The other version said that Grandpa cussed out his mules when they stalled in front of the church just as church was over. Regardless of how it happened, shortly thereafter he was "churched," meaning he was kicked out for cussing!

In her obituary in the *Christian Advocate* on October 13, 1931, it was said that Grandma Emma McAtee, "At an early age . . . gave her heart to God and joined the Methodist Episcopal Church, South, and to the end her church was one of the intimate loyalties of her life." However, her life was filled with many physical hardships: losing her father in the Civil War; losing her first baby, Lifford; losing her adult children, Euna and Bunk, and Bunk's baby son, Walter Preston, who died a month earlier than his dad in the same epidemic; and then rearing Euna's and Bunk's remaining children. The family experienced enduring poverty. At one point they spoke in almost hushed tones about "the year the cow died," remembering how they nearly starved.

My father, William McAtee (III), whom his family called Harvey, was born on March 8, 1889, in a log cabin on Lone Hill Farm, only a month after his dad had inherited the place. The cabin was a one-room rectangular structure with a fireplace at one end, a narrow steep stairway to the loft at the other, and a porch with a well beside it along one of the long sides. A small separate kitchen building stood on the opposite side from the porch and was later attached to the cabin by a walkway. As the family grew, a larger house was built at a right angle to one end of the log cabin. The new house was a typical two-story building with a downstairs room on each side of a "dog trot" and three rooms upstairs with a porch across the front. Many years later, in the 1940s, my daddy tore down the log house, removed the upstairs rooms, enclosed the "dog-trot" and built a small room behind one of the downstairs rooms and a kitchen behind the other downstairs room. Remains of this house, built of heart pine and with a good tin roof, are standing today, the only reminder of life that once existed at Lone Hill Farm.

One time the family had to move into Kosciusko to better their lot. Years later when I was moving to Amory, I ran into a woman who had known the family during this time. She remembered three of the children. Euna was her friend. She also remembered the tall blond-headed boy,

Harvey (William, my father) but could not recall the name of the third child. She said the father was quiet and unassuming. He would come and go and you would never know he was there. He had a beard. The mother was well liked by the neighbors. She was so easy-going and good-natured; one never saw her "ruffled up." She said the family moved away, and she never knew what happened to them, though she had seen the family name in the Memphis *Commercial Appeal* from time to time. I finally told her that she was talking about my family and that this was the first time I had ever heard anyone, other than family, that had known them way back then tell about them the way she had.

My Aunt Doris remembered that, although times were tough, her mother had a quick wit and amusing sayings that helped make life's circumstances bearable. She had a gift for nurturing and a strong awareness of the value of education that she passed on to her children. This she brought to the family from her experience as a governess. There were happy times, especially at Christmas. Aunt Doris described how they made all their decorations and gifts. They always had ambrosia, baked cakes, pies, and molasses candy. They would pick up chestnuts, "chickypins," and hickory nuts. They also raised peanuts. Sometimes they had baked turkey and chicken. In the morning they would have fresh sausage and baked biscuits with sugarcane syrup. Momma's cottage cheese with nutmeg and sugar was "out of this world." Their Christmas tree was a holly tree with red berries and strings of popcorn. There was singing as well as organ and fiddle playing.[8]

By the time my daddy was in his late teens, the two hundred or so acres at The Old Place were not sufficient to support the several McAtee families living off the land there. So he took his leave and went to Canton to work in the city power plant. One Sunday he went to the Methodist church to worship, and no one spoke to him. The next Sunday he went back, and the same thing happened again. The third Sunday he went to the Presbyterian church, and the congregation spoke a word of welcome. That is how he became a Presbyterian!

After a while he felt called to the ministry in the Presbyterian Church and went to Chamberlain-Hunt Academy (CHA) in Port Gibson at age twenty-three to continue his education. He had only completed the eighth grade in the one-room schoolhouse at Zemuly in Attala County. He had a great time playing football and baseball at CHA. His younger brother Claude, called "Little Mac," joined him there and pitched baseball. Daddy, "Big Mac," was his catcher. The crowd would yell, "Get a hit, Little Mac, Big

Mac will drive you in!" On one occasion Daddy was invited to dinner at a local residence. When the hostess heard he was going into the ministry, she turned to him and said, "Let's hear you pray!" Whereupon he did.

Upon completion of his studies at CHA he went to college at Southwestern Presbyterian University (SPU) at Clarksville, Tennessee. His stay there was interrupted by his military service in World War I, when he served overseas in France with a Corps of Engineers unit building railroads and bridges. On Armistice Day he was on his way to Brussels to enroll in chaplains school, but that did not happen because the war had ended. He returned to SPU and completed his college degree. He then went to Louisville Presbyterian Seminary to do his theological studies.

Following graduation from seminary in 1923, Dad accepted a call to the Marks and Lambert Presbyterian churches in Mississippi. While there he met his future wife, Queen Estella Graeber, who had come from North Carolina to visit her uncle, Lewis Graeber, her daddy's brother. The hosts had figured on setting up a date for their niece with a local banker's son, but instead she went off with the preacher to play the pump organ for a service in a chapel out in the cotton fields.

One day Uncle Lewis's wife Neva took their niece aside and said that the "preacher comes from a very good family, but they are poor hill folks." Neva probably knew that the preacher was sending checks to his father at Lone Hill Farm to cover the bills that were not covered by the farm income and giving advice about decisions that needed to be made to survive there. That warning did not deter the young North Carolina woman from accepting the preacher's proposal. On May 20, 1926, she stood in her middle-class home in Kannapolis, North Carolina, with this tall quiet man, dressed in a new suit and high top shoes, and recited marriage vows. Her daddy, Charles H. Graeber, owned and operated the Kannapolis Ice & Coal Company, which supplied these staples to the workers at Cannon Mills.

Daddy served two more years in Marks before he accepted a call to the Presbyterian churches in Shaw and Benoit in 1928. But before they left Marks, my sister Emma Jane McAtee was born on July 27, 1928. By the time I came along, the country was plunged into the Great Depression. Grandma and Grandpa McAtee had long since given up on Lone Hill Farm and moved to Jackson. Aunt Doris had gone to Jackson to help them run a boarding house there for a short while. Grandpa did not like living in Jackson. When Grandma died in 1931, Aunt Doris came to live with us. Grandpa went back to live with his granddaughter's family at Lone Hill for a while before he came to live with us in Shaw.

I was born William Graeber McAtee (IV) on September 18, 1934, in the front bedroom of the small two-bedroom frame house that served as the manse overlooking Porter's Bayou in Shaw, Mississippi.[9] I am told Grandpa McAtee would sit and hold me on his knees and say, "One William is about to leave this world, but another has come to take his place." He died in May of 1936, before I was even two years old. I don't remember much about him or about how hard times were. I do know that we made it through because we had a cow and a garden. My North Carolina grandparents kept us in cars. Clipped securely in black triangular corner brackets in an old-fashioned picture album was a snapshot of me dressed only in sagging diapers pushing my toy lawn mower beside one of those cars, our 1932 Chevy.

I remember seeing ragged people coming to our back door for food. I heard later that there must have been a mark at our house that indicated to hobos that food was available there. I remember standing outside looking up at the chimney by the window of the bedroom where I was born. "Somewhere, Over the Rainbow" had just come out, and I dreamed of seeing bluebirds above those chimney tops. I just knew they were up there somewhere! Maybe that was the sign that marked our door.

My earliest memories of church were formed in Shaw. Of course, I do not recall being baptized, but I do remember going with Daddy on Sunday evenings to the little church in the country where he preached. I remember stretching out on the slat-bottomed pews and falling to sleep. I can still smell the oiled floors and the lit coal oil lanterns up on the walls. They would flicker and make strange light patterns all around. Other times I went with him to a chapel where Mexican farm workers came to worship. Daddy would preach in English and a Mexican elder, who came with the workers from their home church in Mexico, would then translate the sermon for the worshippers. I remember the happy times in the summers we had at Bible school in Benoit. We made plywood birdhouses, sang Bible-story songs, played musical chairs, and drank cooling lemonade.

Most of all I remember sitting in the front row of seats during worship in Shaw. The seats were not pews, but wooden folding two-seaters. You could sit on one side and lift up the bottom of the other one. One day while Daddy was preaching, I was in the front row and got to lifting and closing the side I was not sitting on. I was playing like it was a drink box and I was opening it to get a Coke. Suddenly it got quiet and I looked up and saw that Daddy had stopped preaching. He was looking directly at me. He simply motioned his head toward the side door. That was the high sign that I was to knock it off and take my leave. Walking out of the sanctuary was discipline enough, and nothing else was said. In spite of moments like this, I felt like church was a safe place where I wanted to be. I had no way of knowing that is what it meant to the adults too, a place apart from all the anxieties they were experiencing in those hard Depression times.

After twelve years at Shaw and Benoit, Daddy received another call to serve the Senatobia and Hernando Presbyterian churches. One of the terms of call that the new churches honored was the stipulation that they include our cow in the move and build a cowshed on the side of the garage by the manse in Senatobia. We did not have room for a garden but we had fresh milk and butter! I began the first grade on my sixth birthday in 1940. My sister was in seventh grade, and we lived close enough to school to walk. Sometimes her friend Elise Varner would walk around the corner from her house so they could walk together. Years later Elise became Mrs. William F. Winter.

The world around us began to change dramatically. I can still see the clear blue sky on that cool December Sunday in 1941 when I walked out the front door of the church and across the church lawn to the manse next door where we lived. When I got inside I heard the radio announcement that the Japanese had bombed Pearl Harbor. We spent the next months beginning a scrap metal drive competition at the school. I heard that an old hearse was in some bushes across town, and I thought this was a great chance to add to our team's pile. I got Daddy to hitch up our trailer to go get the loot. When we got there we were very disappointed because the old hearse's body was made of wood! But we continued to flatten cans and save what we could. We would go to the bus station to see the older high school boys leave for the army. We watched strange new stickers put on windshields indicating what type of gas rationing stamps one had. As I recall Dad's was a "C" for clergy. Food was also rationed.

During WW II Daddy would pull our trailer down to Lone Hill and get a load of syrup to take back to Senatobia. He even sent some to Boss Crump in Memphis. When couples came across the state line from Memphis to get married in Senatobia before they shipped out, Daddy would give them a couple of buckets of Lone Hill molasses as a wedding gift. As a child I remember seeing the old log cabin before Daddy tore it down in the 1940s. I remember the smokehouse and the old well before Dad had a new one dug. Years later it fell my chore to have the new well filled in to keep some stray animal or person from falling to a certain death.

Once again, I experienced church in a different way. I always sat on the first pew, which I considered my space, and I would peer over the back to see who else was attending on a given day and "count the house." One day two older children took up seats beside me. It was April 5, 1942, probably right before Easter. I was not sure what was going on. About halfway through the service, Daddy said, "Those who are going to join the church today, please stand up." The two seated beside me stood, so I thought that was the thing to do, so I stood up. Not one word had been said about my joining the church prior to that moment. Daddy did not so much as flinch, but proceeded to receive three new communicants into the fellowship of the church: Shirley Dillard (age twelve), Rita Joe Dillard (age ten) and William G. McAtee (age seven)! Needless to say it raised a few eyebrows when I went down to the communion rail to receive the sacrament in my grandmother's Lutheran church in North Carolina when visiting the following summer. They confirmed communicants at age twelve.

Our stay in Senatobia did not last long, because Daddy received another call to the First Presbyterian Church, Brookhaven, Mississippi. In March 1943, our worldly possessions were loaded up once more, this time without the cow. The back yard of the manse in Brookhaven only had space for a hen yard and a place for Daddy's champion birddogs. I was only in the third grade, but I soon became a young entrepreneur selling eggs to the women of the church at prayer meeting on Wednesdays during the war. I saved up $50, and when I was older I used these funds to buy a dilapidated 1934 Ford to "fix up." It threw a rod before I got much done on it. I sold it as junk for $20 and bought a .22-caliber rifle that I still have packed away in our attic.

Luckily Daddy did not adhere to the one five-year cycle as being optimal time to serve in a pastorate, but was in Brookhaven for three of those cycles. I had the luxury of finishing high school there. The early part of those childhood years was still punctuated with all the rationing and other restrictions imposed by the war. We got to go home from school for lunch. Some days the word would get out at school that a shipment of bubble gum or chocolate bars had arrived at the packing shed by the railroad. We would rush there at lunch to line up for these prize items and forgo lunch.

I remember we had a drawer at the new frozen food locker plant where we took the chickens I raised and butchered. We also packed produce to be frozen, produce bought off the farmers' wagons parked on the street in front of our house when they came to town on Saturdays. My Aunt Hallie, who lived in nearby Wesson, would join us as we canned tomatoes in real cans out on our back porch. My job was turning the crank that sealed the cans after the fruit was properly cooked in the kitchen.

Sometime in the fall of 1944 or the spring of 1945, fog from the smoke-screen devices filled the street between the 5-and-10-cent store and the Haven Theatre. I made my way toward the sound of Ralph Pruitt's voice on the loudspeaker. Mr. Pruitt was an auctioneer plying his talents promoting the war bond drive here in my hometown of Brookhaven. His house backed up to Cherry Street in front of my good friend Bobby Day Sartin's house. I clutched in my hand $18 or so worth of saving stamps I had purchased with nickels and dimes from my allowance. With them I was buying a $25 war bond, a purchase that earned me a much-coveted ride in a "real" tank. All sorts of patriotic props filled the street: jeeps, American flags, "Buy Bonds" posters, recruiters—you name it. I had no idea how nearly depleted the government's resources were at the time, necessitating an all-out appeal to private citizens for their support to continue funding the war.

I got my bond, and I got my ride. Seems like it went down toward the railroad and back—not long, but long enough to give me the feeling of finally being in touch with the real thing, as if I were there! This was as close as I got to the machines of war, even though the prized navy cap that my hero, Billy Hill, gave me sat jauntily on my head. Even at ten or eleven years old I was caught up in the unified patriotic spirit of the war effort. Respect for the American flag was assumed. No one even dreamed of desecrating Old Glory or of the contorted configurations it would be put through in years to come by Vietnam War protestors or with the sport shirt versions worn by twenty-first century Tea Party members.

The war wound down, and on both V-E and V-J days, the fire sirens went off before dawn. That was the signal to gather at the auditorium at Whitworth College for the prayer services of thanksgiving for the end of the hostilities. When the war ended I was eleven going on twelve years old. The global nature of the conflict was beyond my comprehension, for I was now embroiled in my own mini-crises. Rubber gun wars and Saturday afternoon side yard tag football brawls replaced our Saturday afternoon dose of war movies punctuated with grainy newsreels of the action and their re-enactment in the foxholes we dug in the lot out back between the Methodist church and my house. We no longer flew imaginary thirty seconds over Tokyo missions from the B-25 cockpits of our porch swings. One day my cohorts and I were stunned with the gross results produced when Miss Nutt, our sixth grade teacher, ran a "little science experiment" by dropping raw meat in jars of alcohol. Then she issued the sober injunction, "If you so much as drink one drop of liquor, this is what will happen to your stomach!"[10]

Lone Hill Farm was part of my life when I was an adolescent, even though I spent only a week or so at the old place during that time. Tenants living in the house invited Daddy, my cousin McAtee Funchess (Aunt Hallie's only son), and me to stay with them. It was great fun to roam the woods and fields where our ancestors once lived and to imagine what it must have been like for them. We went through the field to Bolatusha Creek to bathe. We used Ivory soap because it floated and we wouldn't lose it.

On Saturday we rode the old wooden school bus with its wooden bench seats with few to no springs on into Kosciusko. The tenant would make a little extra money picking up the hill farmers and taking them into town to do their weekly shopping. The roads had hard washboard beds, making for a jarring ride. My cousin and I bought little helicopter-like propellers which, when you pull a string, actually flew. This visit was as close as I came to knowing what it was like to live on Lone Hill. Daddy put us on the midday Illinois Central southbound train, #3, *The Louisiane*, at Durant to ride back to Wesson where my cousin lived and then on home to Brookhaven.[11] Dad stayed on another week.

My idyllic, youthful days were filled with activities typical of the times: learning to drive; first dates and kisses; Friday night football; Saturday nights at the Teen Tavern; dances at the country club; hunting, fishing, and camping out with the guys; and playing golf with my dad. My gang, the "Troops," made periodic trips for forbidden beer to Dixie Springs, a local watering hole down Highway 51 at the Pike County line. Here, in a perverse fashion, we summarily replicated Miss Nutt's experiment—with differing results!

School days were filled with glee club, band practice, acting in plays, working on the yearbook, and a variety of other activities that enriched our formal learning experience. The skills I developed in the four courses I took my senior year I still use almost daily even now: typing, shop, spoken English, and senior English. In spite of "majoring" in extra-curricular activities, I received an excellent preparatory foundation for college and graduate school. Somehow English grammar stuck with me, most of the time, from diagramming all those sentences and translating Latin to English and vice versa. These curricular activities served me well in later years.

Church occupied an important segment of my life. I participated in Sunday night youth meetings; orchestrated a live Christmas tableaux with the youth group; sang solos in worship; joined in Fifth Sunday youth rallies with area Presbyterian churches. On occasion I "preached" on Youth Sunday. I attended services every time the doors opened. Sunday evening services were a delight. My good friend Dave Swalm and I would sit in the back row. We got good at timing Dad's sermons. On occasion we would slip out the back door just as he was beginning to preach. We would go to our garage next door and roll our 1946 Chevy down the driveway to the street after disconnecting the speedometer. We would then start it and take a quick spin out to the new Highway 51 by-pass. With precision timing we would get it back in the garage, reconnect the speedometer, then slip into our pew before the conclusion of the sermon! I am sure Dad was aware of what went on, but he never said a word.

Swalm did not have enough money to go to college, so he went to Natchez and worked a year at International Paper Co. He worked in the lab, which was responsible for the smell emanating from paper mills. It drifted all the way to Brookhaven, and we got on to him for that! After that year he went to Mississippi State and earned a degree in chemical engineering. He went on to Texas after graduation and worked for Dow Chemical Co. Later he left Dow and used his entire savings, $6,000, to buy a chemical company from Tenneco in 1984. He renamed it Texas Petrochemicals, and it became the largest privately owned chemical company in the USA.

Before he died in April of 2008, Swalm gave Mississippi State millions of dollars in the form of endowed professorships and scholarships in appreciation for his education there. Now the new chemical engineering building at State bears his name: David C. Swalm. He gave fourteen million for that building and another five million for a scholarship fund for Brookhaven students who major in a technical field at State. At one point I wrote Dave and proposed that he endow a chair at Louisville Seminary in the name of his pastor, my dad. He finally sent me a handwritten note saying his foundation did not usually fund projects outside of Mississippi and Texas, but he had some money left from the sale of his company in his personal bank account. Enclosed was a check for $100,000 for my project!

In the summer of 1951, before my senior year in high school in Brookhaven, I was reintroduced to Governor White—at least from a distance. I was selected to go to Magnolia Boys State in Jackson with the likes of Willie Morris. I was elected state tax collector in a mock statewide election and was the only official to receive a stipend for his services. Mrs. Fielding Wright, the actual state tax collector, gave me her earnings from one transaction involving the black market liquor tax. It amounted to about $6.28! When William F. Winter held that office years later, he spearheaded the effort to abolish the office and the tax, which was a contradiction in a legally dry state!

One evening we were marched from Belhaven College to the new Veterans Memorial Stadium, where we stood for hours listening to the speeches of at least a half dozen candidates for governor, including the eventual winner, Governor Hugh White of Columbia. This rally was vintage Mississippi politics in the ranting Vardaman-Bilbo tradition! Compared to it, Barnett's 1959 "Roll with Ross" political rallies were cool lemonade. We cheered wildly and waved the stars and bars as each candidate tried to outdo the others in extolling the virtues of our post-Reconstruction way of life, knowing clearly what that meant. The following winter I joined members of our local Key Club and built a beautiful float proudly representing "Brookhaven—The Home Seeker's Paradise" for Governor White's inaugural parade. On a flatbed "lowboy" eighteen-wheeler provided by a local equipment company, we built two plaster of Paris magnolia trees with live leaves and a water fountain with angel hair "water" flowing from it, surrounded by two white swans. We also covered the skirt of the float with magnolia leaves. Two of our club "sweethearts" donned white formal gowns and long white gloves to wave to the crowd along the parade route. Graduation day in 1952 from Brookhaven High School came much too quickly for me in many ways, but it was time to move on from the days of my youth, and I was ready.

May 1952 gave way to the sultry days of June in that humid Mississippi way. A single floor fan oscillated lazily back and forth creating an illusion of relief from the otherwise stifling stillness of noontime. Only a lone green fly batted itself against the confining window screen, trapping it away from the world beyond. From the den the silence was broken by the sounds of Kay Starr's newest, and eventually greatest hit, *The Wheel of Fortune*, slowly streaming in from WJMB, "1340 on your local radio dial."

Lying on our living room floor I looked up at the boxed cross beams in the ceiling trying to visualize what it would be like if the room were upside down and I had to step over the beams and the tops of the door frames to get from one room to another. It was not as if I were totally bored or without anything to look forward to now. I had yet to start my summer job delivering furniture for T. H. Perkins Furniture Company, which was located across the backyard behind our chicken yard. In the fall I would climb on the Illinois Central's *City of New Orleans* and head to Southwestern at Memphis for my freshman year in college.

Dozing in the hypnotic spinning of Kay Starr's recording and the oscillating fan, I drifted off into a dreamy world only to be awakened by the ringing of 504-J, our "Central operated" telephone. To my surprise, it was my great uncle, Lewis "Pop" Graeber, Sr., from Marks. He went straight to the point: Mr. Grady Clark and he were taking a ten-day cruise from Long Beach to Hawaii and wanted to know if I would like to drive them to California. I could stay with my Aunt Doris, my daddy's sister, who by now lived in San Pedro, while they were in Hawaii. He needed to know soon because they were leaving in a couple of weeks. He gave me a day or so to think it over. It seemed that the arrow on the wheel of fortune had indeed stopped on me. It was my day!

The next day I called him back saying I would be glad to go with them. He said we should meet in the lobby of the Robert E. Lee Hotel in Jackson at 9:00 a.m. on June 15. We were going in Mr. Clark's car and would be gone about four weeks. That was it.

Mr. Clark had a 1949 black four-door Ford, straight stick with overdrive and a flathead V-8 engine, and no air conditioning. It was one of "Whiz Kid" Robert McNamara's contributions that turned Ford Motors around. That thing could fly! Later I found I could accelerate to about 100 mph out in New Mexico or Arizona on two-lane Route 66 with no traffic and chase the sun 'til dark all the way to the mountains.

Little did I know the profound affect these next few weeks would have on my life. I was not to be like the little green fly, "confined behind the window screen, trapped from the world beyond." The summer of '52 provided the first of several major life transformations through which I would pass to a wider world of experience and self-understanding, more than had been afforded by the parochial boundaries of my childhood and adolescence. But best of all was the chance to be with Pop, my surrogate granddaddy, who taught me much about how to be an amateur cultural anthropologist as I followed him around these four weeks and on a trip to Alaska two years later. He would be floored by the title, but nonetheless he was an expert.

Being a "PK" (preacher's kid) was a positive experience for me, not like the negative childhoods and youths some other children of clergymen have alleged they experienced. Growing up in a manse next door to the church has its advantages and disadvantages. I believe for my sister and me the advantages far outweighed the disadvantages. I regret, however, that my older sister and I did not share as many school activities as we might have had we been closer in age. She was six years older than I and this gap meant that she was a senior in high school when I was in the sixth grade. The high school was all the way across town from the grammar school near our house, so our paths did not cross. Over the years, as we have grown older, we have become much closer and do share many delightful memories of those earlier years growing up in Mississippi.

I believe one of the reasons we had such a positive experience as PKs was due in large degree to our parents. They handled raising children in the manse as a matter of course and with great poise. Our mother was an accomplished pianist and organist, having earned her degree in music from Salem College in Winston-Salem, North Carolina. She tried for years to teach me piano, but I was too preoccupied and squirmy to concentrate on her directions. She turned me over to Mrs. Greenwood, a piano teacher in town, to do the job. That went somewhat well until the day of the recital, when I sat down at the piano and played my piece an octave too high. That performance ended my piano playing days!

Mother was big into healthy eating and alternative medicine long before it became the rage. Right after World War II she discovered Soymac, macaroni made from soybeans. She bought it by the case and distributed it to the women of the church. All the visiting evangelists and missionaries were treated to her tuna and Soymac dishes when they came to dinner at the manse. These dishes were staples at family night church dinners. She was, in addition, careful about other things she prepared for us to eat. Over the years, she added various vitamin supplements to her diet. Mother lived to be ninety-five years old. I attributed her longevity to healthy eating and tithing.

Dad was an easygoing person who commanded respect by example. He was active in the life of the community and served as the head umpire for the little league baseball program. His life was a witness to what he believed to be the message of the Gospel, "loving God and your neighbor as yourself, even your enemies." When he died, the whole community poured out its sympathy over the loss of "Brother Mac." The women from the Jewish synagogue participated in the culinary practice of bringing food to the home of the deceased because, they said, they considered "Brother Mac" to be their pastor.

He had great compassion for those who were poor, downtrodden, and hurting—regardless of who they were. At the time of his funeral, the doorbell rang at the manse and I answered it. There stood a man of little means, shabbily dressed and holding his hat in his hand. He simply said that he had heard Daddy had died and he wanted to come by to express his regrets. He said Daddy had found him living in a cardboard box and had helped him get back on his feet. Years later, my sister reminded me that she invited the man to come to the kitchen and sit down with us for a lunch from the bounty of comfort food brought in my friends and neighbors.

"Hey, Boy, where you from anyway?" Earlier generations of my family hold some of the clues as to what formed my personal identity. Time will tell what legacies from my heritage informed a particular moment in my own history and finally demonstrated what my ancestry counted for. The forces that work on us to make us who we are and what we do are still a mystery to us.

But it still matters where you come from.

First Call

Before I could take up my first call to a church in Mississippi to replicate pastor and church as I had experienced it, the turmoil in society in general was beginning to shift from the abstract to the concrete. I was obliged to finish college and get a seminary education in a climate that reflected that shift.

Marsh Calloway, one of my predecessor pastors at Columbia, had a lasting impact on me in my call to ministry. After my daddy, he influenced me most in this matter. I remember the quiet way in which he asked the question: "Have you considered going into full-time Christian service?" This question made a lasting impression on me and was one factor that led me to be taken under the care of Mississippi Presbytery in April 1951, meeting in the sanctuary of the historic First Presbyterian Church, Port Gibson, beneath its distinguished steeple capped with a hand and extended index finger pointing to heaven. Standing under the chandeliers taken from the steamboat *Robert E. Lee*, I declared my initial commitment as a candidate for the gospel ministry less than six months before my seventeenth birthday. I was still a junior in high school.

The meeting was held about the same time, April 11, 1951, that President Truman relieved General Douglas MacArthur of his Far East command and replaced him with General Matthew Ridgeway.[1] At the time our country had been engaged for almost a year in what was known as the "Korean Police Action," a curious term for an undeclared but devastating war. The conflict was extremely bloody during the first year and would remain that way until well over two more years before a cease-fire was signed on July 27, 1953.[2]

Though concerned with what was taking place in Korea, I was not so concerned that my life as a senior in high school suffered—until I received a notice from my draft board during the summer of 1952 indicating that it was time to register for the draft. I would be eighteen years old in September. Memories of the draft that took place in WW II were fading but still fresh enough to make me take my own draft notice seriously. There were several categories in which one could be slotted, one being the 4-D classification for ministerial students, which deferred their military service. This classification required being registered in a seminary, a stretch for one who had just received his high school diploma. I do not recall having grave doubts about military service or trudging off to the combat zone in Korea, though the thought did not capture my fancy. I did not experience the same struggle with my conscience over the morality of an unjust war that faced young men in the 1960s with regard to the war in Vietnam, and I did not feel I was using the 4-D classification as a way out of military service. It was respected as one of several legitimate options to consider. I simply wanted to go to college and to seminary in preparation for ordination into the gospel ministry. Qualification for 4-D classification required being enrolled in seminary.

Enrolling in seminary in 1952 was a very informal process for me. One day my daddy called up his seminary colleague, Dr. Frank Caldwell, who was now the president of Louisville Presbyterian Seminary, where they had attended. Daddy explained the situation regarding the 4-D classification. Dr. Frank simply said, "Consider him enrolled," and that was that, with a minimum of paper work. A letter to the draft board followed, confirming my enrollment, and I was granted the 4-D classification. This status gave me the sense that I could continue my education uninterrupted.

And so in the fall of 1952 I packed my brown Samsonite suitcase and footlocker, said goodbye to my parents and Brookhaven, boarded the Illinois Central's northbound #2 *City of New Orleans* and headed for what the porter called "Memphis Down in Dixie" as we glided into Central Station there. This was long before Arlo Guthrie and Willie Nelson immortalized this dawn to dusk streamliner in a song written by Steve Goodman. By the time the *City* made its run from New Orleans to Memphis that day, at least two dozen students joined me on our way to college.

During my senior year at Southwestern in 1955–56, I decided to begin pursuing my calling in the ministry by doing student supply preaching outside Oxford, Mississippi, at the College Hill Presbyterian Church. William Faulkner was married in its sanctuary, and its grounds became the location where scenes for the movie version of his *Intruder in the Dust* were shot. I preached some thirteen times there, beginning in July of 1955 while I was a counselor at nearby Camp Hopewell.[3] I rented a car and drove to College Hill a couple of times each month during the school year to preach to a very patient and long-suffering congregation.

I preached my thirteenth and final sermon, entitled "Living Monuments," there on March 11, 1956.[4] I declared that it was difficult to be a Christian in these complex times because it "is hard to keep the commandment that Jesus gave us, to believe in his name and love one another."[5] I spoke of the critical times in which we might be faced with using the nuclear armaments we had been building up against the threats posed by the communist world. I also talked about the difficulty of being living Christian monuments in the face of "the situation we are facing here in the South." I indicated that it was not necessary to relate all the facts. Everyone understood my point. I have no recollection of why I chose to deal with these topics and other stories related to them that appeared frequently above the fold on front pages of daily newspapers. Maybe because I knew this was my last sermon, I subconsciously felt I could risk making direct application to contemporary issues of what I believed to be the heart of the gospel.

I proclaimed that God was the only answer to these problems because, "God is to be the only judge of right and wrong." I added, "I fear to think of the things that could happen to us if we continue to go in the direction we are headed." I was doing all right until I said, "Ultimately the victory is not going to be won in a courtroom or by mob rule. These problems are not going to be solved by angry groups of Citizens' Councils or NAACPs. If groups such as these are based on fear and hatred, then nothing good can come from them. The spirit of love is going to have to replace the spirit of hate. . . . The spirit of Christ will have to rest in the hearts of men [sic]. . . . Yes, it is going to be extremely hard to be a true living Christian monument today."

When I walked out the door to greet the worshippers I quickly found out how true that last statement was. I was met by a high-ranking administrator from Ole Miss, who was livid and breathing fire all over me for my remarks about the lack of efficacy of the Citizens' Councils in solving the problems of the day. He was a Delta planter whose home was not too far from where the Citizens' Council had been founded in Indianola. I later found out that he had been a political appointee of Governor Bilbo in the aftermath of the governor's failed purge of the university in an attempt to move it from Oxford, Mississippi, to Jackson in 1936. I may have been a bit naïve and uninformed about the role of the Citizens' Councils and the NAACP in the contemporary turmoil, but I was absolutely convinced about God being the ultimate judge of right and wrong. This was my welcome to the world of emerging realities in our church and society and the price exacted by those realities when challenged.

Marsh Calloway continued to have influence over my life, although I lost contact with him for a while. I knew from what I had observed in earlier days in Calloway's life that ministry was not without its trials and tribulations when one speaks the truth to power as he had done with the governor. But I came to appreciate him more deeply when I later discovered what he experienced as pastor of the Durant Presbyterian Church in 1955–56. What I went through in that moment at College Hill was nothing to what Calloway was experiencing at the same time farther down Highway 51.

Racial tensions were at the boiling point over Providence Farm, a controversial social service for the poor in Holmes County near Durant. A public meeting was held at the Tchula School; one observer called it a kangaroo court to run the leaders of the farm out of the county because of its "subversive activities" in claiming segregation was "un-Christian." A local lawyer, who convened the meeting, offered an "interminable diatribe of proof texts, oblivious to any hint of love in that holy collection," according to Will Campbell. Campbell also said most of the crowd really did not know what was going on. He allowed that "frenzied rhetoric" was one of the favorite tactics the powerful White Citizens' Council used to influence an uninformed populace.[6]

When Dr. David Minter, the farm's clinic physician, and Gene Cox, its resident director, were making statements about its purpose, members of the White Citizens' Council that were present verbally attacked the two men. Minter and Cox had said what they were doing by providing Christian education, social activities, and services that heal the body, mind, and spirit were expressions "of their Christian commitment and denied any violation of local mores or state laws." The White Citizens' Council people took violent exception to this interpretation of Christian commitment and knew well the local mores.[7]

Calloway came to Minter's and Cox's defense, acknowledging he knew little about what was going on at Providence Farm, but vouching for the leaders' and their families' credentials as Christians and Presbyterian ministers and missionaries. As a result of his speaking out in support of the leaders of Providence Farm, the congregation at Durant boycotted services of worship. Calloway printed bulletins and prepared and delivered sermons for a year to a congregation of one: his wife.[8] And then he moved on. My time for all this was yet to come.

My Southwestern days came to an end with graduation on June 5, 1956. The following day, Millicent Bunn and I were married at Evergreen

Presbyterian Church across the street from the Southwestern campus. Dr. W. J. Millard, pastor at Evergreen, and my daddy did the honors. Millard and Daddy were college and seminary cohorts. Millye and I worked in Memphis that summer before we packed up a U-Haul trailer behind our new 1956 Chevy 210 Tutone grey and white four door sedan and headed north to Louisville in August. The car was a wedding gift from my parents that they had bought on special order from Orrick Metcalfe, a Presbyterian elder friend, at Jordan Auto Company in Natchez.[9]

We drove on two-lane highways until we got to Elizabethtown, Kentucky. Then we got on the new four-lane toll road to Louisville that had just been opened. It had been dubbed, "Happy Chandler's parkway to nowhere." It was the only four-lane limited access highway around those parts. The interstate highway system was still mostly a dream of President Eisenhower, but this section would become an integral part of I-65 in years to come.

An apartment in the seminary quadrangle was waiting for us when we arrived. I had been enrolled so long that our name was high on the waiting list. The seminary was located in downtown Louisville at 109 East Broadway. I told people this was my first experience with a northern city, and they would laugh. They would say, "It's not a northern city," and I would reply, "Yes, it is 'cause I drove two days due north to get here." It really was our first experience with living at the heart of an urban setting.

More than the geographical shift, our move marked an ecclesiastical and sociological shift. The northern and southern branches of the Presbyterian Church jointly owned Louisville Seminary. This affiliation gave me my first exposure to Northern Presbyterians. The delightful thing was we didn't wear nametags with denominational designations! I could not tell which professors or students were in which Presbyterian denomination. Furthermore, it really did not matter. The same was true of the little Northern Presbyterian country church I served in Indiana as student supply. I used to say I could not tell a nickel's worth of difference between that church and the ones in which I had grown up in Mississippi. They were just great people who were faithful in devotion to their faith and church.

The student body as well as the faculty reflected the times in the church. We were all male and for the most part white. We had one student from Japan, and there had been a few others international students. During my middler or senior year we did have one woman take or audit a course. She later became the wife of a man who became the governor of Indiana.

We had one African American student in our class, Irvin Moxley. Irv served one of the African American Presbyterian churches and community centers in Louisville. At first, though cordial, we both were not too certain how to take each other in such close proximity. We became friends over time. Finally, before we graduated something very special happened to us. I do not recall the exact circumstances that brought this about, but Irv and his wife Rubee and my wife Millye and I all got together for dinner. It was the first time that any of us had "socialized" in this way, but such socialization became a touchstone for all of us over the years. Irv and I worked together as colleagues in the governing bodies of the Presbyterian Church. We both served on the board of trustees at Louisville Presbyterian Seminary, fifty years after we graduated.

As students we were blessed with very dedicated professors who knew their subjects and knew how to relate them to the pastoral ministry. Most of them had served as pastors at one time or another. That experience helped keep them in touch with what it meant to serve a congregation. One of the professors who taught us New Testament Greek had just completed his Ph.D. George Edwards was demanding but fair. He had been a conscientious objector during WW II and had volunteered to submit to medical malaria experiments on his person as his alternate form of service. He also was very active in the peace and social justice movements of the time. Over the years I told him that I was sure I could not do the things he did or hold some of the views he held, but I always had a deep respect for his convictions because I knew they were a genuine response to the gospel message he discovered in his studies of the New Testament.[10]

Edwards and his wife Jean were good friends of Carl and Anne Braden in Louisville. Carl was a newspaperman. Not too long before I came to seminary, soon after the Supreme Court in 1954 had declared that school segregation was unconstitutional, the Bradens were involved in an incident that fanned the flames of racial tensions in Louisville. They decided as an act of conscience to buy a house on behalf of a black family in a Louisville suburb that "considered itself 'all white'" with the intent to deed it to them after the original sale was consummated. As Anne later wrote in her book, *The Wall Between*, which relates the long ordeal, "[W]e became the recipients of much of the fury that was unleashed."[11]

In the spring of 1959 the Edwardses invited some of the seminary students to meet the Bradens and hear their story. By that time Anne's book was out, so I brought my copy for her to sign. The inscription reads: "For Bill McAtee with my prayers for a creative ministry for you in the years ahead. Anne Braden. 5/1/59." Within a month and a half we would be living in Amory, Mississippi, in my first call pastorate. I did not have a clue as to how "creative" my ministry would become over the next few years.

Upon graduation from Seminary in 1959, three native Mississippians enticed a Kentuckian to join us in calls to pastorates in Mississippi. Frank Brooks, from Lake, Mississippi, went to First Presbyterian Church, Gulfport, as an assistant pastor. He would soon start Westminster Presbyterian Church there as a new church development. Henry Williamson, originally from Water Valley, would serve the Speedway Presbyterian Church in Corinth and the Iuka Presbyterian Church. I would serve First Presbyterian Church in Amory. Our Kentucky friend, Jack Wilhelm, was called to the Sumner and Tutwiler Presbyterian Churches. Another Mississippian, Gordon Smith from Sumner, who started in our class but took four years to finish, would follow us the next year as pastor of the Senatobia Presbyterian Church.

At one point Frank Brooks and I half-seriously tried to talk Irv Moxley into going to Mississippi with us. Recently Irv and I laughed about that event, knowing we had been kidding way back then because of the great risk it posed for him. He reminded me of the time when a generous Presbyterian woman leased a couple of buses to take the seminary student body on a day trip to Nashville to visit the Board of Foreign Missions of the Southern Presbyterian Church. He said with a twinkle in his eyes, "Two things happened on that trip. It was the first time I had been that far south and it was the first time that I had ridden in the front of the bus!"

So the time had finally come for me to return home to Mississippi along with my classmates to begin my service in ministry by replicating pastor and church as inherited from and experienced by my dad's generation of ministers. It was a summer of final examinations given by our presbyteries for ordination and installation. My ordination was on August 2, 1959. It was a season of "firsts" for us: first sermon, first communion, first baptism, first wedding, first funeral, and on and on. It was an exciting time of visiting the members in their homes, being introduced to the community by the congregation, and getting involved in the life of the presbytery. My long-held dream of replicating pastor and church had finally come true. As I was settling in, I felt that the context in which I was doing ministry was but a continuation of the time in which I had grown up. But in actuality that time was in its initial death throes.

Five years had passed since the Supreme Court overturned *Plessy v. Ferguson* (1896) and declared in *Brown v. Topeka Board of Education* in

May 1954 that segregated schools are unconstitutional. For over fifty years *Plessy* held that a Louisiana law mandating "separate but equal" accommodations for blacks and whites on interstate railroads was constitutional.[12] "Separate but equal" was the legal justification for "our way of life" in Mississippi. A crescendo of massive resistance was growing in the wake of the threat *Brown* posed to the status quo.

The summer of 1959 was the beginning of a series of firsts for Ross Barnett, beginning with his campaign for governor against his leading opponent, Lt. Governor Carroll Gartin. The Democratic primary election in Mississippi had been for years tantamount to a general election, and this year was no different—other than the heat and nastiness by which it was conducted. The Citizens' Councils of America was one of the politically powerful organizations that supported Barnett in his campaign. With their backing, he played on the fear that whites had of the advancement of blacks "into their previous all-white areas of schools, neighborhoods and public facilities."[13]

Erle Johnston, the weekly editor of the *Scott County Times* in Forest, observed that this was the first and only statewide campaign in Mississippi where no posters littered the countryside. He also pointed out that Barnett was the first and only governor of Mississippi who never ran for any other office and the first governor to enact a far-reaching bill of rights for industry and business. In addition, he was the first governor to witness the breakdown of racial segregation in educational institutions and to experience an invasion of northern civil rights leaders determined to change Mississippi overnight. In the realm of politics Barnett ended the traditional practice of double dipping, the appointment of a legislator to a state job. In the social realm, he was the first and only governor to have two back-to-back Miss Americas from his home state serve as honorary colonels on his staff.[14]

In the end, Barnett was committed to doing whatever was necessary to maintain segregation as a way of life. In his inaugural speech he made only brief reference to segregation, but brought a roar from the crowd when he proclaimed, "It must be kept at all costs."[15]

By the time Barnett was settled into the governor's mansion in Jackson, we were settled into the manse at Amory and well into replicating pastor and church. The routine of writing sermons, planning Sunday school and youth programs, visiting the sick, and looking ahead to next summer's Bible school occupied most of my time. I did get involved in the presbytery's camp, where we got to make new friends among our colleagues in ministry. In the summer of 1960, Millye and I went to a two-week-long camp directors' training event in Pennsylvania, sponsored by the National Council of Churches to be certified in this work. I wanted to be better qualified to return the favor extended me by Marsh Calloway to the young people in the presbytery through its camping program. It was another enriching experience of integration for us because one in our small group was an African American from Detroit.

The national presidential election campaign was in full swing by the fall of 1960. Institution of Nixon's southern strategy to lure southern white voters from the Democratic Party into the Republican Party was still a decade away, but fault lines were beginning to appear among Democrats. Governor Barnett developed a scheme that convinced "Mississippians to vote for unpledged presidential electors for the only time in history." His was a divide-and-conquer strategy, for he knew that it would divide old-time Democrats in Mississippi. The Mississippi Senate delegation, along with some prominent state officials, had already spoken out in support of the Kennedy-Johnson ticket. Barnett planned to use these electors as bargaining chips to promote his convictions about states' rights when the platform was formed at the Democratic national convention in Los Angeles in July.[16]

The heat and rhetoric from the 1959 gubernatorial election carried over into this presidential election. Not only was the issue of civil rights injected into the campaign, the matter of Kennedy's being a Catholic became a hot button issue. No matter how much he claimed that his religious preference would not impact his political decisions, Kennedy could not satisfy his most ardent detractors. Such an electric atmosphere made one apprehensive about being vocal about one's support for the Kennedy-Johnson ticket. In spite of the tense atmosphere, Millye and I served as polling officials during the November election.

We were ecstatic over the outcome and euphoric at the prospect of the new directions this young president would take us as a nation, a feeling that would be replicated with the election of Barak Obama almost a half century later in a similar generational shift. But we were only able to share this moment of joy mainly with close friends. The hatred for the Kennedys was widespread and oppressive in Mississippi.

The sparkle of inaugural events must have dulled for the new first couple, though no disappointment was publicly evident. Well before his inauguration, Kennedy was deep into his first major international crisis. From the very beginning of Fidel Castro's "Triumph of the Revolution," as it is known in Cuba, opposition was proposed by then Vice-President Richard Nixon because, he said of Castro, "If he's not a communist, he certainly acts like one." The CIA began to develop a covert operation to undermine the Castro government without leaving U.S. fingerprints all over the coup. Kennedy had made promises to Cuban exiles that he would support Castro's overthrow. Kennedy gave the go-ahead to the CIA's plan to land a small paramilitary force at the Bay of Pigs.[17] The invasion was a disaster from the beginning, causing the new administration considerable loss in credibility. This would not be the end of tension with Cuba.

The generally contentious and strident atmosphere at large in Mississippi was having an impact on the Presbyterian Church. In the summer of 1961, the political battle in the Synod of Mississippi was over how to distribute the voting blocs among the adversaries within the five presbyteries. Central Mississippi Presbytery had been the focal point of the conservative voting bloc for years. By this time that bloc was spreading out to the other four presbyteries. The influence of the liberal bloc, the one loyal to the national denomination, was being challenged. So this liberal bloc developed a strategy to contain the influence of the conservative wing by gerrymandering presbytery boundaries to gain a liberal advantage. The five presbyteries in the synod were reduced to three by a fourteen-vote margin. This configuration would last until a major conservative defection from the denomination to the newly formed Presbyterian Church of America occurred a little more than a decade later.

In the meantime, the winners of the battle over denominational reunion in 1954–55 still used theology to cover their racial prejudices as they made various ecclesiastical decisions. The most conspicuous display of this subterfuge occurred when pastors were being called to new congregations. The best-known case developed in Central Mississippi Presbytery in 1962, when A. M. "Mac" Hart was extended a call to the Trinity Presbyterian Church in Meridian. Following the procedure provided in the denomination's *Book of Church Order*, the presbytery exercised its responsibility to "examine" the candidate for reception into the presbytery. The examination lasted several hours and focused primarily on theological topics such as the historicity of Adam, the Virgin Birth, and other matters. The presbytery did not approve the exam, citing Hart's theological views—at least as judged by the majority of Central Mississippi Presbytery, the court of primary jurisdiction in this type of case. Failure to approve his exam prevented Hart from being installed as pastor at Trinity. A series of appeals on Hart's behalf were made over a period of three or so years to the synod, an appellate court of the Church. Eventually the case found its way to the General Assembly, the highest court of the Presbyterian Church U.S.

A year or so after we moved to Amory, the local Plymouth dealer, a member of the church, talked us into buying a demonstrator 1959 Plymouth. When it turned corners you never knew where it was headed. It was nothing but a big V-8 engine! When the front seat was pulled all the way up so Millye could reach the pedals, it was so close I had to sit in the back seat. The dealer could not rest until he got us out of our beloved 1956 Chevy that had only 46,000 miles on it, one of the best cars we ever owned. We were too green to know we didn't have to be that beholden to church members, and we begrudgingly gave up our wedding present. Finally, we put in a special order with George Ruff Buick Company in Tupelo for a new 1962 Rambler Cross Country station wagon. What a happy day it was when we took delivery on our "built for us" new vehicle.[18]

In February I entered in my ministerial log: "John Glenn orbits earth three times—First Presbyterian Missionary in Space!" The rest of the spring was filled with infant baptisms, a men's rally, a visit by a pulpit committee from Franklin, Tennessee, and the funeral of one of our railroad engineers, who died with his hand on the throttle. I directed a junior summer camp at Camp Hopewell outside Oxford. It closed on Saturday morning, July 7. When I went through Oxford in the early afternoon, I learned a hearse had passed through the town square bringing back from Byhalia the body of William Faulkner, who died there the night before. The sun was bright, the temperature was dancing close to a hundred degrees, and the farmers had their produce trucks backed up in front of the courthouse. I stood there on the square thinking what a fitting backdrop for his return.

Our third year in Amory was capped off with a very effective youth week. I had spent the summer outfitting our Cross Country Rambler station wagon with window screens, air mattresses for sleeping on the reclining seats, a foldout cook unit with awning for the tailgate, and a top-mounted carrier for our tent. Look out Seattle! We headed north by northwest on our vacation and were out 31 days in all, including stops at the 1962 World's Fair in Seattle and Banff, in Alberta, Canada.

On Sunday, September 2, the first Sunday after we returned from vacation, Murphy Wilds, pastor at First Presbyterian Church, Oxford, Mississippi, and his family visited in worship that morning. It was the last Sunday of their vacation. Little did we realize how much those days of rest and relaxation in our annual vacations would mean to us as we moved into new, turbulent times. I preached on the "Pilgrimage of the Soul" recalling Moses's "trek across the wilderness of Midian to the foot of Mt. Horeb, not just a carefree holiday to the mountains!"[19]

By fall the Mac Hart case (then in its first year) became overshadowed in what William Doyle referred to as "An American Insurrection," which he graphically portrayed in his book with the same title. It depicted in his words the battle of Oxford, Mississippi, 1962. This battle, of course, was what took place when James Meredith exercised his right to be admitted to the University of Mississippi (Ole Miss). President Kennedy and Governor Barnett, the protagonists along with Meredith and a cast of thousands, played out this epic drama of wills in all its raging sound and fury.[20]

This drama and its ultimate outcome have been well documented. It is recounted here only to illustrate how directly these intersected with my attempts at replicating pastor and church, for this event took place within the bounds of St. Andrew Presbytery, where four of my five classmates from Louisville Seminary had come to serve. It was a very threatening and uncertain time.

❖ ❖ ❖

Late on Sunday afternoon, September 30, when the confrontation at Ole Miss was building between federal and state authorities, I was visiting a friend who was not a member of the church I served in Amory. He was trying to decide whether to give consent to his daughter's return to Ole Miss, where she was a student, after a weekend at home. The situation there appeared to be very dangerous. I told my friend that I did not see how he could deny her the opportunity to witness history up close. He finally agreed to let her go back. Later, we found out that the federalized National Guard entered the campus around midnight, just in time to prevent insurgents from burning down the dormitory where she had gone upon her arrival.

Bill Callicott and Mills Carter were members of the Senatobia Presbyterian Church where Gordon Smith was pastor. Mills and I started the first grade together in 1940. When I was still in high school in Brookhaven, I went back to Senatobia in the summer to visit Nell and Sam Meacham, Bill's aunt and uncle. Bill would take a bunch of the guys, including Mills and me, to Memphis to see the Memphis Chicks play baseball. Bill loved baseball and coached boys' teams. He was an insurance agent and a state legislator.[21] But on this last weekend in September 1962, Callicott was battalion commander Major William E. Callicott, 108th Cavalry Third Squadron, which President Kennedy had just federalized from the Mississippi National Guard and ordered to proceed in convoy to Ole Miss. According to Gordon Smith, he thought Mills was by this time Captain Carter and was with Callicott at the Ole Miss encampment. Callicott later said that he had seen "expressions of absolute terror" in the faces of his men. He said he had "served two years in World War II in England, France and Germany, 1943–45, and I never was as terrified as I was going onto the campus that night." He knew that civilians had come from all over Mississippi, probably including Senatobia, and he was worried that if the shooting started and someone got killed "it could be my next-door neighbor."[22]

By Sunday evening around 11:00 p.m. the situation had significantly deteriorated. Murphy Wilds, pastor of the First Presbyterian Church of Oxford, lived near the intersection on University Avenue between downtown and the east end of the campus. Here, on the previous Wednesday morning, Lt. Governor Paul Johnson, in the absence of Governor Barnett, "stood tall," turning back the U.S. marshals taking Meredith onto the campus to enroll him in college as directed by the federal court. Murphy was not sure what was about to happen in the Sunday evening darkness, because there were snipers nearby taking random shots into the teargassed night. Sometime before midnight, he later told me, the most beautiful sight appeared, coming from downtown through the intersection. Here came the lead jeep of the recently federalized Mississippi National Guard, flying a large American flag and moving west toward the campus ahead of a convoy of now federal troops.

Meanwhile, Major Callicott had positioned his troops at the Sorority Row entrance on the north side of the campus. He ordered the 250 men under his command to march up Sorority Row on foot, three across, in the darkness because the street lights had been shot out. They had had little riot training and were literally shaking in their boots. As they approached the Lyceum, the focal point of the rioting, they were greeted with rocks and pieces of pavement and pipes or anything that could be hurled at them. They managed to make it to the Lyceum about the same time as the 108th Cavalry's First Squadron, led by squadron commander Lieutenant Colonel Guy J. Gravlee, came in from the east. This was the unit that had earlier passed Wilds's house. A November 1962 national guard report later stated, "The situation was still like a scene from Dante's *Inferno*; pitch dark, several thousand men and youths milling around among the trees on the Circle and Grove and among the University streets."[23]

Years later after I moved to Columbia, I made a pastoral visit to a Mrs. Conners, a homebound member of our congregation. We made our acquaintances, and before long she talked about where she had grown up, as Mississippians do. She made the comment that "those carpetbaggers that took over [her] family farm were not so bad after all." I asked where was the farm, and she replied, "You know where those Sororities houses are at Ole Miss? That was our farm." I cannot now help but remember that awful night my friend Bill Callicott spent with his troops on her family's farm!

The following morning, after the situation had been brought somewhat under control, some of the action had moved to downtown Oxford on the square. Robert H. "Bob" Walkup, pastor of First Presbyterian Church, Starkville, dutifully drove up to Oxford to attend a St. Andrew Presbytery nominations committee meeting. He told me later that as he approached Oxford from the south, he topped a hill and there before him was all this glass in the road glistening in the sun. He later figured out it must have been where the rioters collected broken glass to be used somehow in their rioting. He worked his way to the parking lot behind the building on the northwest side of the square, where his meeting was to be held on the second floor. Nobody had called him to say it had been cancelled.

As he turned the corner leading to the square, he came face to face with a tall man in a flamingo-colored cowboy hat. For a moment their eyes locked in near recognition, but the moment passed when he heard the voice of another young man in paramilitary gear shout at the man, "General, what do you want us to do now?" Bob glanced at the stores lining the square and saw backed up in front of the plate glass windows a phalanx of federal troops armed with fixed bayonets. Out in the street before them was a rag-tag group of civilians holding glass bottles filled with gasoline. He assumed the crowd was getting ready to burn those stores.

At this point, Bob decided that it was time to beat a hasty retreat. As he left, it dawned on him that the man he had encountered was none other than former U.S. Army Major General Edwin Walker, who switched sides at Oxford to lead groups of young rioters against the federal marshals. In 1957 he had commanded the 101st Airborne in "the peaceful capture" of Little Rock, Arkansas.[24] At one point it was rumored that Walker had been nowhere near Oxford, but Walkup knew better.[25]

Later, on October 16, after some modicum of order was restored at Ole Miss, even though federalized guard troops were still encamped there, the Presbytery of St. Andrew held its fall meeting at First Presbyterian

Church in Columbus. The presbytery soon became embroiled in a debate over what action it should take with regard to the "crisis and tension following the rioting, and bloodshed within our bounds at the University of Mississippi and Oxford." Some felt that we should take no action, since this was not the business of the church. Others felt that we should take a stand in support of Meredith's enrollment at Ole Miss. It was friend versus friend and family versus family. All sorts of speculations were made about what had happened there and where blame should be placed. For a while it looked as if no action would be taken.

One experience galvanized me when we broke for lunch at Palmer Orphanage that day. One of the elders seated by me made a comment about his perspective on the "race issue." In all sincerity, he said, "We treat our nigras real well." I went ballistic and could not hold my tongue. I had been closely related to his family over the years, and one of its members had played an important educational role in my life, for which I am eternally grateful. In my fury, I proceeded to tell how his family member had told the following story with some pride in my presence a number of years before. He had said in so many words, "I used to go to Parchman [the state penitentiary] and get me a 'boy' and bring him to my house to take care of our yard. His wife would come along and cook for us." Then while assuming a very physically threatening pose, he said: "Boy, if you don't behave, you'll lose your freedom." Then I put in the zinger: "Yeah, ya'll treated 'em real well!"

Even though I had clumsily repudiated a part of my heritage that repulsed me deeply, I knew from the chill around the table that I had violated a common courtesy and cultural norm of not trashing close friends and relations in public. People seated there knew my close relationship with the elder and his family. They also knew that some sort of recrimination would come my way as a result of my damning accusation, no matter how justified. It was ten years before a word passed between the man's family and me, and then the exchange was touchily polite.

After lunch the discussion took on a very serious tenor when Eade Anderson, pastor of the Greenwood Presbyterian Church and Bill Flanagan, pastor in transit from the Byhalia Presbyterian Church to a new church development in Southhaven, Mississippi, strode onto the floor in full battle dress from their encampment at Oxford. They had been called up as chaplains during the federalization of the National Guard. Stories of their first-hand experience at Oxford persuaded the body to adopt a pastoral letter to the congregations within its care to remember, "The spirit of hatred and strife, which manifested itself in the violence, is contrary to the Spirit of Christ."

The pastoral letter admonished each of us "to give the Spirit of God that supreme place in our hearts and minds . . . summon those of our communion within our bounds to undertake such a searching self-examination and to turn to true repentance as the Spirit leads them . . . act only in those ways which promote order and peace . . . use their every influence to the end that those officials charged with maintaining order may pursue their task with dedication and with diligence . . . urge our communicants to pray for God's mercy and guidance for ourselves and for our state and national leaders, that we may praise and serve Him all our days."[26]

We were not aware that only twenty-four hours before we adopted this pastoral letter, President Kennedy first received word that reconnaissance photographs revealed Soviet missiles under construction in Cuba. Seven days later Kennedy announced to the public the existence of the offensive missile installations and his decision to impose a naval quarantine around the island. For thirteen days the Cuban Missile Crisis would bring anxiety and fear over a potential nuclear confrontation to an already troubled people until Khrushchev announced that he would dismantle the installations and return the missiles to the Soviet Union.[27] The anxiety and fear was to a degree assuaged, but those grainy black and white television images of Soviet ships with canvas-shrouded missiles on deck steaming toward Cuba had exacted a toll on the psyche of the American people. Thirty years later, latent feelings deep inside me stemming from these events would strangely rise to my consciousness when I walked the streets of Havana and other locations in Cuba as an international volunteer in mission for the Presbyterian Church, and when I shook hands with Fidel Castro on one of my fifteen trips there.

The next year would bring on more crises. That summer, the Synod of Mississippi was in session at Belhaven College. On the evening of June 12, 1963, Medgar Evers was gunned down in his driveway, and the city of Jackson was plunged into angry chaos. The synod, as church, struggled with yet another timid resolution to address the situation. The minutes of the meeting made no reference to the assassination or any resolution regarding it. A reading of the minutes in their entirety indicates that, "Most of the actions and resolutions made were based on findings prepared by committee months in advance of the meeting."[28]

On the personal front, less than a month later, on July 3, 1963, our lives were blessed with the birth of our son William Neal McAtee (V). He was named for his two grandfathers, William Harvey McAtee and Sargent Neal Bunn. Our son never had the opportunity to know either of these men, because they died before he was born. It was truly a turbulent time in which to enter this world, but the worst was still yet to come.

In August of 1963, Mississippians were immersed in the fractious throes of another primary election. Lt. Governor Paul B. Johnson, Jr. defeated former governor J. P. Coleman in a run-off election. Johnson ran on the famous slogan, "Stand Tall With Paul," derived from his earlier Ole Miss stand on University Avenue. For some, his campaign rhetoric and later actions raised questions about the credibility of statements he made during his inaugural address, when he challenged "the people of Mississippi not 'to fight a rear guard defense of yesterday' but to conduct 'an all out assault on our share of tomorrow.'" And yet later he convened a special session of the state legislature in June through July of 1965 to repeal the state's discriminatory voting laws as a prelude to the August passage of the Federal Voting Rights Act of 1965.[29] Critics viewed his action purely as a strategic move intended to minimize the impact of the proposed federal legislation. The landmark Voting Rights Act of 1965 subsequently bolstered a dramatic increase of voter registrations among blacks.

Following the August 1963 primary election, on September 1, I preached a sermon entitled "Collision Course," based on the text: "They made kings, but not through me. They set up princes, but without my knowledge. For they sow the wind, and they shall reap the whirlwind" (Hosea 8:4a, 7a, RSV).[30] I said that an election year in Mississippi was like nothing else in the world. "On this post election Sunday, I deeply feel that through the words, the speeches, the heat in the past campaign we have established certain elements of our own self-destruction. We have set ourselves on a collision course; we have sown the wind that will reap a whirlwind unless these elements are changed."

The first element that needed to be changed was the deep-seated hatred mainly directed at the personification of the federal government: the president and his administration. The second was the fear underlying the hatred. Was it the fear of giving up something we call our own, or the fear of retaliation at the hands of those from whom we have wrested "our way of life" at the cost of the blacks' integrity? The third was ignorance brought on by being in the clutches of hatred and fear aimed at the two primary targets—Oxford and Washington—effectively excluding the real issues facing us. And I concluded with the recognition "that we as Christians are part of the most revolutionary movement in the world, a movement whose God has little patience with fear, hatred and ignorance, but one whose wisdom demands loving-kindness, righteousness, and mercy; one who calls us to apply our hearts to God's wisdom."

On October 13, Bob Walkup preached in Amory a sermon called "Picture, Promise and Pledge" and chose for his text the two great commandments of "loving God and loving your neighbor as yourself." In the course of the worship service, he administered the sacrament of infant baptism to William Neal McAtee.

In twelve short weeks, the whirlwind arrived. The world stopped, stunned in its tracks, when at noontime on a Friday, November 22, in Dallas, Texas, President Kennedy was assassinated. Millye and I, like the rest of the nation, sat for long hours transfixed before the flickering television screen in shock, in disbelief, with each replaying of those tragic details hoping against hope for a different outcome, but knowing it would not be so. We gathered up our four-month-old son, Neal, and drove to Starkville that afternoon, seeking comfort with our friends Bob and Alice Walkup. Upon arrival we stood in the driveway as our tears mingled with gently falling rain as the twilight of that day turned to utter darkness.

That weekend I was to have been away with a group of college students at a statewide Westminster Fellowship retreat at Tougaloo College. The retreat was cancelled, and I was able to be in the pulpit with my people on that Thanksgiving Sunday. Before I could begin my sermon on Sunday, November 24, I was handed a note from my wife, who was at the manse next door with our son. It read: "Oswald has been shot. No word on his condition or who did it. I just thought you might want to know." I read it to the congregation and prayed for him in the pastoral prayer before I began preaching.

In my sermon, "On the Death of the President," I brokenheartedly proclaimed, "Harvest time has come."[31] The tragic events of the day reminded me of a verse that marked the famous scene when Isaiah was called to prophesy: "In the year that King Uzziah died, I saw the Lord" (Isaiah 6:1a, RSV). I said that in that brief line we see the hand of God moving in history, dated by the death of a national political leader. I wondered aloud how God was working in the death of the president. I noted it was a sad day when even a few school children cheered at hearing the news from Dallas. It was unforgivable to hear grown men say, "I hope he dies," even as the chief executive's life's blood ebbed out, staining the clothes of a devoted wife. It was a sad day, but what could you expect? The dying man had only recently been pictured as a vicious tyrant.

I had no idea at the time how God was moving in this tragic event, but this I knew: In the sadness there was an overwhelming sense of guilt that "engulfed those who silently stood by and watched the seeds of destruction being ruthlessly sown." I confessed I shared this guilt by remaining silent. But in that sermon I finally was beginning to find my voice, as others had done.[32] I acknowledged that I had been a supporter and admirer of Mr. Kennedy from the start, realizing that he was human, susceptible to making mistakes, yet nonetheless exhibiting moments of greatness. I still felt that when I cast my vote for president for the first time, I had made the right choice. Though I felt someone needed to say a kind word for the president, for at least two years and ten months I quietly stood by and bore the bitter barrages of hatred hurled his way by home folks and even family. This paralysis now disturbed and grieved me deeply. I knew I too must share the guilt of Friday, for I had lacked that which I most admired in the late President: vigor, courage, and wisdom.

It was too soon to see how the hand of God was moving in this historical event, the passing of a great American. But in this time of mourning I expressed the hope that, "[W]e at least can remember his courage and devotion to the cause of world peace; his devotion to freedom and justice for all persons regardless of race, creed or color; his courage to attack the status quo and challenge our prejudices and self-interest." I said: "We must stand in judgment before God and not let his passing be in vain."

In writing the speech that he was to deliver in Dallas on Friday, Kennedy chose to close it with a quotation from Psalm 127:1b (RSV): "Unless the Lord watches over the city, the watchman stays awake in vain." I told the congregation that part of Kennedy's greatness came from the fact that he knew that all his tremendous energy and wisdom was of no avail; that all was in vain unless it was a just heritage from the Lord. I concluded by saying that "those of us who rise from deep contrition over the guilt of his untimely death, must lay hold to this heritage that made our late President great, thus not allowing his death to have been in vain. That heritage says that we cannot hate our brother, even Lee Harvey Oswald, and still say we love God. We know that there is no fear in love, but perfect love casts out all fear, even the fear of guilt." On Monday I was asked to offer a prayer at the memorial service held at the Amory middle school.

Bob Walkup, my mentor and friend, was a native Mississippian who was a candidate for the ministry from Senatobia when my daddy was pastor there. Bob had inspired us with his leadership in the church and his response to what was happening in society at large. He said that his big mouth, his stubborn Scottish mind, and his Presbyterianism made him a bunch of enemies in the Synod of Mississippi when he was appointed chairman of the special judicial commission handling the "Mac" Hart case. He said he sat ninety hours on that commission and "saw more 'Christian' hate than I knew existed this side of hell." He defended the National Council of Churches, fought a move to censure the U.S. Supreme Court on the prayer case, and opposed Paul Johnson for governor. He claimed the First Presbyterian Church in Starkville where he was pastor was "the best and freest parish in the Synod. And then came the dawn."[33]

The dawn occurred when the deacons asked the question about seating blacks that came to worship. Initially, the session voted to seat them in a special section, but this was not the end of it. The community, the governor, and the Citizens' Council groups brought unbelievable pressure on the session to change its decision. And it did. Four elders stood fast with Bob, but in the end he said, "[M]y soul sickened and my mind fuzzed over. I grew weary with the struggle and loneliness of it all. There is nothing in this world so profound as the silence of good men."

He went on to say, "[W]hen the President was murdered, the sickness and the hate in Mississippi came out into the open and its sheer ugliness was almost beyond human comprehension . . . . I wept until there were no more tears and a cold anger swept over me. That frightened me for I knew what anger could do." So in the year of our Lord, 1964, Walkup, a lifelong Mississippian, packed up his family and left Mississippi for a call to First Presbyterian Church in McAllen, Texas, way down in the Rio Grande Valley.[34]

The issue of race in the Presbyterian Church U.S. had been at the heart of its identity since its inception in the 1860s, and still was defining its existence in the 1960s. Lines were drawn in session rooms in local congregations and on the floors of presbyteries, synods, and the General Assembly itself, the highest court of the church. The General Assembly, meeting in Montreat, North Carolina, on April 23–28, 1964, took up the issue raised by an overture from the Presbytery of Potomac[35] regarding the designation of "Negro Presbyteries" that "occupy the same district of other Presbyteries [white] of our denomination." One of the three such "Negro Presbyteries," the Presbytery of Louisiana-Mississippi, was located in the same geographical area in Mississippi as the Presbyteries of South Mississippi, Central Mississippi, and St. Andrew Presbytery where I was a member. The General Assembly noted that such an overlap was "not only contrary to our constitution but also weakens our witness by the perpetuation of an institutional form of enforced segregation on the basis of race, which is out of keeping with the consistent stand of our denomination."

The General Assembly's response to the overture was to instruct all its presbyteries [white] where this overlap occurred to bring their procedures into line with the constitution of our church, and to take into their membership and under their care all of the ministers and churches of our denomination [black] within the district for which they bear particular responsibility. The assembly also instructed those presbyteries to begin the process promptly and to present a report of their progress to the General Assembly at its next meeting [in 1965]. Finally, it instructed the three synods in which the three "Negro Presbyteries" were located to take steps to dissolve the three segregated presbyteries as soon as this orderly transfer has been accomplished. In another matter, the assembly began debate over "amending the Directory of Worship to prohibit exclusion of persons from worship on grounds of race, color or class."[36]

For almost five years I worked hard in Amory to replicate pastor and church as I had experienced it, and I had done a fairly respectable job. But the turmoil at Ole Miss and the Kennedy assassination, as well as the growing convulsion in the denomination over race, added a whole new dimension to my first call and was taking its toll. Walkup had been the spiritual and emotional anchor that kept my colleagues and me from drifting off course, but now our anchor was no more among us. Two of my seminary classmates who had come to Mississippi with me had found other calls and left. Little did I know that in two more years the other three of us would be gone from Mississippi. Only two would ever come back to serve there again. Though I could not yet hear the plane bringing Buddy to search for me, I could sense that it was on its way.

CHAPTER 4

Freedom Summer

The sun was beginning to push the shadows of darkness toward the west as I drove out of the parking lot at the Admiral Benbow Motel on Union Avenue in Memphis, Tennessee, on a Monday. It was June 22, 1964. I would not learn until later how dark the night before had been for some. I left my wife and son in Memphis to go home with her mother, who had driven over to take them home to Jonesboro, Arkansas, for a visit. I was on my way to Louisville, Kentucky, to settle in at the Presbyterian Seminary, which had only recently moved to its new campus at 1044 Alta Vista Road. My family would fly up to join me later in the summer. I looked forward to spending a quiet summer retreat writing my master's thesis on what I took to be an erudite topic: "A Study of the Impact of Existential Theology on the Campus Ministry."[1] I had spent the better part of the previous year in dialogue with campus ministers at various colleges and universities in Mississippi and at their national conference at Montreat, North Carolina. All the data from the requisite "questionnaire" were in.

Tuesday morning as I walked to the seminary administration build-ing to make my presence known, I ran into a couple of people engaged in animated conversation in the quadrangle. One was a woman minister from the Northern Presbyterian Church, an aunt of a good friend, and the other was a Lutheran clergyman. When I greeted them, they could tell by the way I spoke that I was from somewhere in the Deep South. Upon finding out I was from Mississippi, they immediately tore into me, as if blaming me for all the ills emerging from that part of the world. I soon found out about the news that Michael Schwerner, Andrew Goodman, and James Chaney, three civil rights workers, had been missing in the vicinity of Philadelphia, Mississippi, since Sunday evening. I knew then that the long, hot summer had gotten much hotter.

Stunned by this revelation, I could barely think about the task that I came to Louisville to complete. I was somewhat reluctant to leave my parish for the summer knowing that Mississippi was bracing for the "invasion" (as it was perceived by some Mississippians) of northern students coming to register black voters and run "freedom schools." These were key elements of the Freedom Summer campaign spearheaded by the Student Non-Violent Coordinating Committee (SNCC). As I wandered around the campus trying to figure out what to do, I found out that the National Council of Churches (NCC) was sponsoring, in coordination with SNCC, a two-week long orientation and training session at the Western College for Women in Oxford, Ohio, for those students going to Mississippi. I had the impression the NCC felt that, if SNCC were going to go through with this plan, somebody had better help prepare these volunteers for what they would face in Mississippi.

Through previous months I knew little or nothing about SNCC other than the virulent attacks against these so-called "foreign anarchists" by arch segregationists. I listened for years to ultraconservatives in the Presbyterian Church rant about the social stance of the NCC. I resented being written off as a stereotypical white southerner by northern liberals and wanted to prove otherwise. These three factors were enough in themselves to get the adrenalin flowing. But most of all, my gut told me I was about to be swept up in something extremely traumatic for which I was ill prepared when I returned to Mississippi.

I pulled out my road map to locate Oxford and discovered it was an easy drive from Louisville, located in the southwest corner of Ohio near Cincinnati. I felt compelled to go north to see firsthand what was taking place. This was motivation enough. It was as simple as that.

Very early, before dawn Thursday morning, I headed north of the Ohio River into what was, for me, uncharted territory. I was the consummate foreigner in an alien environment with all the attendant raging emotions. All the way there, I was very apprehensive about what attention my Mississippi license plates might draw when I arrived. What I discovered when I tried to find a parking place was that the streets were inundated with cars bearing Mississippi plates, so I was able to blend in! I soon discovered that many of those cars belonged to the working class black women, neighborhood organizers in their local communities, who had been brought to Oxford to be part of the orientation teams.[2] Fannie Lou Hamer was one of the prominent leaders present.

The place was a flurry of activity both in and out of doors. All around the lawn small groups simulated the protective positions they might have to assume in threatening situations after they arrived in Mississippi.

Firecrackers were set off from time to time for effect. The Council of Federated Organizations (COFO) and SNCC had recruited students—evenly divided between men and women—from all over the country: California, New Jersey, Michigan, and Massachusetts were all represented. There were a few more whites than blacks, a few Asians, Native Americans, Jews, and Latinos. Most seemed to fit the then current description of Beatnik intellectuals: men with beards, folk singers, guitars, and bare feet, dressed in all kinds of garb. There were some clean-cut young people, schoolteachers, mixed couples, and older blacks from Mississippi. Some were Christian, some non-Christian. Some were political science enthusiasts, while others were old-line agitators. Some were there just for kicks. But for the most part, they all were dedicated to the cause, idealists who believed in the cause of freedom.

The thought crossed my mind: How in the world could such a diverse group of people be molded together in such a short period of time to become an effective force for their cause? Where were the booby traps that would do them in? I had little or no idea what the answers were at the time.

I spent the day walking in and out of various group activities without challenge. As I moved around I engaged individuals in conversation. The first person I met was a black lady who was head of the Freedom House at Canton, and who was having a discussion with a staff member. In retrospect I wondered if that could have been Annie Devine, whom I later learned was in Oxford at Bob Moses's invitation to prepare the students for the racial realities of the Deep South.[3] The staff member was Paul Zimmerman, a Disciples of Christ (possibly United Church of Christ) seminary student assigned as chaplain to the group of students going to Canton, Mississippi, who told me he was a pacifist. At first he was somewhat suspicious of my motives, but in time he took me around to meet different people.

We visited with a small mixed group of people that included a couple of young men from Jackson and a student from Cornell University whose way had been paid by an Episcopal bishop, Ronald and Polly Robinson from Greenville, Mississippi, friends of Hodding Carter, and Charles Walker, by his own admission an "old-time agitator." We talked about their feelings about the NCC and what they were doing here. They were supportive of the NCC. Some had the tendency to lump all whites together. Others said some whites are concerned but are afraid to speak out.

They all seemed almost awed that a white minister from Mississippi would take the time to come all the way to Oxford, Ohio, to find out what was going on. Theirs was almost a feeling of disbelief. They wanted me to make a speech to the whole group, but I declined because of the TV press coverage. I did not want to appear on the evening news back in Columbia when they thought I was cloistered in the seminary writing a master's thesis. I might have been uninformed, but I was no fool!

We went to a general session where two lawyers, one white and one black, were providing background on the legal aspects of the project. The black lawyer had been involved in taking Meredith and others into Ole Miss. They discussed legal points about the uses of cars: speeding, insurance, tags, and lending them to others. They gave specific instructions about what to do when arrested, the types of courts the freedom riders might face, and the various charges they might face: loitering, littering, or vagrancy. The lawyers covered what to plead: no contest, stand mute, or guilty. They talked about bail and what to do if released from jail at 10 p.m.

The lawyers also warned that the southwestern counties of Mississippi—Pike, Amite, Wilkinson, Adams, Jefferson, Franklin, Lincoln— might be the most dangerous sections of the state. This warning hit home emotionally for me, because I grew up in Brookhaven, county seat of Lincoln County. Bob Moses knew this area firsthand owing to the violence and arrests he experienced during his organizing and voter registration work in McComb (Pike) and Liberty (Amite) in the summer and fall of 1961.[4] Summer projects in this area in 1964 were planned only in Natchez (Adams) and McComb (Pike).

A great deal of time was spent on issues such as moral conduct, alcohol use, and travel to their destination. The group was briefed on what to expect from the press, the FBI, and the CIA. Then the lawyers got into the premise for going down to Mississippi, which was to focus attention on opening up lines of communication, even though it was very much a closed society. This was a power struggle in which law and order must go. They reasoned that Mississippi laws were inconsistent; therefore, they did not have to be obeyed. I got the impression they could not seem to answer how this "invasion" would change whites in Mississippi. We were left with the vague impression that if the participants could get enough information reasonably put before the whites, the situation would change. To me the speakers clearly did not understand the situation. The final point was time was running out; this appalling situation had been going on for a hundred years. "We must move now"—though they recognized it could not all be done in a summer. This conclusion offered more ambiguity, but it seemed more realistic to me.

I attended workshops on voter registration and freedom schools, the two main thrusts of the summer project. These workshops proved quite an education for me. In the first, I discovered there were several facets to the voter registration leadership and implementation. COFO, which came into being in 1962, was made up of several civil rights groups whose shared purpose was to coordinate voter registration efforts in the South. This organization was responsible, on paper, for overseeing the voter registration facet of the summer project. However, I found out that SNCC was supplying the vast majority of the staff and funding, based on the work they had done in Mississippi for three years during which time they endured violent retribution at the hands of unrepentant white supremacists. I got the impression these veterans naturally felt a certain proprietorship over this project; it was theirs to run. I also saw large numbers of starry-eyed volunteers who signed on believing optimism and idealism alone were sufficient to bring change to Mississippi. As I watched and listened, I sensed many did not have a clue about what was about to happen to them. I could not help but wonder how this combination of seasoned project staff and idealistic volunteers would work out together on the road.

SNCC and COFO gave their endorsement to Bob Moses's more expansive plans for voter registration efforts in the summer of 1964, encouraged by what they had achieved in the "Freedom Vote" campaign they had conducted in the fall of 1963. Eighty thousand Mississippians had participated in the mock election.[5] But the issue was more than simple registration to vote. In a sense that was a dead end, because blacks did not have access to the Democratic Party. Part of SNCC's strategy was to organize an alternative to the regular Democratic Party in Mississippi; thus the Mississippi Freedom Democratic Party (MFDP) was born. Its immediate purpose was to challenge the party regulars in the June 2 Democratic primaries. Then, if this plan failed, MFDP needed to get enough signatures to get its candidates on the November ballot as independents. This strategy also failed, so SNCC/MFDP held another mock election to challenge the Mississippi regular delegation to the August National Democratic Convention in Atlantic City.[6] The event here in Oxford, Ohio, was an integral part of this larger strategy.

The training leaders' job was further complicated, because there were two parts to the voter registration drive itself. One was an attempt to get individuals registered as official voters, requiring going to the courthouse. This part had very tangible pitfalls and challenges. The other part was to get as many registered as "freedom registering" voters for the MFDP; this could be done in the home. Both parts were difficult in their respective ways for the volunteers to accomplish.[7] All these dynamics were playing themselves out as part of the training sessions at Oxford as I stood by and watched.

The second workshop that attracted my attention concerned freedom schools. Organizers had realized that focus on voter registration, though important, was not enough to bring about change in Mississippi. For too long the separate but unequal segregated education system had perpetuated a devastating effect on the black population. In its curriculum, this bi-level system unabashedly championed "Our Way of Life" for the whites, while degrading the black experience by summarily ignoring noteworthy achievements of black Americans. Freedom schools were the brainchild of Charlie Cobb, a field secretary for SNCC. The National Council of Churches picked up on his idea and called a meeting in March 1964 of educators, clergy, and SNCC staff to generate the details for the basic curriculum.[8]

At the workshop, volunteers were given curriculum packets and introduced to its contents, the final material trickling in at the last moment. A packet consisted of a collection of mimeographed pages, exercises, newspaper articles, pamphlets, booklets, and an assortment of other statistical information. A great deal of discretion in utilizing the material was left to the teachers. The table of contents began with a note of explanation to the teacher regarding the three major content parts: Part I: Academic Curriculum on reading and writing skills and mathematics; Part II: Citizenship Curriculum consisting of seven units with case studies including topics such as the history of the Negro in White America, Mississippi power structure, poor whites, poor Negroes and their fears, discipline in the non-violent movements and the movement itself; Part III: Recreational and Artistic Curriculum.[9] As the workshop progressed, I became very interested in obtaining one of these curriculum packets to take with me. Naturally, there was great hesitation on the part of SNCC staff regarding my request, so they declined it.

Late in the afternoon, all the participants gathered in an auditorium to hear various speakers talk about what life was like in Mississippi, in both the white and black communities. There were some somber and tense moments when the proceedings were stopped to receive reports from the front. At times conflicting messages were received regarding the three missing workers in Neshoba County. National network TV cameras rolled in order to send the story unfolding in Oxford, Ohio, out to all America, and I was careful to avoid their cameras and lights.

As afternoon faded into twilight, the day seemed almost surreal to me. I had gotten caught up in hovering over maps pointing out roads and shortcuts to towns I had known like the back of my hand. It was hard to believe what I was actually witnessing, as hard as it was for others to believe things I had taken for granted all my life in my separate but unequal upbringing. I was flooded with despair born of information overload, from hearing about all it took to plan a full-scale invasion of one's homeland by what I considered an unprepared band of volunteers.

Leaving the auditorium I saw a lost and found table which held three pairs of glasses, one half jar of peanut butter, one half jar of mustard, one banana, and some undelivered mail. Above the table was a bulletin board on which were posted late notices of activities in Mississippi, a letter entitled "Tears for America," and copies of comments from Rita Schwerner. As I was standing by the table attempting to make sense of the juxtaposition of these items and all I had experienced that day, my new friend, Paul Zimmerman, walked up. He could tell I was about to leave. Before I left he asked, "Do you know anyone in Canton I can talk with, a sympathetic white person?" I said, "Sure. Go see Dick Harbison, pastor of the First Presbyterian Church. He will talk with you. He is a native of Greenville, Mississippi and will be sympathetic." As I turned to leave, he said, "Thanks for coming." Then he reached out to me and gave me his curriculum packet saying, "I trust you and want you to have it. I will get another one some way for myself."

We shook hands, and I was on my way south to Louisville with my mind racing in a thousand directions. Could I trust what I had seen and heard? How can I possibly share this day with folks in Columbia? Would I run into any of these people when I got back to Mississippi? Will some I have met not make it back home after the summer is over? What difference will all this make anyway? I had few answers. But somehow things were different now. I was intent on keeping up with the progress of the Freedom Summer project in Mississippi, for what had been an abstraction now came alive for me in a collage of faces, owing to my brief immersion in Oxford, Ohio. I probably would never see many of the people I met there again. However, I would see the faces of other workers and look at them with new understanding and appreciation.

The rest of the summer was uneventful for me, in a sense. My family joined me, and we celebrated our son's first birthday on July 3 at the seminary apartment. I did fly back to Mississippi for a presbytery meeting but did not go to Columbia. Epps was at the meeting and gave me an update on his activities. I felt a thousand of miles away from what was going on and was not quite ready to go back. I did manage to complete the first draft of my master's thesis before we returned to Columbia

Things were beginning to change in Columbia, too. Momentum for change had begun months before the heat began to rise in the "long hot summer of 1964," as it became known. President John F. Kennedy laid the foundation for a civil rights bill he wanted introduced to Congress in a speech he delivered on June 11, 1963.[10] On August 28,1963, Martin Luther King gave his "I Have a Dream" speech on the steps of the Lincoln Memorial during the March on Washington.[11] This gave the Civil Rights Bill much needed support. Kennedy's bill stalled in the legislative process by the events of November 22, 1963, but subsequently President Lyndon Johnson rallied the cause.

Opposition to the Civil Rights Bill before the Senate began to mount across the country—including Columbia. For a number of years, the State Sovereignty Commission (SSC) had been operating widely across the state. The commission was established in 1956 by the Mississippi legislature in response to *Brown v. Board of Education* (1954) and in essence was an arm of state government.[12]

SSC's stated purpose was to "protect the sovereignty of the State of Mississippi and her sister states" from "federal encroachment." It started out attempting to present the state "in a positive light" and to defend segregation, praising the harmony that existed between the races. During all the time it carried out its operations, SSC hired both paid and unpaid informants to spy on civil rights workers and acted as a clearinghouse for information gathered in this fashion. It also channeled money to pro-segregation causes and handed out right-wing propaganda.[13] In 1961, SCC sent its investigators to Columbia to make sure everything was "quiet and under control" with regard to "race relations."[14] With the threat posed to their way of thinking, members of the SSC actively opposed the Civil Rights Act of 1964 as it was being enacted.

Cable television's round-the-clock uninterrupted news coverage was still decades away in the 1960s. Nonetheless, the visual impact of breaking news stories on network TV channels was beginning to have a dramatic affect on viewers' emotions. The shocking clips from filming on the streets of Dallas the previous fall, together with subsequent somber scenes from Arlington Cemetery, were nothing compared with the steady diet of horrors consumed with our suppers during the evening news—the fire hoses of Birmingham, the dogs of Selma, and eventually the blistering napalm of Vietnam and the incendiary flames of Watts. And as powerful as these images were, it was the print media of the 1960s that inflamed our fears and perpetuated our prejudices. On occasion our best aspirations for justice and peace were engendered by the print media.

Newspapers in Mississippi were right in the middle of the struggle between those defending segregation and those aligning themselves with America's demand for civil rights.[15] The state's major daily newspapers in the 1950s and 1960s, under the control of the Hederman family in Jackson (the *Jackson Clarion-Ledger* and *Jackson Daily News* with its editor, Major Frederick Sullens) kept the cause of segregation heated to the boiling point. Jimmy Ward's column on the left side of the front page of the *Daily News* was often the first place many statewide readers turned to get the latest racist jokes and devastating jabs at political moderates, liberals, and "outside agitators." The weeklies followed suit with their unabashed lashing of the outside interference of the federal government and "integrationists." One of the editors most ardently defending segregation and states' rights and delighting in attacking Washington was Mary D. "Hacksaw Mary" Cain of the *Summit Sun*, nearby Columbia.

Newspapers strongly presenting opposing views in Mississippi were few and far between. Bill Minor, the Mississippi correspondent for the New Orleans *Times-Picayune*, who was stationed in Jackson, and Kenneth Toler of the Memphis *Commercial Appeal*, provided courageous and objective reporting in daily papers circulating in the state. The same quality of reporting and commentary came in the weeklies from Hodding Carter, Jr. in the Greenville *Delta Democrat-Times*, George A. McLean in the Tupelo *Journal*, Hazel Brannon Smith in the Lexington *Advertiser*, and in the off-the-charts satire of P. D. East in *The Petal Paper*. Occasionally clandestine student newssheets, like "The Nigble Papers," lampooning the Scotch-Irish that made up the majority of white citizens, showed up on college campuses across the state in hopes of "getting college students whose minds had not yet been closed to laugh at the stupidity around them."[16] News coverage by the *Columbian-Progress* during these years struck a more moderate pose. Although it did not adopt the shrill editorial policies of other weeklies in the state, it did print Thurman Sensing's Column, "Sensing the News," and articles by senators and congressmen touting segregation and anti-Washington sentiments. Although there was limited reporting of civil rights activities, I recall the *Columbian-Progress* printed no pictures related to these activities.

An article run on April 23 in the *Columbian-Progress* announced the opening of the Freedom Writers Office at 324 Second Street. Those who wanted material opposing the Civil Rights Bill to send friends and relatives could "avail themselves of the office." Each was urged to "write his senators and, or, the Senate majority or minority leaders, expressing opposition to the bill." Also available was a copy of an advertisement prepared "by the coordinating committee for Fundamental American Freedoms, Inc., of which William Loeb of Manchester, N.H., is chairman and John C. Satterfield of Yazoo City is secretary." The office said, "All you do is sign a letter! You are urged to respond to this important movement! HELP KEEP AMERICA THE LAND OF THE FREE!"[17]

On May 28, a large ad soliciting votes for Edward A. "Eddie" Khayat as candidate for the Fifth Congressional District seat appeared in the *Columbian-Progress*. The ad challenged Bill Colmer, the incumbent, for taking no action in ten years to stop the advancement of activities pertaining to civil rights: "1954—*Supreme Court Decision Integrating Schools*; 1957—*Eisenhower Sends Troops To Little Rock—Governor Faubus Pleads For Help*; 1963—'*OLE MISS' CRISES*; 1964—*CIVIL RIGHTS BILL Passes House In It's* [sic] *Entirety*." The incumbent claimed, "I have seniority, power and influence." The challenger responded, "Then Why Doesn't he use it? Please Vote for Eddie Khayat, Man of Courage, Action and Abililty."[18]

Khayat failed to unseat Colmer in this election. This did not diminish his involvement in politics. He functioned as an influential cog in the widespread political machine created by Senator James Eastland. In time, Khayat became a legend in his own right because of his service on the Jackson County Board of Supervisors. He was "known on the Gulf Coast as 'The Godfather' long before Francis Ford Coppola made his sequence of movies with that name." From time to time he played fast and loose with the law. In the 1960s Khayat was indicted for evading payment of income taxes "connected with a kickback scheme." Eastland's promise to Khayat that he would serve no jail time was realized when U.S. District Court Judge Harold Cox "took care of it." In the wake of Hurricane Frederic, which devastated the Gulf Coast in 1979, Khayat did what Mississippi politicians had done for ages: He ordered public employees to clean up and restore private property. This order led to an indictment on eight counts of misusing property, issued by a new political rival in the district attorney's office. Though Khayat contested the charges, he eventually pled guilty to a lesser misdemeanor and was convicted in 1982, leaving him broken "as a political leader."[19]

Although some attention was paid to the passage of the Civil Rights Act, the situation in Columbia was rather quiet on the surface. The Freedom Summer project did not seem to have a visible impact on the community at the beginning of the summer, since there was no actual project slated for Columbia. In some ways it appeared as if it would be business as usual at public facilities, meaning they remained segregated. A three-inch column in the *Columbian-Progress* on May 28 noted that the city pools would open on June 7, offering junior and senior lifesaving courses at the City Park Pool (white) on June 1 and 2, with swimming classes at the Duckworth Recreation Center (black) "on the arrival of the instructor, Willie Bradley."[20] Discrepancies in service were obvious and a clue that change had yet to arrive.

Dwain Epps had arrived in Columbia as a summer intern the first week of June.[21] Years later he said that he was "very much aware of the suspicions that people more than ten miles north of the Gulf Coast would have in general about a Yankee nosing about in their neighborhood!" Furthermore, he knew his Oregon license plate on his little blue VW Beetle made his "origins as obvious as did his somewhat unpolished Mississippi accent coming straight out of a year in California!" Although he was not a civil rights worker, he had "strong sympathies with the movement and admired those who had made that choice." On the way to Columbia, Epps "stopped by the COFO headquarters in Hattiesburg for a briefing on how things were and tried to keep some contact during the summer in order to have an idea what was being planned for our neighborhood." Epps said he felt reasonably safe, but it was clear he should keep a low profile. Later, when I found out about this side trip, I thought that it was a dumb thing to do; I figured inquiring eyes had him covered. However, a recent search of the digital collection of the Mississippi Department of Archives and History indicated no entry for Epps in the Mississippi Sovereignty Commission records.

Very soon after I left for Louisville, Epps was faced with the disappearance of the three civil rights workers in Neshoba County near Philadelphia. There was no doubt in anyone's mind what had happened. The next week at the evening prayer service, usually attended by a handful of elderly ladies, Epps prayed for the safety of these three young men, for Mississippi and especially for Columbia. He felt that this act in itself could be dangerous, because he knew word had a way of getting around quickly. He expected the worst but much to his surprise found that the news of what took place at the prayer service came as a relief in many quarters.

It enabled some who were hesitant to talk with him about their fears and their hopes. The fact that these murders were in the press constantly for the next six weeks, until the bodies were unearthed, might have increased Epps's feeling of personal insecurity. But according to his account, he came to feel protected by the community despite the presence of the Citizens' Council and—as he suspected—also the Klan.

Although he never was directly threatened, Epps was aware that the Citizens' Council closely watched him. In addition to experiencing an enormous benefit from the patronage of several families in the congregation, he also felt blessed by the companionship of N. A. Dickson, the pastor of First Methodist Church. A close relationship formed between the two, for they shared the same ideas and commitments both theologically and socially. Epps said he learned a great deal about what one needed to watch for. They developed a pattern of regular meetings, "usually out in the woods where we would not be observed together, to share information on what we were seeing and hearing." Most of all, they gave each other mutual support in what was becoming an increasingly delicate situation, especially for N.A.

The debate over the Civil Rights Bill dissolved into a filibuster that raged on for fifty-four working days and six Saturdays, led by Senator Richard Russell (D-GA) and seventeen other southern Democrats. Finally, as Senator Robert Byrd (D-WV) wound down his marathon opposition speech, Russell privately told Hubert H. Humphrey (D-MN) that he would end the filibuster blocking the vote. The cloture motion was put, and it passed seventy-one to twenty-nine, the first time in Senate history that there had been enough such votes on a civil rights bill. In rapid fashion, the necessary votes were taken in the Senate, the House-Senate conference committee, and finally both houses of Congress, so that the Civil Rights Bill of 1964 was placed on the president's desk for signature on July 2.[22] And so the seeds were sown for the Republicans' "southern strategy," fine tuned later by Richard Nixon, that would hold sway for over four decades.

At the time of this historic event the Presbyterian Church within Mississippi and throughout the nation was caught up in a raging snarl of theological, sociological, and ecclesial kudzu, knotted together in a strange alliance while attempting to untangle the cultural legacies of the times. This theological clash between fundamentalism and liberalism had its origin in the ecclesial conflicts within the Presbyterian Church of the 1920s. At the heart of the controversy were diametrically opposed views concerning biblical authority. Without going into great detail here, I'll note that fundamentalism held that since God inspired the scriptures, every word was believed to be without error and must be taken literally. In its extreme form fundamentalism was very dogmatic and authoritarian. Its "gospel" focused on the "salvation of individuals." Liberalism, in contrast, held that scripture, written by men who were inspired by God, was to be treated as a historical source, leaving room for divergent interpretations. Authority then came, not so much from the actual wording of the text, but from the "facts" behind the text as reconstructed by the historian/theologian through the discipline known as historical and biblical criticism.[23] Its "gospel" focused on the "regeneration of social systems."

Seeking a middle ground, neo-orthodoxy, a camp within which I would place myself if I had to join one, joined the fray. This stance placed neo-orthodoxy between the rigidity of fundamentalism by "arguing for the validity of biblical criticism," and on the one hand, the extremes of liberalism by "asserting the centrality of scripture." Neo-orthodoxy attempted to pull together the sinful character of individuals and of social organizations, both in need of redemption.[24] The theological clash in the Synod of Mississippi during the 1960s was characterized as taking place between the fundamentalism and neo-orthodoxy, since there wasn't much pure liberalism going around.

Race and segregation became the connection, or lack thereof, between the theological and the sociological in this snarl. As indicated, neo-orthodoxy was clear about the social application of its "gospel" when it came to the debate between segregation and integration. But this belief was anathema to the fundamentalists. Rev. G. T. Gillespie, President Emeritus of Belhaven College, championed the biblical basis for segregation. In his speech before the 1954 meeting of the Synod of Mississippi, he had cited eleven passages of scripture, eight from the Old Testament and three from the New Testament, in defending segregation on biblical grounds—according to his interpretation. In summary, he said that for two thousand years segregation was imposed on the Hebrew people by divine command. When this command was broken, the punishment was extremely severe.[25]

Gillespie also held that Christ and the apostles taught the love of God for all mankind, making it clear that the principles of Christian brotherhood and charity could apply to all relations of life "without demanding revolutionary changes in the natural or social order." Because of this conviction, he saw no reason to believe that segregation was "in conflict with the spirit and the teachings of Christ and the Apostles, and therefore unChristian."[26] Was this mere irony or extremely convoluted logic? There was no middle ground for those who held this fundamentalist position, making theological dialogue impossible with those of us who believed differently about the redemption of the social order. Segregation for Gillespie and his followers, who were legion in Mississippi, was a foregone and foreordained conclusion.

The ecclesial snarl played out in battles over realignment of governing body boundaries and who gets in and who does not. Battles over compliance with the General Assembly mandate to receive the black congregations and ministers into presbyteries and responses to periodic outbursts of violence in the streets were yet to come. The basic issue of race was often glossed over when the conflict was couched in terms of power and control of the Presbyterian system. Nonetheless, it was ever present.

Litigation of the Mac Hart case in the church courts had ignited tension and divisiveness among Presbyterians in Mississippi. In late spring of 1964 the General Assembly, the highest court of the Presbyterian Church U.S., sustained a complaint from the Synod of Mississippi in the contest with Central Mississippi Presbytery over the examination of Hart in 1962. The complaint contended the presbytery had erred in permitting improper questions, related to his views on integration and church reunion, calculated to prejudice the presbyters against Hart, related to his views on integration and church reunion. The Synod of Mississippi, an appellate court, requested that the General Assembly instruct Central Mississippi Presbytery to re-examine Hart and ordered that a transcript be made of the proceedings.

In a meeting (which was open to the public) held on July 4, 1964, at the Presbyterian church in Pearl, Mississippi, Hart was re-examined and a 155-page transcript was returned to a commission of the Synod of Mississippi.[27] Hart was never installed at Trinity during the appeals process, although he served the congregation for three years. In 1965, before the case was finally adjudicated, he would accept a call to a church in Little Rock, making the results of the process moot.

On Sunday, July 5, Epps preached on the topic, "Dependence Day." His entry in my ministerial log indicated: "Sunday following Pres. Johnson's signing of C.R. Bill . . .Well received." He entered several interesting remarks about his other sermons, all expressions of his support for the denominational programs of the Presbyterian Church. On July 26, he preached "The One-Horse Rocket," in which he pointed out how the Christian education program lagged behind secular learning. Then the following week, on August 2, he followed up with, "Let the Bible Do the Talking," introducing the new denominational Covenant Life Curriculum, and he encouraged participation in its preview events sponsored by the synod.

Over the summer, Epps developed a significant ministry with the young people, who were mostly high school age, but also included a few young college kids home for the summer. He started out with some Bible study discussions with them, which quickly led into more relaxed general conversations about life. By the end of the summer he was doing quite a lot of personal counseling with individuals, not all of whom were from the Presbyterian Church. They had come along with their Presbyterian friends. Epps said they tended to run interference for him with their families and to ease his way with them. A few of the parents were infuriated with the fact that Epps was sharing translations of the Bible other than the King James Version in the youth study groups. This tended to put him and the Presbyterian Church off limits for those parents.

Meanwhile, with the passage of the Civil Rights Act and reports from other parts of the state regarding the violence related to the Freedom Summer invasion spearheaded by SNCC, opposition rhetoric began to heat up around Columbia. Word was out that the National Council of Churches had sponsored, in coordination with SNCC, the training sessions in Oxford, Ohio. Thurman Sensing, in his "Sensing the News" column in the *Columbian-Progress* on July 9, entitled his remarks "No Precedent For State Invasion," referring to the summer project by SNCC in Mississippi.[28] He wrote: "Indeed the average American planning a peaceful summer can hardly imagine what is involved in the extraordinary combined operation to push through revolutionary changes in the customs of one state." He contended that few churchmen understand why the National Council of Churches invested so much of its resources to work "hand and glove with SNCC, an organization that is insurrectionary in character and infiltrated with communists." He doubted that the "reasonable majority of the American people," regardless of what they thought about the "wisdom of Mississippi's social arrangements," would approve of the "worst type of radical extremism to force through change."

He went on to point out that there were more acceptable ways, in particular amending the U.S. Constitution, to bring about change "gradually without a social explosion." But those wanting radical change, in his judgment, did not want to pursue change in this way, because they were only a "tiny radical group" facing "the great body of the American people" that did not want change. Another way to bring about change was through the states, which provided "50 laboratories" that had their "own special approach to the problems of popular government, allowing progress geared to special characteristics and needs of the people." But this traditional view was challenged by "the liberal intelligentsia concentrated in a few crowded hectic metropolitan centers, . . . determined that everyone must live in the same way and have precisely the same system of state government."

Sensing then proceeded to search for parallel illustrations to explain what was going on by referring to radicals in the 1930s "meeting in beer halls, and when Hitler Youth were being trained to invade communities and destroy law and order and social peace." He topped his remarks off with a nod to the Chinese communists' revolutionary political devices and "what the Soviets call partisan warfare." All the hot button fears and prejudices of the day were trotted out.

Epps made a modest effort to set forth alternate views, constrained by the temporary nature of his involvement in the community. In early August, Syd Armstrong, an elder in the church who was in charge of the program at the Rotary Club, invited Epps to speak to the club. Bobby Buchanan, another member of the church and Syd's nephew, introduced Epps to the club. He noted that although Epps was a native of Oregon, he was "formerly stationed at Keesler Field and has been a resident of Mississippi for a number of years." This seemed a way to ease into the subject of Epps's presentation, "North and South Need Better Understanding!"[29] Epps completed his meaningful service as a summer intern by leading the worship on August 30 and preaching on the subject, "That Your Joy May Be Full." He returned to California to continue his studies at San Francisco Seminary the following week.

◆ ◆ ◆

The Freedom Summer project, which had begun with high hopes and high ideals based on moral persuasion as a strategy for social change, by year's end found itself in a very different place, marred by violence. COFO kept a running tally from June 16 to August 26 of "hostile incidents" across the state that ran "twenty-six mimeographed pages long and covers everything from threatening phone calls to the disappearance of the three workers." Numerous incidents were listed for McComb, Hattiesburg, and Laurel, but none for Columbia. The more prominent incidents were: "4 project workers killed; 4 persons critically wounded; 80 workers beaten; 1000 arrests; 37 churches bombed or burned; 30 black homes or businesses bombed or burned." The sheer volume of incidents and the gravity of the summary do not do justice to "the combination of shock, anger, disillusionment, and fear the volunteers felt in the face of the violence and terror they were witnessing."[30]

The debate about the efficacy of "nonviolence as both tactic and philosophy" was turned on its head by the violence that was encountered in Mississippi. Federal officials, who at times appeared not to be predisposed to do what was morally right, were at a loss to contain the violence served up by white supremacists. By the same token, these same officials had difficulty protecting civil rights workers. So the high ground occupied by moral persuasion was severely compromised, and nonviolence was becoming less attractive to those in the movement. Furthermore, SNCC leadership discovered a long tradition in "a black population that relied on armed self-defense as the ultimate response to supremacist violence." Freedom Summer, on one level, was a failure of moral persuasion, and "the attractiveness of force or self-defense" became a new strategy of choice for many in SNCC.[31] This change merely fueled the notion of some whites that SNCC was "insurrectionary in character."

Choosing sides between non-violence and use of force as a means of self-defense would not bode well for the future of SNCC. The "Beloved Community" was being torn asunder. This eventuality, along with the increased hostility toward whites in some of SNCC's ranks, led to a decline in involvement by northern students in the movement. The momentum built among activist students during Freedom Summer was lost, though this loss took a couple of years to become evident.[32]

I resumed my pastoral responsibilities on September 6 and preached about new beginnings in my sermon, "Pilgrimage of the Soul," a revised version of the sermon I had preached two years before to the day, when Murphy Wilds and family had visited in Amory.[33] The new beginnings had to do with new and fresh goals for the next twelve months that would give vitality and renewed life to the congregation's pilgrimage of the soul. I recommended new goals for a vital program of youth work; new teachers for the church school; new special study groups using the new curriculum; a renewed emphasis on stewardship; and fresh signs of encouragement to others in fulfilling one's Christian commitment. I plunged headlong into answering my call of replicating pastor and church as business as usual. No mention was made of any new beginnings called for by the turmoil that had wracked the state during the summer months I was absent.

Because of the new duties I had assumed and the fact that the manse was some distance from the church, it seemed imperative that we become a two-car family. David Laverty, a friend and pastor of the Trinity Presbyterian Church in Laurel, was leaving for the mission field and needed to sell his black 1961 VW Bug, which he had bought secondhand from another preacher. It was inexpensive, and I paid the $24.94 *ad valorem* tax on a very used vehicle valued for tax purposes at $350.[34]

During the summer unknown arsonists burned to the ground thirty-three church houses of black congregations across the state, possibly motivated by the fact that "outside agitators," as part of the Freedom Summer activities, had used some of the buildings. Epps, upon resuming his theological studies in California, was asked to join Keith Chamberlain, a Presbyterian campus minister at the University of California at Berkeley, to speak at San Francisco Seminary concerning their civil rights activities in Mississippi. Chamberlain, who worked in the Freedom Summer project, described Mississippi as "a foreign land." Epps, speaking of his summer activities as a student intern in Columbia, said, "[I]t was amazing how 'oblivious' whites were in the burning of black churches until the latter part of the summer when burnings became more frequent." He said, "They figure 'It's propaganda' . . . or 'So what' . . . or 'It's not here.'"[35]

Finally the religious community in Mississippi was incensed with these mean and cowardly acts, feeling that they were "attacks on *all* houses of worship, on religion itself, indeed upon our Constitutional guarantee to assemble and worship" and accepting the "losses and suffering as *our own*." On September 9, 1964, the Committee of Concern was formed as "an expression of the religious community in Mississippi: Roman Catholic, Jewish, Protestant, from both races." The executive committee was made up of heads of communion and local pastors from ten mainline religious organizations.[36]

The executive committee produced a brochure, "Beauty For Ashes," in which it stated its two purposes. The first was "to make it possible for men, women and children of goodwill to respond to violence, hatred, and destruction with concern, compassion and construction" by initiating "a united effort for concrete and personal action in response to the physical losses and personal injustices and indignities suffered by Negro congregations." The focus was to collect and dispense "materials, labor, equipment and financial aid . . . only when requested by a congregation and then after a responsible investigation." The committee wanted local communities first "to answer the needs of the deprived congregations" before it got involved. The second purpose was stated this way: "Through personal acts of concern and compassion by Jews and Christians throughout our state we hope that a new spirit of goodwill springs up to 'let justice roll down like waters, and righteousness like an everflowing stream.'" The committee's prayer was that "all people will be guided by a sense of wisdom and justice which will destroy the will to violence of any sort." Funds and resources, including work teams, showed up in response to the committee's appeals.

The chairman and coordinator of construction for the Committee of Concern sent a memo to student advisors on Mississippi campuses indicating, "[W]e would like to see Mississippi campuses become a ferment of concern about the burning of houses of worship."[37] In it the committee reported that Mennonite masons and carpenters and San Francisco Quakers had teamed with local volunteers to do both construction and landscaping at various locations around the state. The "Carpenters for Christmas" came from Oberlin and other colleges, bringing with them $7,000 for the construction costs. Eight students from Queens College, New York, committed to come in late January. Eight volunteers from the Wesley Foundation at the University of Illinois and Washburn College committed to contribute labor during the Easter vacation. Out of state volunteers were urged to consider coming on weekends prior to the Easter break. Places where help was immediately needed were listed. Competent construction supervisors in the faculty were encouraged to accompany the students. The committee prepared some guidelines for volunteers working under its supervision, and these were included with the memo.

As the heat of the turbulent summer began to moderate, the temperature of national politics began to rise. Time had come once again to ratchet up the litany of criticism of the federal government—especially in terms of taxes paid to it, "undefined federal spending, federal waste, federal extravagance." The irony was that, if the aid from the federal government to Mississippi were cut off, such cessation would create an economic disaster for the state, because the aid far exceeded state income tax revenue sent to Washington.[38]

The political leadership in the state had faced a growing dilemma in its relationship with the national Democratic Party since the days of the Dixiecrat Party in 1948. Governor Paul Johnson's endorsement of Barry Goldwater for president led to a curious decision to allow the Johnson-Humphrey Democratic ticket to be placed on the November ballot so that "it would make it easier" to defeat. "Angry, and seemingly in vindictive mood," the state's political leadership "displayed hostile banners and pledged to vote G. O. P."[39]

Bill Minor, manager of the *New Orleans Times-Picayune* bureau in Mississippi, told the Columbia Lion's Club that "the Arizona senator can count only three southern States—Alabama, Mississippi and Louisiana—in his camp with Florida a doubtful fourth." He added, "Even in Goldwater's 'sure' Dixie states, President Johnson was gaining followers." Minor went on to say, "The Goldwater trend has stopped." Concerning segregation, this change translated into a shift in strategy "from one of massive resistance to one of tokenism." Shouting "never" is something that no longer would get candidates elected with the certainty it used to. He concluded, "Integration in this state is a reality."[40] In the days before the election, I got the feeling from the conversations I heard in Columbia that Goldwater was a "lead pipe cinch" to win. But when election day, November 3, was over, Johnson won by a landslide, even though there were only a few votes for him in our precinct. I knew where two of them came from.

Details of the Civil Rights Act of 1964 began to trickle down to main streets across America and were soon announced on the pages of the *Columbian-Progress.* The statute, which was aimed at resolving local problems, created two key groups. One was made up of several hundred private citizens, appointed by the president and called the National Citizen's Committee (NCC). Its purpose was to "foster improved communications between those of different race, color, religion and national origin."[41] The other group was the Community Relations Service (CRS), charged by the U.S. Department of Commerce with performing a conciliatory role. It had the authority to "arbitrate disputes referred to it by the courts . . . be invited to help by community leaders or . . . step into a local situation without invitation." Its authority went beyond what was assigned by the 1964 law. It was given "the task of aiding communities where racial discrimination has impaired the rights of persons 'under the Constitution or laws of the United States of America' or which affect or may affect inter-state commerce."[42] I do not recall experiencing the presence of the NCC in Columbia, but I soon would be involved with the CRS.

Even though the summer had been relatively quiet in Columbia, such was not the case for McComb to the west. SNCC had been conducting civil rights activities in McComb and Liberty since 1961, focusing on voter registration and school issues. Violence and intimidation reached a peak during the summer. According to COFO's running tabulation, six houses and a super market were bombed, with most, but not all of these incidents related to the movement. Three churches were burned and the SNCC office raided because of a warrant issued to search for "illegal liquor." Though none was found, officers used the opportunity to read letters and literature found in the office. Numerous arrests on bogus charges were made, and harassment of all sorts was committed.[43]

As 1964 wound down, it became evident that a majority of the citizens of McComb had been subject too long to the "acts of terrorism" committed "against citizens both Negro and white." They decided to break their silence and to speak out "for what is right and against what is wrong." They maintained there was only one responsible stance they could take: support equal treatment under the law for all citizens regardless of race, creed, position or wealth; make protests within the framework of the law; and obey the laws of the land regardless of personal feelings in the matter. They felt that "Certain of these laws may be contrary to our traditions, customs or beliefs, but as God-fearing men and women, and as citizens of these United States, we see no other honorable course to follow."[44]

A public statement captioned "Citizens for Progress" ran as a full-page ad in the *McComb Enterprise Journal* on November 17, 1964. It was authorized by the 653 persons who signed it. It urged: "1) order and respect for the law; 2) end of economic threats and sanctions against people of both races; 3) both races to reestablish avenues of communication and understanding and that the Negro leadership cooperate with local officials; 4) widest possible use of our citizenship in the selection of juries and that men called for jury duty not be excused except for the most compelling reasons; 5) fellow citizens to take greater interest in public affairs, in the selection of candidates, and in the support and/or constructive criticism of Public Servants; and 6) all of our people to approach the future with a renewed dedication and to reflect an attitude of optimism about our country."[45] This was a big step in shaping public opinion and would have a significant impact on the community and the surrounding area, including Columbia, though it did not solve all the problems.

Throughout the summer and fall I wondered if I would ever see Zimmerman again. I never did, but I heard about him one more time. I had not given much thought to whether or not he would meet up with Harbison, but later I found out he did. When I initially suggested he meet with Harbison, I assumed it would be on a personal basis and not by attending a public congregational worship service. The session of the Canton church—as so many other church's governing bodies had done across Mississippi that summer in face of the "invasion"—had approved policies keeping their houses of worship closed to blacks and those who came with them seeking admission. I could not help but imagine what the scene must have been in the session room when the struggle over that decision was made. One of the little ironies for me was my daddy's picture hanging on the wall in the session room overlooking the debate. He was the only candidate for the ministry from that congregation in over fifty years.

Zimmerman was in a group from Freedom House that decided to visit the Presbyterian church one Sunday morning at 11:00 a.m. in late summer. They were turned away from worship, and Harbison refused to lead the morning worship. The group came back the following Sunday and were turned away again. This time Harbison laid his robe across the pulpit with his letter of resignation and left Canton to accept a call to First Presbyterian Church, Lexington, Kentucky.

Soon after I returned to Columbia in September to resume my duties as pastor, I discovered that I could very well be faced with the same moral dilemma that Harbison, Walkup, and other ministers had faced. On Friday evening of the week I was in Oxford, Ohio, June 26, the session of the Columbia Presbyterian Church adopted the following resolution: "It is the opinion of the Session and we so instruct the Diaconate, that should colored people and/or their associates attempt to enter our Church during regular services, that they be turned away in a very kind manner, unless otherwise instructed by the Session."[46] Epps, not being eligible to moderate the session meeting, did not attend and did not know about this action until well after he had left Columbia. I have no idea why they decided to handle the matter in this way. Was it to prevent me from being put on the spot, or were they afraid I might object? I never found out. For whatever the reason, they put Epps in an awkward position that summer by not making him aware of the action.

The moment of truth, where we had to decide what we would do if this policy were tested, never occurred for either Epps or me. I remained silent. I did not challenge the decision at the time and have wondered for years if that should have been the moral battle for me to fight. At the time I chose not to, but remained, only to be later engaged in many more significant struggles with moments for truth.

PART II

Engagement

CHAPTER 5

Moments of Truth
in the Making

The waning days of 1964 gave way to the dawn of 1965 with more than the usual feeling of relief that the old had passed away, but it was not clear what prospects the new would hold. Some were thrilled that Columbia was spared the violence and traumatic experiences other parts of Mississippi had suffered in 1964 as the result of the activities of Freedom Summer and the formation of the Mississippi Freedom Democratic Party (MFDP). They hoped that 1965 would be business as usual. Others, however, were committed to bringing MFDP and all it stood for to the streets of Columbia. Moments of truth were in the making.

Through the late fall and early winter, I pursued with vigor my ministry of replicating pastor and church. My ministerial log indicates that I must have come to terms with one of the least exciting aspects of ministry for me: stewardship season. On the Sunday before Dedication Sunday, I preached on "One Man Can Try," to which one parishioner commented, "best stewardship sermon ever heard." The following Sunday on Dedication Sunday, I preached on "Much Given—Much Required," about which I noted, "best ever preached!"[1] It is all a matter of perspective.

Thanksgiving Sunday 1964 fell on November 22, the first anniversary of JFK's assassination, but I stayed with the traditional theme of thanksgiving with a homily on "5 Grains of Corn."[2] Unbeknown to me, on the following Tuesday, Virgil Downing, investigator for the State Sovereignty Commission, visited Sheriff John H. Willoughby of Marion County for the purpose of "determining any and all activities of the NAACP and COFO organizations that may be active at this time." Willoughby told Downing that these organizations "were not creating or causing any trouble in Marion County." He went on to say that he knew of "no voter registration schools in progress in the county." Willoughby's perception was that "relations among the races were very good in Marion County at this time" and he really did not expect "any trouble whatsoever from the colored citizens." He took a measure of credit for this because he had hired "lots of colored help during the 25 years he was superintendent of road construction crew," and they respected "him and the laws of Marion County."[3] No doubt for him this made for a great time of thanksgiving.

The *Columbian-Progress* ran a story on December 17 that seemed to speak of business as usual. By title it announced, "City Schools Begin Re-Evaluation Study." As a member of the Southern Association of Colleges and Schools, the Columbia Schools were committed every ten years to self-study and re-evaluation by a visiting team. The last time this had happened was in 1952, although the local school system had done its own self-study five years earlier in 1959. The high school had a double A rating, and was designated a "Big Eight" school (a category of school districts in Mississippi), but the junior high was not accredited because its old building had been lost to fire. Several committees had been working since the summer to get ready for the visit that would take place April 26–28, 1965. Improvements, including a move into its new building at the junior high school, had been made in hopes that it would receive accreditation. B. F. Duncan, Superintendent of City Schools, was chairman of the steering committee overseeing the project.[4]

At the church, with Thanksgiving behind us, Advent season leading up to Christmas began in full swing. Young J. J. Haney lit the first candle in the Advent wreath on November 29, and I led the congregation in the "Pilgrimage to Advent."[5] On December 6, during Advent, I baptized Sandra Downing from the Columbia Training School. The "Nine Lessons and Carols for Christmastide" was celebrated on Christmas Day. The following Sunday new deacons were installed. On the first Sunday of the New Year we celebrated the sacrament of Holy Communion.

The second Sunday in January I set up a tape recorder to tape the service, because I thought I had something to say that was relevant to the times we were experiencing and that it needed to be reprinted. "SO YOU WANT FREEDOM!"[6] I said, "posing this as a question to people today in the 1960s, the resounding answer was, 'YES, WE WANT FREEDOM.'" I reminded the congregation that we had heard much about freedom in recent months from many persons, adding, "You will know the truth, and the truth will make you free." (John 8:32, RSV). I proclaimed that "Pseudo religious prophets, political extremists, social reformers, status quo-ites have filled the airwaves and bookstalls by day and the driveways and door steps by night with tracts in which they have carefully SET FORTH THE TRUTH—the 'truth' about their cause, the 'truth' about their point of view, the 'truth' about their reason for being—which is the ultimate guarantee of *THEIR* freedom."

My problem was that these people, who filled the airwaves, book-stalls and driveways with their "truth," discrediting the opposition, point-ing out its weakness and showing where it was wrong. But mainly their truth sowed the seeds of suspicion and distrust, claiming that the oppo-sition was "misleading the people." Their "truth tract" was usually filled with "exposes, shopworn catch-words; selfish, petty, eroded clichés of their cause." They extolled their own righteousness for having revealed the "truth," claiming they alone were trustworthy. Therefore, in some extreme cases, they wanted to destroy the opposition.

I made it clear that I was not supporting or denouncing by implica-tion one movement, or one cause, or one side "in our current struggle" to the neglect of others. Anyone—and I included myself—chanting words about "truth" and "freedom" doesn't make these words divine simply by voicing them. I did say that such misuse of Holy Writ as a cheap trick to bring prestige to one's narrow cause was far from the heart and intent of God and therefore was blasphemy. I did not go so far as to say one would go to hell for use of such tactics. But I did say that such use has caused much of the hell on earth, the chaos, the strife, the contention, because in such a way misguided people have attempted to champion freedom in a sense that has misled so many others. "WHEN FREEDOM IS PRO-CLAIMED APART FROM THE FREEDOM OFFERED IN THE GOSPEL, NOTHING IS PRODUCED BUT HELL-RIDDEN BONDAGE! You know it because you are experiencing it! SO YOU WANT FREEDOM? YES, WE WANT FREEDOM! Well, do you know what you are demanding?" It is not a freedom to do anything you want. Christian freedom is summed up in the two great commandments: "Loving God and loving your neighbor as yourself." One may claim to love God with ease, but how one loves one's neighbor is more difficult. The real catch is how to treat those who oppose us. How do we look on those who differ with us? In other words, how do we love our enemies? I concluded by saying, "[L]iving out this truth today, here and now on the streets of Columbia in ways we never dreamed, is what will set us free." Thus ended the word for the day. The only remark in my ministerial log was: "Got to the point, but was it missed?"

Back on the street, John Homer Willoughby, sheriff and tax collec-tor, ran a quarter-page ad trimmed in black in the *Columbian-Progress* on

January 14, 1965, announcing: "IMPORTANT NOTICE, Poll Taxes Must Be Paid by Feb. 1st. POLL TAX RECEIPTS for two years are necessary in qualifying as a voter in this year's MUNICIPAL ELECTION."[7] Little irony was connected with the collection of poll taxes in state and local elections, despite the Twenty-Fourth Amendment to the U.S. Constitution, ratified on January 23, 1964, which ended the poll tax in federal elections. State and local poll taxes were adopted decades ago, in some southern states as early as the 1800s, even though the Fifteenth Amendment had been adopted on February 26, 1869, granting former slaves the right to vote. Through the intervening decades poor blacks and whites alike were disenfranchised because they did not have the money to pay these taxes.[8] And even if they did, they had to pass stringent literacy tests in order to vote.

Both the Columbia City and Marion County school boards were faced in mid-January with a decision that had far-reaching implications, both for financial reasons and for the social mores of the community. The boards had to decide whether to present plans in less than six weeks to desegregate both school systems. Failure to submit a plan meant the loss of federal aid. According to an article in the *Columbian-Progress* on January 21, 1965, "[I]t would take about a 4.5 mills increase in the city and about 12 mills in the county to offset the loss of federal aid to local schools according to studies currently underway by the school boards of the two districts." The school boards had until March 3 to sign a voluntary compliance statement agreeing to desegregate the schools or lose all federal aid. The same column quoted Erle Johnston, director of the State Sovereignty Commission and an elder in the Presbyterian church in Forest, as saying "refusal to sign a pledge does not exempt a school district from being desegregated by court order." He also said that "signing does not mean desegregation unless some person asks to cross color lines."[9]

The featured guest speaker addressing the Marion County Citizens' Council on January 25, 1965, at the Marion County courthouse was former Governor Ross Barnett. The focus of his speech was states' rights and the encroachment of the federal government based on powers it is not, in his judgment, granted under the U.S. Constitution. He warned that "local governments are in grave danger due to minority blocks [*sic*] who have support of the federal government officials and that there are too many pussy-footing politicians who would sell us down the Mississippi River to get the support of these blocks."[10] Barnett clad his hopes in cloaks of "individual freedom" and "self government" as the proper attire in which to "save our state from destruction." He applauded the Citizens' Councils for offering "a great contribution in perpetuating liberty for both white and colored races." Concerned that his audience might become "discouraged due to the present state of affairs," he offered a challenge: "Let's fight in a dignified way. Ultimately, we will have to obey the law but let's organize now to get these civil rights matters changed."[11]

Other voices offered a different way to respond to the "present state of affairs." W. F. Minor reported in an article published in the *New Orleans Times-Picayune* on February 4, that "Mississippi industries and businesses were advised . . . to begin taking steps to comply with the equal employment provisions of the Civil Rights Act, which becomes effective July 2." In a conference sponsored by the Jackson Chamber of Commerce, a panel made up of Mississippi lawyers and two federal representatives challenged the industry and business conferees not "to balk at compliance, but face the need for community understanding because of the racial changes the act will bring." Specifically, they were told they "should move now to go into absolute detail to ferret out your payroll and hiring practices and eliminate *de facto* discrimination." Furthermore, "you don't want to risk being forced to comply with the act."[12]

On February 5, 1965, Rev. J. M. "Jack" Bemiss, regional director of Christian Education for the Presbyterian Synod of Mississippi, sent a letter to ministers (clerks of vacant churches) in which he enclosed a mimeographed copy of a letter from Dr. William P. Davis, chairman of the "Committee of Concern," concerning volunteer help by students from Mississippi campuses in reconstructing burned out churches and including suggestions for response. With the letter was a reprint of the brochure, "Beauty For Ashes," concerning the purpose and work of the committee. Bemiss, a native Mississippian born at Rodney, was very careful to explain that this mailing was something he was doing purely on his own initiative. What he did was not approved by the synod's executive committee on Christian education, or by the synod's executive committee on campus Christian life, or by any other presbytery committee, council or group in Mississippi or the denomination's board of Christian education, as far as he knew. He asked to be corrected by any individual or by synod if he was out of order. His hope was that this action would not affect his working relationship with any of these groups, for he wanted to be of continued service to the congregations of the synod and to the Presbyterian campus ministries on the five state campuses.

The lengths to which Bemiss went to qualify his action were but an illustration of the growing tension in the delicate balance of perspectives within the Synod of Mississippi. He closed his letter by saying, "I trust my sharing with you these matters will not be misunderstood . . . because I believe this is one of the first and few ways Mississippi students can become involved in a worthy cause and can also help to change the image of Mississippi campuses."[13]

◆ ◆ ◆

The winter lecture series at Louisville Presbyterian Seminary had played an important role in the continuing education of its graduates and an opportunity for them to gather and renew old acquaintances. The deadline for me to present the final draft of my thesis was getting close, so the final oral exam for my master's in theology degree was scheduled for this time. On Sunday evening, February 7, Frank Brooks and I boarded northbound the L & N Railroad's train # 98, the *Pan American*, in Gulfport at 10:51 p.m., headed for Louisville. It was Brooks's thirtieth birthday, and what a way to celebrate! We had been lifelong rail fans and had engaged a double bedroom on a Pullman car traveling on our clergy permits. Standing on the rear observation platform in an eerie fog, we watched as the train crossed the causeway over Biloxi Bay between Biloxi and Ocean Springs. When we got to Mobile at 12:40 a.m., we stepped out on the loading platform looking for Bill Shenk, the seminary cohort we thought was joining us, but he was a no-show. Finally, we climbed back aboard and settled in for the night.

After sunup the next morning, we had a fine country ham and eggs breakfast in the diner and then retired to our room to read and look at the Alabama scenery. Frank lit his pipe, and I ended up like a smoked ham in the upper berth. Years later after he quit smoking, he apologized profusely for putting me through all that. At 12:30 p.m., the *Pan* had a short layover in Nashville. We had arranged beforehand to have our friend, Spencer Castle Murray, meet us at the station for a quick visit. Spencer had been my predecessor at Amory and was from Starkville where Frank, during his college days, had known his family and him.

We re-boarded the train and continued to Louisville, arriving at 5:55 p.m. at the Broadway Station, a short distance out Broadway from the seminary. The time spent there met our expectations for inspiration and fellowship. I concluded the final step in my master's program. All that was left to be done when I got back to Columbia was for Millye to type the final draft of my thesis on my dad's Royal manual typewriter. On Wednesday about 12:30 p.m., we boarded southbound L & N Railroad's train # 99, the

Pan American. We arrived in Gulfport the following day at 6:45 a.m. after another night on the sleeper. I picked up my VW Bug and drove home to Columbia fully exhausted. I did not realize at the time this would be my last long distance overnight rail trip in a Pullman car.

My sermons during this period were on the Beatitudes. The one on Sunday following the Louisville trip was "Happy are the Slave-Drivers."[14] My record showed it as being "[v]ery good, but I was dizzy!" Too much railroading I guess. That week the *Columbian-Progress* had an article announcing the grand opening of two Sunflower Stores in Columbia: one in the former National Food store in Gardner Shopping Center, which would later become the target of picketing, and another in the former Moore's Shop Rite Food Market on Broad Street, near the high school. The announcement assured customers that the store in Gardner Shopping Center "will continue to give S and H Green Stamps as formerly done by the National Food Store."[15]

The next Sunday's sermon topic was "Happy are the Trouble-Makers."[16] The notes in my log included a simple cryptic entry, "annony-call." Sometime during the previous week I had been away overnight at a synod committee meeting. My wife's mother was visiting, since it was close to Millye's and her mother's birthdays. That night my wife received an anonymous phone call in which the person calling, presumably a black woman, said something to the effect, "You tell your husband to meet me tonight where he met me last night." My wife said, "You must have the wrong number. What was the man's name you are talking about?" The voice on the other end replied, "[T]his is the right number and I know his name," and hung up.

My wife was petrified and did not even tell her mother what had happened. She got out the old phone book—luckily a small one, like our town—and went through every listing until she found the number that had been given to us when we moved in. When I got home she showed me the address listed and I located it on the city map. It was in the white part of town that was near the black part of town, the two divided only by the railroad tracks. All I could figure was that there had been some "crossing the track" activity going on here in the past and that the number we had been assigned had previously belonged to the man involved. Nonetheless, the episode was unsettling because of the present tension in the community. We had been anticipating personal harassment and were not sure if this was part of the expected smear tactics. This event, however, was not the inaugural of such antics.

On the last weekend of February, Brooks and I drove over to Mobile for the Bill Walker-Gloria Merry wedding. On the way into town we drove by the Shenks's to see why Bill did not go to Louisville with us on the train. Daughter Lauren, who said her father was not available, greeted us at the door. We told her who we were and that we suspected he was in the back somewhere sitting in his rocking chair. That got us in the door, and we found him right where we expected him to be. After a short visit, we changed into our clerical collars and suits for the wedding, even though we had no roles in it.

The wedding was stately, and the reception was a grand affair at the Mobile Country Club. A small distraction arose because the candelabras held real white candles, and the room was so hot the tallow dripped all over the guests. For a while we wondered if a flock of birds had passed overhead! We did not stay long because we had to make the long drive back to Mississippi in order to preach the next day. However, before we left we had to change a tire on Frank's VW Bug. We had parked the Bug on the edge of one of the golf course greens, thinking we were so smart. It seems that we had ignored paying the parking attendants a tip for parking the car and we had been rewarded with a deflated tire. When I entered the pulpit the next day, I looked out and saw many parishioners who also had driven back from Mobile in the wee hours of the morning, but were in their pews at the appointed hour. The sermon was on "Happy Are the Wise-Guys."[17]

Sometime that spring a lone black man came to town with nothing but a backpack holding his worldly possessions. Curtis Styles had been living in Biloxi, but was originally from Jayess, Mississippi, a country village between Tylertown and Brookhaven. He was involved with Dr. Gilbert R. Mason, Sr., in voter registration drives and desegregation protests of the segregated beaches on the Mississippi Gulf Coast in the early 1960s. These acts of civil disobedience seemed highly dangerous, because the protesters felt trapped on three sides by racists with only the Gulf on the fourth side making for a dubious and damp escape route. For some reason, Styles felt drawn to Columbia as the location where he would test the laws and customs he felt were unjust and oppressive. The first fearful night in Columbia he slept in the rain out in the nearby woods until he could make contact with sympathetic local residents. Styles had been given the names of these persons, but he had written them in code on a piece of paper he carried just in case he was picked up by the police or the Klan.[18]

In nearby Hattiesburg, Rev. Bob Beech, a graduate of McCormick Presbyterian Seminary in Chicago and an ordained Presbyterian minister, was director of the Hattiesburg Ministers Union from 1964 to 1966. This organization, under the auspices of the National Council of Churches, was associated with a group of ministers across the country that volunteered to help blacks register to vote.[19] Beech was the kind of guy that was known at times "to help the 'COFO kids' with a balky movie projector" or at others "to interrupt anything to offer pastoral counsel to a Negro Mississippian, or a white one, or a homesick civil rights worker." He had attended a white Presbyterian church in Hattiesburg on several occasions when the pastor "politely asked him please not to come there on a regular basis and to refrain from bringing his children to Sunday school." It was stewardship season and "the minister thought that friendly Bob Beech would have a bad effect on receipts."[20]

In early spring 1965, Beech paid a visit to Vernon Dahmer at his home in the Kelly Settlement north of Hattiesburg. He took Ira Grupper, a member of the research staff of SNCC working in Hattiesburg, along with him to meet this prominent civil rights leader whom the Ku Klux Klan frequently threatened. When Beech and Grupper arrived at the Dahmer residence, they were faced with a ten-by-thirteen-inch red, white, and blue poster of an Uncle Sam figure pointing at the viewer with caption, "The Klan Wants You!" nailed to a tree. Dahmer would die in January of 1966 as the result of the Klan's firebombing his home.[21]

On March 4, the *Columbian-Progress* expressed the sentiment that it was "No Time for Street Protests." The writer felt that the Civil Rights Act of 1964 opened the door "to give not simply rights but special privileges which the great majority of citizens did not enjoy . . . and that minority protest and agitation may flare anew in the summer of 1965." He claimed the Community Relations Service, a federal agency created by the act, was "established to force American communities to get rid of established social customs and meet the demands of street agitators and professional protest leaders." He declared that "professional voices of protest must learn that there are limits to the patience of the American people," having put up for too long "with an outrageous amount of arrogant pushing about by those who, as a minority, regard themselves above the law or as people for whom the law has special concern . . . . It is time to call a complete halt to the lawless protest movements and actions."[22]

I suspect the writer had no clue that his words were laced with irony. One has only to consider what thoughts Curtis Styles might have had that cold, wet night sleeping out in the woods about patience with those who have enjoyed special privileges for the past one hundred years. What might

Vernon Dahmer have thought as he lay dying in the hospital about "putting up with an outrageous amount of arrogant pushing about" by those "for whom the law has special concern"?

March was greeted in Columbia with the announcement that the city and county school boards would take no action at that time on the civil rights school desegregation pledge. The boards released similar statements, one written by the city and one delivered orally by the County, in which they declared that they had been "giving careful study to all facets of the various problems related to future acceptances of federal aid to the school program," including how to respond to the compliance and agreement forms. They were aware that the state school board had signed the compliance agreement prior to March 4 in order to assure federal funds would be available for the remainder of the school year. However, this action by the state board was in no way binding on local school boards.[23] Officials for the state school board said they signed "because our school children would have suffered loss of school support immediately." J. M. Tubb, state superintendent of education, explained that local school boards could comply at any time. But because they needed enough lead-time to make plans for their schools, they would have to comply by April 15. In order to count on federal aid, tentative budgets had to be submitted by July 15.[24]

Not long after the school boards declined to take action on the civil rights school desegregation pledge, N. A. Dickson and I concluded that such a stance would only aggravate relations within the community, especially when there was obviously poor communications between the aggravators and the aggravatees. N. A. had grown up in nearby Bassfield and knew from very painful personal experiences the sort of difficulties that haunt one's past. He also knew the difficulties that come to one who dares to be a prophet in one's own country. His names, Nathan and Andrew, were descriptive of his character: Andrew, after the apostle known as the one who brought people to Jesus; and Nathan, after the prophet who spoke the truth to King David's power. In addition, N. A. had such a winsome smile and contagious chuckle!

In January of 1963, he had joined twenty-eight Methodist ministers in the state to sign the "Born of Conviction Statement" based on their Christian commitment, calling for freedom of the pulpit and welcoming all people to the congregations they served. Bill Lampton, a son of the Methodist church in Columbia, was also a signatory. In addition the ministers clearly communicated their support for the public schools and opposed the creation of segregated schools operated by churches. Retribution for this act by many of their congregations was swift and final. Two ministers were immediately dismissed, and by mid-1964 eighteen of the statement's signers had left Mississippi. But not N. A. Dickson. He withstood the initial criticism and declared he would not be driven out of Columbia.[25]

N. A. and I decided the time had come for us to explore ways of setting up communications with some persons in the black community. Through his connection with the Mississippi Rural Center at Lampton, a few miles south of Columbia, he contacted an acquaintance, Rev. I. C. Pittman, the first director of the center. According to Rev. Pittman, the center was organized to serve the large black rural community around Lampton. Blacks and whites worked together to plan and administer its programs of spiritual, social, educational, and recreational experiences to enrich the lives and attitudes of those involved. Rev. Isaac Pittman, a native of Sandy Hook and an ordained Methodist minister, was very open to the idea that we needed to establish more effective lines of communication between the black and white communities. His work as the first director and community organizer at the center had shown him the importance of effective communications and the medium through which it works. He had a special way of becoming the medium. At times I saw him dressed in overalls, going about his chores, identifying with workingman, but calling attention only to the quality of the task being performed and not the performer. At other times, he put on the director or pastor's suit—white shirt and tie, as the circumstance required—clearly communicating the authority of the role.

The second minister we contacted was Rev. L. Z. Blankinship, a native of Foxworth and pastor of Friendship (Missionary) Baptist Church and member of Christian Hill Baptist Church.[26] His years as Quartermaster in the U.S. Army gave him a commanding appearance, much in the style of Dr. Martin Luther King, Jr. It was obvious that Blankinship was an administrator by nature and very attuned to the way organizations functioned— or at times, how they were dysfunctional. He served as moderator of East Pearl River Baptist Association and chairman of the Mississippi Baptist Theological Seminary in Columbia. I observed that he was a polished leader, outgoing in his relations with people.

The third minister we contacted was Rev. Amos G. Payton, Sr., who was born in Marion County, and was pastor of Owens Chapel (Missionary) Baptist Church. Payton was drafted in May 1942 into the U.S. Army during World War II and served for more than three years, including more than two years in Europe. After his service in the military, he began

serving pastorates in locations all across south Mississippi before coming to Columbia. He was a recognized leader in various local, regional,
and national church and civic organizations. Payton was quiet and dignified in his demeanor, presenting the classic image of a black preacher
from an earlier generation. A fourth black minister met with us a few
times, but his name and church affiliation do not show up in the records
or in my memory.

Our meetings took place during the same time that the violent Alabama guardsmen, police dog, fire hose, teargas, bullwhip, nightstick, pro-
testor, "Bloody Sunday" drama was being played out on March 7 at the
Edmund Pettus Bridge in Selma, and in the March 21 aftermath procession
on the highway to Montgomery. As the six of us talked about the potential violence and turmoil facing our community, real understanding was
reached quickly that we did not want this to happen here. Over a period of
time we began calling ourselves simply "Six," even though the fourth minister only met with us for a short time and then for some reason dropped
out of the group. Though only five in number, we continued to refer to ourselves as Six for purposes of identity and communication. The black ministers were identified at times as "Four." It was evident Six would become a
very important group in our lives.

◆   ◆   ◆

E. D. "Buddy" McLean, Jr., was born on January 23, 1925, in Gastonia, N.C.,
to Earl D. McLean, Sr. and Fay Lampton McLean. In 1928 the McLeans
moved to Mobile, Alabama, and then to Fernwood, Mississippi, Mrs.
McLean's Lampton family home, in 1930. Finally, they moved to Columbia
in the mid-1930s. Mr. McLean was employed by the Fernwood, Columbia,
and Gulf Railroad until his retirement. He was active in the community,
the chamber of commerce, the Mississippi Jersey Cattle Association, and
the United Methodist Church. Mrs. McLean in later years became librarian at the public library. Buddy graduated from Columbia High School in
1943 and immediately entered the Army Air Corps in June. He received his
wings at Luke Field in Arizona and served in the Air Corps until 1946. He
attended Duke University, which his father had attended when it was Trinity University. Upon graduation from Duke, Buddy returned to Columbia and became a partner in the T. C. Griffith Insurance Agency. Soon
thereafter, he married E. Justina "Tina" Walker. To their union were born
Justina W. McLean and Earl "Danny" McLean III. Buddy was the president

of the Columbia Rotary Club in 1959–60 and president of the Marion County Chamber of Commerce in 1961. The McLeans were members of the Columbia Presbyterian Church, where Buddy served as a deacon.

On March 11, 1965, after "great thought and consideration," Buddy McLean formally announced his candidacy for mayor of the city of Columbia in the municipal Democratic primary to be held on May 11. "Having made Columbia my home I am deeply interested in our city, its government, and the welfare of the people," he said. He went on to declare that, "The conditions of our city, county and nation are such that we can no longer take our government for granted." He was very realistic in his estimate of the situation when he said, "I am not unaware of the fact that the next four years, as have been the past four, will be filled with problems and perhaps turmoil. No one can accurately foresee the future." His only platform was his "promise to use every ounce of my ability and the entirety of my time and efforts in our behalf" and "with your support we can grow and prosper in our city."[27] Though this sounded like standard campaign rhetoric—albeit without the usual Mississippi nastiness—it was far more than that.

One of Buddy's campaign strategies during these two months before the election was to knock on the door of every house in Columbia, both black and white, simply saying, "I want to be *your* Mayor and I ask for *your* vote." He accomplished this goal. He was driven to run for mayor by his vow to find ways personally to meet the challenge of the words he had used during his Kennedy memorial speech: "[H]ow utterly man [*sic*] has failed in learning to live together . . . . [We] MUST GO FORTH . . . promising ourselves that we shall overcome our complacency, we shall examine our beliefs, we shall face our image, and the guilt of last Friday can never again be placed on our shoulders." It was obvious that Buddy's deep commitment caught the imagination of Six and our support in his campaign.

A week after Buddy's announcement, Wiley Wolfe, member of the Columbia school board and the Columbia Presbyterian Church, told the Rotary Club at its luncheon meeting that the school board was faced with a decision regarding school desegregation that would impact the community for generations. Wolfe stressed that no matter how one might individually feel about the new civil rights law, it is the law of the land, unless it is repealed or struck down. He added, "And the present administration will see to it that this law is enforced." Federal aid was a significant part of local schools' operating budgets, but with this law, Wolfe said, "[Y]our own tax money [is] returning home with strings attached and it is in these strings we are becoming hopelessly enmeshed today . . . [and] the ultimate outcome is clear despite what any local board will do."[28]

Some seemed to think that local school boards' signing a compliance agreement was merely an acknowledgment of intent to abide by the public schools section of the civil rights law. But Wolfe contended compliance was more complex than that. School boards were objecting to signing compliance agreements due to "the inference that we will comply with an interpretation of the law by federal agencies—not only now, but in the future." Such interpretation by these federal agencies had direct consequences with regard to whether or not local school districts would receive thousands of dollars in funding for a variety of programs: commodities for lunch programs; vocational training programs; programs in science and language departments; and practical nursing programs conducted in conjunction with the local hospital.[29]

According to Wolfe, three choices facing the board regarding school desegregation were: "1) Sign the compliance agreement of the Health, Education and Welfare Department and submit a plan for desegregation beginning in September, 1965. 2) Submit a plan to desegregate without signing a compliance agreement. This plan would also be effective this fall. 3) Do not sign, submit nothing, and await the action of the federal court." In conclusion, Wolfe strongly emphasized that the board, in meeting its responsibilities, "WILL make the decision at the proper time and pray to God that it will be the right one."[30]

B. F. Duncan, Superintendent of City Schools, reported on April 1, 1965, that the Mississippi Education Association had recently adopted sweeping new accrediting standards that school districts must meet within the next five years. These changes had to do with the following: membership on the accrediting commission; when a particular school's accreditation may be dropped; what constituted the number of required days in the school year; approval for operating split sessions; requirements for storage of student records; requirements for administrator certification; audit standards; health certificates for teachers; certification of lunch program managers; and several other requirements.[31] It would be hard to tell from this report that anything other than business as usual was facing the Mississippi Accrediting Commission or the Columbia School District.

However, on the same page in the *Columbian-Progress* where Duncan's report appeared, a very different story reflected what the Marion County School Board was facing. That board was concerned about the possible loss of significant federal funds for its vocational education program in the county as a result of the Civil Rights Act. These funds had been used in the past for "home economics teachers and departments, as well as vocational agriculture in the high schools." As of January 3, 1965, the State Board of Vocational Education could neither "commit nor designate any additional funds for any purpose to any school that is not in compliance with the Civil Rights Act." The United States Office of Education declared by regulation consistent with the regulation of the act, that "Beginning July 1, 1965, there can be no federal funds expended in any school that is not in compliance."[32]

On the political scene, on April 15 A. E. "Buck" Webb announced his candidacy for the office of mayor in the municipal Democratic primary in the *Columbian-Progress*. Webb had lived in Columbia for about twenty years and was "proud to be a citizen." He declared his belief that "all other citizens of Columbia are interested in better government, better business management, more and better streets, a better and more adequate fire department, an efficient police department and better drainage for all of Columbia." He touted his "working knowledge of management and business" gained from "over 25 years experience in the equipment and construction business" and as "Superintendent of Mid State Paving Company." He felt that his experience "will be of great value to the city of Columbia."[33] No doubt this last would be true, especially when it came to fulfilling his campaign promise of "more and better streets." There appeared to be little if any acknowledgment of the potential problems and perhaps turmoil facing the city and county.

In an unrelated article in the same issue of the *Columbian-Progress*, Thurman Sensing warned that, "Of all the weapons in the arsenal of the social and political agitator, [no] one is more dangerous—for the user—than the economic boycott." In his judgment this weapon "inflicts injury on whoever picks it up," and "when used or threatened frequently antagonizes the American public." He cited the activities of Martin Luther King, Jr., "a master of organizing conflict where there previously has been peace, order and gradual progress," as having "unquestionably overstepped himself when he urged boycott of Alabama products." Such efforts "can only increase bad feelings in this country and multiply the divisions that already exist as a result of revolutionary street action bordering on civil insurrection." Obviously Sensing's feelings were inflamed by the highly publicized violence associated with the Selma-Montgomery march the previous month, the purpose of which was, he said, "to shock people, to break down established customs, and to promote chaos."[34] Sensing, in essence, was warning the "responsible citizens" of Columbia that, "the people attempting to reduce Alabama to conditions of permanent strife and chaos want to reproduce those same conditions from coast to coast," raising that fear that it can happen here. He concluded that, "Every responsible citizen of the United States needs to understand how the boycott plan fits into the overall scheme of breaking down American capitalist society."[35] Once again the alarm of ominous threat to the status quo was sounded.

Meanwhile, in my world of replicating pastor and church, I was heavily involved in the busy Lenten season leading up to Easter. I conducted the annual communicants class for several of the eligible boys and girls in the congregation who were to be received into membership. On Palm Sunday, April 11, they were admitted to their first sacrament of Holy Communion. Buddy and Tina McLean's daughter, Tina, was in the group. I incorporated several experienced based activities in the curriculum for the class. One especially meaningful segment concerned the church and what this community means to its members. I brought my charcoal grill to the church and built a fire in it with finger-sized twigs stacked together in wigwam fashion. After I blew on it and got it blazing, I took a stick and scattered the burning twigs around the grill. The young people watched as the fire died down. I then scooted the twigs back together, blew on it, and the flames began to pick up again. I told my audience that the word for wind and spirit are the same in Hebrew. This exercise illustrated how in the church the spirit of God moves through us, releasing a powerful energy in the community and allowing us to be more faithful when we stick together rather than when we try to go it alone.

On Easter Sunday, April 18, at the sunrise breakfast we served fifty persons. The junior high choir sang during the eleven o'clock service, and the young people in the communicants class were admitted to full membership. There were 140 plus worshippers in attendance, the largest crowd we had had since the 120 who attended the previous Christmas Sunday's worship. We averaged around seventy on ordinary Sundays. Then, at the "typical, yet excellent service" that evening there were eleven worshippers to hear my favorite sermon, "The Day Far Spent!"[36]

April 21–26, 1965, the 105th meeting of the General Assembly of the Presbyterian Church (US), known as the Southern Presbyterian Church, was held in Montreat, North Carolina. Of the many items of business before the assembly, there was one that had particular relevance to the Synod of Mississippi. This had to do with "overtures" (requests to the General Assembly for official clarifications, rulings, or responses to issues) from the Synod of South Carolina, the Presbyteries of Asheville,

Tuscaloosa, and East Alabama relative to the 1964 Assembly's action "to instruct" presbyteries with regard to Presbyterian (US) Negro churches within their bounds. This 1965 assembly response to these overtures was as follows: "[W]ith all Christian Compassion and understanding, [we] request all presbyteries [white] that have Presbyterian US Negro churches within their bounds to take immediate action to receive said churches into their membership if this has not already been accomplished." The assembly also instructed the "aforementioned presbyteries to report this action or progress toward it, to the Stated Clerk of the General Assembly prior to the 1966 meeting of the General Assembly."[37] This instruction was tantamount to ordering the desegregation of the Southern Presbyterian Church.

Shortly thereafter, the school accreditation process begun in 1964 entered its last phase when the visiting committee came to town on April 26 to conduct its on-site re-evaluation of the Columbia city schools. The Mississippi Accrediting Commission and the Southern Association of Secondary Schools had rated Columbia High School for a number of years as an "AA" school. The committee, made up of forty-three persons, held its organizing meeting, followed by a banquet in the high school cafeteria that included faculty, school board and representatives from the board of aldermen. The committee worked in several sub-committees dealing with administration and related subjects, student services, programs of stud-ies, and instructional material services. On Tuesday, committee members visited classes and talked with teachers. Following preparation of their sub-committee reports, an oral report was made to Superintendent B. F. Duncan and E. E. Pope, principal of Columbia High School, with a com-plete report to be filed with them at a later date. Although schools for black students were under the jurisdiction of the city school district, no explicit mention was made in the article of any accreditation activities associated with these schools.

As the mayoral campaign was winding down in the spring of 1965, Six invited Buddy to meet with us. At the time Six began to meet with Buddy, Payton (58) and Pittman (57) were the "old-timers," N. A. (46) and Blankinship (43) were the "mid-lifers," and McLean (39) and McAtee (30) were the "youngsters." A long discussion centered on what Six might do to support Buddy, assuming he won the election. Buddy indicated that it would be helpful if we could serve as a very unofficial group of advisors. In the course of the conversation, Rev. Pittman said he saw our role as that of a catalyst, similar to what he and Blankinship had observed in chemistry experiments. Rev. Payton described our role delightfully as being that of "enhastening agents," a vernacular precursor of what would later become known in organizational development parlance as "change agents!" We would do things in indirect ways that would "enhasten" what others would be convinced to do directly to bring about change.

Buddy also said we needed to figure out some way to develop a communication network, especially in the black community. He understood there was difference of opinion in the black community over how to achieve these first steps in complying with the new laws of the land. Some believed in a gradual approach, fearing recriminations if we moved too fast. Others believed that enough discrimination is enough, that there is no middle ground in applying the laws equally for everyone, so let's get on with it. Nonetheless, Buddy knew that disseminating and receiving accurate information as quickly as possible is essential for effective governance. Buddy wanted the black ministers to compile a list of fifteen local blacks who were recognized by the black community as leaders. Rev. Blankinship indicated that there were "clusters of influence" in all sectors of the black community that could be tapped for such communication needs. A phone tree system was devised around these leaders so that if the mayor had a message to send needing a quick "sense of the community" response, it could be easily activated through N. A. or me. We would contact our black minister colleagues, who in turn would use the phone tree contacts they had established to get a timely response from those clusters of influence—sometimes within thirty minutes. As the summer unfolded this plan turned out to be critical to what the mayor needed to accomplish.

There was nothing much for Six to do now but wait out the results of the election. I have always found in times of emotional distress that some form of physical exercise proves therapeutic. In those anxious days of late April, I launched into a fencing project in the backyard of the manse. Our son Neal was rushing headlong into being a rambunctious two-year-old and needed lots of safe space to roam freely. So I procured all the needed materials and began the task of digging postholes, setting posts, and stringing wire with the able assistance of Neal. On May 1, the task was completed. Since the manse was church property, I wrote the church treasurer, who happened to be Buddy McLean, notifying him that the fence had been installed and gave the church a fence around part of its property at an actual cost of $98.86, which included wire, posts, staples, gates, and rails. I threw in the labor for free because I figured exchanging the cost of materials for therapy was a very good deal![38]

Later that week I received a letter from Dwain Epps posted May 3 at Selma, Alabama, telling me how he got to Camden, Alabama, and the small black Camden Academy and what he had been involved in since he got there. A Vanderbilt Divinity School graduate student, currently on leave from his mission in a Japanese university, was living at Camden Academy for four months, working with blacks who had been put out of work or out of their homes because of their civil rights activities. He contacted Epps to see if Epps could take his place, since he needed to get back to his work and family. He looked for some mature, reasonable person who had lived in the South and understood the position of whites, but who also was concerned as a Christian that all people should be able to live with the benefits of God-given American freedom and opportunities.

Within a short forty-eight hours, Epps had made the decision to quit three jobs and fly to Alabama, bringing with him $7,000 in cash that had been collected by concerned seminary students in response to the Selma crises and intended to be applied to civil rights efforts in Alabama. It was a dangerous time for Epps, but nothing compared to what the blacks had been and were experiencing. I was profoundly touched by the stories he told in his letter, giving me new perspective on what others were experiencing here in Columbia. He wrote: "I am no new person. I'm the same one who preached in Columbia last summer." Now he was involved in what some may describe as "working the other side of the street" in the name of reconciliation and peace. Then he went on to say, "But I am not ashamed of what I am doing, and I feel comfortable sitting with the D. A., the mayor, president of the bank, Baptist ministers, superintendent of schools, and other whites who saw me standing at the head of a march on Monday. I can feel that way because even though they know I'm living with Negroes, they also know I am trying to avoid violence and that I love and am concerned about them *too.*"[39]

❖ ❖ ❖

An article in the May 6 *Columbian Progress* reported committee chairman E. R. Ford's announcement that Marion County Agricultural Stabilization and Conservation (ASC) would employ four Negroes as temporary field crop reporters during the summer, an action complying with the equal opportunity employment provisions of the Civil Rights Act. "Each county in the nation will employ Negroes this summer in the same proportion that there are Negroes engaged in farming in the county," in addition to the employment of five white reporters. "ASC state and county committees will also see that Negroes are placed on the ballot for ASC committee elections in the same percentage as there are Negro farmers in the county."[40]

The same month, the municipal Democratic primary had a new feature occasioned by a law enacted by the Mississippi State Legislature in which for the first time, "all qualified voters will vote for all five aldermen" as well as for alderman at large and for mayor. Up to this time voters had cast ballots only for a candidate running for alderman in their respective wards. One had to wonder if this change by the legislature was motivated by the fear that voting in predominantly black wards with increased voter registration might produce black aldermen, whereas the new plan could nullify that possibility. The city of Columbia was divided into four wards that "all come together where West Avenue crossed Dry Creek." Poll managers, who had served in previous elections, were: Ward One, Will Cooper; Ward Two, John Watts; Ward Three, Shelby Regan; and Ward Four, Van M. Morris, Jr. The polls were opened from 7 a.m. to 6 p.m.[41]

At one point speculation raged that a run-off election might be necessary, brought on by the new law, but it did not happen that way. Candidates for mayor and alderman won either by a clear majority or because also-rans withdrew from the run-off. McLean defeated Webb 1,081 to 454.[42] By law, a general election had to be held, but the result of the Democratic primary was tantamount to election. No contenders were on the ballot. Nonetheless, election officials were named, polls were open on June 8 for the usual hours—this time for a light turnout. McLean, the alderman at large and the five ward aldermen were elected once again.[43]

The spring activities related to my replicating pastor and church were winding down to what I anticipated to be a slower paced summer. I went to Louisville for graduation on May 16 to receive my masters in theology degree. On May 30 I delivered the Columbia High School baccalaureate sermon, "Fiddle-Dee-Dee," to a class that included four seniors from the church.[44] I officiated at the only wedding I was asked to perform while in Columbia on June 5, 1965, for the daughter of our next-door neighbors, a family I had known when they lived in Brookhaven. On June 20, I was in Memphis teaching in the kindergarten department of the teacher training laboratory school sponsored by the Presbyterian Board of Christian Education.

The mayor and board of aldermen took their oaths of office in a brief ceremony at city hall on July 5, Circuit Judge Sebe Cale presiding. Mayor McLean announced, with no reason given, that an employee at city hall and three policemen had not been rehired. He did say that the city clerk, the city attorney, the chief of city police, the head of the street department, the head of the waterworks, the tax assessor, and the fire chief had all been rehired. The mayor expressed his hopes that "the city officials can develop a system of harmony and have an efficient city administration." He also announced that he would be in his "office at City Hall on Wednesday mornings and evening." In this way he wanted to devote more time to discussing city business and hoped that this arrangement would be convenient to citizens "interested in discussing improvements and problems."[45]

Four days before he was sworn into office on July 1, 1965, the mayor-elect wrote five names on a Pearl River Valley Electric Power Association memo pad he found on his desk: Sam Gross, Curtis Styles, Ann Marsh, Richard Atlee, and Shana Shumer. The only other marking on the memo was a bracket beside the five names on the right-hand side, with the word *one* beside it with no indication where the information was from or what it was about.[46] Before the summer was over, Buddy would become well aware of who these people were and what they were about.

In early July, the Columbia city school board voted three to one not to sign a compliance agreement or submit a voluntary desegregation plan. There was practically no response from the public. In fact only a few people knew what was going on. The stage was now really set. The aggrieved, the clueless, the powerless, the powerful, the skeptics, the resisters, the die-hards, the activists, the enhancers, the compliant, the officials, and the authorities were present now, each facing his or her own moment of truth. But truth is a matter of perspective, and Columbia was on the cusp of being immersed in a confluence of perspectives.

CHAPTER 6

A Confluence of Perspectives

Faced with the possibility of the impending passage of new federal voting laws, Governor Paul Johnson called for a special session of the Mississippi legislature in June of 1965 to redraft sections of the state constitution that were in violation of the proposed Voting Rights Act in the U.S. Congress, explicitly intended to correct issues of discrimination implicit in the federal Constitution. The prospect of amending the state constitution caused great dismay to those in the Mississippi Freedom Democratic Party because they felt such changes weakened "their claims about Mississippi's intransigence in regards to race relations without eradicating the problems inherent in the state's social and political system." The MFDP was in the midst of an attempt to replace Mississippi's congressmen with their candidates at the national Democratic convention, even though the MFDP was "losing sympathy" on a national scale.[1]

Nonetheless, a peaceful protest of the special session was organized by the MFDP. The city of Jackson recently adopted an ordinance "restricting distribution of leaflets and flyers in the city." This ordinance was used to arrest over five hundred of these demonstrators, causing additional ones to protest and be arrested. More than one thousand were eventually arrested and herded off by police to the state fairgrounds, where they were placed in cleared-out stalls where livestock were usually on display during the state fair. Treatment was harsh and conditions unsanitary. The National Council of Churches conducted an investigation, but the mayor of Jackson and the governor did not repudiate the violent tactics of the Jackson police or make further inquiries in the matter.[2] Ira Grupper, a field worker for SNCC, was among those arrested.

More was at stake than just voting rights on the local level. Social arrangements between the races reflected the dominant cultural values of the South. In this structure a multi-tiered social order existed among both whites and blacks. Whites were divided by inequities between the powerful, wealthy class and the working, poorer class. Discrepancies existed among blacks, such that some had economic and educational advantages that distinguished them from the poorest of the poor. In our separate but unequal society blacks at all levels suffered from racial discrimination. The civil rights movement became active to address a whole range of discrepancies and inequities among blacks evident in almost every dimension of life. Some seemed more crucial than others and there were differing opinions as to what those might be. Battles to overcome all inequities were staged on many fronts. Annie Devine, a respected civil rights leader in Canton, expressed her feelings about what was the most "detrimental thing" in the civil rights movement. She charged that politicians had played with school desegregation like a toy as a way to maintain the divide between the races and thereby avoided dealing with the real issue. "She felt that the controversy over desegregation masked the deeper issue of poverty."[3] To her it was a matter of economics.

In June 1965, the Student Non-Violent Coordinating Committee in Columbia, concerned about blatant inequities between blacks and whites that continued to exist in Marion County, had compiled some statistical information in terms of population, school enrollment and years completed, occupations, median family incomes, and voter registration.[4] But the time was rapidly approaching to move beyond mere statistics to nonviolent protests in the streets.

Almost immediately after the city school board's decision in early July not to submit a plan, N. A. and I decided the time had come to jostle the white leadership. We agonized over how to do this. We finally came to the conclusion that we needed to write a letter to key businessmen spelling out what we thought the alternatives were that we could expect in the fall, and what must be done to fill the vacuum created by the school board's decision not to comply. Our hope was that somehow this letter would break the silence and tip the balance toward a more favorable response. For several days we drafted letter after letter and revised them once more. We drew up a potential list of recipients, again with numerous revisions.[5] Although we decided that this letter should be from us as individuals, we also decided it would be wise to focus mainly within our own flocks and on people we knew well. We ended up with twenty-eight persons, all Presbyterians and Methodists, with the exception of two Baptists. The mailing consisted of three parts: A cover letter, a list of recipients, and a page entitled, "For Your Consideration."[6]

The letter clearly stated that while totally unofficial, it represented the effort of two individuals vitally interested in the life of the community. We acknowledged the recipients' leadership positions and asked them to consider honestly and carefully the realities presented in the enclosed sheet. We let them know we had no proposal, and that the decision about how to respond was completely theirs. We offered to work with any group if that were desired. We underscored the urgency of the situation, noting that, "By our action or inaction we will set the future direction of life in our city." We urged recipients to share the enclosed information with those interested in the welfare of the community, then to contact our city officials "expressing your concern and offering them your support."

"For Your Consideration" was intended to be non-judgmental of the school board. It laid out several concerns: districts not submitting a plan might be subject to court action as early as the next fall; implementing a court order may incite local resistance; public apathy would create a vacuum inviting lawlessness; publicity surrounding a court order would invite outside extremists to action in our community; and normal life would be destroyed, leaving behind bitter feelings and leaders unable to exert control over the situation. We called for a broad segment of the community to insist publicly on peaceful compliance, so that order might be maintained and law justly applied to all citizens. We urged the recipients to spread the word, give permission to use their names in a public statement urging peaceful compliance, and consider any constructive ideas that might bring about peaceful solutions to the problems we all faced. We emphasized our belief that, "A healthy community atmosphere beneficial to all individual citizens and businesses will not just happen, it must be worked for." A list of recipients was included because we wanted to model openness as well as let each know who else had received the letter. It was a way of generating a buzz that would not let anyone off the hook by claiming anonymity. The letter was dated July 17, 1965, and dropped in the mail on Sunday, the next day. The mayor was aware of what we were doing and had suggested names to us. The only other person we talked to about the letter prior to its mailing was the chair of the school board, who gave his hearty unofficial approval. We shared the final draft with the mayor in person immediately after we mailed the letters, even though he was on the list to receive one.

On Sunday, July 18, N. A. and I gently prepared our people for what was to come without spelling out the details. My communion sermon was entitled, "Almost Dead, and Don't Know It."[7] It was based on the text, "Awake, and strengthen what remains and is on the point of death, for I have not found your works perfect in the sight of my God. Remember then what you have received and heard; keep that and repent" (Rev. 3:2–3, RSV). In my sermon I said we too often shut our eyes to the poor and the effects of poverty, then condemn the poor for being undeserving; we claim the business of the church is saving souls and not social reform; we do not recognize that charity without love destroys the giver and the receiver; we denounce any effort to meet the needs of the poor and refuse to recognize alien voices that capitalize on the plight of the poor.

As I began to bring my sermon to a close I said, "Would to God that this day I had in my power to set before you specific steps as how to bring to reality what we ought to do." I went on: "Never before has this church been faced with the opportunity to witness to the redeeming love of Christ in this place. We are rapidly approaching our rendezvous with destiny, the reason why God allowed this congregation to be established some 50 years ago, the reason why God has poured into it so much leadership ability, so much resources." Then I declared that I had reason to believe that before we come again to this sacred communion table, "[W]e as a community may enter a profound period of stress which will make young men old before their time." I said this advisedly, reading the signs of the times, and not as an alarmist. "How we go through this time will depend largely on how we as Christians act, whether or not we will utilize the good gifts we have received by God's gracious hand." I concluded, "This community is on the brink of having to find a loving and just way to live together, loving one another or no one will be able to live with any meaning . . . . It would be staggering to describe the impact on this community if this church out of Christian conviction, together and individually, would take the lead in all areas of our life, doing things we have never done before and in certain ways because it's right to do it that way. But this won't just happen, it must be worked for."

On the very night of the day we dropped the letters in the mail, a group of SNCC members rented a house on Nathan Street. The letter received a good hearing. Only three or four said anything to N. A. about the letter. I heard nothing before I left the next week around July 19 for several weeks vacation and study leave. After we got back to Columbia around August 16, not one recipient said a word to me about the letter.

I attended an alcoholism seminar at the Presbyterian School of Christian Education in Richmond, Virginia. Millye, Neal, and I had an apartment on campus. One day we drove up to Washington, D. C. I made arrangements to meet and visit with Mac Seacrest of the Community Relations Service at the Department of Commerce. Epps had introduced me to him by phone back in June. The meeting with Seacrest established a personal contact, and he gave me more information about the service and how to access it.

Back in Richmond, Millye and I decided one day to see the movie, *The Sound of Music*. Neal went with us and enjoyed the singing and dancing. We also took a Korean student who was attending the seminar. After the film ended, he was very quiet. As we talked we discovered that he had fled his home in North Korea by walking across the mountains to South Korea, very much like the von Trapp family had done, as depicted in the movie. It was a sobering moment to think what it must be like to have to leave your home and all you had known all your life and start over in a new place.

After the seminar was over we came back to Montreat, N.C., where we visited with friends and sat in on a conference. We were staying in a college dorm that was filled with high school students. Neal thoroughly enjoyed that experience, but we did not get much sleep, and we moved to a local motel. We had to stay for an extra night because something broke on our station wagon and we were lucky to get it fixed before we headed to Mississippi.

The mayor had been very active while I was away, dealing with the challenges of his office including the SNCC activities that were becoming more numerous and public. I did not fully appreciate what took place during this time until I reconstructed the sequence of events decades later, primarily from thorough notes the mayor kept about what was going on. Close to midnight on Friday, July 30, the Freedom House was fired on fifteen times, according to some accounts, and set on fire. The number of shots fired and the manner in which the conflagration—some called it a firebombing—was set varied widely. The following Thursday the *Columbian-Progress* reported, "A fire of more than passing interest was brought under control by Columbia's efficient fire department," which responded to the alarm around two o'clock Saturday morning. The article was short on details about the fire itself, but very detailed on the location of the house and its occupants. It noted that the house was at "623 Nathan Avenue, one block from Owens street and near Lafayette street . . . . It was occupied by a group of out-of-towners." The article went on to say that records identified the occupants as "representatives of the Mississippi Freedom Democratic Party here to encourage Negroes to vote and otherwise help them." It was very specific in identifying the individuals as, " . . . two white women: Ann Marsh, Goalsburg, PA and Sarah Shumer, UCLA, Berkeley, CA; Two white men: Samuel Gross, Columbia University, N.Y., Richard

Atlee, Monroeville, Pa.; and one Negro, Curtis Styles, 769 Main Street, Biloxi, Miss."[8] Some discrepancy existed in reporting as to whether Shana or Sarah was Shumer's first name, but she was one and the same person.

E. E. Johnson, chief of police, received three telegrams on Wednesday, August 4, from Huntingdon and College Station, Pennsylvania, sent by families and friends expressing their deep concern that the "civil rights workers in Columbia have been harassed by night riders" and that the Freedom House had been bombed. They urged the chief, "to use immediately whatever means at your disposal to guarantee the safety of the civil rights workers in Columbia." The following day, the mayor and the police chief telegraphed the concerned families and friends: "Protection being given Ann Marsh and co-workers in keeping with that given other citizens in Columbia. Miss. Hway Patrol and FBI alerted to circumstances surrounding their presence. Bombing and resulting fire of their residence most regretable [sic]. Under full investigation by FBI."[9]

On Monday, August 2, the mayor met with a group from SNCC that wanted to use the library. The mayor's mother, the librarian, agreed each SNCC patron was welcome to check out five books. That night, the mayor attended a meeting at the Pearl River Valley Electric Power Association building to hear presentations by several people about the Community Action Program, part of President Johnson's War on Poverty. The mayor welcomed some thirty to forty white and seventeen black community leaders. Someone noted later to me that the group of whites was encouraged to attend the meeting by some of those that earlier received the Dickson-McAtee letter. Several officials from Lamar County were also in attendance. The mayor stated that the purpose of the meeting was to hear about the anti-poverty programs and make plans for how to take advantage of them in our area. Marion and Lamar were working together to meet the federal guidelines regarding size of population and were looking for another county to join them, presumably Forrest. J. O. Cagle, Columbia, manager of the Pearl River Valley Electric Power Association, moderated the meeting and introduced the presenters.[10]

Cagle gave the background on how the county organization got started. State Senator Ed Pittman, Hattiesburg, outlined the proposed organization for the Marion, Forrest, and Lamar County area. Gene Triggs, Hattiesburg, assistant director of the A & I Board, led a discussion on what other areas were doing in this program. O. H. Simmons, Jackson, chief of operating functions for the Mississippi Employment Security Committee, covered the different phases of the program including a complete explanation of the Community Action Program (C.A.P.).[11] According to the mayor, Simmons reported that the Mississippi Employment Service Program was pitched toward youth but was not related to the Job Corps. Some projects under the anti-poverty program were: early childhood education, adult education, nursing care, mobile health services, and food distribution. Simmons also described the Neighborhood Youth Corps (NYC) for those sixteen to twenty-one years of age. Participants had to be in school fifteen hours a week and work outside the school for thirty-one hours a week for any governmental agency, but they would not replace any current government employees. A counseling service related to the NYC was described. The floor was opened for discussion.[12]

Following the discussion, it was announced that a steering committee of five (three white and two black) had been appointed earlier by county supervisors J. O. Cagle, chairman, M. C. Connerly, L. Z. Blankinship, Glyn Tynes, and I. C. Pittman. An advisory committee of some thirty to forty persons, known as the Marion County Action Committee, volunteered to survey the needs of the local community, locate projects that qualified under the law, and recommend them to the steering committee as suitable applicants for government grants. A chartered corporation had to be formed to govern the projects and receive and disburse the funding: "Funds received from the Office of Economic Opportunity will be administered wholly by the community and no outsiders will be sent in or permitted to have any part in the decisions made."[13]

❖ ❖ ❖

The evening circle of the Women of the Presbyterian Church held its monthly meeting on Monday, August 2, at 7:30 p.m. in the church fellowship hall. In addition to Bible study and reports on various projects, the circle announced that it had purchased an individual communion set for in-home communion. Miss Mary Wolfe reported that, "Rev. William McAtee, pastor, desired that the communion service be dedicated in the near future."[14]

❖ ❖ ❖

In preparation for what the mayor assumed might take place in the near future, he invited a group of restaurant owners and operators to meet with him on Tuesday, August 3, to discuss the situation they were facing. He brought his audience up to date on what was taking place in town. He then shared with them the history of the economic problems faced in other towns. He reported that other merchants were considering hiring black clerks. He talked about the law of the land and legal action that would ensue if it were not followed. He laid out his vision of the image "we want to build in Columbia." Most of all he hoped that "individual café and restaurant owners [would] stick together and not play one another's misfortune against each other." He closed by giving a report on the community action meeting from the night before.[15]

That same day a group of fifteen civil rights workers visited the library for one hour, sitting and reading material. They checked out books to read. Later, Mrs. McLean, the librarian, fined one of the workers two cents for being overdue in returning a book. The following day, Wednesday, August 4, approximately fifteen civil rights workers were refused entrance to the Marion Theater. They proceeded to go to city hall to talk with the mayor about the incident. He promised to speak with the manager of the theater to see what could be worked out.

Sometime during this week, Dr. Vernon L. Terrell, the county health officer, wrote a letter to the mayor, with copies to the board of aldermen and the executive officer of the State Board of Health, advising that the swimming pool at City Park be closed immediately because of the high level of coliform organisms that had shown up in recent water samplings. He noted that, "[T]he automatic clorination [sic] equipment has been inoperative for the entire summer, so an attempt to clorinate the pool by hand was attempted." He advised that the pool should remain closed "until adequate clorination [sic] equipment is installed."[16]

Friday, August 6, was a historic day. President Lyndon Johnson's efforts to get Congress to enact anti-discrimination legislation that would enforce the Fifteenth Amendment had finally borne fruit. Hearings held regarding this legislation clearly indicated that case-by-case litigation was not successful in opening up the registration process. President Johnson signed the Voting Rights Act of 1965 into law on this day. Section 2 of the act, which closely follows the language of the Fifteenth Amendment, "applied a nationwide prohibition against the denial or abridgement of the right to vote on account of race or color." The act also outlawed literacy tests and appointed federal examiners with the authority to register qualified citizens to vote. Although poll taxes in national elections were abolished by the Twenty-fourth Amendment (1964), the act did direct the attorney general "to challenge its use in state and local elections."[17]

Mayor McLean called a meeting of key leaders in the community in the chamber office on Friday, August 6, at 10:00 a.m. to discuss with him what needed to be done to create a positive atmosphere and what leadership they must give the community as it faced the dramatic changes before it. Many ideas and opinions were expressed, and the groundwork was laid for what would soon become a public statement.

On Wednesday, August 11, eight to eleven civil rights workers went to Ja-Gee's restaurant to be served. Then they went to the Marion Theater. The mayor indicated that extra highway patrols were on hand, but he gave no indication of what happened at the restaurant or the theater. The mayor also reported that he had recruited ten private citizens as observers to be in the area.[18]

Up until Friday, August 13, the civil rights workers had worked within the bounds of the framework outlined in meetings with the mayor where they shared with him the moves they intended to make. The mayor had vouched for them, as they had tested a couple of restaurants, the theater and the library, all without incident. That day a trial was held for two civil rights workers who earlier had been accused of shoplifting, but had not been picked up until later. Accounts vary as to the discretion used in the detentions. The alleged shoplifters never denied the charges but contended that the wrong individuals had been arrested. They would not reveal the identity of the actual shoplifters. About the time the trial was to close, the sheriff came in with some petty charges of tearing up screens in that jail and the like. These allegations struck the civil rights workers as gross injustices. All of a sudden they walked out of the trial unannounced and went to Autry's Café where "Klan types" hung out. To protest the sheriff's action, they demanded to be served. The protest came off without incident. It was not clear to me if their choice of location for protest underscored their desire to disrupt the status quo or to exercise their rights as citizens. Neither did I understand how they thought integrating this white hangout would counteract the outrageous behavior of the sheriff.

Saturday night, August 14, approximately ten civil rights workers entered Autry's Café around 11:00 p.m. without incident. The following day, Sunday, August 15, civil rights workers went to the Marion Theater in pairs without incident. One police officer in street clothes was in the theater, along with an undetermined number of private citizen observers. Years later when Grupper and I talked about these incidents, he seemed totally surprised by the mayor's advance involvement and how it had possibly contributed to the way the above encounters played out.

On Tuesday, August 17, Columbia's District Attorney Maurice Dantin, also a former mayor, was invited to speak at the Laurel (MS) Rotary Club, where he made clear his perspective on the activities of the civil rights workers. He told the Rotarians that race riots like the ones in California happened because federal officials and civil rights leaders encouraged the Negroes of America "to seek to obtain their objectives through unlawful means." He believed the end result of such a tactic was "chaos, rioting, civil strife, and the destruction of personal property." To bolster this claim he cited rising crime statistics in the country reflecting a massive growth of disrespect for constituted authority in society. "People take to the streets in demonstrations of walk-ins, sit-ins, lie-ins, wade-ins, many resulting in violence; others retaliate by taking the law into their own hands. Both contribute to the growth of chaos in our orderly, democratic society." He concluded that the only way for our nation to survive and remain strong was for civic leaders "to insist on the maintenance of law and order, and the orderly processes of government for the redress of any grievances that may exist in our society."[19]

The *Columbian-Progress* carried in its August 19 edition a front-page editorial entitled "A Time for Leadership." The piece recognized that it would be "wishful thinking" to think Columbia had not been affected by the turmoil in neighboring communities. It went on to note there had been no flagrant incidents worthy of recognition here in Columbia. It referred to the fact that "workers from outside Columbialand" had been discouraged by leaders in the Negro community, "and we commend them for having the confidence they have in local white leaders." It then expressed the belief that "at the proper time these leaders would come out for strict law enforcement, and that the 'laws of the land' would be recognized and enforced even though some of them are not popular locally."[20]

The editorial applauded the leadership of our "young and capable" Mayor McLean, "who is working untiringly with all citizens who have problems." It referenced the "Statement of Beliefs" that appeared in this same issue as "proof that local leaders feel that it is time to go on record for rigid law enforcement, regardless of who might be involved." The statement was, the editorial went on, a recognition that, "We needed sound, sensible leadership. Now we have it in the group who signed the statement and the hundreds of others who did not have an opportunity to sign, but who endorse the statement." The editorial concluded by philosophizing about the potential Columbia had as a community and the difficulties that come with changing a way of life, concluding, "We have every reason to be proud of our past, and we should look forward to a great future."[21]

The "Statement of Beliefs" covered an entire page of the paper, with five statements in large bold type and some 150 names attached, all belonging to business leaders, city aldermen, and county supervisors. Only a couple of main street businessmen did not sign on: two druggists and one grocer, who ran the store where the shoplifting took place. The five beliefs were: 1) to abide by the law until declared unconstitutional; 2) to leave law enforcement to officers and ask all people to do the same; 3) not to condone punishing those with whom we disagree as individuals, but if such events happen, the aggressors should be prosecuted; 4) to discourage gathering of citizens to view "events"; and 5) to approve actions of our elected officials and ask others to do likewise.[22]

On Saturday, August 21, the civil rights workers—some from outside, some local—began picketing the Sunflower Store from 10:00 a.m. until 3:00 p.m., demanding a public apology for the shoplifting false arrest, the hiring of one of the ones falsely accused of shoplifting as a clerk in one of the stores, and a few other expected stipulations. There were also pickets at Ja-Gee's all day.

W. E. "Bill" Walker, Jr., wrote a letter to Bud Sowell, a member of the Columbia City School Board, on Monday, August 23, in which Walker said in his business he had no alternative to integration or segregation and felt that our local school situation was the same. He went on to say that he earnestly believed our local schools were going to be integrated, and he hoped that we would take action resulting in the least number of overall problems for everyone in our community. Walker emphasized that he felt voluntary integration was our best course of action at this time. He concluded by saying he would be glad to discuss his concerns with the recipients at length if he could be of further service. Walker sent the same letter to two other board members, Ray Pittman and Bert Lawrence, with a blind copy to Buddy McLean.[23]

On Tuesday, August 24, the Columbia Municipal School Board met to reconsider its noncompliance with the desegregation order. Other school boards in the state had opted to comply. According to what I heard at the time from those close to the situation, the public "Statement of Beliefs" and the letter N. A. and I had sent to key leaders put pressure on the board. In this "rounder of a meeting," one member, who had originally voted against compliance, changed his vote, leading to a tie and making it possible for the chairman to break the tie in favor of submitting a plan.

The civil rights workers picketed the Sunflower Store and the Marion Theater again on Thursday, August 26, and in the process five workers were arrested. Sometime during the day the mayor called Mac Seacrest at the Community Relations Service in Washington, inquiring about trespassing laws and how they relate to churches. Some discussion regarding "trespassing" and "arresting juveniles" took place. It was noted that the U.S. Supreme Court had ruled in a couple of cases in Alabama that an "invitation to use" the sidewalks dedicates them to the city. On private property, a warrant must be issued in order for an arrest to take place. The "rule of reasonableness" must be followed in defining ground rules for picketing, such as: 1) exits and entrances must not be blocked, 2) picketers must keep walking, 3) picketers can't block streets, etc., and 4) numbers must be limited to available space. Seacrest informed the mayor that Jim Draper, an employee of the Community Relations Service, would be arriving in Columbia sometime later in the day and would be in contact with him.[24]

Friday morning, August 27, the mayor called N. A. and me to come to his office to meet with Draper and him to discuss the situation before he met with the civil rights workers the next day. Our long session covered a myriad of questions that the mayor wanted addressed: Can we have agreed upon ground rules regarding picketing; does the group of picketers want to be arrested; are they going to push to the limits; will there be moves to follow, as Columbia has been chosen for the next major focus of planned publicity; what is the mayor's responsibility to citizens to keep their confidence in order to accomplish anything; what is the mayor's responsibility to church and school; how quickly is total integration forecast to take place; what are the identities and relative sizes of some communities that have made the transition in the South; how responsible are the Snick [SNCC] leaders and can we depend on any agreement, etc. made with them; are they sincere in their desire to promote this evolution peacefully as long as we proceed with efficiency and speed?[25]

As best I recall, the conclusions reached in the discussion were that certainly there could be ground rules for picketing, and we had no indication of the picketers' desire to be arrested. Up to now the SNCC leaders had honored agreements, indicating willingness to work for peaceful solutions as long as progress was being made. However, there was no guarantee that they would not push the mayor to the limits if progress were not made. Keeping the leaders of the community informed about positive steps the mayor was taking and what was taking place were important to maintain confidence in his leadership. A great deal of uncertainty surrounded answers to questions about SNCC's intentions regarding being arrested and action plan. Who could make forecasts regarding total integration?

The mayor then filled Draper in on the steering committee for the anti-poverty program, with its advisory group and the two meetings scheduled for the next weekend out of which it was hoped that a bi-racial committee, the "Committee of Concerned," could be formed. The mayor promised to give Draper three days notice when it was finally decided that these two meetings would be a go. There was a discussion about the FBI talking with the local police about how to handle the arrest of female civil rights workers and about the police's remarks to the "kids" [civil rights workers]. The mayor discussed a meeting to be held with the civil rights workers to discuss local employment opportunities. Finally, the mayor asked more about court injunctions ordering picketers to cease blocking entry to the stores.[26]

At a duly called meeting on Friday, August 27, the Board of Trustees of the Columbia Municipal Separate School District adopted a plan of desegregation. A letter to all parents was drafted by the Office of the Superintendent stating, "A plan for desegregation of our school system has been put into effect so that our schools will operate in all respects without regard to race, color, or national origin." The letter went on to announce that the plan would commence with the 1965–66 school year, and that all students in the district eligible to attend grades one and two should have freedom of choice to attend any school or attendance center in the area of their residence. The plan specified that the third, fourth, seventh, and ninth grades would be integrated beginning in September 1966. All other grades would be integrated beginning in September 1967, so that "the maintenance of separate schools for white and Negro children of said Columbia Municipal Separate School District shall be completely ended as to all grades."[27]

A choice was required for each child. It was clear that parents were not to receive any advice or recommendations or otherwise be influenced by any teacher, principal, or other school official in their decisions about choice of schools for their children. And there would be no favor or penalty as a result of their choices. Overcrowding was the only reason a request would be denied. In that case the child would be offered another choice in any of the other schools in the system where space was available in his or her grade. School bus routes would be charted on a desegregated basis, and transportation would be provided for all pupils eligible for it. It did not matter if a choice were made for the formerly white or formerly Negro school nearest to the child's residence.[28]

This was a very timely decision on the part of the Columbia school board. Sometime around noon on this same Friday, August 27, Federal

District Judge Harold Cox of Jackson "dashed the last—and legally base-less—hopes of holdout districts in a suit involving the North Pike County School District." When any suit was filed, he had to order desegregation almost immediately. But Cox did not wait on a lawsuit.[29] The North Pike County school board thought that by rejecting federal aid and not filing a plan it could "preserve segregation." There was no question in Cox's mind that federal school aid was not the issue. This ruling was quite a shock to the school board, since there had been no applications for admission to white schools by any local blacks. No mention had been made about any suit. The whole registration process could have been derailed when regis-tration occurred Monday, and it would be too late to clear up the confu-sion to make the plan effective in the fall. Judge Cox gave the board until September 10 to come up with an acceptable plan for desegregation.[30]

Picketing was scheduled to begin at the Sunflower store at 9:00 a.m. on Saturday, August 28. However, prior to that time the mayor convened a meeting at city hall. The mayor met with Lester Haddox, City Attorney Ernest Duff, a person named Moore, and Jim Draper from the Community Relations Service. Civil rights workers Ann Marsh, Shana Shumer, Richard Atlee, and Curtis Styles were also present. Two other names were written off to the side of his notes of the meeting, in this fashion: <Ashley and Watts>.

The civil rights workers presented three demands: a) repay the $218.00 fine; b) apologize for the false arrest in the shoplifting case; c) hire Negro employees. The mayor responded that those picketing should cease parad-ing in front of the door at the Sunflower Store. He did not question the privilege of picketing. He only requested that they confine parading to the defined area. There was some discussion about not arresting the picketers, but no decision was reached during the meeting. The mayor told me that Jim Draper later confirmed that fact off the record.

The police complained about vulgar language used by the protest-ers. The police also admitted that they had arrested the wrong persons in the shoplifting incident, and that they knew who the true culprits were. They said they had apologized and confirmed their suspicions with a civil rights worker. A certain amount of levity entered the meeting when "all laughed when Moore confessed to be a Christian." The civil rights work-ers complained they were called "boy" or "girl," and said they should be called "young lady" or "Mr." or "young man." They also described the police force as "lousy," and requested that Negro policemen be hired. The final complaint reiterated objections to the police shoplifting action as false arrest. The mayor's final entry on his notes was, "meeting very distasteful."[31]

N. A. and I stood by all Saturday morning, August 28, to see what was needed of us. Downtown on a Saturday in a southern town was the place for everyone from across the county to gather. It was a time to socialize with family and friends and to share the latest gossip and rumors. The sidewalks were filled with black and white shoppers doing their weekly shopping, and parking was at a premium. The public mores of southern culture were still politely adhered to in Columbia. However, there was no guarantee that this kind of behavior would continue in light of the violence erupting across the state.

Around noon the mayor called, telling me that things had gotten worse on the picket line. The protestors refused not to block the door, and he was going to arrest them. The mayor recognized that "blocking the door" was hard to define. He wanted to inform community leaders about what he was forced to do and why. He spent the morning trying to effect a compromise, but to no avail. He was concerned about the presence of the usual Saturday crowds.

N. A. and I got part of Six together and spent a great deal of time trying to determine the affect an arrest might have on our planned meetings. The large gathering of whites was scheduled to meet on Friday, September 3, and the black gathering on Saturday, September 4. We activated our phone tree to determine the reaction of the black community to an arrest. Word came back in a very short time—thirty minutes or so. There seemed to be widespread support, assuring the mayor they were still behind him even though he was forced to act. While we were conferring, things were developing downtown. We found out later through sources in the black community that word on the street was that the local leader was not producing, so a civil rights "hard-core head" was sent in to take his place. We did not know the identity of this person. It was never clear to us if the local leader was actually circumvented, or if in reality the outside person was invited in to generate leverage to achieve the objectives of the picket line. Nonetheless, as the arrests began, this new outside leader managed not to cross the chalk line and so did not get arrested. He immediately demanded police protection, which was refused. The members of the group went limp and had to be carried off to jail. The mayor had ordered the city police not to manhandle any of the arrestees, but a county deputy jumped in and started roughing up one civil rights worker on the ground. The mayor reached down, pulled away the deputy, who was emotionally out of control, and made the arrest himself. A couple hundred spectators had gathered, including a local Baptist preacher who was laughing it up on the front line. I was standing nearby and heard him say, "This is enough to make a preacher cuss." Finally the area was cleared without further incident.

I left the shopping center, got N. A. at the Methodist Church, and went to the home of one of Four—the black contingent of Six—who lived close to the Freedom House. Looking through a curtain in my friend's home at Freedom House across the adjoining backyards was as close as I ever got to it. We were briefing him on the latest developments when he mentioned he thought his oldest son was in the group arrested. At that point I was not sure what to expect next.

N. A. and I looped through downtown. It was dark and raining by then. Things were quiet. After I let N. A. out at the church, I went looking for the mayor, only to reach him at his home by phone. He said he was making headway with the local kids in jail, but was still not getting through to the outsiders. He then informed me that the civil rights worker who had carefully not stepped across the line that afternoon had asked for a parade permit for Sunday afternoon at 3 p.m. This man alleged that four busloads of civil rights workers were converging on our town and that he had notified CBS plus all networks. A new stage was set. The mayor granted the permit and outlined the route.

At this point I could tell only N. A. the details of the march and indicate its potential impact. The mayor and I talked about the necessity of getting a group of white and black leaders to stand with him in case of an emergency. He was getting some rumble and lip from a few local white leaders—not that they were against him, but they had not reached the point of supporting him. The mayor notified the FBI, the highway patrol, and local police about plans for Sunday. Those were the only organizations he contacted. He wanted to keep it quiet in order to avoid a crowd. Late Saturday night, with the mayor's approval, I conferred with one of the black leaders and briefed him, getting clearly established in his mind the need for a group of blacks that would stick with us. He confirmed that following this strategy would not to be a problem.

The mayor went to his office on Sunday morning, August 29, to request highway patrol support, only to learn there was just one patrol car in the whole district. All others were in Natchez because a NAACP official had been bombed. That morning there also had been an announcement on

TV calling for a big Klan rally with Robert Sheldon in Columbia. Finally, this announcement provided the motivation for the highway patrol to pull twenty-seven units and send them to Columbia.

◆ ◆ ◆

That morning I preached a sermon entitled, "Who is a Minister?" never once giving a hint as to why the mayor was absent from worship or what was unfolding downtown.[32] Rather, I focused on not confusing the ministry of the church with the work of the clergy. I pointed out that through baptism God has acted, and we are all welcomed into the church. The church's ministry or task is to serve the world and has no being, except as a servant. Everyone who is baptized then is a minister who shares in that task. Failure to recognize and exercise one's ministry is another matter. Then I stressed that, "The main reason the Church obviously fails in being a servant—in being the Church—is that ministry is seen as the prerogative of the clergy rather than all the people 'serving' in all areas of their lives!" I concluded, "We flounder in fear because we do not know who we are. When we know who we are, we live out our convictions without fear of the consequences."

As late as one o'clock that afternoon there had been no buildup downtown. But when twenty-seven patrol cars rolled up to city hall, traffic picked up. At a briefing with the mayor, an FBI agent reported there was reason to believe that some three hundred Deacons for Defense were also coming. He reported it was not clear who the deacons were, but he said the common perception in law enforcement circles was that they were armed and dangerous militants. At some point the agent also told the mayor that the guy who had refused to be arrested the day before was on their list and was under surveillance as a communist. The agent pointed out that not all the civil rights movement had been infiltrated, but the area in the Natchez-Laurel-Bogalusa triangle was.

Later, in a letter I wrote my friends describing in detail what was going on during these hectic ten days, I seemed to buy into this "official" line by inserting "(THIS IS QT)"! At the time, the surveillance activities and credibility of the FBI were neither questioned nor verified. Decades later I got another perspective from Ira Grupper as to the identity of the deacons. He experienced them firsthand as hard-working folk who wanted to be treated fairly under the law but who, due to the hostile environment of the times, took defensive precautions to arm and protect themselves.

The mayor indicated he had been informed that the highway patrol officers were ordered to shoot first, because the deacons and Klan were expected to shoot and then ask questions. Whether or not this order can be confirmed, the potential for violence was real, and atmospheric fear permeated the day for most all involved. Still, some "good ole Columbianites" gathered to watch the show. Only nine marchers showed up, led by the "tough agitator." He did not produce. No four busloads. No Robert Sheldon. No Klan. No Deacons for Defense.

Late Sunday afternoon, Four met to come up with their list of 150 for the meeting planned for the following Saturday. All along, we were dealing with the immediate, but trying to keep our previous plans intact. The mayor wanted to meet at 9:30 Monday morning with Four plus the fifteen key leaders they had identified in the spring. Having to work fast, we got our signals crossed, so that by Monday, August 30, only Four was notified of the meeting. At any rate, I activated Four to pull together as many of the fifteen as they could in thirty minutes. This group was to meet at 9:30 a.m. with the mayor and a small number of other white leaders. We decided that N. A. and I would give up our seats to those who had not been informed. We had to explain to our counterparts on Six that the status of the white minister was different from theirs when it came to certain matters.

The meeting was held, and it was one of the most fruitful to date. The mayor laid all the cards on the table and brought everyone up-to-date on what had happened in the previous week. For the first time, there was a free exchange of ideas, not glossing over the bad or the impossible. Some from the white side criticized the mayor for his frankness, but by and large he continued to build support. That afternoon the mayor met with thirty other white business people and informed them of what was going on.

At 4 o'clock the mayor sat as judge in city court, hearing the case of those who were arrested on Saturday. It lasted for four hours. A sharp federal attorney represented the accused. He was more than kind to the mayor, who himself claimed he was not a "legal eagle." The mayor had a note that prompted him when it came to the swearing in of the defendants. It read, "Affirm, not swear to tell the truth and nothing but the truth, so help you God." The names of Ann Marsh and John Atlee were written on the note.[33] There was nothing in this note indicating that they were the defendants, but there were other indications that they probably were two of the five arrested and on trial. The end result was that the mayor fined the defendants the minimum, suspending their sentences so that they would not go back to jail. Later the mayor told me that the federal attorney had commented during the proceedings that this was the first time he had ever heard a white southerner talk like our mayor and complimented him. He also told the defendants that the judge had bent over backwards on their behalves.

Monday night was another long night of reevaluation for the mayor, N. A., and me. We felt we had made some mistakes in getting our signals crossed about the meeting and had some fences to mend. But even when things were at their hottest, some wise decisions had been made, like how the black and white leaders were informed about what was going on in the community. Years later, looking back on the events of this week, I came to the conclusion that this may have been one of the pivotal points in the whole adventure.

The mayor had faced a potentially volatile mix of perspectives that could have created a disaster for the community. Fear of this possibility was real for everyone because of the uncertainty involved, even though enough certainty did exist. The rhetoric of anticipated violence had replaced notions of civility in the press and with some public officials. Black power advocates were beginning to discard the rhetoric of non-violence. The Freedom House was firebombed. However, no evidence existed that any acts of violence were initiated in return by the MFDP in Columbia, even though years later Grupper confirmed they were armed as a matter of self-defense out of fear for their lives. The NAACP official in Natchez was bombed. Then the Klan, known for violence, announced its march in Columbia, countered by the presence of the Deacons of Defense, a group purported by some law officials to be militant and dangerous.

Critics then and in later years might have viewed the mayor's desire to keep things quiet as evidence of his being primarily interested in preventing protest and minimizing or slowing change. Other leaders in the white power structure may be rightly accused of those aims, but this was far from the truth as I experienced it with Buddy. His first order of business that weekend was to avert total chaos and public disorder that could have greatly diminished any possibility of achieving his primary goal: the series of firsts that would begin to open access for all citizens to public institutions and facilities as provided by law. His leadership as mayor during events that followed gave witness to his commitment to this primary goal. No extensive organized public opposition to his leadership ever emerged or was widely voiced in the white community, though no doubt some vehemently disagreed with his actions.

As so often happened during this whole adventure, high moments of achievement soon gave way to low moments brought on by new challenges and an uncertain future. Tuesday, August 31, was a low day emotionally, a day to regroup and take soundings as to whether it was feasible to continue with the mass gatherings planned for the weekend. I feared these meeting might be called off. Our black colleagues were sounding out their networks, and according to them support in the black community was high. The mayor tested his sources and found growing support over the need for bi-racial talks, but a disagreement over how to bring them about. Also, there was growing distaste for having the Feds come talk to whites at this point. N. A. and I ran off the invitations for the blacks, and Four were to have envelopes addressed and waiting for the word to go. I pulled away to get set up at the church for the beginning of our weekday kindergarten.

At 3:00 p.m. this Tuesday, fourteen civil rights workers proceeded to picket at the Sunflower Store. Curtis Styles called the mayor's office at 3:45 p.m. about the $550 bond for those who had been jailed on Saturday, saying the Western Union money order was to be cashed Wednesday morning. Styles agreed with the mayor to picket only in front of the glass window of the store, for four hours per day, on two mornings and two Saturdays. He also agreed to allow the pickets to be roped in whenever "our people" (I assume police or other citizens) gathered. "Their people" (civil rights workers) would stay in the fence; our people would stay out.[34]

We scheduled a meeting of Six on Wednesday morning, September 1, to reevaluate and plan for the weekend meetings. By now the mayor was convinced these two meetings must take place. He wanted to get the maximum number of people informed and involved, not just the old power structure, so the invitations had to go out. Earlier the mayor, N. A., and I had discussed the need to get women involved in this meeting. N. A. and I learned in conversations with our own women parishioners that many of them were more progressive in their views about race than were some of the men. But because they did not hold positions in the white power structure, these women's voices were not always heard outside the home, only in small private groups and certainly not openly at church.

I went to Miss Mary Wolfe, my unofficial pastor's aid, and asked her to draw up a list of women in the white community she thought should be at the meeting on Friday night. She gave me a handwritten list of sixty-seven names: ten Presbyterians; thirty-four Methodists (with note to "ask N.A).;" seven from "schools" (with note to "see Wiley," her brother, a member of the school board); two from Foxworth (the community across the Pearl River from Columbia); four from outside the city limits; and ten others without any designation. From this list, twenty-one were chosen to receive invitations.[35]

That morning's meeting with Six was the best yet. We had reached a deep fellowship that was unequaled as far as I was concerned. We felt we were under constant danger, for we felt certain we were being watched, but these black men taught me the meaning of living with fear without being crippled by it. Also, we had received the word the previous Monday that there was a strong possibility that the mayor's, N. A.'s, and my phone lines were all tapped. At the time I assumed this was done by the Klan or White Citizens' Council, but years later I wondered if it might have been the FBI. This news produced a problem in communication, but we worked through it. One of the black ministers at the meeting said, "[T]he blacks were more interested in hearing what local white leaders are saying than the Feds."

Wednesday afternoon I got the go-ahead from the mayor to get out the invitations to the list of 169 white leaders to meet Friday night. I gave Four the word to send out their invitations to the list of people in the black community they had identified. We suggested that each group set up methods of choosing representatives from these two meetings so that they could sit down together and begin to talk.

Thursday, September 2, came, and as I had not been out of the office during the morning I was unaware of the latest developments. This quiet period provided a serious time for reflection on what N. A. and I had been through since we first decided to establish lines of communication with the black community. I made a note that I intended to see that the "good friend in high level of state government" we all wanted to run for governor got to know Four, because after seeing them operate we felt they could hand him a segment of the vote in this county. Our friend William Winter would lose the election in 1967.

I took the opportunity to send a very detailed letter, that later became known as the "Tiredly Bill" letter, to close friends as a way of capturing a written record of the past ten days and the run-up to them.[36] I left out thousands of incidentals, which were nonetheless most interesting. I had been involved fifteen hours a day for all those days. It had been a time of elation and despair. I had written a highly elated letter to someone right after the school board had reversed its decision on August 27, but then the bottom dropped out with the activities of the following weekend. I was reluctant to be too elated over the outcome of the Sunday march, for fear the bottom would fall out again and despair would come up to bite me. But I knew I must write the story while it was fresh on my mind, for someday

I would forget the details. It was also my way of reaching out for support when I said to my friends, "I would appreciate your taking time from your busy schedule to write me." I promised to answer them "in the next lull," and noted that "next week right now seems like next year."

With both sets of invitations to the weekend meetings sent out, N. A. and I felt momentary relief. Each of these two meetings now must succeed on its own, and both had to work together. The two of us had set in motion a series of events and relationships that made these two meetings a possibility. We had done what we could to make them happen, and now our roles in them were receding into the background. As we were stuffing invitations, N. A. and I came to the sobering realization that, as "enhastening agents," we had actually played a role along with others in changing the political structure of Columbia and Marion County. The dynamic within this confluence of perspectives had accelerated to the point where the age-old deafening silence of separation was on the verge of being broken in a way far greater than we ever imagined.

CHAPTER 7

Broken Silence

Silence can be a peculiar thing. At times some people yearn for silence after being caught up in the cacophony of sound, maddening sounds that disturb or make no coherent sense, hearing the same thing over and over with no rhyme or reason driving one to distraction. Sometimes other people, through no fault of their own, hear nothing and must sign with their hands as a way to communicate with one another to overcome the silence. In either case, the lack of silence or the ever-presence of it can be deafening to the soul, killing the spirit unless some creative intervention changes the patterns through which silence is experienced. It is only when the silence is broken, literally or figuratively, and honesty prevails that mutual respect and forbearance is possible.

Effective communication is critical to such creative interventions. Gestures sent and responses made do not constitute effective communication in and of themselves. It is only when common understanding is reached through these exchanges that authentic communication takes place.[1] Other variables are involved that make common understanding possible, such as trust or even self-interest, with only a fine line separating these two at times. Silence or its absence plays a critical role in all forms of interpersonal communication, in that too often either version creates a barrier to or distortion of common understanding. Such silence may be fueled by fear or hatred or ignorance or other emotions that engender mistrust. Patterns of problematic communication emerge in the form of veiled or coded messages open to a wide range of misunderstanding. Dividing walls of hostility mount up, one's place becomes defined through accommodation, and a veil of mendacity descends upon the arrangement, becoming nigh on impossible to break through. Society becomes closed, and productive relationships among people become fractured.

Such was the state of the separate but unequal cultural arrangement that dominated Mississippi's relational landscape for decades. The sound of silence was deafening, overwhelming, and unchallenged, reminiscent of the song Paul Simon, the popular folk singer, wrote in 1964 that would later propel Simon and Garfunkel into prominence: ". . . People talking without speaking, People hearing without listening . . . . No one dared disturb the sound of silence."[2]

In recent months, initial gestures and responses were heard in the exchanges between the mayor and Six that began to bring about common understanding and break the silence. Trust and mutual respect grew based on promises made and promises kept, having a ripple effect that flowed out into the community. We learned later from Six that on Sunday, August 29, announcements were made in black pulpits regarding the protest march set to take place that afternoon. They said in so many words that the announcements were made but were "editorialized." It was their opinion that several hundred people could have showed up, but I assumed that turnout was squelched by the leadership of Four. Not everyone in their congregations agreed with what their pastors said or were doing, but pursued other forms of overt protest. Others in the community looked on them as "Uncle Toms" or as personal opportunists who had curried favor with the white power structure.[3]

On Tuesday, August 31, Curtis Styles, the local leader of the civil rights workers, met with the mayor and the two agreed again on certain ground rules for picketing. Although the community had a long way to go in facing and solving the issues before it, at least for the moment, the agreement on non-violent protests greatly enhanced the prospect for holding the two meetings on September 3 and 4, where it was intended that the silence would be broken even more definitively. From the very first time that Buddy McLean met with Six, when he was campaigning for mayor, to talk about how to develop a system of communication with the black community, it was evident that he knew that open communication was essential in working for the welfare of the city. At the heart of achieving this goal was breaking down the walls of suspicion and silence by involving the largest possible segment of the community, both black and white, in face-to-face conversations about the issues confronting us. These two early September meetings were part of a fragile two-step process to get to those face-to-face conversations. They were designed to elicit information about a variety of concerns and problems. Also, a plan would be presented for the formation of a bi-racial committee to continue the conversation and begin to find common understanding about how to find solutions to the issues. The mayor, in his signed invitation to white citizens to attend the meeting at the primary school on Dale Street, on Friday, September 3, at 7:30 p.m., simply stated that the purpose was "to discuss with other interested citizens problems facing our local community and county. *YOUR ATTENDANCE IS URGENTLY REQUESTED*."[4]

More than 150 whites, including twelve women, were in attendance. N. A. and I decided not to attend the meeting, but we heard from those who did that the mayor got an excellent response. The discussion was described as "out in the open" and "things were said that some never dreamed of hearing" in support of the mayor. The group requested that the mayor appoint the twelve white members to a bi-racial committee that would be organized in the near future. Numerous voices were heard saying they were "willing to serve." It was noted that the Feds were in attendance.

The invitation to black citizens to the meeting at Jefferson High School on Saturday, September 4, at 7:30 p.m., was not signed by anyone but stated that the purpose was "to discuss programs for improvement of community developments." It noted that "Federal and local officials will be present to bring information" on a long list of issues ranging from economic development, to the future of the schools, health programs, voter registration, and inter-racial relationships. Ways "to help both races progress in harmony and understanding" would be discussed. The recipients were invited "to attend and bring others of like interest to come."[5] One hundred and sixty plus black citizens attended. I was told later that there were women present, but no definite numbers were given. Following the information and discussion portion of the meeting, twelve representatives were elected to serve on the bi-racial committee, including one woman, Mrs. I. C. Pittman. Participants characterized it as "an excellent meeting."

The following week the civil rights workers, who came from outside Columbia for the summer, left town. Many of them were college students who were returning to their schools for the fall semester. The resolution passed on August 27 by the board of trustees of the Columbia Separate School District stipulated: "(1) That the maintenance of separate schools for the Negro and white children of Columbia Municipal Separate School District be completely ended as to the grades and at the times following: (a) With respect to the first and second grades during the school year commencing on or about the first week in September, 1965 . . . ." Three black students were to have entered the second grade on September 15, but their parents declined out of fear for the safety of their children. Mrs. Bess Pope, a member of the Presbyterian Church, was to have been their teacher. She was well qualified and expected to handle the situation with sensitivity.[6]

On Thursday, September 23, the mayor convened an organizational meeting of the representatives selected by black citizens on September 4 and those white citizens he had appointed to serve on the bi-racial committee.[7] There was some question as to what the name of the committee would be. Some called it a "Committee of Concern," some called it the "Committee of Concerned Citizens," while others referred to it as a "watchdog" committee. The mayor's reminder memo for the meeting included the following notations: 1) name plates, 2) steno pads, etc, 3) seated in between (alternating blacks and whites), 4) "Mr." and "Mrs." (way to address each other), 5) Organization-Procedures-"office" terms; 6) Items of business. 7)_____.[8]

The front-page article reporting the meeting in the *Columbian-Progress* lauded Columbia and Marion County for taking "another step last week toward good citizenship and better relations when a 'Committee of Concern' was organized here" at the initiative of the mayor. The article noted that several community meetings of local leaders had been held recently, indicating there was a need to talk about how to comply with all federal and state laws. The piece also indicated that the committee had no authority to speak for the city, the county, or the chamber of commerce, although at some point it could give advice and make recommendations to any of these groups with the hope that tensions might be eased in order for worthwhile projects to be developed by these organizations.[9]

The mayor made it clear that the Committee of Concern would in no way duplicate what the Community Action Committee was organized to do in making certain Marion County qualified for grants from the Anti-Poverty Program of the federal government. The article pointed out that "Marion County Negroes already enjoy many advantages covered in the new civil rights law. For example, Negroes, who registered and wanted to do so, have voted here for years. Four hundred voted in the last election. Over seven hundred are on the poll books now."[10] As admirable as this assessment of the voting record sounded to the writer of the article, it left much to be desired by some in the white community and many in the black community.

The committee agreed that the officers would rotate every three months. Mr. Sedgie Griffith, a white wholesale grocer, was elected moderator, Professor William J. Rice, a vocational teacher at Marion County Central School (black), was named vice-moderator, and Mrs. I. C. Pittman, a director of the black rural center at Lampton, was chosen secretary. The committee also agreed on monthly meetings, where Marion County citizens of both races will be heard.[11]

The organization of the committee attracted attention far beyond Columbia and Marion County. W. F. Minor, writing in the New Orleans *Times-Picayune* on October 2, quoted the mayor: "Maintaining good communications between the races is not only the practical thing for a town like ours to do, it is the only thing." McLean went on to say, "When I came in office I knew some racial problems were coming and I was convinced the only way to solve them was by an honest approach by both races." He believed that it was up to local citizens to find lasting solutions because he did not believe "any outside party or parties can truly solve these problems" for us.[12]

The mayor readily acknowledged that the formation of this advisory committee to the city administration had already prompted calls from "Kluxers," but he guessed that was to be expected. These hecklers did not disturb him "as long as we are doing the right thing." The committee's vice-moderator Rice, a graduate of Mississippi's Alcorn A & M, was quoted as saying he was surprised "when the Mayor initiated the move to form a bi-racial committee . . . . We were not expecting it."[13]

Years later, critics who had experience with radical techniques of community development might contend that such meetings as the one described here were but an effort by white moderates to limit outside involvement and active protest. Such restrictive meetings in their view would not be the most effective way to generate real change. However, as a first-hand observer of these events, I held a different view. I agreed with the mayor that acts of civility to break the silence with honest and open conversation were truly essential as the beginning point in building the kind of mutual trust and respect that was sorely needed to bring about lasting change. Only from some distant future could the validity and efficacy of those techniques be judged. Nonetheless, both then and now I marvel at the fact that a group of black leaders was chosen by the black community to sit down with a group of white leaders in the community to begin conversations about the welfare of the city and county. What took place that night in this first and subsequent meetings—the way they were conducted and the atmosphere that prevailed—was in my judgment truly radical, taking into account the relational landscape in Mississippi in 1965.

◆   ◆   ◆

There was more to my study leave in Richmond in August than the alcoholism seminar. We made several side trips, including a tour of Williamsburg.

Prominent in the visit was a movie about the American Revolution, filmed in the restored section of Williamsburg, which made one feel like one was part of the action. Moreover, it was an inspiration for the sermon I delivered on September 12, 1965, entitled "The American Dream Comes Home," because the times seemed so similar to ours.[14] The notes in my ministerial log read: "If it don't do any good, it sure won't hurt! Not subtle, not meat ax!" I told the congregation that the film reminded me that the rebellion of the founding fathers was not an attempt to overthrow, subvert, or deny the authority of the government, but that their rebellion was against the abuse of that authority: being ruled without representation. They rebelled in order to gain admittance and take possession of the government they felt was rightly theirs. They wanted simply a continuation and expansion of constitutional democracy.

I pointed out that, according to the film, our revolution was in direct contrast to another development in eighteenth-century revolutionary thinking. In France, the Jacobin Party advocated and promoted the overthrow of the government and the liquidation of the governing class. There was no continuation or expansion of the government. It was completely destroyed and replaced altogether. As I understood it, our founding fathers wanted to make the government more responsible by getting more people admitted to the governing class and voting electorate. The next step was to revise unequal and unjust laws, so that eventually all people would have equal opportunity to enter the government and be represented. This principle was carved into the Preamble of the Constitution in the opening phrase: "We the people . . ." I fully recognized that all people did not mean all people living at that time, for the right to participate and be represented via the ballot was limited primarily to white male landowners. Nonetheless, the principle was embedded in the Constitution, inviting wider interpretation of "all" in the 1960s.

In summary, I proclaimed, the American dream, "by having more citizens participating in the choosing who will govern, representatives will be produced who will represent and govern more equally and justly on behalf of ALL THE PEOPLE." Clearly in the minds of the Founding Fathers, the "DREAM was not brought to reality by simply adding more people to the voting rolls." It would not happen "if the decent respect for the opinions of others was not at the heart of the electoral process." I went on to say: "The real problem came then and now when a group of people is not allowed to participate in choosing who will govern them." Often those in power act only "on the basis of the special interest of the few, but not in the best interest of all." They get "an exaggerated sense of their own worth and develop all sorts of rationalizations on how to silence the opposition" and exclude them "from the electoral process by intimidation, threats, and in extreme cases extermination." Those out of power are at the mercy of those who show them no respect. "They nurse being ignored and there is nothing more humiliating. They lament the fact that they are not respected and develop all sorts of abnormal attitudes and patterns of behavior. When the threat becomes too great, many remain silent."

I pointed out, however, that "some few may find ways to break this isolation; make noise, attract attention as best they can; make all sorts of attempts to overthrow those in power, displacing them without the respect they themselves aspire." I said, "Contrary to popular belief, the American Revolution did not end in 1776 or 1789. It is still in full swing. As a matter of fact it has finally reached Columbia in recent weeks and months. We finally have entered the life and death struggle of whether we will lay hold of our heritage—The American Dream—or whether we go the way of tyrants. We are struggling with whether or not we really believe in liberty and justice for all as we chant our Pledge to Allegiance to the American flag." I continued: "To date only a few have ruled in Columbia. I am not calling them tyrants, but giving them the benefit of the doubt, they like the Founding Fathers, attempted to act in their way for the best interest of the people . . . . But from now on that will not be sufficient . . . . For today we are faced with the American Dream at its best. We are having more citizens represented and choosing who will govern us."

In conclusion I charged: "[W]hether we will produce representatives who will govern more equally and justly on behalf of all of the people, regardless of public opinion, depends on how we bring to bear upon the situation a decent respect for the opinions of others. This qualifying dependency falls full-square on the shoulders of the Church and we as Christians." In the words of the text, "For freedom Christ has set us free; stand fast therefore, and do not submit again to the yoke of slavery. . . . For you were called to freedom, brethren; only do not use your freedom as an opportunity for the flesh, but through love, be servants of one another" (Gal. 5: 1, 13, RSV). At the time I preached this sermon I was not aware of the particular activities of other persons struggling to bring the American Dream of freedom to the streets of Columbia. Years later I discovered that sometime in late September or early October, Curtis Styles invited Ira Grupper to come to Columbia to work with the FDP, the local chapter of the MFDP.

A rare opportunity came my way on Saturday, October 16, when I was invited to speak at the Mississippi District YWCA fall conference of Area V meeting in Columbia. The conference had sessions for senior Y-teens, junior Y-teens and adult advisors and sponsors, with the overall theme of "This Is Your Life—Live It." Area V covered much of south Mississippi, including Brookhaven where I had grown up and Hazlehurst where my Aunt Hallie, Dad's baby sister, taught math in the junior high school. She was a Y-teen advisor and was in attendance at the meeting. I was not sure how she would take what I had to say in my presentation, but it turned out that she was pleased at the accolades I received for it, even though I never knew what she really thought personally.

They asked me to talk at the luncheon held at Tay's Restaurant for the adult advisors and sponsors on the "Challenge of Change" facing school systems at this moment in history.[15] I opened by saying that the challenge of change was the story of my life in every living moment. I launched into the story of the four generations of William McAtees to establish my credentials and show how the challenge of change had been our story. I said, today each of us may feel like our school is teetering on the brink of disaster. I pointed out the obvious, that "there are those today who do not want to meet the challenge of change for they have chosen the way of tyrants . . . . I do not need to identify them for they identify themselves as they resort to fear, distrust, hatred, revenge, threats, intimidations, blatant disregard for the opinions of others, loving darkness rather than light." I said that "you leaders of Y-Teens may be the key in your school and have the power to swing change from destruction to construction, your finest hour."

My message had three points. First, the change taking place in our schools, though we may not like it and have struggled to resist it, is here to stay. The sooner we accept this fact, the sooner we can get back to the primary task of education. Second, the change coming does not necessarily guarantee a better quality of education. It is not the change itself, but what we make of it, how we face it creatively and make the most of it. What is crucial are our feelings toward those who were a part of that change, those with whom we differed. That meant wrestling with the reality of loving our enemies. Third, our youth will find and follow leaders. They will follow tyrants, or they will follow those who have demonstrated a genuine desire to understand and work out the situation in the best interest of all concerned.

I closed by challenging the advisors and sponsors to set the pattern for their youngsters by demonstrating common courtesies and avoiding cheap humor about the situation. "Whether we realize it or not, our young people want to be adult, and they fulfill this want by acting like adults. What will they see in us? This is the challenge of change! It will not be easy, not without considerable cost—cold stares, animosity, vicious hatred, separation from family and friends. The challenge before us is that we must find a loving and just way in which to live. We must all find a way to live together, forgiving and loving one another or none will be able to live with any meaning at all. Any other consideration is secondary."

◆   ◆   ◆

On Thursday, October 21, the Committee of Concern met for the second time, moderated by Mr. Sedgie Griffith.[16] The minutes were read, and Mr. Tom Watts moved that the words "concerned citizens," referring to the bi-racial committee, be struck. Some uncertainty about the proper name for the committee prevailed. Under old business it was suggested that the name Committee of Concern be retained for the time being. It was suggested that the mayor be interviewed about the background of the committee and that the interview be used to publicize the committee's work. Vice-moderator Rice suggested that a scrapbook be created for the committee news. A letter was read from Mr. Charles Otis, one of the black representatives, indicating that he was moving from the community and would not be able to serve.

The moderator indicated that the committee would spend some time in small groups identifying the issues before the community and any suggestions about how the committee should function. After a considerable amount of time, the groups made reports about a range of concerns. Major topics centered around the schools and education: what's best for the blacks; more improvement in attendance; better school administration; getting parents to value education; having the mayor visit the schools and answer students' questions; the sewage problem at Marion Central; patrols at school crossings; peaceful integration. Other topics were: employment and job opportunities; trade schools; water service; street signs and improvements; rest rooms at the court house; how the Community Action Program (C.A.P.) could help us and how we could help C.A.P.; and some discussion about the March of Dimes campaign. Joe Boucher from the Employment Security Commission shared information about job opportunities in Columbia. He concluded that there were plenty of jobs available for persons who wanted to work.[17] The reality of decades of discrimination still made many of these job opportunities problematic for black citizens in Columbia. Suggestions concerning how the committee was to function included: continuing informality; using name badges; organizing subcommittees around issues; tabling the decision about what to name the committee until we have more experience with it; and having Mr. Rice, the vice-moderator, moderate at the next meeting.

Because serious discussion had begun, it was decided to meet again in two days, on Saturday, October 23, and with the vice-moderator presiding, continuing to raise and address issues. At that meeting considerable time was given to the issue of voter registration. According to my notes, it appeared about seven hundred out of about eight thousand blacks (approximately 33 percent of the total population in the county) were registered, an increase of late but not significant enough. Also, some teachers reported there was a suspicion that a quiet reprisal campaign was under way to discourage registration. Someone questioned whether it was possible to find out who was registered as a way of determining how best to go about targeting voter education and also finding a way to thwart the reprisal campaign. Someone reported that there was a growing attack on the "administration" (referring to the mayor), to which someone else responded, "They fail to realize the pressure on him." Another commented that, "[T]hings at Duckworth [Recreational Center, historically for blacks] is not all as rosy as you think." These issues were not pursued in great detail.

Other agenda items included: finding out what the term "in conjunction with" meant as it pertained to the March of Dimes campaign; replacement of inactive members on the committee; and remembering to address each other as "Mr." or "Mrs." The issue of intersection safety for black school children was raised, with the possibility of conducting a traffic count—especially at Owens and Marion, Owens and West, and Dale and West. If warranted, the possibility of creating a "ladies patrol" to work these corners was suggested. Also, it was important to hire Negroes in the police department. Reaction to the "union activity" at the New Orleans Furniture factory was sought. Concerns were raised as how to inform a larger group about the committee's activities as a way of gaining more support among skeptics for the work of the committee. It was noted that by next summer the record of the committee would stand for itself if the committee produced, because "we cannot expect 'them' to get in our corner if we have not."

At the close of the meeting I was asked to offer observations about how the committee was progressing. First, regarding the selection of a name for the committee, I suggested that the name should issue from the purpose of the committee, which may not be defined well enough yet. Second, I said it was essential to set up subgroups for further study and discussion of particular issues. On the basis of what I had heard so far, there were six possibilities: 1) public utilities—streets, water, lights, sewage; 2) schools and facilities; 3) voter education—registration and information on issues like the half-cent sales tax proposal called for in the upcoming special election; 4) employment—what jobs available were in the private sector and the additional hiring of Negro policemen; 5) publicity—how to keep the public informed; and 6) an orientation of what C.A.P. had to offer, such as adult education, and C.A.P.'s relation to this committee. These suggestions were basically pursued. Members of the committee, though they realized there was a lot of work to be done, felt progress had been made through the open discussion of the issues.

Dr. Russell Bush, Jr., a white dentist who served on the initial bi-racial committee, recalled his experience with the group and its significant accomplishments.[18] He explained how in early meetings the mayor set the tone for how they should relate to each other. By way of introduction, the mayor went around the table and asked each member to state his or her name and occupation. He emphasized that not only should they address each other as "Mr." or Mrs.," they should show respect for the blacks on the committee by using the term "black" rather than "Nigra." Bush told of a moment when they were helping one of the white members learn to pronounce "Negro" properly, but try as he may, all the man could utter was "Nigra"—thinking he had demonstrated how he had progressed on that point. His genuine attempt at pronouncing the word properly, although he was not able to do so, somewhat relieved the tension of the moment because of the way the issue was openly addressed.

Bush recalled the discussion in small groups about the most important issue facing the community and the committee. When it came Dr. Bush's time, he wanted to be honest and did not hold back. First he said, "I don't like the language you speak and I don't want your teachers teaching my children that kind of English." In his opinion, not too many of the black teachers at that time were qualified to teach English, simply because of the way they spoke. Then he made a few remarks about "their" perceived morality. He finally said that he drove over every day to pick up his maid, whose "house was in terrible repair. They threw the dishwater out the window." It was not because she did not know better, because "she came to my house and kept it well." To Bush, this was not an isolated case.

When he was finished, it came time for Mr. Lindsey Walker, a black member of the committee, to speak. Dr. Bush recalled that Walker looked at him and said in a quiet, measured voice, "Dr. Bush, I want you to know I do get dirty because I am a brick mason [who worked for the Wolfe brothers' construction company]. When I come home at night, I take my bath, I put on clean underwear, I put on clean socks, and I put on polished shoes for my evening meal. I am a deacon in my church and I have sent my daughters to the University of Michigan." He noted they had graduated. He continued: "You can come to my house after nine o'clock any morning, and the rugs will be vacuumed and all the beds will be made up. And anytime after nine o'clock you would be welcomed to come to my house to drink coffee with me." Finally Walker said, "What do I have to do for you to accept me?" The silence had been broken. Bush said he looked down at his own unpolished shoes and thought Walker had really put him on the spot. He didn't know what else he could say in response. Finally he said, "[T]he only thing I could think of was, 'you'd have to change the color of your skin' and I said that in jest because he had already torn up all the arguments I had!"

A few years later, when Bush retired from his dentistry practice in Columbia, he became a Baptist preacher, serving a congregation in Hattiesburg whose Sunday morning services were broadcast on television. One Sunday Bush told the story of his exchange with Walker in that early bi-racial committee meeting and made the point "Lindsey Walker taught me more about race relations in that moment than any other person in my life; and it changed my life." A few days later Bush was walking along a downtown street in Columbia, when he saw a red pickup truck approach him and heard a voice from it holler, "Hey, Dr. Bush." When he got over to the pickup he saw that it was Mr. Walker. Walker got out of the truck and said, "I want to shake hands with you. You know I heard what you said on TV and my wife and I appreciated that more than you will ever know." Bush was deeply moved and said, "Mr. Walker, I want to take you out to eat, would you go with me?" Walker said, "[I] would, where can I meet you?" Bush said, "I don't want you to meet me, I want to come to your house to pick you up." And he went to his house and picked Walker up and took him to the most public restaurant he could find in Columbia and sat down at a table in the middle of the room. There were a lot of other people in that restaurant, and Bush said, "I was the one eating with a black man and they were all giving me the once over." When the staff members from First Baptist Church sat down to eat, Bush took Walker over and introduced him to them, breaking the silence: "I want your to meet my friend, Lindsey Walker."

The two men's friendship and mutual respect grew even deeper and would continue to blossom through the years. It all started that night around the table at the first meeting of the bi-racial committee. Bush said, "I'm not saying how good I was because I was opposed to all that. It was a great lesson I learned that night and I have not changed my position."

◆ ◆ ◆

Senator John Stennis was in town on Saturday, September 25, to address the annual meeting of the Pearl River Valley Electric Power Association. The senator pointed with pride "to the record of our Rural Electric Cooperatives as conclusive proof of what can be done by responsible people who are willing to work to help themselves." The senator seemed to be somewhat disparaging when comparing the achievements of the electric cooperatives with "other recent efforts such as the war on poverty programs." In bringing about better living conditions and improvement of our economic welfare, "by good planning, hard work and applying the blessings of a hot electric wire to every home and every need," our electric cooperatives were "unlike other recent schemes." The cooperatives were "not conceived in a Madison Avenue public relations office as a political campaign gimmick." Stennis concluded by proclaiming his "faith that the American people will rule themselves and urged that more attention be paid to the value of family groups, authority of and respect for law, and for fine Christian morality and help from on high, which is the only thing which can 'lead us through' these troubled times."[19] The same day Stennis spoke in Columbia, four civil rights workers picketed the Sunflower Store again, causing no problems.

Although Six continued to touch base from time to time about how things were progressing in the community, our activities had now become dispersed among several organizations that had grown out of our earlier activities. Blankinship and Pittman were on the steering committee of Five of C.A.C., the anti-poverty program group. Dickson, Payton, and Pittman's wife served on the Committee of Concern, while I served as advisor to that committee and to the mayor. On Monday, September 27, N. A. and I conferred with Mr. Sedgie Griffith, moderator of the Committee of Concern, about the agenda for the next meeting of the committee.

My involvement with Six after returning from vacation had tapered off, and I gave more attention to replicating pastor and church. All the usual fall programs such as introducing the new Christian education curriculum and getting a new youth choir started took up my time. On Worldwide Communion Sunday, October 3, we dedicated the new home communion ware at the quarterly celebration of the sacrament. My mother and my Aunt Doris had driven over from Hazlehurst to spend the day and worship with us.

All the demands of office had weighed heavily on the mayor during the summer and into the fall, taking time away from his family. I decided to devote some of my time and attention to his son Danny, one of my parishioners. Danny had just gotten a big red Labrador retriever but did not have suitable quarters at home for him. So I offered to supervise this young, energetic teenager in the construction of a new doghouse for the Lab. After Danny had roughed out the dimensions of a very large house for his charge, with his dad's approval to charge to his account what was needed for the project, we went to the Wolfe Lumber Yard on South High School Avenue to buy supplies. Danny loved the look and the feel of redwood, and so he loaded up my station wagon with the requisite number of boards and other items. I was not paying attention to the numbers, but before we got out of there he had charged over $100 in redwood to his dad's account! It turned out to be a mighty fine home for the dog. Although it was almost big enough to hold us, Danny and I did not land "in the doghouse" for our extravagant spending on materials. Working with Danny to see him develop his carpentry and relational skills was time well spent. The mayor was very appreciative for my acting as his surrogate.

While Danny and I were engaged in the building project, the mayor received a visit from A. L. Hopkins, investigator for the State Sovereignty Commission.[20] He had received instructions from Director Erle Johnston to meet with the mayor, the chief of police, and the sheriff of Marion County to let them know that on Thursday evening, October 7, the Freedom Democratic Party was having a meeting "for the purpose of organizing a local chapter of the Deacons for Defense." The mayor was familiar with the "militant group of young Negroes" that had been active in Bogalusa, Louisiana, and other parts of the South, but was unaware of the meeting scheduled for that night in Columbia. The mayor checked with the chief of police and the sheriff, and they were not aware of the meeting either. Hopkins later indicated in his report that, "This group of Negroes arm themselves [sic] usually with pistols and advocate violence." Hopkins stated that, "There is evidence that this group is connected with the NAACP, COFO, and Martin Luther King dispite [sic] the fact that most of these civil rights groups deny that they are affiliated with the Deacons."

After meeting with the mayor, Hopkins rode with the police chief on a surveillance run to see what was happening at Freedom House. They saw "42 folding chairs" set up in the yard, indicating that a meeting would be held there later. Around 8:00 p.m., "[T]wo late model Cadillacs bearing Louisiana license plates" pulled in. By that time forty young "colored males and very few colored females" had gathered, which did not include any whites. Hopkins was able to get the plate numbers on one of the Cadillacs (15L-192), but not the other one because of where he was sitting.

The meeting adjourned around 11:00 p.m., but it was unclear to Hopkins and the police chief what had taken place. The chief speculated there was a good possibility "that preliminary steps were taken at this meeting to organize the Deacons for Defense." The chief indicated that he would find out later, since he had an informant in the meeting. He also assured Hopkins that the police department, sheriff's office, and the highway patrol would keep a close eye on the situation. Hopkins reiterated in his report to Johnston that "this militant group of young Negroes are [sic] extremely dangerous." He closed by stating that, "The local officials expressed their appreciation for the cooperation of the Sovereignty Commission in furnishing them this information." It was not clear if indeed this were the case or if it were some self-serving gesture aimed to secure the approval of Hopkins's boss. Nothing was ever mentioned in my presence by the mayor about this or any further activity of consequence on the part of the Deacons for Defense.

Two articles of interest appeared in the October 21 edition of the *Columbian-Progress*. The Marion County Ministerial Association announced that at its monthly meeting on Monday at the First Methodist Church, a report would be made by a committee working on plans for a countywide Thanksgiving service. Serving on the committee were the Rev. Charles Brister, the Rev. George Lee, and the Rev. William McAtee. It was noted that "the association, which is inter-denominational," will announce details "after plans are completely formulated." The Marion County Ministerial Association was for ministers serving white congregations. Another ministerial group, the Interdenominational Ministerial Alliance of Marion County, was for ministers serving black congregations. The announcement did not mention what the black congregations were planning for community Thanksgiving services. The other article announced that "Columbia and West Marion high schools will both observe Homecoming Friday with parades that afternoon and the crowning of the Homecoming Queens at the football games that night." Linda Thompson was the homecoming queen at Columbia High School, which hosted the football game between the Columbia Wildcats and the Jackson Central High Tigers. Robin Dunaway was the homecoming queen at West Marion, which hosted the game between the West Marion Trojans and the Liberty Rebels. No mention was made of homecoming activities at Jefferson High School.

That year Halloween fell on Sunday. Trick-or-treat was scheduled for Saturday night. It was quite an evening. Neal, a two-year old, got very much involved in answering the door with me. Millye watched from the couch, since the birth of our second child was near. The manse on Orchard Drive was on an oval drive somewhat larger than the size of a college athletic track around a football field. It seemed as if every car, truck, or bus—anything from out in the county that could run—made a bumper-to-bumper parade around the drive, with intermittent stops for trick-or-treaters to canvass the neighborhood carrying open sacks for goodies. The parade seemed endless so we finally closed the door and turned out the lights.

The next day was Reformation Sunday and a busy day for me. I had the usual Sunday morning responsibilities at the church, before I drove to Gulfport to participate in the dedication of the new sanctuary at the Westminster Presbyterian Church in Gulfport, where Frank Brooks was pastor. It was a grand affair. I am not sure what I was called—maybe the grand marshal. At the appointed hour, in full clerical garb, I led the liturgical procession up to the closed front door of the sanctuary and rapped on it loudly. A voice from within inquired, "Who is it and what is your business." I made some flowery remark to the effect that we had come to dedicate this sanctuary properly "to the Glory of God and for purposes He hath ordained." The doors swung open, and we processed to the chancel to the jubilant wails of a bagpiper for the service. Afterwards, I returned to Columbia at midnight, welcoming in November as I wearily drove into the driveway at home.

❖   ❖   ❖

The mayor received a letter dated November 2, 1965, addressed "To the Honorable Mayor, Leading Business Men of Columbia, Miss." from "Responsible Negro's of Marion County," in which the "Negro Citizens of Columbia would like to submit Plans for our city which we are tax payers and are not able to get benefits on." The letter asked that three major streets in the black community, "Nathan street, Kings ave., and Corners Avenue" be "paved before the month of December which Citizens on these streets for years has been trying to get paved and already know what is expected of them." The signers also stated, "We would like to have Negroes on the Jury for November's Court." To underscore the seriousness of their requests, "If these demands can not be meet or if there is no Plans drawn up in the next weeks paper showing that you have plans we will stage one of the largest boycott's in Marion County which will hurt the economy of both (Race's). We are prepared for the out come what ever God see's fit." There was one more sanction. "We are planning a major boycott for Christmas if these demans are not in effect."[21] Judging by this letter, not all blacks in Columbia were satisfied that sufficient progress had been made through the efforts of the bi-racial committee.

On the same day the letter was written, Millye decided that she was ready to go to the Marion General Hospital to deliver our child. I got her settled there, and Neal and I spent the night at home in anticipation of what the next day might bring. The following morning I took Neal to friend Grace Melvin's house and went to the hospital to continue the wait. By noon nothing had happened, so Millye encouraged me to go get something to eat. I went over to Broad Street to Flora's, a sandwich shop across from City Park, and got a huge hamburger. The weather was mild, so I sat out at a picnic table and ate. When I got back to the hospital, I found Walter Bunn McAtee had entered this world, breaking its silence anew in his definitive way! We chose the name Walter after Uncle Bunk's son, Walter Preston, and Bunn was Millye's maiden name. Late in the afternoon I picked up Neal and his new baby doll, which Grace had given him for the occasion. After several days, we took the newcomer home, and the residents of the manse now numbered four as new sounds filled what little silence there was in our young household.

On November 10, 11, and 12, the forty-ninth annual session of the South Mississippi State Baptist Convention (black) was held at Owen Chapel (Missionary) Baptist Church, where Rev. Payton was the pastor. The motto of the host church, printed on the convention program brochure, was, "The Church that Cares," and the theme of the convention was "Christ the Source of Brotherhood."[22] A musical pre-convention program featuring the One Hundred Voice Chorus was held at Jefferson High School the day before the convention convened. The program began with a rousing trumpet call, followed by the singing of "America the Beautiful," the national anthem, and the theme song for the convention, "Blessed Assurance." Solos, instrumental music, anthems by the chorus, and hymns by the Youth Choir filled the auditorium, uplifting the spirits of all present.

No piece could have been timelier than the anthem, "If You Ever Needed the Lord Before You Sure Do Need Him Now!"

Morning, afternoon, and evening sessions on Wednesday, Thursday, and Friday covered an array of activities: enrollments of messengers, associations, and conventions; evangelistic services, sermons, offerings, and devotionals; and business sessions and reports from a variety of its committees and boards. The Wednesday evening service included a local program in which a variety of persons brought greetings to the convention. When I introduced the mayor, I learned that one needed to be prepared for a very vocal response to rhetorical questions from a black congregation![23] I asked one such question about whether or not they had seen something on TV, and Rev. Blankinship, who was sitting in the choir, answered me in a loud and emphatic voice that he had. His response undid me for a minute, because I was a bit nervous having seen through the outside door at the back of the sanctuary a line of pickup trucks passing slowly back and forth along Marion Avenue, and I was not sure who their occupants were. I soon regained my wits and really made a connection with the congregants in a rhythmic interchange of sounds.

The mayor, in extending the convention a welcome to the city, expressed his pleasure at their coming to Columbia and said how proud he was of the "opportunities offered our citizens in all areas of their activities," especially "our many fine churches and their membership." He expressed special appreciation for the leadership of Rev. Payton, not only in his role in this congregation, but also in the larger community. As mayor, it was his "every good wish that your convention will be a most successful one and that you shall again return to our fine city." N. A. brought greetings from First Methodist Church of Columbia without incident. The mayor, N. A., and I felt well received and were honored to be included in this special occasion since it meant so much to our dear friends in Six to have us there.

On Monday, November 15, the mayor met with Louis Ashley from SNCC to talk about a black family that needed help. Ashley was also concerned about finding a room for an adult education program in which he was interested. He shared with the mayor the name and address of Septima P. Clark, a teacher and training director in an Atlanta school and affiliated with the Southern Christian Leadership Conference, who might be of help with this program.[24]

The following day, Tuesday, November 16, the mayor met with Ira Grupper, Sarah Shumer, Johnnie Ray Lee, and Mary Spencer to discuss an upcoming parade route they were planning for December 17 and 18.

Streets mentioned were Owens, Marion, West, Lafayette, Main, and Second to city hall, with the same route going back. They would spend twenty minutes at city hall.[25]

The Committee of Concern met on November 18, 1965, and officially adopted its new name, "Marion County Community Relations Committee" (CRC). It also heard a report from the subgroup meeting with the county school board regarding the problem with the rest rooms at Marion Central. Another group was assigned to meet with city officials about paving streets in the Owen Street area in the black community and also about water mains there. This group also would talk with the Power Cooperative about installing more streetlights in that location. Another group was asked to talk with the police about the possibility of designating streets around Jefferson High School as one-way and about training for crossing guards.

Word of the productive results of the work of the CRC spread beyond Columbia. The mayor received a phone call from a person in Bogalusa on Tuesday, November 23, inquiring about how to put together a bi-racial committee. The caller said there was an increase in picketing in Bogalusa, but that the white leadership was not willing to take part in setting up such a committee.[26] Leadership from the white community had been key to the success here in Columbia. The following week the New Orleans *Times-Picayune* reported that in Bogalusa, "Negroes picketed stores here and in a shopping center on Monday. They also were served at two restaurants and went almost unnoticed." The newspaper also reported that "Jim Warren Richardson of the 22nd Judicial District court for the third time extended a temporary injunction against the Bogalusa Voters League banning the group from enticing school children from missing school for the purpose of civil rights demonstrations."[27]

W. S. Griffin, director of administration and finance of the State Department of Education announced in the November 25 edition of the *Columbian-Progress* that Marion County's basic grant allotment of $317,665 under Title I of the federal Elementary-Secondary Act of 1965 had been awarded. In making the announcement, Griffin said that this grant made possible projects "limited only by the imagination." He went on to say, "These may include preschool or summer programs, after school or weekend classes, health and nutrition services and special programs for dropouts—so long as they are concentrated on children in low income families." He specified that grants could be used for "Children between the ages of 5–17 years from families with less than $2,000 incomes." The grants may not be more than 30 percent of the current budget.[28]

❖ ❖ ❖

Rev. Robert G. Patterson baptized Walter Bunn McAtee during the morn-
ing worship service on November 28, 1965, at the Columbia Presbyterian
Church. Patterson, the husband of Walter's aunt, Jane McAtee, was a Bible
professor at Southwestern at Memphis. Walter's grandmothers, Velma
Bunn and Queen McAtee, were also in attendance, along with brother
Neal and parents Millye and Bill.

❖ ❖ ❖

During the first week of December, a typewritten flyer circulated through
the black community in Columbia: *"ATTENTION: ALL NEGROES OF
MARION COUNTY*—THE BLACK CHRISTMAS BOYCOTT HAS
BEGUN IN COLUMBIA." It said, "[W]e have fallen short on ourselves
for not helping ourselves . . . . Negroes cannot work Downtown and we
are treated like second class citizens . . . . BLACK CHRISTMAS means
we Negroes of Columbia should NOT buy where we can't work . . . .
DO NOT SHOP AT THE DOWNTOWN STORES. Buy less and BUY
FROM NEGRO STORES. NEGROES ARE BOYCOTTING WHITE
STORES ALL OVER MISSISSIPPI, AND BOGALUSA TOO! You may
not like your Negro merchants but the white merchant is a segregationist
and may belong to the White Citizens Council or to the Ku Klux Klan—
and THE MONEY YOU SPEND AT THE WHITE STORES MAY BUY
THE BULLETS THAT KILL YOU." It concluded with an invitation to
come to a meeting at the FDP office on Nathan Street "this Wed., Dec. 8,
1965 at 7 P. M. . . . AND BRING YOUR FRIENDS."[29]
    Willis McLendon, Ira Grupper, Johnnie Ray Lee, Mary Spencer, and
Sammie May Weary met with the mayor on Wednesday, December 8, to
follow up on the flyer. McLenton inquired about his Social Security card.
Grupper asked for copies of certain city ordinances and building permit forms. They presented a printed list of demands to the mayor that
included a wide range of subjects: stop the tampering with MFDP mail;
remove phone taps; establish non-discriminatory policy; hire at least three
Negro policemen with power to arrest equal to white policemen; accord
courtesy to Negro citizens by addressing them as Mr. and Mrs.; get local
radio stations to accept ads on non-discriminatory basis; pave streets in
Negro neighborhoods; end police harassment of Negroes; insure pay for
maids of at least $7 per day; end discrimination against FDP participants

at the employment office; and stop cutting welfare checks. The statement alleged that it was within the power or influence of the mayor to address these grievances. The authors also expressed a willingness to discuss their demands in detail with the mayor or anyone else.[30]

The December 9 edition of the *Columbian-Progress* contained an announcement by the mayor and the board of aldermen about plans for improvement in the Owens Street area. The plan included replacing two-inch water mains with six-inch mains. The announcement said this process should begin in January, having been delayed because of a late delivery of pipe. A complete resurfacing of Owen Street was to begin in early summer of 1966. Representatives of the Community Relations Committee, Lindsey Walker, W. T. Maynard, and Wilton James, were asked to survey the situation and recommend to the city possible locations for new streetlights. The power company was determining whether or not to use mercury vapor type lights throughout the city.[31]

W. F. Minor, writing in the December 12 edition of *The Times-Picayune*, stated that, "COFO—the Mississippi-created radical civil rights organization whose demise had been predicted a year ago after its quick rise to national significance, no longer exists." After trying to regroup its strength and structure, "[I]t died because of lack of funds, loss of a broad base of local support and the departure of the strong leaders in the movement." Rumors alleged "in 1964 on possible Communist links among the imported civil rights workers" did not help its cause in some quarters. In the wake of COFO's departure from the prominent leadership role it displayed in Freedom Summer in 1964, the Mississippi Freedom Democratic Party filled the void. The article reported that, "Last week, authoritative sources said that not more than a dozen people, most of them Mississippi Negroes, are left on the payroll in the state." Efforts were made by local civil rights leaders "to minimize, if not eliminate, the SNCC influence in the FDP." Hard-core out-of-state volunteers of COFO remained and attempted "to start a new group—the Freedom Information Service."[32]

The Marion County Community Relations Committee held its last meeting of 1965 on Thursday, December 16. L. Z. Blankinship from the Community Action Committee (CAC) explained what his committee did, what it could mean to the county and city, and the progress and failures made in the effort to secure the CAC's programs for this area. The major focus of the meeting was on the hiring of blacks to work in the stores. Sentiment was expressed that the time had come to go beyond what the law requires; that it should be done on a voluntary basis; that decisions should be made now; and that hiring should be made, not on a temporary basis, but on a permanent one. A committee made up of Thomas Watts, Ben McCraw, and Bill Walker was appointed to follow through on this recommendation to hire blacks as cashiers and clerks during the Christmas holiday rush. The committee elected by ballot its new moderators for the first quarter next year: Mr. H. H. "Hessie" Wolfe, moderator, and Rev. A. G. Payton, vice-moderator.[33]

The first installment of a new hiring policy was made during the next day or so. I remember I milled around Bill's Dollar Store at the corner of Main and Church Streets and watched as the first black woman clerked at the cash register. Other stores soon followed suit. A small ad in the December 17 edition of the *Columbian-Progress* touted a "Good Breakfast at Ja-Gee's Worth Eating! Only 78 cents!"[34] Nothing in the ad indicated that the restaurant had adopted an open hiring policy.

The mayor reviewed the conditions under which the MFDP parade that day would be conducted.[35] The time for starting the parade needed to be firm. Traffic flow was a major concern, even though a judge ruled the previous week that parades could not be stopped because of the Christmas season. In case of a violent attack, the police were to re-route or cancel the parade as a safety measure. One police car would proceed in front of the parade and one in the rear to cut off traffic as needed; the police were to take them on through and not try and stop. Marchers were to march two abreast for their safety and keep moving. Blocking an intersection was considered civil disobedience. With regard to picketing during the black Christmas boycott, two hours' notice must be given as to where the picket would be held. Demonstrators must keep moving and must not harass people for attempting to shop. A warrant must be used to arrest for harassment.[36] The parade proceeded without violence or arrests.

New cacophonies of sound had broken the silence during the previous days and weeks, in the streets and in the hearts of people. For some, these maddening sounds made no sense. For others, the absence of silence was a sign of hope, however fleeting, that created new ways of communicating. Had the line been crossed, literally or figuratively; would there be creative intervention lifting one's spirits, where honesty prevailed, making mutual respect and forbearance possible? Or would there be more disappointment, heartbreak, and walls of hostility mounting up with little common understanding reached?

Mayor E. D. McLean, Jr. in the early 1960s. Portrait by Phyllis Moore. McLean family archives.

Rev. William G. McAtee on the day of his installation service at the Columbia Presbyterian Church, May 10, 1964. McAtee photo archives.

Rev. N. A. Dickson, pastor of First
United Methodist Church, Columbia,
Mississippi, ca. 1960, Dickson family
archives.

Rev. I. C. Pittman, first director of
Mississippi Rural Center, Lampton,
Mississippi, ca. 1976. Courtesy Marion
County Historical Society.

Rev. L. Z. Blankinship, pastor of the
Friendship Missionary Baptist Church,
Columbia, Mississippi, ca. 1965.

Rev. A. G. Payton, pastor of the
Owen Chapel Baptist Church
Columbia, Mississippi, ca. 1965.

The Lampton Co., site of the FDP picketing on January 8, 1966. Photo Bill McAtee, 2010, McAtee photo archives.

The Marion Theater and Autry's Café. The theater (l) integrated on August 11 and 15, 1965, and the café (r) on August 14, 1965. Photo Bill McAtee, 2010. McAtee photo archives.

The McAtees: Bill holding Walt, Neal standing by Millye, on Sunday, October 16, 1966, after Bill preached his last sermon in Columbia, Mississippi. Family photo album.

Irv Moxley (l) and Bill McAtee (r) conducting "Fireside Chat" at their Louisville Seminary's Fiftieth Class Reunion, April 2009. Photo Jonathan Roberts.

Left to right: Ira Grupper, Bill McAtee, and Dwain Epps at Bill McAtee's seventy-fifth birthday party, September 18, 2009, Louisville, Kentucky. Photo Ian Husk.

Bill McAtee (l) and Ira Grupper (r) teaching a class on civil rights at Bellarmine College, November 18, 2009, Louisville, Kentucky. McAtee photo archives.

CHAPTER 8

Crossing the Line

It finally happened. Monday, January 3, 1966, was a historic day. According to a report in the *Columbian-Progress*, "An 8-year-old Negro girl was registered at the formerly all white Columbia Primary School Monday without incident." Her mother walked with her as she went to her assigned classroom. The line was finally crossed, the one that for decades had been a barrier to equal education under the law. This was the first time the Columbia Municipal School Board's desegregation compliance policy of integrating first and second grades was implemented.

Regardless of the mounting pressure and sea of emotions that undoubtedly swept over them, the Weary family came to a different conclusion than other black parents had reached the previous September, when they had withdrawn their three children when they reportedly "did not think the children would adjust."[1] No doubt fear overrode even a chance to adjust. But now the Wearys made a different decision. What must have been their daughter Dorothy's emotions the moment she stepped across the threshold of history that Monday morning? Her life was changed forever and so was life in Columbia.

Later that day the mayor met with twelve ministers of the Marion County Ministerial Association at the First Methodist Church, where he led a discussion centered on "ways in which both races can learn to live a peaceful existence."[2] Mayor McLean gave a report on "the state of community relations" and the way in which his administration had "conducted the business of city government, especially in regards to community relations." After the mayor's presentation, the president of the association announced that at the next meeting on January 31, a roundtable discussion would be held "by a bi-racial committee made up of mature local people." The association "approved wholeheartedly a resolution to send letters of commendations to the City officials and the Police department."[3] N. A. Dickson hosted the meeting.

On Saturday, January 8, Willis J. McClenton (erroneously referred to as Willie McLendon in some documents), along with other persons from the Freedom Democratic Party (FDP), began picketing Lampton's Department Store (the Lampton Company) at the corner of Main and Second Streets in downtown Columbia. According to the picketers, their purpose was "to protest unequal hiring practices at Lampton's."[4] The sidewalk on which the picketing took place was approximately nine feet wide. The store had four entrances: two opening on the Main Street sidewalk; one on the Second Street sidewalk; and one at the intersection of the Main Street and Second Street sidewalks.

The picketing, according to a petition for removal, was conducted in the following manner. A single file consisting of all the picketers was formed, with approximately two feet separating each person from the next. The line proceeded along the sidewalk approximately one foot from the side of the building. It would pass in front of the door or doors on one side of Lampton's, then turn the corner and pass in front of the door or doors on the other side of the building. After the entire file passed the door or doors on either side of the building, moving in the direction away from the corner, the picketers would reverse direction, pass by the same door or doors, turn the corner, pass by the other doors or doors and reverse its direction again.

This was the plan, but there were differences of opinion on how the plan was actually executed. The picketers later claimed that at no time did the file stop in front of any of the doors or reverse its directions in such a way as to have two lines of pickets in front of the door at the same time. They also claimed that at no time did the file stop in front of doors when customers were trying to gain passage into the store, but stopped or stepped toward the curb to let customers in. In addition, they claimed that at no time was there physical contact between the picketers and any other persons, threats of any kind to anyone, inflammatory or profane songs or jingles, or language of any kind used by the picketers.

City officials took exception to all these claims. They claimed that songs and jingles were sung, "designed to express opposition to the unequal employment practices at Lampton's and opposition to unequal treatment received by the Freedom Democratic Party volunteers at the hands of local police." They also claimed that the picketers carried two signs stating in substance that Jim Crow must go, urging that others not buy where they cannot work, and asking if others will always be "broom pushers."

According to the picketers, three of their associates left the picket line around 1:45 p.m. and did not return. The remaining group continued to picket until around 2:05 p.m., when two or more others left and did not return. The four remaining picketers continued marching until around 2:44 p.m., when they stopped. The four said they walked down the Second Street sidewalk away from the corner, some twelve feet beyond the side door to talk about whether to take a thirty-minute break or stop for the day. Shortly after they stopped picketing and began to confer, they claimed they were approached at this location by Chief of Police Earl Johnson, who in a rude and profane manner told them to leave the area if they were not going to picket. The chief later denied he had exhibited a "rude and profane manner."

Chief Johnson gave a different account of both the timing and the manner in which the exchange took place. He claimed that some time had elapsed between when the marchers stopped picketing and when he approached the group. He told them they were blocking the side entrance to Lampton's and must cease blocking it, which they refused to do. Curtis Styles, one of the picketers, "in a moderate tone of voice, without profanity or disrespect," told the Chief that he "thought he and his associates were entitled to remain on the sidewalk so long as they did not block the sidewalk or entrance to Lampton's." Styles then claimed that the chief, without further comment, physically restrained and arrested him, then placed him in a nearby police car. The chief claimed that he informed Styles he was under arrest for blocking the entrance to Lampton's and that the arrest was made only after Styles, along with his fellow picketers, was requested not to block the entrance.

After Styles was placed in the police car, Ira Grupper approached the chief and asked, "in moderate tones and without profanity," the reason for Styles's arrest. Those arrested later claimed that at this point the chief directed two other police officers to arrest Willis McClenton and Grupper without informing them of the reason. The chief claimed he reiterated for them that they were arrested for blocking the store entrance. Grupper was placed in the police car with Styles and taken to the Marion County Jail, which was also used by the city. McClenton was taken to the jail in another police car.

Those arrested claimed they were not permitted to communicate with anyone by telephone or otherwise. The chief said he allowed each of them to make one phone call. According to those arrested, the only way they communicated with their associates was by speaking to them through the windows of their jail cells. They claimed they were finally able to talk with their counsel by phone on Sunday, January 9, the day after their arrest, and then only after the chief had refused several requests. Claims were met with counterclaims.

The original trial date was set for Monday, January 10, but it was postponed until Monday, January 17. Those arrested were released from jail on a one hundred dollar bond on Tuesday, January 11. None appeared before any "magistrate, judge, justice of the peace, or any other judicial officer in connection with these matters," because they had never been served with a warrant or other documents. The only papers they had were the receipts for their cash bond, and these did not specify the charges against them. Those arrested only got a copy of the affidavit and warrant when their counsel obtained them from the city clerk's office on Thursday, January 13.

Before the court could convene on Monday, January 17, to hear the case, the attorney for those arrested took action to have the case removed from the Police Justice Court of the City of Columbia to the United States District Court for the Southern District of Mississippi, Hattiesburg Division, under Title 28, Section 1443, of the United States Code.[5] The basis for this change in venue was that the civil rights of those charged under affidavits and warrants would be denied equal protection if their cases remained in the police justice court. Another line had now been crossed—the line to legal action.

The January 13 edition of the *Columbian-Progress* carried two notices indicating the signs of the times. One was an alert to "customers needing payrolls or other matters attended to please take notice" that the Columbia Bank and the Citizens Bank would not be open on Wednesday, January 19, "in observance of Robert E. Lee's Birthday (A Legal Holiday)." Without the slightest hint of irony, the notice also stated that these banks were "Members of the Federal Deposit Insurance Corporation."[6] The other important notice was a repeat of one that had been run the previous year by John Homer Willoughby, sheriff and tax collector, urging citizens to pay their poll taxes before February 1. The notice stressed that, "Poll Tax Receipts for two years are necessary in qualifying as a voter in this year's elections!" The notice also announced that the "Tax Rolls are now open to receive payment of poll tax, personal property taxes and real estate taxes. Pay Now—Avoid the Rush!!!!"[7] The U.S. Supreme Court would later declare poll taxes in local and state elections unconstitutional.

Paul Pittman's column, "Outlook On Mississippi Politics, Economy," printed right next to the poll tax notice, said, "The possible effect on elections that widespread registration of State Negroes may have is a subject which stirs considerable interest these days in Mississippi politicians of every description." He also stated that, "There is little doubt among state officials that the constitutionality of the new federal voting rights act will be upheld by the courts and that county registrars will be forced to put hundreds of recently registered Negro voters on the eligible voter lists." One surprise that federal election examiners discovered in several Mississippi counties was the "large number of older voters they were listing, and the very small number of voters in their early twenties and thirties being added because of the new federal law."[8]

I later heard about stories that had circulated at the time relating how some of the older blacks, who had paid their two dollar poll tax for years, had not crossed the line to register before 1962, much less actually voted. After some women finally went down to register, some of their husbands were encouraged to do the same, only to be confronted with ridiculous tests given to blacks along with a registration form. These tests asked prospective black voters to interpret some obscure point in the Fourteenth Amendment and all sorts of crazy questions like "how many bubbles in a bar of soap," or "how many dots on the point of a pencil." Those restrictions rapidly began to disappear following passage of the Voting Rights Act of 1965.

❖ ❖ ❖

On January 18, Rev. A. G. Payton penned a beautifully scripted handwritten letter to me acknowledging "the receipt of the Scholarship and additional funds in behalf of our daughter, Sandra L. Payton's college fee," funding I had arranged, and expressed "to you and co-workers our *sincere thanks* and *deepest appreciation* for the same." Payton made a solemn pledge of his "honesty to use it *only* for the purpose which you designated it to be used." He prayed that, "God's *richest* blessings be accessible to you and yours. And may your leadership be Divinely guarded, protected and provided for." He closed by saying, "I shall forever *strive* to be useful and rewarding to *each* of you and mankind. Humbly and affectionately yours, A. G. Payton."[9]

❖ ❖ ❖

The Marion County Community Relations Committee met on Thursday, January 20, at which time the mayor gave a report of the court case arising out of the arrest of those who had picketed Lampton's.[10] He stated that the case had been removed from the city court to the federal district court in Hattiesburg because of allegations that Negroes had not been represented in the mayoral election. Mrs. Pittman made a motion that this report be made part of the permanent record of the committee, and the motion passed.

A question was asked about how merchants fared during the recent Christmas shopping season in light of the black Christmas boycott. Tom Faust, chairman of the Retail Merchants Committee of the Marion County Chamber of Commerce, reported that according to the merchants it was the "best Christmas ever." One indicator of this success was a very signifi-cant increase in sales tax receipts over the previous year.

Rev. Pittman told me earlier that he received calls from black friends in nearby towns, such as Bogalusa, where the boycott disrupted regular shopping patterns. They asked him if it was safe to shop in Columbia. He told them, "Sure it's safe downtown. Just park on Main Street and put your money in the parking meter!" Later in March, in response to several com-plaints to the city regarding police feeding meters, the mayor issued an order immediately suspending the practice. He said that "in the past police gave parkers an extra service by taking coins from a vehicle's dashboard or from under the windshield wiper and putting the money in the meter to save the driver from getting a ticket."[11]

Again I was called on at the close of the meeting to make observa-tions about how the committee was progressing in its working relations. I pointed out that there was a reduction in give-and-take in the discussions, as well as fewer members actively participating. I suggested several pos-sible reasons for these changes: First, a natural "post-success slump" after the Christmas hiring of black employees; second, having a new modera-tor and not being sure how the group would be run; and third, the effect of guests on black participants. For example, two guests spoke regarding personnel hires that sounded defensive, saying they were unable to take on new help and implying ignorance of the workers who were hired.

I made several suggestions for consideration. First, I suggested the committee be more alert and sensitive to those poised to speak. I noted that at one point when a motion was made to replace members who were inactive, one black member was trying to get the floor before the vote was taken, but was ignored. Second, I suggested it would be more productive to hear all sides or views by drawing people out who had not spoken. I offered several illustrations. Several whites wondered why blacks were so interested in working on Main Street but got little response. This was a good opportunity for more blacks to speak. I also pointed out there was a minimum of discussion as to whether or not the group wanted to explore the possibility of providing a bus for black students to commute to the Prentiss Institute.

Regarding employment, I said, if whites have to interpret the need to be courteous for some merchants, maybe some blacks need to interpret why some who apply for work may be turned down and others accepted. Finally, regarding voter registration, it seemed that whites were emphasizing to blacks that nothing would happen if they came, so it was as simple as that. But this approach failed to recognize the fear in the minds of some blacks and the need for whites to make overtures to them, demonstrating their support. In summary, I said there was a tendency for whites to offer quick solutions before really hearing what the blacks were thinking. I observed that black reticence was very subtle, not deliberate in the pattern of "Uncle Tom." This attitude was a natural result of years of working in a given framework where whites dominated decisions.[12] Progress was being made in improving civil discourse, but there still was a ways to go.

❖ ❖ ❖

Now that the McAtees were a two-car family of four, the little black "Missionary" VW was not big enough to act as a second car. On January 26, 1966, we purchased a new 1966 VW Square Back station wagon from Steadman Motor Company in Hattiesburg for $2,520, with radio, seat belts, and outside mirror extra.[13] We sold the black VW Bug to N. A.

❖ ❖ ❖

The machinery of the War on Poverty in Washington was beginning to be mobilized so that results from that legislation were being felt across the land. Carl Loftin, Marion County Superintendent of Education, announced in the January 27 edition of the *Columbian-Progress* that Marion Central had received a Title I Grant of $61,674. This was a grant to be used for "educationally deprived children, or children in families which have an annual income of less than $2,000." Loftin said that these funds would be used "to purchase classroom equipment, teaching equipment, materials and supplies needed for six new teachers." The timing could not have been better because "the final inspection was held last week on a new addition of six classrooms, offices, rest rooms and storage area." All this was "designed to reduce the class load in the first six grades and improve reading." Bids for the equipment and material were already being received.[14]

With the award of these funds, new coordinators for the Title One programs were named for Columbia Separate Municipal and Marion county school districts. Mr. James Brewer, a graduate of the University of Southern Mississippi and band director at the high school, was named to the city position. Rev. B. Alfred Jones, a graduate of Mississippi College, a county teacher, and pastor of the South Columbia Baptist Church, was named to the county position. "Both [white] men will be responsible for supervising the administration of the Title One projects and working up new ones."[15]

R. D. Reeves, superintendent of the Marion County General Hospital, spoke to the Marion County Ministerial Association at its meeting on January 31, at First Methodist Church, on problems faced by the hospital. A roundtable discussion by a bi-racial committee "made up of mature local people" filled the remaining time, as had been suggested at the previous meeting on January 3.[16] Clergy members of the Community Relations Committee and the Community Action Committee were included on the roundtable panel. This was the first time that an integrated meeting of clergy had been held, and again N. A. hosted the group, supported by the officers of the church.

Rev. Amos Payton, our friend from Six, gave the closing devotional, in which he elegantly related a moving story that illustrated his feelings about current race relations in Columbia. He said there was a man who was having some difficulty with vision and memory. Finally, he decided that he could not continue to live this impaired way, but had to do something about these two maladies. So he sought the services of a chiropractor. The doctor put the man on the adjustment table in his office and began to manipulate his back. Something interesting developed. When he moved him one way, the patient regained his memory, but he could not see. He moved him another way, and he regained his sight, but he could not remember a thing. This happened several times, until the doctor concluded he could not fix it. The man could not have both his sight and his memory at the same time. He told the patient he had to make a choice, so the man chose his sight. The doctor asked him why he made that choice. The man replied, "I had much rather see where I am going, than remember where I have been!"

On the fifth day of February, Ernest R. Duff, attorney for the City of Columbia, filed a motion to remand with the U.S. District Court in

Hattiesburg in the case involving Ira Grupper, one of the civil rights workers arrested in January at Lampton's. The city attorney's motion was based on his contention that the case was not properly removed from the police justice court to the federal court under Title 28, Section 1443 of the United States Code. He maintained that this action to remove was "not predicated on any provision of the Constitution or statutes of the State of Mississippi which deny civil rights of the accused." He also maintained that the Columbia police officer had acted under valid laws and ordinances.[17] It is assumed that the Styles and McClenton cases were also removed to the U.S. district court in separate motions. It is interesting to note that Title 28, Section 1443 of the United States Code originated as a post–Civil War civil rights bill enacted in 1866.

Without getting bogged down in the details of these legal maneuverings it must be noted that these were not the only cases where civil rights lawyers attempted to remove similar cases from state courts to federal courts. One such case originating with civil rights workers in Greenwood, Mississippi, was working its way through state courts, the U.S. District Court for the Northern District of Mississippi, and the Supreme Court for resolution beginning in 1964–65 and continuing into 1966. The High Court agreed, "to consider the case on 'the important question raised by the parties concerning the scope of the civil rights removal statute' enacted in the 1866 Civil Rights Act (Reconstruction Acts)." Resolution was being sought for the same issues regarding removal and remand based on the same provisions of the law that were in the Columbia proceedings. Resolution eventually came in favor of remand from the federal courts to the state courts in the Greenwood case.[18] Short of digging through the old court records in the district court in Hattiesburg, I assume that the Grupper case and the others were remanded to the police justice court in Columbia. In a recent conversation, Grupper could not recall how the legal process ended. All he could remember was that he did not get his one hundred dollar bond money back.[19]

◆   ◆   ◆

On the McAtee home front during the first week of February, Walt was getting sick with a head cold and congestion. As it got progressively worse, we took him to the Marion General Hospital for treatment, where he was given a shot. This did not give him any relief. My ministerial log indicates Dr. Cleland, President of Belhaven College, was the guest preacher on

Sunday, February 6, to tell "The Belhaven Story." It also says that I had literally lost my voice, and the evening service was cancelled. This was Millye's
birthday, but she tried not to let on to her brother and mother how upset
she was about Walt's condition when they called to wish her a happy birthday. Our main attention was given to Walt, who was very listless, feverish,
and getting worse. We were getting desperate and did not know which way
to turn.

On Monday we parked Neal with our friend Grace Melvin, got the
name of Dr. Mary Clark, a pediatrician in Hattiesburg, and took Walt to
see her. The minute she looked in his ears, she immediately lanced his
abscessed eardrums, which were on the verge of rupturing. She said he had
pneumonia and made arrangements to admit him to a nearby hospital *post
haste*. Millye stayed with Walt overnight, and I drove to Hazlehurst to get
my mother to keep Neal while I drove back and forth to Hattiesburg. Millye and I took turns staying with Walt. On Thursday I brought Neal over to
stand outside the hospital window to wave to the young patient, who soon
recovered and was released to our care on Saturday. The doctor felt like
the basis of Walt's problem was an allergy to house dust. Addressing that
problem required stripping his room, and dusting and mopping the floors
daily. Walt even had to give up his beloved "Humpty" for a while. Before
long we had weathered that scare, and things were back to normal. We were
relieved that we had not crossed the line that no parent wants to cross.

❖ ❖ ❖

In mid-February, as a platform to give a progress report on the city's
affairs in a variety of areas over the past eight months, the mayor chose
the weekly meeting of the Columbia Rotary. The Rotary Club was a key
location, where issues of the day were presented for consideration to leaders of the white community. By way of introduction, the mayor reported,
"[T]he city is in good order, well managed, is honestly facing the problems
before it, and is planning for a better tomorrow."[20] Then he proceeded to
highlight various departments' physical accomplishments. Included in the
fire department's future plans was "an additional fire station or substa-
tion located in the residential area of the city." A study was being conducted by the Mississippi Power Company over the kind and locations
of new streetlights across all the community. The water department had
completed "enlarging several of our major water lines, a complete renova-
tion of the water plant, the drilling of two new wells and the erection of

a 250,000 gallon stand pipe in the northeast section of the city." The antiquated water filtration system was now upgraded and the control system fully automated. He noted specifically that the department is "completely reworking most of the water lines in the Owens Street area [the black residential and school area]," work that was begun in December and expected to be completed by summer. Two major problems in the sewage system were addressed "with the elimination of Columbia Training School waste from a main sewage line that transgresses the city and the removal of sewage disposal from the Pearl River."

The mayor reported he was proud of the police department, which over the past several months had worked "extra hours at tasks that certainly were far from desirable." Each officer was personally challenged to control his emotions "at times when I am sure they and others present did not approve of the action which the police were called upon to perform." He noted he hoped all policemen in the department would have the opportunity to attend the new state police academy for additional training. Over the past six weeks the department had been taking applications for one or more black policemen, giving no indication when the hire would take place. He expressed his hope "that it will be in the near future."

The street department had completed a major repaving project, begun last October, which left 50 percent of the streets in the city in "good shape." Major projects in 1966 would focus on reworking and paving West Church Street, old North Main through Popetown, and Owens Street. Several other streets would be improved in the prominently black Owens district of the city through special property assessments. The mayor said the city had received bids on a new larger capacity garbage truck that he hoped would be in service within a month. Finally, he said that a major problem that had to be addressed by 1970 was the garbage dumping in the Pearl River. He hopes to initiate a landfill operation, but doing so would "require the purchase of land suitable for that purpose and the purchase of a caterpillar-type tractor."

The mayor completed his report by discussing briefly the challenges the school system was facing in the immediate future and the way "each of us is handling our race relations." He emphasized: "No longer can we afford the luxury of facing these problems with a negative attitude and waiting until we have to do something. This community thus far has shown remarkable progress in facing these issues honestly and doing the things that should be done to continue to have law and order."

In a separate action that week, the mayor announced that the board of aldermen had appointed Dean Noblitt to a five-year term on the Columbia Municipal District School Board, replacing Bert Lawrence, whose term had expired. Lawrence "had served on the local school board for the past five years."[21]

In early March, the mayor and board of aldermen would pass "a resolution declaring necessary special improvement in the city of Columbia and have fixed a date to hear objections." The legal notice specified that, "the Mayor and Board of Aldermen may borrow money and issue negotiable notes or other obligations to raise funds to pay for the improvements."[22]

A special report from Washington, D.C., which appeared in the *Columbian-Progress* on February 24, stated, "Congressman Wm. M. Colmer (D-MS) charged on the House Floor that both the attacks on the State of Mississippi recently and on the war effort in Vietnam are part of a Communist-inspired conspiracy." As supporting evidence, Colmer said that "one-third of the 150 lawyers who acted as counsel for the Mississippi Freedom Democratic Party in its challenge of the Mississippi Delegation in Congress last year" had communist or communist-front records. He also alleged that, "the [Communist] Party and its affiliates had taught draft dodging in its 'freedom schools.'" He was appalled when some members of the House had supported the MFDP and SNCC. He concluded that, "The poison of Communism, of black nationalism, of racism, has been labeled 'Civil Rights,' and some well-intended members of this House have looked no further than the label."[23]

Mrs. Seaborn Hasson, president of the Columbia Education Association, sent a letter on March 3 to members of the "club" announcing a joint meeting of the Marion County Education Association and the Columbia Education Association at the Crystelle Ford Auditorium on March 15, at 7:00. She stated, "The purpose of the meeting is to inform the local political leaders, patrons of the schools, and teachers of the responsibility for professional improvement and how they should exercise citizenship duties. We want to secure the support of patrons and local political leaders." The guest speaker would be Mr. Otis Allen, Superintendent of Education in Leflore County (Greenwood), who "is widely known for his ability to inform the public of the problems facing schools today." She concluded the invitation by saying, "We would like very much for you, or a representative of your organization, to meet all the teachers of Marion County and Columbia City Schools, both white and colored, for this important meeting."[24]

During the weeks following Dorothy Weary's enrollment in the second grade, the Weary family had been faced with threats of varying degrees. The insurance policy on their house at one point lapsed due to some misunderstanding. Apparently the Wearys were turned down by several insurance agencies in their bid to get their coverage reinstated. It was not clear if these rejections were a direct result of their involvement in the civil rights movement. Nonetheless, the Wearys contacted the Lawyer's Committee for Civil Rights Under Law in Jackson, seeking assistance.

In his day job, the mayor had in 1964 become a partner in the T. C. Griffith Insurance Agency, Inc. after he left the employ of the W. E. Walker Stores. Edward E. Ellis, a civil rights attorney in Jackson, contacted McLean in his capacity with the insurance agency regarding the reinstatement of the Weary's policy.[25] McLean, in a letter to the insurance carrier, reported that the Weary property was "above average in appearance for this class and the values are present." He noted that his agency had "written the coverage for three years prior to this without loss." He also shared the fact that Mrs. Weary had "been active in the civil rights work and that her daughter had recently enrolled at the white primary school." McLean added that he did not personally "fear any reprisal against her and [felt] that normally this risk would be alright." He said after weighing all the facts and talking with Mr. Ellis, the lawyer, and with Mrs. Weary, "I am of the opinion that we, as the agent, had no other choice [but to write the policy]."[26] McLean responded in writing to Ellis: "Frankly, under normal business operations, I would not have renewed [the policy], but as Mrs. Weary cannot obtain coverage from another company, I am writing today an insurance policy to replace the policy referred to in your letter of January 25, 1966." McLean also told Ellis that he had "discussed this matter with Mrs. Weary and she is in agreement with these proceedings." In addition, he requested of Mrs. Weary "that if in the future she had any questions concerning this insurance," she personally contact him and "not rely on a third party to relay any request."[27] A year later, the mayor would write this shard-like "artifact" on a memo pad and place it in his file: "3-16-67 Dr. Henderson, Washington, Mrs. Weary—threats to blow her house up. FBI has been notified."[28]

◆ ◆ ◆

In early March I traveled to Brookhaven to attend the funeral of "Miss Mary" Abshagen, aunt of my high school English teacher, "Miss Ab," who opened a world of literature, drama, speech, and writing to a less than attentive seventeen-year-old. While at the funeral, I watched my educational past file before me and remembered the quality education I had received in that place. I had a long talk with "Chief Lipsey," our school superintendent, who had assembled an exceptional core of professionals— Abshagen, Mathison, Burns, Daily, Jenkins, Smith, Hendricks, Granberry, McNair, Lofton, Roach, and others—who through the years affected the lives of countless young people at the start of their quest for truth and love of knowledge.

Miss Mary Bracey, the black woman who had looked after "Miss Mary" Abshagen in her failing years, made a profound statement after the funeral: "We have something good here in Brookhaven that has gone all around the world." This sentiment was true, and it gave me pause to consider the paradoxical nature of our situation, which gripped legions of people in numerous ways. It was a contributing factor in the irony of our superintendent's present circumstance. So I sat down and wrote him a long letter.

He was hurting because he had to cross the line to retirement during this turbulent time, and was not able to carry the school system through this transitional period. In my letter, I tried to console him by talking about the host of white youths who had gone out from Brookhaven High (B.H.S.) to the ends of the earth. Our preparation there had helped bring about the surge of technological development and growth experienced in the early and middle years of the twentieth century in America. I complimented him on his hard work to raise the level of education for the black people of the community by providing an outstanding center of learning at their school, Alexander High (A.H.S.). Even in that separate but unequal world, I wrote, there still was a degree to which the youth from that school were "freed from the shackles of ignorance which imprisoned and impoverished their parents. They no doubt have played an important part in the coming of their people to first class citizenship."

I summed my thoughts up by saying, "[Y]ou provided enlightened grist for the twin mills of technological advancement and the emergence of the dark peoples of the world which characterize the vibrancy of the second half of the twentieth century. Both have produced certain conditions, which make change inevitable and irrevocable—conditions over which no one person has control as to how it comes or in what order. This can be confusing and disheartening, even distasteful at times."

I apologized for launching into "a lengthy treatise, but merely wanted, as one of the many whose lives have been enriched by your efforts, to say—thank you for a job well done." I said it was only natural, when the time comes to step down, to feel that the job has not been completed, to "question if any contribution had actually been made." I hoped that he would "not allow disappointment, frustration, or bitterness to creep in and over shadow the good which you have achieved." Speaking on behalf of many B.H.S. graduates, I said, "In receiving the torch from you we know we are better equipped to face the demands of change and to meet the responsibilities of our generation than we would have been had you not tried to give us your best. You see, your influence will not soon cease, for it has engendered purpose and proficiency in countless lives."[29]

After a week, I received a handwritten letter from Mr. Lipsey stating his appreciation for my "expressions" in regard to him, and saying "that they are not at all deserved." His humility rested in his belief that he had been "very fortunate to have capable, dedicated and consecrated teachers." He was surprised that he had "disclosed any of this frustration that I feel. But evidently it could not be entirely concealed." He stated further, "Most of all I was impressed by the depth and direction of your thinking. What a pity that there are so many supposed Christian leaders who seem to forget the basic teachings of the Bible in regard to God's love and Christian love." He closed by saying he would keep my letter "by me and read it with interest and benefit in later years. Wishing for you great success and satisfaction in your work, I am, sincerely yours, Crawford Lipsey."[30]

❖ ❖ ❖

Another federal program found its way into Marion County when plans got under way in mid-March for vocational training through the Manpower Development Training Act. When up and running it would "provide job training in seven occupations for 200 people." An article in the *Columbian-Progress* making the announcement said, "Employment service figures reveal the need for trained people to fill existing jobs and that hundreds of people in Marion County and surrounding areas are unemployed." A. P. Fatherree, vocational and technical education director Orville Simmons, the Employment Security Commission's chief of operations functions, and Tom Cole, a Commerce Department representative, met with Columbia Chamber of Commerce official Jimmy Cagle to lay the groundwork for establishing the job training program. The visitors said the "job training program should begin within 60 to 90 days."[31]

◆ ◆ ◆

One of the special features of replicating pastor and church was the annual week of services in the spring, the Presbyterian version of what others labeled a revival. On the week of March 21–25, 1966, the session of our church invited Eade Anderson, pastor of the First Presbyterian Church in Greenwood to be our guest preacher. Anderson had held a week of services in Amory April 1–5, 1963, during the time I was deciding on how to respond to the Columbia call, and we had an excellent time together. To Millye and me, he was a special friend whose personal warmth brought out the very best in people, and his caring spirit helped one make it through the darkest of nights.

Anderson had held a front row seat during some of the most critical events of the 1960s in Mississippi. As an army reserve chaplain, he observed the aftermath of Meredith's entry into Ole Miss, when the national guard was federalized in October of 1962. He provided pastoral care to a young Le Flore County farmer who faced threats of physical violence and general community shunning when the young man identified the rifle used to assassinate Medgar Evers in June of 1963 as the one he had recently sold to Byron de la Beckwith. This revelation led to Beckwith's arrest. The young man had not had a clue as to the rifle's intended purpose when he sold it, but nonetheless he eventually had to move to another city as a result of the sale.

Anderson had a sympathetic understanding of what we had been experiencing in Columbia over the past months that added a depth to his messages. But the most significant thing about his time in Columbia was that he was engaged in deciding whether or not to accept a call to the Memorial Presbyterian Church in Montgomery, Alabama. Some might say that was like going from the frying pan into the fire! Eade and I spent many hours between services struggling with issues of leaving or staying in Mississippi and deciding which would most faithfully fulfill our calls to ministry. He spent a great deal of time on the telephone with the Memorial pulpit committee, getting clarity on expectations and conditions that had to be met before he accepted.

In the end, he accepted the call and moved his family to Montgomery on May 31 to begin a new ministry there. An additional void was created in the leadership pool loyal to the Presbyterian Church U.S. in Mississippi. In leaving when he did, he just missed another critical event, when James Meredith's somewhat peaceful march turned violent, and Stokely

Carmichael with SNCC arrived in Greenwood, electrifying the world with his demand for "Black Power."

❖ ❖ ❖

Miss Evelyn Gandy, commissioner of public welfare for the state of Mississippi, announced, "that 76 of the state's 82 [counties] are taking part in the surplus commodities distribution program. Six other counties . . . are participating in USDA's food stamp program which replaced the commodity distribution program in these counties." With this, "Mississippi became the first state in the South to have U.S. Department of Agriculture food assistance program in operation in every county." Under Operation Help, a recently launched expanded food surplus distribution program, "$24,000,000 worth of USDA donated foods will be made available to half a million low income Mississippians within the six month period which began February 1." Secretary of Agriculture Orville L. Freeman hailed the demonstration project and its service to the needy as one that "will develop methods and procedures that can be adapted by other states for the benefit of more of their needy citizens."[32]

All was not rosy to some observers with regard to the anti-poverty programs coming out of Washington. Thurman Sensing in his weekly column in the *Columbian-Progress* warned that "if local government officials are wise, they will be taking a close look at the plans being devised" by the Great Society's anti-poverty agencies in American communities, claiming that these plans "offer little but trouble to the communities concerned." He challenged the theory that "taxpayers should provide concentrated training and concentrated benefits to residents of slum areas in hope of eliminating what they call 'cultural lag.' But this theory means the productive citizen is penalized in order to confer privileges on the non-productive citizens." He also warned: "[L]ocal school boards would be well advised not to invite outside groups to take over special summer educational projects in their communities." He feared that "local and state officials who let anti-poverty programs operate without public inspection may be letting the anti-poverty warriors set up political units developed to take over political control of cities."[33]

The following week Sensing approached his concerns from a different angle when he claimed that Chief Justice Earl Warren, speaking in support of the Voting Rights Act of 1965, "wasn't so much endeavoring to affirm the constitutionality of a law as to make sure that a political revolution is accomplished in Southern states." The bottom line for Sensing was that, "the new reconstructionists on the Warren Court are hoping . . . that the voting rolls of Southern states will be so packed with illiterates who can be manipulated by the liberals on election day, that the proven quality of conservative leadership will be defeated next fall in congressional races." He pointed out that in the past "this type of voter was bought by unscrupulous politicians with a pint of cheap whiskey." But times have changed. Today said voter "is enrolled in an anti-poverty program or otherwise made a financial beneficiary of the political bosses of the Great Society . . . who prefer to live by handout than by hard work."[34] If true, only the bait and perpetrators had changed, not the practice.

Spring Break was a rite of passage for college students all over the country. Recently, students from up north had trekked to the South to engage in all sorts of activities, some serious and some frivolous. In 1966, a group of college students from American and Temple Universities came to Columbia during their spring break to help with voter registration. Rev. Charles Rother, campus chaplain at American University, accompanied the group. It was Holy Week on religious calendars, although that designation was not all on their minds. They made contact with the MFDP and stayed in Freedom House while they were in Columbia.

Years later, Ira Grupper told me that he was responsible for the students' orientation to the community. Incidentally, this time was the closest Ira and I ever came to crossing paths until years later, but we did not meet during this week. In his orientation Grupper urged the students to pay careful attention to how they conducted themselves so as not to detract from their primary purpose: fighting for justice for everybody. In governing their personal conduct, he said it would be wise to follow and to respect the "duality of the puritan religious mores of the community," especially as it related to their sexual behavior.[35]

Early in the week the group went to the courthouse to help some local black citizens register to vote. When they got there, the potential registrants were not able to complete the process because the tax rolls were not anywhere to be found. For a while they thought they had run into the stereotypical white resistance used to keep blacks from exercising their constitutional rights. Fortunately, the person in the registrar's office activated the volunteer "rapid response" system that the Community Relations Committee had set up for just such an occasion. The volunteer on call was Hessie Wolfe, a white member of the committee and a businessman whose construction company office was nearby. In a matter of minutes, he went to the registrar's office to inquire about the problem. He soon discovered that the tax rolls were upstairs being used to prepare a jury list. He arranged for the books to be brought back downstairs so people could register to vote, which was done without further complications.

Chaplain Rother, in conversation with someone in the community, indicated that the group was interested in getting a well-rounded view of the community and wondered if a meeting might be arranged with white citizens that were not spokesmen for any official group. Word of this request came to the mayor, and he asked N. A. and me to help him set up such a meeting. So N. A. and I arranged a meeting at city hall on Good Friday, April 8, at 8:00 p.m. We invited ten white citizens, mostly members of the bi-racial committee, who agreed to meet with the ten students and the chaplain.

At 7:30 p. m., prior to meeting with the guests, I told the local participants what this meeting was about, how we should proceed, and how to mingle the groups in scattered seating arrangements.[36] I reminded them that our attitude should be non-judgmental. We should answer their specific questions and carry on a discussion with our guests by asking our own questions. I said the stated purpose was "to get to know each other as individuals in an informal, frank discussion about the interests in and goals of the community." I declared, "Communication is essential to understanding."

At 8:00 p.m. the students joined us, and Rother gave an opening prayer. Each person introduced himself or herself. Local people stated their occupation, role, and service in the community. Guests stated their school, class, major, and reason for making the trip. Rother gave background about how his group became interested in coming to Columbia and how students were selected to make the trip. After a lively, constructive discussion and a brief summary, N. A. offered a closing prayer.

In the course of the evening we discovered the visitors were put out with a couple of members of their group, including a black student who had helped recruit them for the trip. The two had secretly taken one of the rental cars the night before and gone to the French Quarter in New Orleans for a night on the town. It appeared that this had been their plan all along, leaving the impression that this was sort of a spring break lark for those two. The rest of the group was very serious about their intentions. Years later, Grupper told me that the two that took off to New Orleans, despite their momentary lapse of judgment, were nonetheless committed to the purposes of their trip to Columbia.

The following morning Doc Wolfe, brother of Mary, Hessie, Wiley, and Karl Wolfe, came by my house in a huff about what he had felt as one of the participants in the meeting the night before.[37] He said he did what I asked, maintaining a "non-judgmental attitude." He said it was all he could do to hold his tongue about some of the things he heard from the guests, but he did. After we talked for a while, he was "able to laugh about it now!" Another personal line had been crossed.

Later in the spring, N. A. had a tense encounter when he met a bus-load of churchwomen coming to assist in voter registration. Around dusk he met them at the city park on Broad Street. They were seeking directions to the Methodist Rural Center at Lampton, where they were to be housed while in Columbia. As he was talking with the group through the door of the bus, a vehicle approached, occupied by members of the KKK. One of the occupants angrily jumped from the car and shouted at the women, "You set one foot off this bus and you won't see the light of day." N. A. stood his ground. After the intruder backed down owing to N. A.'s courageous "line-in-the-sand" routine, he got back in the KKK car and left. The bus then proceeded to the rural center as directed without further incident.[38]

Another shard-like "artifact" appeared on a memo pad in the mayor's file. At the top the date, "4-13-66," is written over "5-19-66," which has a line scratched through it. The only other words on the pad are: "Resist arrest dismissed, Disturb peace, 15.00, 2.50 jail, Docket #835." It is reasonable to assume that this notation had something to do with the mayor serving as judge on the police justice court, but it is not clear if this refers to the Lampton's picket cases, remanded from the U.S. district court in Hattiesburg.[39] After search of the city court records recently, Chris Watts indicated that he could "find absolutely no court records at all." He also reported that the present mayor, Harold Bryant, indicated that sometime around 1989, the mayor no longer acted as judge. He was not sure if that was only in Columbia, or if every mayor in Mississippi or all of America lost that power.[40]

Although the threshold to a desegregated school system had been crossed the previous fall in the Columbia city system, the volume of foot-steps on that path would dramatically increase when the 1966–67 school session would begin in the coming fall if all went as planned. The first eight grades in the Marion County system would be desegregated, and grades one through five, plus seventh, ninth, and twelfth grades in Columbia city schools. In mid-April, patrons of Marion County and Columbia city schools received a detailed notice about the procedures to be used in filing choice of school forms for the students involved in those grades. The city school deadline for returning the forms was May 9, with May 13 for the county schools. It was again made clear that school choice is solely the responsibility of the parents of each child. Teachers are not the only persons not allowed to influence the choice of schools.

The city school board had submitted its plan for desegregation that it assumed complied "with the requirements of the Civil Rights Act of 1964 (P.L. 38-352), particularly Title VI." This plan "was accepted last year and . . . provided for desegregation of four grades per year, beginning with the first four grades this session." But a "revised statement of policies for school desegregation as issued by the U.S. Department of Health, Education and Welfare in March of 1966" sought to accelerate "the desegregation of all schools, including staff, transportation, athletic fields, meeting rooms, and all 'school-related services, facilities, activities, and programs, such as commencement exercises, and parent-teacher meetings, which are open to all such persons other than enrolled students.'"[41] Many lines were now crossed.

What was accelerating in the state was also accelerating in the church with more than "deliberate speed." The 106th General Assembly of the Presbyterian Church, U.S., meeting in Montreat, North Carolina, April 21–26, 1966, received a commissioner's resolution, one of the signers being commissioner George A. Chauncey from Transylvania Presbytery in Kentucky, where years later I would be Presbytery Executive.[42] The resolution noted that, "[T]he Church was troubled by evident disorder in the life of the Synod of Mississippi." Several examples were given: the failure to resolve the A. M. Hart-Central Mississippi Presbytery case; the creation of an unauthorized theological seminary within its bounds; and the unwillingness thus far of the presbyteries of the synod to receive into their membership the Presbyterian Negro churches within their jurisdiction, as requested the previous year.

The General Assembly, the high court of the church, acted within its prescribed authority "to appoint a committee to visit and examine this portion of the Church affected with evident disorder, to inquire into the difficulties therein; and to report its findings and to recommend appropriate action to the next meeting of the General Assembly." Rev. Charles L. King of Houston, Texas, was named as chairman of this five-man interim committee, informally known as "the Charlie King Committee." A minority report was filed by the six commissioners from Central Mississippi Presbytery, focal point of much of the disorder, stating that, "It is our feeling that this situation in Mississippi is not such as to warrant the appointment of this committee . . . but we would welcome such a committee if it comes with a pastoral concern, and can help quiet any unrest there may be in our Synod, and perhaps any unrest concerning us outside our Synod."[43]

Signs of continued progress in the development of new local anti-poverty programs and improvement in educational facilities in Columbia and Marion County began to appear. Frank K. Sloan, director of the Atlanta Regional Office, Office of Economic Opportunity, announced that a $32,046 anti-poverty grant was awarded to Pearl River Valley Opportunity, Inc. (PRVO), "for studies, surveys and investigations into the causes and nature of poverty and the means by which poverty might be eliminated." John Paul Roblin, executive director of the three-county agency, PRVO, served as director of the new programs.[44]

In a special election on May 17, qualified electors in the Columbia Municipal Separate School District voted 427 to 93 to approve a $300,000 city school bond issue "to make improvements at the John J. Jefferson School and to build an office building across from the Crystelle Ford Auditorium . . . to provide office space for the superintendent of city schools, lunch room director, the assistant to the superintendent, board meeting room, and other facilities."[45]

An announcement was made that three Head Start centers would begin classes on June 13 and run for eight weeks. They were located at the Mississippi Rural Center, Friendship Community Center (Mt. Bethel Church), and at Owens Chapel Church. I. C. Pittman received applications for teachers, resident aides, cooks, kitchen helpers, and janitors by May 30. A special training program for Head Start teachers was scheduled for June 6–10.[46]

On Friday, May 27, sixty seniors graduated from John J. Jefferson High School after hearing Haskell S. Bingham, Director of Public Relations, Jackson State College, give the commencement address. The evening was inaugurated with "Pomp and Circumstance" and an invocation by Rev. Amos Payton. Barbara A. Brewer was valedictorian, and James Burrell was Salutatorian. Principal W. S. McLaurin presented the class to Superintendent B. F. Duncan, who bestowed diplomas on the graduates.[47]

Across town on Monday, May 30, ninety-seven seniors graduated from Columbia High School in the Crystelle Ford Auditorium. Rev. Paul H. Shell, pastor of East Columbia Baptist Church, gave the invocation, and class president Mike Dickson, N. A.'s son, gave the welcome. Mike received the Boy's Leadership Award and the American Legion School Award. William F. Winter, State Treasurer, gave the commencement address before the diplomas were awarded by Superintendent B. F. Duncan.

Winter told the class, "[W]e live in a world that will not let us forget that we don't 'have it made.' There is no guarantee." He went on to remind the class that "each person is personally accountable for what he or she does with his or her life and that nothing corrupts as much as blindly following the crowd." He challenged the graduates to "use your gifts of personality, mind, and body to the fullest, free of confused values, vanity, and misplaced pride to maintain the heritage of free men and free women."[48]

The spring of 1966 was punctuated with many crossed lines that led to the beginning of new realities in the world: the first integrated class and plans for others providing equal education opportunities; legal action challenging denial of equal protection; the first integrated ministerial association meeting; new federal programs providing Title I aid to local school districts, vocational training, surplus food distribution, Head Start and other programs designed to eliminate poverty; and the opportunity to listen to others with whom one differed. Not everyone in the community celebrated these new realities. Some were suspicious and angry.

Seniors graduating from high school this year crossed another line into the new world of adulthood. But they would never experience what those coming behind them would experience, for they had spent their educational career in separate but unequal segregated circumstances. Their school days were drawing to a close. But theirs were not the only ones whose days were dwindling.

CHAPTER 9

Dwindling Days

Sometime in early June, Buddy asked if I wanted to fly with him up to Chattanooga to take Danny to summer school at McCallie, a Tennessee prep school. I agreed and we loaded Danny's gear in the Twin Beech and flew off north to Tennessee on a clear blue summer morning. Upon arrival we went over to the school in a rented car and deposited Danny and his things there. On the way back to Mississippi we swung by Atlanta to get a part installed on the door of the plane. It was exciting to listen to the air traffic control instructions to the company pilot as he worked his way into landing pattern between all those big commercial birds as the afternoon traffic picked up. We taxied over to hangar one, where the service on the door was performed. While that was happening, I walked around among all the corporate planes in the hangar, enthralled with the beauties parked there. A perfectly restored World War II P-51 fighter converted for private use—the kind the Tuskegee Airmen "Red Tails" of the famed 332nd Fighter Group flew with great distinction—graced one side of the hangar.[1]

By the time we got back on the tarmac, the late afternoon air traffic had become heavier. After we lifted off, we flew a direct course, chasing the sun to its setting hovering over the western horizon. The air was unusually calm for summer. When we reached cruising altitude, the Twin Beech felt as if it were sitting still as the lengthening shadows slid across the south Alabama countryside below us. The bright rays of the setting sun streamed through the cockpit's windscreen into the cabin, where Buddy and I were sitting. Down below the evening lights were beginning to blink in Montgomery and Selma as we headed to Columbia. The peace and serenity of the moment belied the upheaval that had taken place below in recent months.

I thought of Eade Anderson's decision to move to that part of the world, and what the future would be like for him. I thought of the tragedy at Selma's bridge and Epps's subsequent stay at Camden Academy. But most of all, I remember looking across the aisle at Buddy as he quietly gazed out the window at the dwindling light. I thought of all we had been through since first I sat in this plane with him. It seemed like an eternity ago, but it had been only a little over twenty-four months. Neither of us wanted to break the tranquility of the moment, which was in such stark contrast to the turmoil of the previous weeks. The scene had the feel of a private mount of transfiguration, one that we were reluctant to leave to go back down to earth. But the Twin Beech could not fly on forever, and we touched down once again in Columbia in the dark.

◆ ◆ ◆

Summer was an eventful time for our young family, though when it began we had no idea what dramatic changes lay ahead. One day Millye took Neal to see *Mary Poppins* in Hattiesburg, while I kept Walt for the afternoon. On the way back from Hattiesburg, the radiator cap that had not been properly replaced by the service station attendant came loose. The engine of our beloved Rambler overheated and blew, turning the block into molten sculpture. Neal loved the steam geyser spewing from the radiator as he and his mother sat on the side of the road! Somehow word reached me about their plight. Walt and I went to fetch the other half of my forlorn family. I arranged to have the crippled Rambler towed to a shop where the engine was replaced. It survived the repair and continued faithfully in our service.

Days in Columbia were dwindling down for N. A. and his family. The annual conference of the Methodist Church met at the Galloway Memorial Methodist Church in Jackson in mid-June. The highlight, at least for local pastors, was to find out if the bishop would reassign them to another charge. Methodists tended to follow the five-year pastoral cycle, with no vacancy that lasted more than a week. In some conferences all the pastor's family had to move were their personal belongings, because the parsonages were furnished. N. A. had been transferred from a church in Laurel to Columbia in 1961, so his five-year cycle was up. He was transferred this year to the First Methodist Church in Yazoo City, where Willie Morris's mother served as his organist. Dr. J. D. Slay, who had been the district superintendent in the Meridian district for the past six years, was reassigned to the First Methodist Church in Columbia where N. A. had been. Slay had been the pastor at the First Methodist Church in Brookhaven when I was in high school.

An article in the *Columbian-Progress* noted N. A.'s accomplishments as a church leader: "the construction of a new parsonage; enlarging the pipe organ; enlarging the air-conditioning of the entire buildings; removal of two houses for increased parking area; and increased giving to the Methodist Church and its programs." A church-wide picnic was held, and N. A.'s family was given "a beautiful TV set." Though not a word was said specifically about his contributions in community or race relations, the paper noted that, "Rev. Dickson and his family have contributed much to the local community and its activities," for which "best wishes and warm regards" were extended "as they move to a new field of ministry." Both Slay and Dickson assumed their new duties on Sunday, June 26.[2]

And so the rich personal and working relationship that meant so much to N. A. and me came to an end, as the Dickson family and the missionary VW Bug moved on to Yazoo. I do not recall how and when we said our good-byes, for I was gone from Columbia for the Sundays of June 19 and 26 and July 2. During that time I served on the staff of the Consultant Service Session in Memphis, a program of the Board of Christian Education of the Presbyterian Church U.S., which trained master Sunday school teachers of teachers. This period was also part of my allotted vacation time. I preached at the Senatobia Presbyterian Church on June 26.

June 26, 1966, was a red-letter day for the Columbia Municipal Separate School District and the State Board of Education of Mississippi. This was the deadline for either or both to file a request for a hearing to answer charges that the city schools were not in compliance with Section 602 of the Civil Rights Act of 1964 and the regulation of the Department of Health, Education, and Welfare. Failure to comply meant the district would lose all federal funds, amounting to approximately $150,000. The school lunch program was not affected at present. The Columbia district had submitted a desegregation plan in the fall of 1965, but the commissioner of education held that it was not adequate to accomplish the purposes of the Civil Rights Act and federal regulations. However, he would determine the adequacy of compliance for school years after 1965–66. He now alleged that although some parts of the plan were followed, the Columbia district did not comply. It did not give him assurance that its program would be conducted or its services operated in compliance with all requirements as currently written, as well as with any future modifications that might be made to them.[3]

Superintendent B. F. Duncan had received a letter on June 3 from Harold Howe II, the U.S. commissioner of education, outlining the details of the notice of noncompliance. Howe concluded by stating that "the matter is being referred to the General Counsel for further action and that 'all Federal agencies extending assistance to schools will be notified of this action . . . . [W]e shall notify these agencies in addition that efforts to secure voluntary compliance have failed. They will be advised of their opportunity to join in enforcement proceedings if they wish.'"[4]

The commissioner of education received several complaints about the free choice procedures used by school authorities, about school officials' attempts to influence choice, and about alleged corporal punishment by a school official of one black girl who chose to attend a white school. The staff of the commissioner's office made several attempts to urge school officials in Columbia to follow the revised guidelines, but to no avail. In addition to the complaints, Congressman William Colmer, Senator John Stennis, Superintendent B. F. Duncan, and the Office of General Counsel all wanted the Office of Education to initiate compliance proceedings. The department took steps to initiate an onsite review later in the summer.[5]

During the first week of October Harold Howe II, U.S. commissioner of education, wrote Congressman William Colmer a detailed response to the congressman's request concerning the compliance review conducted in Columbia. His request was made at a rules committee hearing on House Resolution 826, investigating the guidelines and policies of the commissioner of education on school desegregation, held on September 29–30.[6] Howe was very specific in describing the reasons for the noncompliance notice, saying although it had been accepted last year, "only minimal progress was made under the plan. No steps were taken to begin the desegregation of the faculty and very little was done to create the kind of atmosphere in which Negro parents would feel free to choose a formerly all-white school for their children." He added, "Under the plan only one Negro student was assigned to the white school. In other words, after a year's operation of the plan all of the faculty and more than 99% of all students were still assigned to Negro and white schools as has been the practice in the past."[7]

In other school related matters, a short article in the *Columbian-Progress* noted that, "Over two hundred students have been enrolled in the remedial program which will run for ten weeks at Marion Central." This was a program for students in the first six grades that "need special help to prevent failure in their respective grades." There was also a vocational technical program for high school students who, if they completed the program, "will earn a high school unit of credit." The newspaper noted that, "The entire program, including transportation, is being paid for by the Federal Government under Title I of the Elementary and Secondary Education Act."[8]

In early July, Frank Brooks and I went back to Memphis by train for the evaluation of the consultant service session we had worked with in June. After it was over, we rushed down to the Central Railroad Station on South Main to catch Illinois Central's No. 1, the *City of New Orleans*, to return to south Mississippi. Not long after we left Memphis, we passed Senatobia a little after 5 o'clock. I looked out the west side of the chair car and saw the old platform by the station where I had stood in the early 1940s behind bales of cotton to watch the fly-by of the new streamliner, the *Panama Limited*. We were told it was so fast that it could suck you into its side if you were not protected. We were very disappointed when it came through town at five miles per hour.

Before we got to Batesville, Frank and I made our way to the diner, where there was only one table left. Everyone else in there, including the waiter, was black. In a few minutes a couple of young black women came in and had no place to sit, so we invited them to join us. We found out they were from Detroit and that this was their first trip this far south. While waiting for an indeterminably long time for our food to arrive, we had a delightful conversation, answering their questions about Mississippi and what was life like here. When our meal was over and we were about to leave, one of the young women—in a loud voice clearly heard in the rest of the diner—complained about the service, which everyone had expected to be better. In determining the tip, she said, "To send the strongest message, the best way was to leave two cents rather than leave nothing." As we walked out of the diner, I noticed two cents prominently displayed on every table!

Frank and I took our leave and walked back to the club car. By then we were somewhere near Durant or Goodman. The *City* was rocking along at close to ninety miles per hour according to the speedometer in the club car. A white couple was sitting in the very back curved lounge with their daughter, whom they were taking to New Orleans to celebrate her sixteenth birthday. They had a birthday cake sitting on the coffee table and invited us to join in the festivities. Many a time in later years on the way to the Old Place as I crossed those tracks at Goodman—now used only for freight service after the Amtrak passenger service was moved to the Delta Division—I thought of what took place on the *City* that delightful evening. As we passed Brookhaven around 9:40 p.m., I was flooded with memories of the many times I had gotten off the *City* through the years, coming home from college or other far away places like California and Alaska. But this time I remained on board thinking about all the things that had taken place in the town where I grew up.

Around 10:30 p.m., we pulled into the McComb station, where ghosts of silent steam engines mothballed in the IC division point shop yard haunted my mind. As we piled into Brooks's VW that steamy night for the drive to Columbia, I could not help but think about the turmoil the community had endured of late and how it had changed since I first knew it. It seemed eons since the annual turkey day football game in 1951, when I came as team statistician to McComb with my Brookhaven High Panthers, who beat the McComb team for the first time in sixteen years, with a final score of 34–6. But my world was about to change again in ways I never thought possible.

◆   ◆   ◆

The temperature was again rising on the streets of Columbia this July. Efforts were made by the mayor to ease tensions, cutting some slack by printing up flyers the police were instructed to use. The text of the flyers read: "Welcome to Columbia—You have violated a Traffic Ordinance—Be More Careful Next Time—If we can make your visit more pleasant, Please Call us. E. D. McLean, Mayor, E. E. Johnson, Chief of Police." On the back of the flyer he placed in his file, the mayor had written some notes about a FDP parade on July 6. He noted that there were fifteen participants, "4 white girls, 1 white boy, Willis McClenton, mostly small negroes, <30 minutes at the Court House> Court House, 2:30—Main Street, 2:50—over, 3:15."[9]

On Friday, July 8, the mayor had a visitor, a law student from the University of Wisconsin, who was working with the Lawyer's Committee on Civil Rights. The two talked about the proper procedure for checking books out of the library and the use of restrooms and water fountains. The mayor cautioned about the use of the telephone, saying, "We expected rules of courtesy" to be followed.[10]

On Saturday, July 9, one of the most respected black educators in the state died at the age of ninety-six in the home of his niece in Columbia. Professor Preston Sewell Bowles, Jr., president emeritus of Alcorn A & M College, was a longtime educator and resident of Marion County. Funeral Services were held the following Thursday, July 14, at the New Zion Methodist Church, with interment in the Jefferson Cemetery. One of the presiding ministers was Rev. Amos G. Payton.

Professor Bowles was born in Claiborne County on September 29, 1869. He and his brother, L. F. Bowles, who was principal at Marion County Training School (now John J. Jefferson School) for twenty-two years, received their formal education by alternating years in school. Professor Bowles graduated from Alcorn A & M and attended Cornell University, after which he returned and taught at Alcorn, where today Bowles Hall stands in his honor. His presence was felt statewide, as he crisscrossed Mississippi establishing vocational-agricultural shops in rural schools as a representative of the extension department of Alcorn.[11] He taught for a while at Lampton in Marion County. No doubt the legacy of his opinions directly or indirectly influenced the character of that community and also the county.

Professor Bowles was teaching in Monticello when Marion County contacted him around 1898 about establishing the "first" Negro school in the county. Local historian Chris Watts, in doing research recently for a column he was writing about Bowles, said that it is inaccurate to say that Bowles started the first Negro school in Marion County, because some Negro schools were begun soon after emancipation. Watts contended that what might have been meant was that Bowles established the first "constructed" school.[12] Professor Bowles "believed a man should be judged by his character, as an individual, and how he worked to take advantage of opportunities." According to those who knew him well, "[H]e didn't mind expressing his opinion," as he did on occasion in letters to the editor of the *Columbian-Progress* and other newspapers.[13]

Although Professor Bowles was not directly involved in our efforts to bring about better communication between the races and the establishment of the bi-racial committee during 1964 and 1965, he was a strong advocate for such action. In the May 28, 1960, edition of the *Jackson Advocate*, he penned an article entitled, "An Appeal to the Christian Conscience of the White Citizenship of My Home County, Marion," in which he described bi-racial committees as the "Unquestioned Urgent Need of the Hour." He picked up on President Eisenhower's appeal "to all the people in all the States to set up bi-racial committees to work together, on the community, city, county and State levels, to study, to handle and solve our inter-racial problems as the only Fair and Christian approach to the situation that we are facing." He noted that a couple of weeks before he wrote this article, "our Mississippi State Teachers Association [black] numbering close to 8,000 members, in their annual meeting . . . in Jackson, reading the signs of the times, made an earnest appeal to the top-level white citizens of the State, to set up bi-racial committees at all levels where the interests of the two groups meet, as the only brotherly and Christian approach to the solution of our inter-racial problems."[14]

Sunday, July 10, the day after Bowles's death, was the time for the quarterly celebration of the Lord's Supper. It was the first Sunday since I returned from my vacation, and I decided to start serving up my three-part version of Walkup's sermons on the prodigal son, the elder brother, and the loving father. The first one that day was titled "A Fatal Demand," with the younger son's actions as the primary focus, based on the idea of "give me all that is due to me." I talked about how that fatal demand spelled the death of happiness, harmony, and peace when it becomes operative in the home. I said the same was also true of business and industry, where "give me" rules, whether on the part of the owners or workers, are fatal to prosperity. I noted that, "We are learning the lesson at the present time and are likely to learn it more thoroughly as time goes by" because "it is a demand that cuts short the consideration of others."[15] My point was that, "The greatest among you become . . . as one who serves." (Luke 22:26–27, RSV), a lesson sorely needed in a broken world where the spirit of 'gimme' must yield to the spirit of 'use me.'"

The following day, July 11, the U.S. Department of Education's review team, led by Mr. Lloyd R. Henderson, arrived in Columbia. The team had hired summer law students to assist in the review. Their duties included examining "various records in the Superintendent's office, visit the schools, and interview[ing] Negro parents and students to determine the manner in which the plan was being carried out and whether they under-stood their rights under the plan." They were not to give "expert advice on school desegregation to school officials." Neither were they "authorized to 'crusade' or 'beguile and entice people to use their choice one way.'" Lists of discrepancies were found regarding free choice forms and information about the plan. There were also irregularities in how requests by forty Negro students to enroll in formerly all white schools were handled and how transfers were to take place. Only fourteen of these students were admitted. The department made it clear that, "All pupils will be assigned to the school of their choice." There was, in addition, "some evidence that school officials attempted to discourage or prevent Negroes from attend-ing formerly white schools. They did not find, however, that all parents had been spoken to, as had been alleged." With regard to the corporal punish-ment charge, the black girl who had chosen to attend a white school had received such punishment, but there was "no conclusive evidence that it was related to her choice of school."[16]

On the church front, Dr. Charlie King, beginning the assignment given to the Presbyterian General Assembly's interim committee "to visit and examine this portion of the Church affected with evident disorder committee," on July 1 wrote James V. Johnson, Jr., Stated Clerk of the Synod of Mississippi, to make the appropriate visitation arrangements. Dr. King was of the impression that there was dialogue going on in all three presbyteries in Mississippi. If this impression was accurate, he hoped to meet with those groups. King asked if it would be wise for members of his committee to visit the presbyteries in the fall, and if so, could Johnson share with him the dates of the fall meetings? He closed his letter by writing, "I will be very grateful for your help in this delicate matter."[17]

Jim Johnson responded on July 14, indicating that he was uncertain if dialogue was being conducted between the two sides in each of our three presbyteries. He knew there was no such dialogue in the Presbytery of South Mississippi where he and I were members. He told Dr. King that the situation in St. Andrew Presbytery in north Mississippi was favorable to the group loyal to our Southern Presbyterian program. The situation in the Presbytery of Central Mississippi was extremely unfavorable to the group loyal to denominational programs. The Presbytery of South Mississippi was fairly evenly divided on denominational support. Johnson gave King the names and addresses of the stated clerks of the three presbyteries so that dates for visits could be confirmed.

Johnson expressed his feelings of disappointment that no one from King's committee attended the June 1966 synod meeting. Johnson was convinced that many things took place there that probably would not have happened had the pastoral committee been present. Johnson hoped the committee would want to attend the 1967 synod meeting. In order for the committee to attend, the General Assembly would be required to grant permission for it to continue laboring for an additional year. After Johnson chronicled some of the "inner turmoil" he had experienced during the eleven years he had been in the synod, he shared the fact that a group of ministers loyal to our denomination got together during the 1966 synod meeting and appointed a steering committee to meet with the pastoral committee and represent their views. Johnson expressed his gratitude to the General Assembly for appointing Dr. King to investigate the disharmony in the Synod of Mississippi.[18]

On Tuesday morning, July 19, nine days after I preached my "A Fatal Demand" sermon, some members of Local Union 2692, United Brotherhood of Carpenters and Joiners of America, were walking the picket line "at the New Orleans Furniture Manufacturing Company here as management and union leaders scheduled more discussion sessions in an attempt to iron out their difficulties." The main issue was over "pay hikes for employees who are union members and a request for a 'check-off' system whereby the union is asking the company to deduct union dues by payroll deduction." It was noted that the "picketing was orderly, and there were no indications of violence."[19]

◆ ◆ ◆

Jim Nisbet, former regional director of Christian Education for the Synod of Mississippi, had gone to the PCUS Board of Christian Education in early 1963 to help Will Kennedy launch the new Covenant Life Curriculum. Part of the program included a Department of Home and Family Nurture. J. Moody McDill, pastor of the Fondren Presbyterian Church, where William Winter was an elder for many years, left his pastorate early in 1966 to become an associate in that department. This left another void in the leadership pool loyal to the Presbyterian Church U.S. in Mississippi. McDill had been an outspoken advocate for racial justice, and this stance had taken a toll on him, as it had on so many other pastors.

The pulpit committee from Fondren, elected to find a new minister, came to Columbia to hear me preach at the morning worship services on July 17 and 24. I was truly honored, but I was not sure I was up to replicating pastor and church in another location in Mississippi.

◆ ◆ ◆

This last week of July turned out to be a busy week for the mayor and members of the Freedom Democratic Party. The mayor issued parade permits to the MFDP for five days this week, Monday, July 25, through Friday, July 29. Each permit outlined precisely the time, the route to be taken, and manner in which the "marches," as they were known in civil rights parlance, were to be conducted.[20]

The FDP still was not satisfied with the progress being made by the bi-racial committee, or with their own efforts to bring about change as a result of their Christmas boycott and picketing at Lampton's Department Store. On Monday, July 25, "Willis McClenton and one white girl" met with the mayor at city hall to present a list of grievances. McClenton complained bitterly about the bi-racial committee and asked permission to appear before it. The mayor told him that would be possible "by appointment only." The mayor noted that, "Sidney [was] threatened by 6 white boys on Owen Street," and that in the future "another patrolman [would be assigned] to go with Sidney" [assumed to be a black policeman].[21] The printed list of demands presented to the mayor by McClenton included: opening the swimming pools to the public; reforming the bi-racial committee answerable to the community with regular reports, meeting dates set, and regular elections; hiring three more Negro policemen who could arrest colored people and whites, acting as more than just "Negro catchers"; adding permanent Negro clerks and cashiers downtown, not just "broom pushers"; asking all Negro parents to register their children in "so-called white schools" with no further intimidation of children who enroll; receiving a report on streets that were supposed to be paved in June; installing more street lights, water plugs, and adequate sewage disposal; and making bathrooms public at city hall. And there was one final item: "Last but not least, we support the workers in their right to strike at the New Orleans Furniture Factory, and their right to organize." The FDP also circulated a flyer promoting this first march.[22]

The first protest march started with thirty-three marchers, including "4 white girls and 2 white boys, at the FDP house at 1:30 p.m. By the time the group reached city hall at 2:15 p.m., the number of marchers had increased to forty-five."[23]

A newspaper clipping in the mayor's file, identified only as a "Reprint From Yesterday's Final Edition" with "7-26-66" written on it, described this meeting and the staged "protest march on city hall." In it the mayor, responding to McClenton's demands, was quoted as saying, "All problems we discussed are under study by our bi-racial committee and have been for more than six months." He went on to say that "one Negro policeman is already on duty and another will be added to the force in the near future." He was further quoted as saying, "[T}he city schools are complying with the law governing their operation; and streets in both Negro and white sections are being improved as rapidly as possible. Regarding the swimming pools . . . they have been closed for some time and there are no plans to reopen them in the near future." The mayor reiterated that, "Our bi-racial committee . . . is well aware of all existing problems affecting citizens of both races. Any credit due for dealing with these problems should go to these members and not to some other group which may or may not represent the community."[24]

The mayor's file also contained a handwritten note from McLean marked "10:00 a.m. Tuesday morning," referring to the second march on July 26, spelling out the details in cryptic form: "FDP House—Nathan—East

Ave.—Lafayette St.—Park Ave to City Park—1:00 hour—Broad St to Main St to Lafayette St. Marion St. to Owens St. to West Ave to Nathan St to FDP House."[25]

Local police, along with Patrolman Flynt, Patrolman Tyrone and Inspector Henderson from the highway patrol, escorted approximately thirty-three marchers. The mayor learned via radio that an auto from Bogalusa joined the marchers when they passed the Park Avenue and Church Street intersection. The marchers reached the city park a short time later, then scattered to picnic tables throughout the park, with some standing near the tennis courts where seven or eight whites were playing. At 1:55 p.m., an FBI agent arrived at the park. The parade resumed along Broad Street at 2:45 p.m., passing the Texaco station at 3:00 p.m. and arriving at Main Street at 3:05 p.m. There were "4 white girls, 2 white boys. 43 persons in parade, 10 of these children, 13 years and under."[26]

I was away from Columbia on Tuesday, July 26, attending the meeting of the steering committee appointed by the group of ministers loyal to our denomination to consult with Dr. King's committee from the General Assembly. The committee met in the session room of the First Presbyterian Church, Starkville. The steering committee was deeply concerned over the need for reconciliation. If reconciliation were possible in some areas, the committee needed not only to study synod but individual presbyteries in great detail. Calling a mass meeting or visiting various stated meetings of presbyteries or synod seemed to be of limited value. We were of the opinion that it might be advisable to obtain from the general council of the General Assembly a full time staff person to hold interviews, and collect and organize the material. But most of all, we felt any delay in the work of the assembly's committee was ill-advised in that oppressed churches needed immediate help in obtaining the kind of ministers they wanted to serve them. The steering committee requested an early audience with the assembly's pastoral committee to convey the seriousness and extent of the feelings of disorder.

Specifically, the steering committee outlined several areas that needed special attention: the Commission of the Minister and His Work's contribution to the disorder in the way it assisted churches with vacant pulpits; the basis for determining suitability of pastors (i.e., which side they were on); issues created for ministers by Reformed Theological Seminary and how it related to Presbyterian churches for field work; stewardship records of presbyteries and church (i.e., the degree of dollar support for the denomination); and the actions of the 1966 synod meeting.

The steering committee also wanted the pastoral committee to pay attention to some miscellaneous items: distribution of the ultraconservative *Laymen's* publication; the Mac Hart case transcript; and the minutes of synod's special judicial commission.[27] The steering committee concluded its work by creating an extensive list of persons and groups we felt the assembly committee should interview to obtain different perspectives on the situation. We identified a dozen or so key loyal ministers, who had recently left the synod and needed to be heard.[28]

As I sat in that session room where Bob Walkup had lived out his courageous convictions, I was overwhelmed with the enormity of the challenge that lay before the steering committee and by my role as chair. This moment, in which I was being asked to lead the group, I felt the leadership mantle finally being passed from my daddy to me, though I had not actively sought it. Before I left that room that day I was overwhelmed with a deep sense of peace. What I thought I wanted, when I got it, I no longer wanted. It was not clear as I drove home to Columbia what that discovery meant for my future in the synod—or in Mississippi, for that matter.

The third march took place on Wednesday, July 27, leaving FDP House at 1:30 p.m., passing along S. High School, then on to city hall. The highway patrol contingent of Henderson, Flynt, and Tyrone was again present, along with Martin of the FBI and all the local police. The make-up of the group was very different from that of previous parades. There were no adults, although at one point there was a possibility two servicemen, one marine and one airman, were participating in the parade. Fourteen children, eight years old or younger, were among the fifty or so marchers. Teenagers, including two white youths, one of whom was very young, made up the balance. The parade arrived at city hall almost on schedule at 2:25 p.m. and was back at the FDP House at 3:04 p.m. The margin of the mayor's notes about the event contains a long list of license plates, some indicating from Louisiana and others labeled "on lookers." The mayor's final remark in his notes: "No Problems."[29]

By the time the fourth march took place on Thursday, July 28, it carried a routine feeling of familiarity. The group left FDP House at 1:30, escorted once again by Henderson, Flynt, Tyrone and Martin. The mayor noted that he "Put our men [local police] in autos and let them [the marchers] walk." The group started out with twenty-two marchers, but the ranks had swollen to thirty-three by the time they arrived at the police station. The mayor made a curious note: "Grupper missing." He did note that there were "two white girls and one young white boy present." Also, he indicated that there were three or four persons from Hattiesburg present, "including a Chineese [*sic*] girl." Although the group was smaller in number than the previous ones, the note concluded with, "Parade too long, cut out trip to City Hall."[30]

The same day, Mayor McLean, commenting on the recent closing of both city swimming pools in the *Columbian-Progress*, said the action was taken "in an effort to preserve harmony among all citizens of the community and to avoid possible strife being instigated by outsiders." He went on to report that, "[I]n recent cases of this kind—where communities were faced with unwanted problems demanding immediate action—the courts have held that the control of such city-owned facilities is up to the individual cities." He added, "The city of Columbia felt that it was in the best interest of all concerned that both pools be closed." He expressed regret over the action, "but it appeared there was a probability that incidents would occur if we did not," adding that such action denied "responsible citizens of Columbia the enjoyment they had in using the pools in the past."[31]

For some, this decision seemed to indicate that moderate white leaders were not fully prepared to deal with integration or the law of the land. It also may have seemed to infer that the mayor was claiming those pushing for enforcement of the law were causing the trouble by denying "responsible citizens" access to these public facilities. I can see now how this interpretation may have had some validity for some people, but I do not remember that such blaming was the mayor's intent. I believe, as he did, that the decision had more to do with his estimate of the "probability that incidents would occur" at the hands of those objecting to the protesters; in that moment this consideration—justified or not—took precedence over enforcing the law with regard to the operation of the pools. But I don't remember hearing much talk along these lines at the time the decisions were made.

On that Friday morning, July 29, in my capacity as chairman of the steering committee, I wrote Dr. King, chair of the General Assembly's pastoral committee, a letter in which I summarized the notes of the July 26 meeting. I expressed the committee's hopes that the assembly committee could get under way with its work as soon as possible, because there were situations that need prompt attention and would probably deteriorate with prolonged delay. I concluded with our request for an early audience with his committee so that we could give our perspective on the situation.[32] I would not be part of that meeting because this was my last official action on behalf of the steering committee. I still believed in the importance of its mission, but shortly after writing this letter, I resigned my position as its chair and walked away from the imaginary leadership mantle I had once thought so prized.

The fifth and final march of the week commenced three minutes behind schedule at 1:33 p.m. on Friday, July 29. Grupper and McClenton , along with "10 very small [children] 10 years and younger," were among the twenty-four initial participants. The route this time was more direct, going from the FDP House to city hall and back "with no trouble," even though, as always, the group picked up additional marchers along the way. Henderson, Flynt, Tyrone, and Martin were again on hand to help with the march. The only other comment the mayor made in his notes was: "Attitude of all police good & joking about marchers. General public seemed to ignore marchers."[33]

The following week the activities of FDP shifted to picketing stores on Main Street. On Monday, August 1, the FDP began picketing on Main Street in two groups, with ten persons in one group and six in the other. The groups communicated with each other using walkie-talkies. They walked the length of Main Street on the sidewalks with posters carrying a message along the lines of: no buying, as no hiring on Main Street. Around 4:30 p.m., fifteen protesters went to the city park to play tennis and baseball, leaving there around 6:00. The mayor simply noted on a piece of paper, "No Sweat." The same note included an entry that read: "August 2, 1966—eleven in one group on Main Street picketing at 1:30 p.m.–3:30. City Park—4:30."[34]

On Tuesday, August 2, John Paul Roblin, executive director of Pearl River Valley Opportunities, Inc. (PRVO), announced that, "Anti-poverty projects costing more than a million dollars [have been awarded] for the three county area of Walthall, Marion, and Lamar." He stated that the package included "a 52-week Neighborhood Youth Corps program and a nine month Head Start program for pre-school age children from low income families." The Neighborhood Youth Corps targeted "youths, age 16–21, from low-income families who have quit school before receiving their high school diplomas." They would work thirty hours a week for some public agency, "but will be required to receive at least six hours of education toward completion of requirements for a high school diploma. Pay will be $1.25 per hour." The director said that about 450 youths in Marion County could qualify for the program, and he "stressed that the program does not encourage dropouts as some critics have claimed." He also noted that there were three new Head Start centers planned for Marion County, creating many new job opportunities.[35]

The Thurman Sensing column in the August 4 issue of the *Columbian-Progress* made a quantum leap by assuming that, "The real authors of the riots are the hundred of professional agitators and their amateur 'do-good' helpers, some in clerical garb one is sad to say, who in recent years have shouted such slogans as 'freedom now' and 'we shall overcome.' They have incited the ignorant into believing that the public must provide them with instant contentment, instant wealth, and instant freedom to do as they please." These agitators and do-gooders, according to Sensing, "have preached civil disobedience and recommended lie-ins, kneel-ins, sit-ins and other forms of assault on the rights of the public. They laid the trail of powder that finally resulted in massive urban explosions in the Northeast and Middle West."

The riots Sensing referred to were the "looting and arson that have swept over Cleveland, Chicago and other northern cities in recent days." He had a point when he maintained that "This great nation . . . is entitled to civic order and a national life free of the kind of terrorism that engulfs many backward regions of the world." But he trivialized legitimate concerns by claiming that, "The leaders of the 'civil rights' movement of the Great Society have encouraged the notion that equality can be handed out like tickets to a movie." He concluded by asserting, "[T]he pendulum has swung far, far to one side. It is time that it swung back in the direction of strict law enforcement, hard work, and civil responsibilities instead of civil 'rights'"[36] His take on reality was somewhat different from what had been happening in Columbia.

The Office of General Counsel of the U.S. Department of Education wrote Superintendent Duncan on August 5, making four specific recommendations to bring the Columbia Municipal School District into compliance: 1) admission of all Negro children who chose a formerly white school; 2) new choice period with adequate notice to parents; 3) mail transfer applications to all students with those who requested transfers being admitted if qualified; and 4) provide for more faculty desegregation than proposed to date.[37]

On August 5, the FDP was issued one more parade permit, which had been granted by the mayor. The march was to be held on Saturday, August 6. The permit read like a carbon copy of all the others issued the previous week, laying out the times, the route, and the "orderly manner" requirement for the demonstration. It must have been uneventful, because the only record of it kept by the mayor simply says, "August 6, 1966, Parade—1:30 talked at Court House."[38] The season for FDP public demonstrations and marches had evidently dwindled and now come to a close, creating little attention.

Erle Johnston, Jr., Director of the State Sovereignty Commission, entered a memorandum in the commission files on Tuesday, August 9, indicating, "We have been informed that this subject [Ira Grupper] has been instigating marches in Columbia, Mississippi, and has been active in soliciting members for the W. E. B. DuBois Clubs, cited as communist front groups by J. Edgar Hoover." He also alleged, "We have been able to determine that Grupper and other members of his family are in Columbia and that they came to Mississippi from their home in Brooklyn, New York. We expect a more comprehensive report within a few days." The memo was copied to Honorable Herman Glazier.[39] Years later Grupper looked at the memo and informed me in good faith that the only truth in it was that he was from Brooklyn and that he was involved in the marches in Columbia.[40] The days of Grupper's involvement as an outside advisor for the local FDP were also dwindling, and only local leadership remained to provide guidance. Grupper told me he left Columbia some time in the fall of 1966, possibly in October, but returned to visit occasionally.[41]

❖   ❖   ❖

The Columbia McAtees joined the Bunn family (Millye's) at Many Islands Cabins on the Spring River at Hardy, Arkansas, on Sunday, August 14, and Sunday, August 21, for the balance of our vacation. Our days were filled with all sorts of activities, such as shooting the rapids in canoes and taking Neal to the doctor in Thayer, Missouri, one night to treat his burns from falling in the campfire. It was a great time to reflect on our time in Columbia. We were searching for clues to determine if it were time to move on and seek another call.

Frank Brooks was in the process of interviewing for a position with the Board of Christian Education in Richmond, Virginia. Jim Nisbet had invited Brooks to interview for the new position of Director of the Department of Worship. Brooks was worried about leaving Mississippi because he did not want to be far from his mother, who was seriously ill. He accepted the position, and as it turned out his mother died before he moved his family to Virginia. Her funeral was on September 4.

When Brooks went for the interview, I had asked him to check with Nisbet to see if there might be a position there for me. We finally realized that we would not hear anything from Frank before we returned from vacation, so we gave thoughts of a new call a rest.

◆ ◆ ◆

The Community Relations Committee got together for its monthly meeting on Thursday, August 18, with a variety of items on its agenda. These included a discussion of a hospital and doctor bill for Ray Hill in the amount of thirty-five dollars. More substantial items were: a discussion of economic opportunities for Negroes; having a joint meeting with people of the county to explain the problems before us; a resolution to the Chamber of Commerce concerning Negro employment on Main Street; seeking Negro workers on poll boxes in next elections; and getting Negro workers employed at city hall. The final item was to schedule a public meeting at John J. Jefferson High School to "Report to Our People."[42]

On August 31, at the request of the Office of General Counsel, a member of the EEOP staff phoned Mr. Duncan to see what action the school board had taken regarding its recommendations. Mr. Duncan reported that only fourteen of thirty-nine Negro students who had applied to a formerly all-white school would be admitted. He also said the board had not authorized a new choice period and had not authorized him to distribute transfer applications, acknowledging that, "[W]e are not complying with the letter of the law here." Desegregation of the faculty would be pursued only if the district received additional federal funds. Duncan made it clear that the "Board preferred to lose Federal financial assistance and submit to a court order rather than to take remedial action to meet the concerns set forth in your letter of August 5, 1966." In light of this information, the Office of General Counsel concluded that, "[T]he enforcement proceedings should continue against the school district."[43]

PRVO, Inc. continued to conduct studies in September that would lead to more projects aimed at reducing poverty in its three-county area. In addition to Head Start programs and the Neighborhood Youth Corps already under way, the studies now focused on: a program of remedial education for adults; a program to develop more job opportunities for low income or unemployed persons; health services to provide examinations and clinical care for low income adults and children, with special emphasis on rehabilitation and training of the physically and mentally handicapped; welfare services; consumer education to help low income families budget and buy wisely; a legal service to provide advice and counsel on contracts, financial agreements, and rights of the accused; and a program to establish multi-service neighborhood centers to co-ordinate and focus different service programs at the neighborhood level. John Paul Roblin, executive director of PRVO, Inc., indicated that, "We want our program to reflect the desires and wishes of the local people in this three county area," and to that end he welcomed "constructive ideas and suggestions from any citizen."[44]

With the special "wet-dry" election coming up on September 13, the dry camp was out in force. On August 25, the Improve Baptist Church ran an ad in the *Columbian-Progress*, stating that it "Unanimously Urges YOU to VOTE DRY. The Church on August 1, Voted as a body AGAINST liquor."[45] J. L. Watts was listed as chairman of the Church Dry Committee. The September 1 edition of the local paper printed "An Open Letter from Rev. Lloyd Weiss to Negro Voters." It said, "Negro civil rights leaders were urging Negroes to vote Wet in local referendums. Please hear us . . . . VOTE DRY!" The United Drys of Marion County, heavily supported by local Baptist churches, sponsored the ad.[46]

A different kind of ad appeared in the same edition of the *Columbian-Progress*. This W. E. Walker Stores ad read: "*WANTED* EXPERIENCED SALES LADIES for New Discount Store—Paid Hospital Benefits, Profit-Sharing Retirement Plan, Paid Vacations, Advancement Opportunities." After the contact information, the ad concluded with a special last line: "An Equal Opportunity Employer."[47]

In the second week of September, the U.S. Department of Agriculture expanded the number of counties in Mississippi, including Marion County, in which low-income families would be eligible to receive food stamps, replacing the commodities program.[48] By the end of September, the state Department of Public Welfare was advertising open competitive examinations for positions in the food stamp program in Marion County: food stamp visitor, food stamp cashier, and clerk I (typing).[49]

◆   ◆   ◆

On Wednesday, September 14, I flew to Richmond, Virginia, to interview for the only position that was open at the Board of Christian Education of the Presbyterian Church U.S.: editor of pre-school curriculum. Brooks had passed my inquiry about a position on to Jim Nisbet, who passed it in turn to Will Kennedy, the secretary for education. When I got to Richmond, I met with a Realtor by the name of Thomas Jefferson III, who showed me several houses on Wednesday night and Thursday morning. I was taken by the house at 1417 Bellevue Avenue and phoned Millye about it that night. She was a bit suspicious when I said I was contracting with Thomas Jefferson to buy a house! But the house sounded good to her. Tom took some Polaroid pictures of it to show her when I got back to Columbia.

I interviewed for the position on Friday morning and was reasonably sure that I would get it, but my application had to go through channels for official approval. They would notify me later. That was good enough for me. I called Jefferson, made an offer of $17,750 with $2,125 down and assumed the loan for the balance at 5.75 percent at $127.00 a month, gave him $500 earnest money, signed the contract, and flew back to Mississippi later in the evening.[50] This would be the first house I had ever lived in that was not a church manse. The words that Sinatra had crooned on a new release a year ago earlier kept flooding through my mind, something about not having time to wait for things to unfold when September days grow short as "autumn weather turns the leaves to flame."[51]

Sunday, September 18, was my thirty-second birthday. The sellers accepted our offer on Wednesday, September 21. William B. Kennedy, secretary of education of the board, and Harmon B. Ramsey, secretary of the Division of Systematic Study, signed the formal letter, dated September 22, extending me the call to be editor of children's work literature in the Division of Systematic Study.[52] Ramsey was a close boyhood chum of Millye's daddy in Jonesboro, Arkansas. I accepted the call.

❖   ❖   ❖

On Wednesday, September 28, Mayor McLean and the Board of Aldermen appointed Tom T. Rainey, Jr., as chief of police to replace Chief E. E. Johnson. Rainey, "well-known in this area," moved to Columbia ten years before, when he became the manager of the local A & P store. He now owned a grocery store. Rainey stated that, "[H]e will do the best he can, will enforce the laws of the city impartially, and asks the cooperation of the public in maintaining law and order in our city."[53]

❖   ❖   ❖

The Session of the Columbia Presbyterian Church met on Friday, September 30, to call a congregational meeting for October 9 to vote on my request asking the Presbytery of South Mississippi to dissolve the pastoral relationship between the Columbia congregation and me, so that I could accept the call to the Board of Christian Education. The announcement of the congregational meeting was made on Sunday, October 2, in keeping with the provisions of the *Book of Church Order*. On October 9, the congregation unanimously concurred with my request.

In leaving, I felt I had not completed everything I set out to do in replicating pastor and church in the usual five-year cycle, though I achieved a great deal. Circumstances required another kind of ministry, one that focused on seeking the welfare of the city. These two emphases in ministry were not mutually exclusive for me. Some wanted them to be. In spite of my mixed emotions about being tugged between the two, I received a great deal of solace from the fact that an overwhelming majority of the congregation expected me to be involved in the kind of ministry I had pursued while there. For this support, I was eternally grateful to them.

❖   ❖   ❖

Members of the Columbia PTA, in order to be "better informed on legislation regarding schools," gathered in the Crystelle Ford Auditorium on the evening of Tuesday, October 11, to be presented with different perspectives on school systems "operating under voluntary compliance with Health Education and Welfare Department Guidelines" and those operating "under court orders." Julian Prince, superintendent at McComb, presented the advantages and disadvantages of the former, while Kirby Walker, superintendent of Jackson, schools presented the latter. Prince contended that school boards "could possibly maintain more authority by voluntary compliance and that there would be less [*sic*] expenses because of court costs and . . . get every dollar possible from the federal government." Walker said, "Much of the time is spent in court—time that needs to be devoted to running the schools—and is very expensive . . . . [T]he court road is rocky."[54]

Columbia Schools began under the voluntary compliance system but later balked. Something happened between August 31, 1966, and February 14, 1967, that prompted the school board to change its position on revising its desegregation plan.[55] On that February day, Superintendent Duncan would mail a letter to all parents that had a one-line note at the bottom of the page: "Content of this letter required by U.S. Office of Education." That "content" closely resembled what the Office of Education had stipulated in its July compliance review: "[T]he purpose of the plan is to eliminate the dual structure of separate schools for children of different races."[56] The last legal step in the eradication of the separate but unequal educational system in the Columbia city schools had been taken.[57]

Adoption of the plan did not mean that it would be easily implemented, for there were forces that still did not want change. On March 7, 1967, Erle Johnston, Jr., of the SSC, would write a "personal" letter asking Duncan on behalf of Senator Jim Eastland's office "for the names of any of these [Negro] families who were in any way pressured by these [HEW] representatives urging that they send their children to the white schools." Johnston assured Duncan, "that we would have to get affidavits on an individual basis . . . if you can furnish this office, confidentially a list. . . we will make direct contact with the families."[58] I never knew what Duncan's response was to this request.

Thursday morning, October 13, Mayor McLean joined Bill Walker, his brother-in-law, for the ribbon cutting ceremony at the grand opening of Bill's new Walker's Discount Center, located on South High School Avenue at South Main Street on the site of the old canning plant. Bert Lawrence, president of the Marion County Chamber of Commerce, welcomed the new store to the city.

❖   ❖   ❖

I preached my last Sermon in Columbia, "I believe in the Forgiveness of Sins," on October 16, 1966, and wrote in my ministerial log, "C'est Fini!"[59]

The next day, Monday, October 17, Johnny Stringer sent his movers once again to load our household belongings on to his trusty moving van. We sold the smaller VW Squareback, with 9,000 miles on it, to Mrs. Daly for $2,000, packed our Rambler Cross Country, with its 80,000 miles and new motor, and drove out of Columbia north toward Richmond, Virginia, and our new home. We all were exhilarated with the spirit of high adventure that comes when a significant part of one's life is in the rear view mirror and greater unknown challenges lie ahead down the road!

Frank Brooks and I began work on November 1 for the Board of Christian Education of the Presbyterian Church U.S. in Richmond, where the autumn leaves had turned to flame. The days and years as Mississippi residents for these McAtees "dwindled down to a precious few" and were now history.[60]

CHAPTER 10

Another Reality

So, that is the story I promised to tell when Chris Watts, the curator of the Marion County Museum and Archives in Columbia, Mississippi, asked me to contribute to his documentation of the town's history during the mid-1960s struggle for civil rights. As I was telling the story, however, I became ever more aware of the fact that even the telling needed to be a collaborative task bringing together people with perspectives other than my own, who also sought at that time to promote not just peace in the moment, but lasting peace based on justice for all. My accounting was limited from the perspective of those active in the civil rights movement, who in a sense were "working the other side of the street." Although all of us were living in a climate of extreme violence and fear, I could in no way depict from personal experience what that experience was like for the black citizenry of Columbia.

Those born after these events might find it difficult to comprehend the magnitude of the cloud of fear that hung like the heavy humidity of a hot August afternoon over any person of color in those days. The ravages of the separate but unequal culture at its worst were still very much in evidence in those years. Violent events in Hattiesburg, McComb, Bogalusa, and many other communities across Mississippi fueled an all-consuming fear that was pervasive among blacks in Marion County.

In this highly charged climate during the period from 1964 to 1966, the local chapter of the Mississippi Freedom Democratic Party was a powerful player in the larger Columbia story. Curtis Styles, W. J. McClenton, and Ira Grupper were prominent leaders in that group that was more a movement than a structure with organization charts and a hierarchy of officers. It was a "free association." Just as I am the only living survivor of Six today, Ira Grupper is the only living survivor of that core group.

Summer workers and students came and went, but Styles, McClenton, and Grupper were the glue that held the Columbia version of the movement together. Local blacks were deeply involved in the movement, people like Mary Spencer, the Dukes family, and the Weary family. A few of the children and grandchildren of these families, and living descendants of other black families that were involved, certainly have memories of the time or have heard stories about the reality of the fear that was pervasive among blacks in Marion County in the mid-1960s. Without their perspectives, my narrative would be at best lop-sided and incomplete. I hope that others, especially in the black community, will one day complete this picture I have started to paint.

When Chris Watts was studying McLean's "Race Relations" file in November 2008, he ran across several names of people active in civil rights whom he then tried to locate via the Internet while performing research for me. The only relevant living lead he found was Ira Grupper, whose name popped up on the Civil Rights Movement Veterans website, which listed him as being with "SNCC, COFO, MFDP, 1965–66, Georgia, Mississippi." To our surprise, the site listed an address and phone number in Louisville, Kentucky. Ira was living an hour's drive from Lexington where I live! We also learned that after Ira left Columbia in the 1960s, he returned to New York for a time to "become a union organizer, among other things." Then he moved to Louisville to work with Carl and Anne Braden on the staff of SCEF (Southern Conference Educational Fund). He has been in Louisville ever since.[1] Our long delayed reunion journey for Ira and me to find each other took over forty years, but it was a remarkable extension of the original story itself, the story within the story.

When I first heard about Grupper from Watts, I was not sure if Ira were black or white. I was a bit skittish about what kind of reception I might get if I made a cold call to him. So I called my friends George and Jean Edwards, close friends with the Bradens in years gone by, to see if they knew this Ira Grupper. The Edwardses and Bradens were very active in the civil rights and peace movements in Louisville in the 1950s. The Edwardses knew Ira and his wife, Pam, well. I told them about my project and asked if they would be willing to call him and introduce me to him. They agreed to do so. After several days Jean called back to say she had reached Pam, but that Ira was in Vietnam on tour with a group of international socialists and would be back the following week. I could call him then, which I did. The first thing I said to him was, "You don't know me, but I know all about you!" This raised his defenses to high alert unnecessarily. We had a long phone conversation in which our tentativeness about each other gave way to respect that led to a visit in his home in January of 2009. He agreed to let me tape record our conversations.

This visit led to two more visits there, one in February and one in April. Ira was very cautious about accepting my initial proposal to place the tapes in the Marion County Museum and Archives because, he said, "[I]n reality, what I experienced in Columbia with the white power structure was less than hospitable." He wanted to know more about Chris Watts's role as its archivist and wanted to be assured that what he was doing at the museum was a "righteous" cause. In late February we set up a three-way phone interview so that Chris and Ira could share their feelings and expectations about the project. This call went extremely well, and we said we hoped that one day we might meet face-to-face.[2]

And so, with these events, a new relationship between Ira and me began to grow.

During my first visit with Ira, I asked him to tell me about his background and his motivations for becoming involved in the civil rights movement. Ira, in his own graphic and sometimes salty way, freely shared all sorts of stories about his early days and family. He was born in New York City in the Borough of Brooklyn in 1944. His family lived in a tenement building. His father was a welder who made a living that way during World War II and later became an accountant. According to Ira, his family never had much money but always had something to eat. As he put it, "People thought Jews had lots of money, but somehow that passed over our house!" They had to move out of the tenement when it was due to be demolished to make way for an upscale development. The family then moved into an integrated city housing project, "one step up the caste system."

Ira, as the child of Orthodox Jewish parents, went five years to Hebrew School when he was eight to thirteen years of age. He told me two things that stood out in his memory: the day he had his bar mitzvah, and the day after it, when he swore never to set foot in a synagogue again. He became radicalized when he learned about movements for social change in Africa, Asia, and Latin America. Because of this knowledge and his own experience growing up, he was well aware of the economic and social differences among people. His first recollection of the civil rights movement—beyond the activities in his housing project—was seeing Rosa Parks, in the mid-1950s on TV, refusing to move to the back of the bus. Later his interest was sparked by the sit-ins at Woolworth's in Greensboro, North Carolina.

His daddy was a progressive, but not a real activist. But one day he came in and told Ira that there was a picket line going up in the neighborhood, and asked if he wanted to go join in. Ira was legally blind, but with correc-tive glasses he could get by. Ira described himself as "a skinny little kid with pimples and did not want to be seen on TV like that." Nonetheless, he was excited by the prospect of the picket line. He went.

He said he was not one to go to the South thinking that everything was OK in the North. He knew better; racism was a universal phenomenon. However, he soon discovered that the focal point was "when the pimple burst in the South," where racial contradictions heightened to the point of antagonism and violence. He had to be involved. Ira was never arrested in New York because his mother was not sympathetic to civil rights. She did not want black people bitten by dogs in Birmingham, but she did not want her son involved "in that mess." Her idea of a way out of poverty for her son, who was smart, was to major in English literature, get a Ph.D., and then a good teaching job. But Ira said (in so many words, here redacted), that "was not my cup of tea, not because I was anti-intellectual."

In time, he headed south to Atlanta, where Ruby Doris Smith (Robin-son) hired him for his first job with SNCC. "I was not a major player," Ira said, without false modesty or self-deprecation. Ira worked in the research department of SNCC, where he learned some valuable skills and lessons. His boss had written a piece on "Life with Lyndon" about the good things that were accomplished in the cause of civil rights. What was troubling to Ira was that SNCC foot soldiers, who played an important role in bring-ing change about, were never properly recognized. One of the lessons he learned about doing research was, "When they screw you, they like it recorded!" He learned how to trace money flows, decipher demographics and voter registration rolls, and a host of other topics. This was not just a desk job. He got involved in demonstrations at Rich's Department Store in Atlanta to learn more about what happens on the street. He also got to know John Lewis, Julian Bond, and other notable young civil rights leaders who worked in the SNCC offices.

One day Stokely Carmichael was engaged in a debate at some SNCC conference being held in Atlanta and made an outrageous comment. Everyone seemed in awe of "the Lord" and no one spoke up to challenge the comment. Ira stood up and held his own with Stokely, although he personally did not consider himself a good debater. After it was over, a black woman came up and got in Ira's face and said, "I am Johnnie Mae Walker and I'm from Hattiesburg, Mississippi, and you are coming with me to Hattiesburg, 'cause you are pretty smart for a white boy!" Ira looked at her like she was out of her mind. "I go where I want to and nobody tells me what to do." A couple of months later, in February or March 1965, Ira was on a bus to Hattiesburg, because "there is a whole lot of trouble there and they needed Civil Rights workers." Ira discarded his official SNCC staff title when he went Hattiesburg, but he still thought of himself as representing SNCC, COFO, and eventually, MFDP.

In June of 1965, one of the largest demonstrations that ever happened in the movement took place, protesting what SNCC considered the illegal convening of the Mississippi state legislature to deal with voting laws because of the disenfranchisement of African Americans from the process. The protesters did not trust the governor's motives. They felt that his way of addressing voting inequities did not coincide with theirs. The protest culminated in what Ira referred to as the "Fairgrounds Motel." He was in the first wave of the 950 protesters arrested and crammed into big semi-trailer trucks to be carted off to the fairgrounds. The trucks had fencing on their sides, and their drivers would speed up and slam on the brakes on purpose. But these maneuvers did not stop the chanting and singing going on inside. The male foot soldiers were taken to large buildings on the fairgrounds that were used to house cattle at show times. The buildings were hosed down and the men placed in a large compound. The women and the leaders of SNCC were taken to the city jail.

After the protesters were booked in one compound, they were moved to another one nearby. To get there they had to navigate a human corridor, where they were prodded and jabbed with weighted batons by highway patrolmen and city police as they were herded along. Ira said he was 5 feet 9 inches tall and weighed about 136 pounds at the time. He was jabbed so hard in the back that he stumbled and fell to the ground semi-conscious. The next thing he knew he was being dragged or carried into a building.

The arrestees were trying to organize themselves in integrated groups, but the police would not allow them to carry through with this plan. One incident Ira would never forget involved a particular form of humiliation at the hands of the police. Officers forced the white men to line up to get their food, such as it was: two stale slices of bread with a stale piece of bologna in between—"and definitely no mayo!" They also received a cup of tepid water with some powdered milk sprinkled in it. The white guys then marched in line to one side of the building and sat down cross-legged on the floor. Not a word was said. They placed their cups in front of themselves, with the sandwiches on top. Then the black guys went through the line, and after receiving their sandwiches and cups, returned to the opposite side of the gigantic room. They sat down cross-legged on the floor in silence and placed their cups on the floor with their sandwiches on top. Without any pre-arranged signal, all the whites and blacks picked up the sandwiches and cups and "broke bread as one." Ira said that if he were a Catholic that would have been as close to holy communion as he had come. When Ira was telling me this, he was moved to tears remembering the thought that came to him at the time, "I'm a Jew and I am with those who are in distress . . . and that is what the Civil Rights Movement meant to me."

His injuries were such that he was sent to see an orthopedic doctor, paid for by the Medical Committee for Human Rights. The exam revealed no broken bones, only bruises and contusions. He was dismissed with instructions, "Don't go on any demonstrations for a while." He went to New York to stay with his parents to recuperate. When he healed enough to move about, he went to Washington, D. C., where he worked on legislative lobbying in the D.C. office of the MFDP at the time the Equal Employment Opportunity Commission was being set up. The creation of this agency resulted from civil rights activities and was, according to Grupper, "a concession made by the ruling class." After about six weeks, he headed back south to Hattiesburg.

Sometime during the spring or summer of 1965, while working out of the Hattiesburg civil rights offices, Ira met Curtis Styles at a conference. Curtis, the project director of the FDP in Columbia at that time, began talking with Ira about the possibility of coming to Columbia to work with him. Curtis was "a graduate of Southern University of Louisiana and a veteran of many civil rights campaigns," just returned from integrating the beaches in Biloxi on the Mississippi Gulf Coast.

In July, Curtis rented a house in Columbia at 623 Nathan Street from a courageous family by the name of Dukes, who lived nearby on Hendrick Avenue. The Dukeses did not walk the picket line for the movement, but renting the house, little more than a shack with no indoor toilet, was their contribution. Grupper emphasized that "having anything to do with the Civil Rights workers could mean serious trouble, even death . . . . In the winter, the only heat was from the fireplace. We chopped our own wood." That house became known as the Freedom House and was the hub of FDP and civil rights activities in Marion County.

A few days after Curtis had set up shop in the Freedom House, in walked Willis Johnson McClenton. Curtis would tell Ira later that all he said was, "My name is W. J. McClenton. I just quit my job. I am here to fight for freedom." W. J., "at best functionally illiterate," made it as far in school as the third grade, then dropped out to make a living as a pulpwood hauler. He was a powerful man with "massive physical strength." This was the beginning of a team of local leaders who would train and guide young northern whites who came to Columbia to engage in civil rights activities. Then in early August the Freedom House was firebombed. Curtis was listed in the newspaper as one of the occupants, together with other summer civil rights workers. McClenton's name was not mentioned.

In a long conversation with Ira, Curtis finally persuaded him to come to Columbia to work with him in the FDP in the fall of 1965. "You are an experienced civil rights worker and you are here for the long haul." The student summer volunteers were headed back north to school, especially the white guys who wanted to protect their 2-S student deferment and not be drafted to go to Vietnam. Ira took Curtis up on his offer and moved to Columbia, where he became fast friends with Curt and W. J. They "walked the dusty roads together; where the sidewalk ended and the dirt road began."[3] They would work together for a little over a year. During that time Ira became co-project director.

Life for them was far from a spring-break lark. Ira was very intense when trying to get across to me what it was like for them. After the firebombing and shots were fired into the Freedom House, the activists positioned their mattresses on the floor "below the bullet line," easily identified by the bullet holes left in the wall from the previous shooting. Ira's favorite saying, used to underscore their situation, was: "Paranoia is the fear of the unreal. This was real." The presence of the KKK was real. The local Klan leader, who lived nearby, was aligned with Robert Shelton, Imperial Wizard of the United Klans of America from Laurel, Mississippi. Their lives were in grave danger on a daily basis.

The occupants of the house were constantly watched, and they received threatening phone calls. They would get word passed on by some blacks, who worked for the city and were "considered 'Uncle Toms' but were not," that more bombings and shootings were about to take place. Rarely did these threats materialize; they were at best scare tactics. They felt these informants were "unbeknown to the white power structure," but one had to wonder if this were totally true, because the police chief had bragged about his "informants" watching the Freedom House. Were some informants working both sides of the street? Even if this suggestion were true, it in no way diminished the real threat that was ever present. The police had perpetrated vicious threats of their own.

Many times, Ira said, the occupants of the Freedom House engaged in gallows humor as a way to survive and used sophomoric pranks to divert their attention from their constant fear. On the day they got word that the Klan was going to blow them up or shoot the house up, he said, they decided to take turns staying up standing guard. Ira took the first turn for two hours or so. W. J. snuck out of the house when Ira was not looking and threw pebbles against the windows. Ira said, "It scared the [bleep] out of me." When his two or three hours were up, Ira said, "Curtis, it is your turn." Curtis responded: "[Bleep] you, white boy, I'm tired, they ain't coming tonight," and went back to sleep. Ira did not know what to do: take another turn or go back to sleep? He went back to sleep. Ira remembered "they" used to listen in on phone calls. Today you can't tell if your phone is being tapped, but then telephone taps were very crude. Ira remembered they would pick up the phone and say something derogatory about "Chief Johnson's momma," and then they would hear a throat clearing and the clunk of the phone hanging up.

At other times they sang songs to sustain themselves. One song was particularly poignant: "This may be the last time," meaning this may be the last time you will see us alive. Was this paranoia fueled by the fear of the unreal, or was this real? They saw the world in terms of black and white; there were no grays. In the middle of one of our interviews, Ira broke into singing a freedom song to make his point: "They say in Mississippi no neutrals have you met, / You are a freedom fighter or a Tom for Ross Barnett. / Tell me which side are you on, boy, which side are you on?" There was no middle ground!

For the FDP it was very clear. There was no nuance, no subtlety, no gradation. The law of the land said you should not segregate the races. There would be either segregation or no segregation, and the FDP was going to test the law. Ira said that did not make him a revolutionary or anarchist; it made him a law-abiding citizen, someone who wanted justice the way it should be according to the law. The law of the land was in direct contradiction to the laws and customs of Mississippi. It had to do with public access to schools and stores and jobs and the electoral process—all as a matter of justice. What the public perceived as anarchy in the streets was simply a battle against the segregated system, itself the antagonist of justice. And Ira said for challenging this unfair system, "I was regarded as a 'n——-loving outside agitator' who should go back to New York and take [your] 'commie views' with you." But he did not go.

There was "very little social intercourse" between the FDP and the white community in general. The FDP's desire was to gain the full benefit of law. They were committed to nonviolence, a concept they derived from Martin

Luther King's "Beloved Community." They were not interested in getting arrested as an end in itself. However, if the tactics of the "Beloved Community" did not work, they were forced to engage in different tactics to achieve their goals, and these tactics might lead to arrest. In their view, it came down to "us-against-them" so "we charged, taking the rams horns up to the walls of Jericho." The fundamental question was, "Which side are you on, boy?"

The pain and suffering, the visceral indignity and humiliation, the fear and injustice were universal and real. In 1965 the social structure in Columbia still was very much separate but unequal. Not all blacks subscribed to an us-against-them view, though there was no question that rejection of Jim Crow was universal in the black community. However, for many reasons some blacks sought other ways to "overthrow Jim." For this they were considered by the either/or hardliners to be "accommodating," a polite way of implying they were Uncle Toms.

There were other divisions within the black community. There were the educated, those with financial means, and some who owned property. Then there were the poorest of the poor, the have-nots at the bottom of the socio-economic scale. Each group chose different tactics, with varying degrees of risks, to respond to the dramatic social changes taking place about them. Some became activists, and some remained silent and invisible. Others sought a middle ground and they stayed away from trouble, working to improve their lot in life. Still others just continued to work to build a better world in the only way they knew how. Regardless of tactics, many were concerned not only for themselves but also for the welfare of their community. All were very much a part of another reality.

Ira came to know and love Miss Mary Spencer, "one of the most dedicated freedom fighters" he had ever known. "She was tenacious, determined—and kind and gentle as well." She did not have an easy life, for "she worked long hours in a white woman's house, cooking, cleaning, and then some." Then she would come home and do the same thing for her own family. She had little formal education, but she had "a real education in true life, in the struggle for a world free from racial segregation." She tried to "organize a maid's union in Columbia," but that effort did not work out because there were "too many separate workplaces." Nonetheless, this attempt showed her determination to build a better world. According to Grupper, her involvement with MFDP cost Miss Mary her house when the bank foreclosed on it.

She had fed Curtis during his earlier days in Columbia, and sometimes she fed W. J., too. She soon invited Ira to come with Curtis for a meal. She had a habit of standing while her guests sat down to eat. Curtis and Ira felt uncomfortable with this, but "did not want to disrespect Miss Mary in her own house." Another day they decided when the meal was served, they would stand up and eat. As gently and determinedly as he could, Curtis said, "Miss Mary, if you have to stand while you eat, so do we." She finally sat down with tears in her eyes, and Curtis and Ira did too.

When they got up to leave, Curtis gave her a big hug. After Curtis left, Ira, a self-confessed uncouth fellow with "a big dirty mouth," let out "a bad four-letter word." In response Miss Mary let out a set of instructions. "Boy, get you into the bathroom." "Boy, fill that glass with water and put the bar of soap in the glass." "Now, drink the water." At that point Ira balked and said, "I ain't gonna do that." "You what?" she said with her hands on her hips, blocking the bathroom door. So he drank some, and by the time he reached the front door he was sick to his stomach. She had one more question for him. "Now, boy, what have you learned today?" He answered, "I learned not to curse in your damn house!" She made a move and he took off. Looking back he saw Miss Mary "shaking her head, but also smiling like a Cheshire cat!" Years later Grupper told this story as part of his eulogy for her at her memorial service at Owens Chapel Missionary Baptist Church. She was eighty-four years old when she died.[4] A white woman she had raised was in attendance at the service paying her respects.

COFO disbanded in Mississippi in late 1965, and that had a significant impact on funding from outside sources for SNCC and other civil rights groups. Grupper said, "I lived for four or five months by my wits." Before that he had received financial support from friends of SNCC at Vassar and New York City sources. He would send them reports telling of what was being accomplished in the field. One report entitled "Two Counties" detailed Grupper's perceptions of the events he was experiencing in 1965–66.[5]

His perceptions about some events varied widely at points from my own. He offered other insights that gave new dimensions to some of those events. For example, he described in this report that it was his opinion that the 1965 black Christmas boycott "was very successful—80–85% effective among Negroes." It is not clear what he based that opinion on, but no doubt this sentiment could have been reflected among that segment of the population with whom the FDP had contact. The larger community did not appear as widely affected as hoped. From an economic standpoint, Grupper's view seemed to be in contradiction to the report given to the bi-racial committee concerning the very significant increase in the sales tax revenue during that period and the participation of non-resident blacks from the surrounding area.

Ira noted the FDP felt that, "Our demands were met with only token gestures." Ira said he conducted financial research utilizing the skills he had learned earlier and discovered that Lampton's Department Store was owned by one of the wealthiest families in Columbia. The tactic was to "hit them where it hurt the most," in the pocketbook, in hopes of getting FDP's demands heard and acted on. These families had to demonstrate to the black community and its white allies some effective form of change. Because of this goal, "they decided to continue the boycott," but limited it to one store: Lampton's. But before this tactic could be implemented, FDP had to concentrate its attention on the integration of the schools.

Ira spent long hours with Sammie Mae Weary—who was active in the FDP—agonizing over the decision to enroll her "sweet little girl, Dorothy" in the previously all-white elementary school. The Wearys had two children. Sammie Mae was a quiet person, but tough as nails. She and Ira talked about all the possibilities of what might happen. She would break down at times and cry, saying, "I don't want my daughter hurt." Ira was at a loss for words to describe the tension he felt as a white guy sitting there "encouraging the mother of this black kid to go into the belly of a monster, not knowing what might happen." Ira confessed it was difficult for him to function in the black community. Yet the black citizens had accepted him to the extent that he forgot he was white.

The decision was finally made to go ahead and enroll Dorothy. On the third morning of the New Year, 1966, Dorothy walked into that school and had no trouble from her classmates or anyone else. This did not mean that it was a fear-free environment for the little girl. What was not commonly known, according to Grupper, was that a segment of the black community was heavily armed when she went in. They continued to guard the Weary house well after that day. This protection became more significant when their house received bomb threats later in 1967.

One incident Ira related that may have played into the decision to be heavily armed occurred one day when he and several other civil rights workers drove to Bogalusa to meet with the Deacons for Defense. As they were approaching Bogalusa, he noticed that on either side and behind the car in which he was riding, several cars appeared out of nowhere and hemmed them in. It was obvious that the occupants of these vehicles were armed. His fear level rose, and he thought he was really in for it as the only white guy in the car. The escort took them to the location of the meet with the Deacons. What he soon discovered about the group was that they were not the dangerous group of militants portrayed by the white power structure, but in reality ordinary blue-collar factory workers and day laborers who wanted to be treated fairly, and who had decided to protect themselves in the hostile environment where they lived and worked.

Five days after Dorothy Weary integrated the public school system in Columbia, the FDP began the boycott of Lampton's that led to the arrest of Styles, McClenton, and Grupper. It was an experience that was forever ingrained in Grupper's mind, especially because of his ensuing arrest and incarceration. One rumor Ira had heard was that Chief Johnson was one of the biggest purveyors of liquor in the city of Columbia, and that his supply was stashed in the jail. During the time Ira was in jail he saw no evidence to confirm this suspicion.

After they were booked and frisked, the most significant part of his stay happened. Ira was put in a "white" cell by himself. Curtis and W. J. were placed in a "negro" cell next to him, but there was little, if any, difference between the two grimy cells. Ira made no bones about the fact that he was scared. Soon after the group was locked up, they started to sing along with their compatriots, who had gathered outside the jail. The chief soon put a stop to that. In a while a big, black, hostile trusty brought them something non-descript to eat. The only thing in the cell was a Bible, so he read that. He also managed to find a nickel in his cuff with which he etched on the wall, "Ira Grupper, Civil Rights jailbird." He wondered years later if what he wrote was still there.

Later that evening Chief Johnson came into the cell where Ira was sitting on his bunk bed. The chief was acting strangely. He said, "Boy, you ain't singing so much now," and turned his body so that his pistol was almost in Ira's face, a move that Ira interpreted as life threatening. He was now petrified and did not move a shadow. Ira glanced to the side of the chief and saw the deputy standing outside the open cell door with his hand on his holster. He then suspected that this was some sort of set-up. When Ira did not respond they left.

After what he had learned from me about what Buddy had been trying to accomplish as mayor, Ira understood that probably what happened to him in the jail cell with the police chief and deputy took place in secret. He still was furious that there had been no right to *habeas corpus*, no constitutional rights protected in that moment when his very life was in danger, as were those of Curtis and W. J. He said to me, "The white power structure should have known this was going on, and that included you!" I had never heard of any of this.

Much of the problem Grupper had with the mayor grew out of what took place around the Lampton's protest, his experience in jail and with subsequent legal issues. Part of the problem was that Ira did not see eye to eye with Buddy during the latter's service as judge at Ira's hearing. Grupper felt he should not have been found guilty of disturbing the peace because, based on his understanding of the First Amendment, he felt he had acted in a lawful way. He was protesting something egregious, not breaking the law by blocking the entrance to the store.

Grupper acknowledged to me years later that Buddy changed the dynamic in the community, yet not enough time had elapsed to change all his perceptions of what had happened in Columbia during Ira's time there. But he said what I had told him gave him insight into things he had not been cognizant of before. He asked, "Are you trying to tell me that what Buddy McLean did probably stopped the KKK from killing me?" That was a good probability, if only in an indirect way. However, Ira was not forgiving of Chief Johnson. Which side were you on?

It was clearly us-against-them. In Grupper's understanding of the situation there was no room for "syllogistic reasoning or polite conversation attempting a meeting of the minds," as Ira put it. There was no place in his world for the bi-racial committee, though in retrospect he confessed, "Thank God for small favors." Now he could agree there were certain things that had to take place so other changes could follow. But back then he felt the committee was so caught up in trying not to antagonize either side that it became impossible to do anything constructive. He did not see in the white community elements with which to form a meaningful joint relationship or a middle ground. Whites were in control; blacks were not. In the words of an old Yiddish saying duly translated in Grupper fashion, "With one ass, you can't dance at two weddings!"

From his perspective, the existence of the bi-racial committee did not immediately assuage fear in the black community. Too many people who registered to vote were denied. Applications for crop allotments from the ASCS were still rejected. People lost their jobs, and were otherwise harassed. Mortgages held by those owing the banks were foreclosed. Ira said he "saw this happening over and over and could not tell the number of times." It was not always clear that these things resulted from involvement in civil rights activities. They may have happened anyway for legitimate reasons. Nonetheless, they happened.

Furthermore, he was incensed that "his small ragtag group fighting for justice in Columbia" never was asked to meet with the bi-racial committee, whose members included the "most accommodating black ministers too afraid to march but only talk in meetings." Ira, during my interview with him, asked me why the local FDP leaders were not invited, along with the students from American University, to meet with the group of local whites on that Good Friday in 1966. He said the leadership of FDP did not approve the meeting, because they were afraid that, by itself, the meeting might give the students the impression that things were not as bad as they really were. I responded that the presence of FDP leaders would have changed the dynamics, and we had wanted the students to be exposed to a different set of citizens than they might otherwise have been or that they had imagined because of the southern stereotypes.

Ira and I did not agree that us-against-them was a lose-lose proposition. It was valid to hold an either/or position when it came to justice or no justice, to segregation or no segregation. But when it came to finding ways to make societal shifts a reality—dependent as we were upon building relationships critical to effecting change—the us-against-them proposition built a wall of separation that became impregnable. With little social intercourse between the FDP and the white community, the line separating the two sides became more distinct. Ira's axiom on paranoia—the fear of the unreal—became fear of the unknown. As so often happens, separation spawned speculation and in time became lethal when fear of the unknown degenerated into behavior that attacked or discounted the other person. It was only fair to recognize that both sides at times were capable of bad behavior.

Ira maintained that the FDP's outrage about the bi-racial committee was justified at the time. No doubt there were those in the white community who felt similar outrage about the FDP. But as Ira and I reflected on it years later, he was beginning to wonder "if there are times when you don't have to be so strident . . . Maybe we should have found a way to utilize that [opportunity with the bi-racial committee] in a way we didn't, rather than rejecting the whole thing." Which side were you on? I wondered: Could there have been a third side that could possibly have been win-win?

It must not be forgotten that there were other foot soldiers who were part of the fight for freedom. Some were very young and may not always have fully comprehended what was going on. Yet they knew the deep feelings of fear and humiliation common to the black experience into which they were born. Such were the eight children of Ned and Lucille Dukes. One of their daughters, Lillie Lowe-Reid, whom Ira knew as Elaine, recently wrote an article for Ira's column, "Labor Paeans," that told about her struggles in the civil rights movement in Columbia.[6]

She wrote that one of her earliest memories was of a march down Main Street. It very likely had been one of those that took place in the summer of 1965. "I don't remember how old I was, but I was very young. Almost too small to keep up with the pace, feeling like I had to trot. I remember we were running a little late, because my mother had eight of us to get ready, and when we arrived the march had already started. We ran to fall in with the others. I remember my heart pounding so fast and feeling panic because there were police present." Sometime later her parents announced that three of their daughters would be going to the all white school in the fall. Lola would be in the second grade, Elaine in the fourth, and Delores in the seventh. They were in the next wave after Dorothy Weary to integrate the schools. When the time came, they boarded the bus that first took Elaine to the wrong school. They "could hear name calling stereotypes shouted at us" along the way. "That entire week was hell for me," she wrote. Elaine was academically bright "but can remember getting low grades for work that I knew to be correct."

In later years, those who knew some of her history would ask: "Did they prepare you for what to expect?" Her answer was always, "How do you prepare someone to be discriminated against? Even an adult cannot be prepared for that. No matter what you say to someone, especially a child, you are never prepared." She was profoundly changed by her school years; some of what happened, she said, "I cannot remember or choose not to remember." In spite of all her difficulties she became a cheerleader, was in the National Honor Society, was elected into the Hall of Fame, and was senior maid and editor of the Annual Staff.

Her sister Delores had another unique experience when she reached the twelfth grade, by which time the school was fully integrated. She was among three nominated in the homecoming queen election and was the only African American running. The white vote split, and she was elected because there was no run-off. The family immediately began receiving threatening phone calls, "telling my mother if she wanted to keep her daughter alive, she would not let her get on that float." Her mother asked Delores if she wanted to ride the float and she said, "I won and I am riding the float," and she did. There was lots of tension, but no violence.

A very different expression of another reality took place in other communities across the South when religious leaders came from far and wide to join local people in their struggles for justice. The National Council of Churches of Christ in the USA (NCC) set up offices that operated programs such as the Delta Ministry Project in Mississippi. Volunteers staffed those offices temporarily to co-ordinate the influx of ministers and laypersons that came to work under the auspices of the NCC for a week or so. Many times these workers would be assigned to the projects COFO workers had going at the time. Local ministers, especially when the volunteers were members of the same denomination, would be greatly agitated by their presence and say, "You don't understand the situation here. You come in, just scratch the surface, then go home to write your glowing 'triumphalistic' reports of all the good you accomplished for the cause of justice, and retire from the fray proudly basking in warmth of thinking in that moment you did not bow to Baal." I even remember saying at the time to my northern liberal friends, "When they run you out of town, you can just leave; when they run me out of town, I have to go by my house and get my wife and babies before I can." These short-termers were making a contribution, but it took me years to understand the full significance of their presence.

The nearest NCC location to Columbia was in Hattiesburg, where Bob Beech, a Northern Presbyterian minister I referred to earlier, took Ira Grupper to visit Vernon Dahmer in 1965. Beech was part of the original Hattiesburg Ministers' Project from 1964 to 1966. The NCC's office where he worked was diagonally across the street from the COFO office, the one that Dwain Epps checked with on his way to Columbia in the summer of 1964. In early 1964, a stream of short-termers came to Hattiesburg to make their mark for the cause of civil rights. Not all fit the stereotype harbored by local ministers. The Reverend Dean Hay, minister of the College View Presbyterian Church, Lincoln, Nebraska, recorded the best example of this recognition in "A Hattiesburg Diary," where he detailed the experience he and other ministers had in early February 1964. His unpublished diary is worth a careful reading and helps one understand the significance of another reality.[7]

Hay expresses his sincere appreciation, "first of all, to the Session of College View Presbyterian Church, without whose knowledge I would not have gone." The session did not hinder Hay from going to Hattiesburg, because it believed "that freedom of the pulpit also implies the freedom for a minister to act where conscience compels him." Hay expresses his gratitude to members of the congregation for contributions made toward his expenses for the trip. Also, in the event of his arrest, a family expressed willingness to post bond for him. His diary started "as a very simple recapitulation of daily notes," but soon became something very different. As is the case with many such journals, it does not include every detail of the trip. He simply shares what he thought important with those who could not go themselves, because the experience "meant too much to me to be kept to myself." His daily log describes his mission of service and the risks it entailed: working with the Justice Department in voter registration; canvassing door-to-door, encouraging black people to register to vote; participating in "tea parties," so named because of the beverage served, that were pep rallies to encourage the disenfranchised; joining a picket line around the court house, protesting the failure of the county registrar to certify black applicants as literate or eligible, even though some were seminary professors, school teachers, and other professionals; sharing in meetings that focused on building self-respect; enduring all sorts of harassment by the white community; and yes, taking time to fix a cranky mimeograph machine in the SNCC-COFO office!

But all was not work. To their delight the short-termers were exposed to real southern cooking on occasion. It was delicious, consisting of "the inevitable fried chicken, black eyed peas with ham hock, green beans with large chunks of sow belly, turnips chopped with the greens and cooked with pork, hot spiced peaches, spiced pears, several kinds of potato salad, several kinds of cake, a plate of fancy club sandwiches, skillet bread, and lots of chicory coffee."

As he prepared to leave, he writes, "So, you ask, 'What did you accomplish?' In all honesty, I must answer, 'I do not know.'" But this he does know: "I could not help but think about the ease with which the ministers would soon be out of the community and free of the tension, barring some unexpected incident still possibly to occur; it was humbling to consider the dedication of those who could not leave, but who would stay here in Hattiesburg day after day, week after week, year after year, fighting for their rights until they were won, at the risk of their lives."

Dwain Epps, reading the diary years later, gave it good marks saying, "The Hattiesburg write-up is not bad at all. It conveys a good sense of the SNCC training they got, showing that the operation was well-organized and disciplined to keep individual visiting hot-shots from stepping over the line." It does not claim more than was done. One example is the way Hay admits that the results of his group's voter registration efforts "were meager." Epps contended that these efforts still had long-term value. National

awareness about such problems were raised by this and other similar recit-
als in local congregations around the country, going a long way towards
fostering a political climate supporting the Johnson administration's civil
rights legislation. Hearts and minds do change, and congregations remember the universality of the church. All would be worthwhile if, in hearing
these stories, doors are opened for interracial contacts between blacks and
whites in congregations in their own communities beyond the South.

A sense of serendipity colored the experience of Ira and me finding
each other after these intervening years since Columbia. Together we
watched in awe as the initial reticence between us became transformed
into a special new relationship, as each let go of preconceived notions
about the other. Each of us had looked at what was accomplished in the
cause of civil rights and justice in Columbia during the 1960s as if it were
solely dependent upon what our own respective group had done—for me,
the mayor, the bi-racial committee, and Six; and for Ira, Styles, McClenton,
and the FDP. Ira and I came to believe that both groups were vital in keeping a creative tension in play. Had the mayor and his initiatives not been in
place when FDP took "the rams horns up to the walls of Jericho," the situation might have deteriorated into violence and destruction. By the same
token, had FDP not engaged in peaceful and nonviolent tactics, the white
power structure might have been less open to change. Authenticity existed
in both group's experience, and each needed the other to bring out the best
in both.

Ira and I came to realize that this process of changing separate but
unequal to liberty and justice for all required many different tactics.
Sometimes each of us thought that the tactic with which we were involved
was the tactic that made the difference, to the exclusion of the tactics of
the other. When one was relied on to the exclusion of the other, the first
became counter-productive and at times oppressive

The tactic employed by SNCC, the Mississippi Freedom Democratic
Party, and the local FDP, as I have come to understand, was nonviolent
exercise of constitutional rights of freedom of speech and assembly to protest egregious injustices brought on by unjust laws and customs perpetrated by the dominant power culture. The civil rights activists took to the
streets especially on behalf of the poorest of the poor, the disenfranchised,
and the under-educated. Theirs was a simple and elegant position: "Grant
us what the law of the land—the Constitution, the Civil Rights Act of 1964,
and the Voting Rights Act of 1965—says rightly belongs to every citizen."

The tactic the mayor and others of us employed, as Ira came to understand, also repudiated egregious injustices brought about by unjust laws and customs of the dominant power culture. Yet, our approach involved working within the dominant power structure to bring about changes granting to all citizens what rightly belonged to them. This tactic was committed to bringing about change in the most peaceful way, with the least violence possible, so that the fabric of the community was held together in order to create a more just and civil society. It took a great deal of political savvy and finesse to navigate those turbulent waters in the separate but unequal culture.

Although some of us in the white community were involved in working within the dominant power structure to bring about change, some of us remained silent. Others violently and vocally resisted change. Those who held this last position viewed the tactic of taking to the streets as anarchy, and viewed the tactic of working within the dominant power structure to bring about change as traitorous, with both approaches constituting an assault on our way of life. For this group, it was "them against us."

As our conversation unfolded, Grupper was surprised at the accomplishments of enlightened whites. He acknowledged, "I am now coming to understand your position, and more and more its vision. Although I don't completely agree with it yet, I now see the significance of your book. The value of the two positions, yours and mine, remain in creative tension." My own estimate of what he had done grew exponentially. We totally agreed that there was no middle ground between justice and injustice. We both were about moving the culture from one condition to another, to repudiating injustice in all its forms, to establishing justice for all as guaranteed by the Constitution and by all moral and spiritual standards of God and humanity. That was our goal, and it was no small or simple undertaking. Equal opportunity was win-win; anything less was unacceptable.

However, it was a very dramatic and volatile undertaking to work for that goal, given the separate but unequal environment in which we lived. There were great risks for all involved, which varied in intensity according to individual circumstances. I came to learn firsthand that Ira's experience was far more dangerous and traumatic than mine ever was, yet he still remained committed to nonviolence as a tactic. He came to believe, as he listened to me, that I was a righteous Christian. I was opposed to violence as a revolting anathema to Christian beliefs, yet I realized that had I taken a public stand, as he did, I would have been put out of the community.

We came to understand from our later vantage point that although we had played a part in moving that process along, we did not finish the job despite the great risks we had taken. Each generation must learn the necessity of contributing to moving change along, and it became clear to Ira and me that it was incumbent upon us to tell our stories.

As I listened to Ira talk about his experience with the Columbia Freedom Democratic Party, my whole perception of the phenomenon became radically humanized. He described that "rag-tag group of freedom fighters" as "a band of brothers (now add sisters) and a circle of trust." He made it clear it was "not over dramatic to say we learned to love one another; learned how to respect people of different sex, origin, nationalities, as human beings." He went on to say, "I like to think people are not intrinsically good or evil. Given the proper atmosphere, people will behave well toward one another . . . . I would like to think under most dire circumstances, people could love one another and we did in the midst of such terror. [He started to cry as he spoke.] It was all so surreal. You talk about ways the white and black communities tried to work together, we did not know if we were going to live." Ira acknowledged, "All of us in the civil rights movement were victims; we had racism. There was no purity; we were not inoculated because we got wasted or faced dire circumstances. But the 'Beloved Community' was not some sappy stuff. It was true. It changed my life. We thought we were building it. Those of us still living remain friends after all these years."

It felt like a sacramental moment, and I felt drawn into Ira's band of brothers and circle of trust because it was so akin to what I had experienced in Six. We now were reliving in a small way a twenty-first-century version of those "bands of brothers and circles of trust," thanks to risking an open dialogue, the stuff out of which true reconciliation is made. We both lamented the fact that we had not met long ago—but we both knew that probably could not have happened. Ira and I got almost euphoric thinking about what might have been if Curt, W. J., Isaac, L. Z., Amos, N. A., and Buddy could have lifted a cup and broken bread with us, but the wall of "us-against-them" was too tall to climb at that earlier time. At least the two of us now, decades later, were willing to listen to each other and were growing in mutual respect despite divergent experiences and beliefs. In that process, we were learning anew that it was possible for something special to take place, whereby hearts and minds were transformed.

Some may look back over the almost half century since these events took place and ask, "What was the lasting impact of these two different efforts to bring about justice for everybody in the community in the mid-1960s?" Some may have good reason to answer, "very little, especially in attitudes toward race." Sometime during the 1980s, Grupper had a conversation with his good friend, Anne Braden, herself a longtime advocate for racial peace and justice, when this question came up. She approached it this way: "When you look back at the economic situation and the racial divide and say, 'what has changed?' If you look at the 1950s, would you really want to go back to that time, and if you don't, then you have to say, 'something did come out of it.' And so for those who say 'nothing has changed; well, there's the economic system, there is this and that.' But there were things that happened. If you minimize those, ignore those, if you don't pay attention to them, then nothing has changed. Then you are not really understanding the historical context."[9]

Here was an additional reason why capturing another reality was such a critical part of the overall narrative of this book.

PART III

Reflection

CHAPTER 11

Thank You, Mr. Mayor

As memories of Buddy McLean flood over me, something Ted Kennedy said about his slain brother Robert seems also to be a true and fitting remembrance of Buddy: "[He] need not be idealized or enlarged in death beyond what he was in life, to be remembered simply as a good and decent man, who saw wrong and tried to right it, who saw suffering and tried to heal it . . . ."[1] In his own way, Buddy faced conflict and found creative ways to resolve it. What he did in those years as mayor of Columbia did not reward him with the acclaim bestowed on other high profile leaders of his day. He certainly did not seek adulation, though it certainly was deserved.

Buddy was ordinary, ordinary in the sense that during his tenure he left no collection of papers outlining his understanding of the intricate working of municipal government, or a record of speeches he made stating the positions he had taken on with quiet dignity regarding the weightier aspects of race relations. As with so many other moderate white southerners, the positions he took and the transformations in his personal life are hard to know. Yet it is fair to ask what personal qualities he possessed that made him capable of making a difference in the situation that prevailed in Columbia in the mid-1960s. Glimpses of his wisdom and the thoughts that motivated his life and public service can be found in three places: in his eulogy for John F. Kennedy, in the way he approached his responsibilities as mayor, and in his brief report of his first eight months in office.

For Buddy, his public tribute to John Kennedy at the memorial service on November 25, 1963, was not merely a moment of private introspection, but an opportunity for public inspiration. From "the thoughts that have come to my mind during these dreadful hours," he hoped "that in some way we might leave here more dedicated to share our responsibilities as citizens of this great nation." He went on to say, "[t]he first real shock and feeling of guilt in this horrible event" was when his ten-year-old daughter came home and told him that students in her classroom cheered when they were told of the death of President Kennedy. His first thought was, possibly to ease his conscience, "Well, they are just too young to know better." But then he asked himself: "Wasn't this really a reflection of my image, a mirror reflecting my beliefs, my degrading the highest office in the land? Am I not guilty?" He continued: "Haven't I said in jest that we would be better off if Mr. Kennedy was dead? Haven't I just supported a political campaign whose paramount theme was to do away with the Kennedys?" He went on to ask, "Must I not share the guilt for the attitude of the youth of my community?" Although he felt many in the community might see his concern as insignificant, to Buddy it crystallized his failure. It was obvious he did not want the cheering of the death of the leader of the greatest land on earth to be his image. But he questioned, "If I allow this to continue where shall it end? Shall I not reap what I sow?"

On hatred and vengeance he was equally eloquent. As he watched the tragedy of Kennedy's death unfold before him, he thought of the hate and vengeance portrayed by such an act, and how this same hate showed "its ugly face throughout our beloved Southland today." One of the most common remarks he had heard recently was, "Thank God it didn't happen in Mississippi." He felt the question should be, "Could it have happened in Mississippi?" For him, this was the real concern of responsible citizens. He was appalled at how far as citizens, "and above all as Christians," some had gone, degrading themselves. He wondered if true Christians could hate with vengeance and still have Christ share their hearts. He believed Christ felt nothing but compassion for those who crucified him, as witnessed in the scripture read that day: "Father, forgive them, for they know not what they do." Then he asked the congregation, "Can we as followers of this Christ leave here today with hate in our hearts? Where are we headed? What is our image?"

Reaching deep inside, he uttered a prayer of thanksgiving and poured out a lament of compassion, then called for a season of public contrition. "I thank God that he has given to me the feeling of compassion for those about me, that I can actually shed tears for both sorrow and beauty." He was deeply saddened by any individual who could not feel compassion; such a person "is indeed unfortunate." In striking and poetic prose, he said, "One of the most beautiful remarks of yesterday was that the quietness of the rotunda was so still it almost cried." He acknowledged that, "Though we in the South differed greatly in our beliefs from those of our late President, IF we could not in the last few days feel compassion for his loved ones, we had best examine closely our own hearts."

Finally, he could not help but marvel as he watched current events, some only moments after they had happened and others unfolding before his very eyes. Yet, even as he thought of the progress made in communications, he was struck by the thought of how we have "failed in learning to live together." He concluded: "We have had the blueprints to accomplish [living together] since the first year of our Lord—Our Holy Bible—but we have never learned to follow them. How Tragic." Buddy was not satisfied simply to wallow in personal or communal guilt as some white southerners have done over time. He chose to move forward in positive ways by taking action.

This eulogy is not the only record he left of his take on what was happening around him. Another was the pragmatic and principled way in which he approached his responsibilities as mayor, making first attempts to shape and direct the tectonic societal and cultural shifts taking place. Buddy, totally rejecting what Gladwell in later years described as a violent "culture of honor" mentality and behavior,[2] made the most of Gladwell's "being a beneficiary of hidden advantages and extraordinary opportunities and cultural legacies" for the good of the community.[3] He was a quick learner and a keen observer whose gifts helped him work smart and make sense of the world around him in ways others did not.

As part of the economic power structure of Columbia, Buddy used his position for positive change. For that reason, he was not vulnerable to financial intimidation when taking the stands. So many other politicians across the state were not as fortunate. His decision to run for mayor was not a matter of satisfying personal ambitions or an expression of his feeling of competence in the field of governance. Buddy was a competent licensed pilot with World War II flight experience, but he was the first to acknowledge that he was not perfect and that too often he later had to fly by the seat of his pants in administering the business of the city and was no legal eagle when it came to functioning as a judge in the city court. But he ran for mayor out of a deep concern for righting wrongs and injustices of the past. He received criticism from certain segments of the white community, but he said that did not bother him "as long as he knew he was doing the right thing."

He had an innate understanding of the proper use of power and influence and used both to good advantage in exercising his authority and fulfilling his responsibilities as mayor. He knew clearly what parts of the system had the power to make binding decisions, and what parts of the system could rightly be partisans, either in influencing that system to function well or in disrupting it.[4] Fundamental to his approach to governance was his belief in organizing the entire community behind responsible leadership. Key to that was encouraging wider participation in the electoral process by all citizens. He sought the guidance of law enforcement agencies and legal experts in the proper protocol regarding the rule of law and due process, concepts to which he was firmly committed. He also reached out to Six for advice about building an informal communication system linking the natural centers of influence in all sectors of the black community.

Another way Buddy got the wider community involved in creating change was by involving himself in the selection process for members of the bi-racial committee. He saw to it that the larger gatherings of whites and blacks determined the process. He made sure the bi-racial committee's mandate and responsibilities were clearly defined, and that equality was established in the way the committee was oriented. The existence of this committee underscored his belief that this was the most constructive vehicle for successfully negotiating improvements in the community by means other than demonstrations, picketing, and marches. That is not to say he underestimated the significance of those other methods, and he openly engaged with those from SNCC and FDP. His approach proved productive in that these groups did not feel it necessary to seek help from outside civil rights organizations and individuals in exerting pressure on the white power structure to accomplish their goals.

Buddy demonstrated his commitment to fair and just application of the law in many ways, including: his instructions to the police on how they should conduct themselves; his willingness personally to step into a volatile situation and make an arrest when it was being mishandled; his bending over backwards to reduce the sentences he rendered in court against civil rights workers; the concern he exhibited with parents of summer civil rights workers when their children came in harm's way; his thoroughness in advising those engaged in picketing on the acceptable boundaries for those activities; and his precision in defining and issuing parade permits. He testified to his belief that the greater the involvement in preparation for what was coming, the better the results in briefings he held with business, school, and civic leaders, keeping them up-to-date on recent and unfolding developments. He encouraged compliance in both private and public sectors with the new civil rights legislation regarding hiring practices and access to public accommodations. In his administrative role as mayor, he worked with the fire department, the water department, the sanitation department, the police department, and the street department to see that they were implementing all policies and decisions of the board of alder-men in all sectors of the community as fairly and as promptly as possible. He utilized the newspaper, churches, and civic organizations as commu-nication channels through which to make regular progress reports to the community. These were some examples of how the mayor conducted him-self that gave a clue as to the measure of the man.

He presented a glimpse of how he perceived the problems of the future in a report he made about what he had learned in his first 250 days in office.[5] "The greatest challenge to each of us is the handling of our race relations. No longer can we afford the luxury of facing these problems with a negative attitude and waiting until we have to do something," he said. He was proud of the fact that "This community has shown remarkable prog-ress in facing these issues honestly and doing things that should be done to have law and order." His use of law and order here was not uttered in the old sense; it was not used to perpetuate racial segregation through the legal means, as in the past. His whole approach to leadership in local gov-ernance was based on the fact that, in order to avoid chaos, there must be an enforceable structure based on laws that make sense, providing protec-tion for the rights of all citizens, not just the privileged few. This approach gave new meaning to the term "law-abiding citizens."

The mayor inserted parenthetically in his report, "I have had leaders from both sides tell me that our city is a rare one indeed, that both races should be proud of the relations we share together. I hope and pray that we can keep it this way." He was proud of what had been achieved by the bi-racial committee, "a perfect vehicle for communications between the races." He cited the fact that "during the recent Christmas holidays I am sure that members of this committee were responsible to a great extent in preventing a partial boycott of this community."

He hastened to point out that he had learned a couple of things in his "brief experience with civil rights matters." First, "the comment that we have the best Negroes in the South and they don't want any part of this 'Civil Rights movement' is basically incorrect." He felt that statement was an underestimation of "just how responsible our local Negro citizens are, for this community owes them much." Again, he was not merely say-ing that "accommodating Negro leaders" were doing "our bidding." "Our Negroes are very happy here in Columbia," was something he was keenly aware was not the case. He knew well that during the previous months, "they could have blown the lid off this town if they had so desired and there would have been nothing we could have done." It was obvious to the mayor that, by far, the majority of the blacks of Columbia wanted "all the rights of first class citizenship that are guaranteed under our present laws . . . and deserve them . . . and are entitled to them."

The second thing the mayor said he learned during these eight months had "to do with who will control what action the community will take concerning civil rights requests, or the implementation of the new civil rights laws." In saying in his report that "You must keep control of your local citizens of both races," his use of "control" referred to his understanding of law and order, one making it possible for a community to remain civil by establishing an enforceable structure based on laws that made sense, providing protection of the rights for all citizens. I heard him say on several occasions to various leaders in the community, both black and white, "We can do it ourselves, or somebody will come in from the outside and do it for us. It is as simple as that." He wisely knew that, "When local communication breaks down and the outsiders step in to help either side, then you are bound to have trouble." For him, that was "why our bi-racial committee was so very important" to keep the conversation going.

Buddy would be the first to admit that the progress made under his leadership must not be overstated. He knew these small first steps, for some, were far too great a departure from "our way of life." At the same time, he would also acknowledge that for others these steps were far too small to get us beyond the injustices of the past. Yet he was very proud of Columbia, as was clear when he said, "I feel that we are way ahead of most communities and if we will continue on the pattern that we have set over the last eight months, we will develop within our confines a way of living together that all others will eventually realize is the only logical way."

This was Buddy's leadership moment in time when he edged Columbia along the spectrum from a closed, secretive society to one that was more open and collaborative—at least as far as institutional change was concerned. He brought leadership segments of the community, both black and white, together to face difficult challenges and to prevent the community from being destroyed by violence and division. Through it all they found a way to work together to make it a better place. He knew that attitudes were another matter, requiring more than a couple of years to change, yet his contribution was a welcome beginning.

There is no question that when he came into office the moderate white leadership of which he was a part was not fully prepared to face the impact of the Civil Rights Act of 1964. One can appreciate the extraordinary role he played in helping Columbia face the wider problems of society and the implications these raised for everyone involved when one contemplates the historical and contemporary context in which he had to operate. As mayor of Columbia, he overcame powerful obstacles in an extremely complex and volatile environment. The progress made in Columbia was a tribute to his wise and courageous leadership.

Buddy McLean served a second term as mayor of Columbia. He continued to administer the office in the same manner he had during his first term, although he was not faced with the same kind of events. Some of the events from his second term were mentioned in news stories in the *Columbian-Progress*. There are a few letters and notes in his race relations file. He received one somewhat ironic memorandum dated July 7, 1971, in his day job at the T. C. Griffith Agency, from Charles H. Otis, Planning and E. O. Officer of PRVO, Inc. Otis was checking on equal opportunity practices in various local businesses. He had been one of the original members of the bi-racial committee in 1965. He pointed out in his memo that businesses were prohibited under Title VI of the Civil Rights Act of 1964 from receiving "federal funds to be spent and deposited where vendors practice discrimination. Therefore, I am suggesting that you forward to this office a copy of your firm's EEOC to determine it's [sic] hiring practices. I am also suggesting that your agency establish an affirmative action program relative to equal opportunity employment." He went on to outline the consequences of lack of compliance.[6]

The day following receipt of the memorandum, McLean sent a reply to Otis concerning his equal opportunity employment inquiry. "Dear Charles: We discriminate, like hell! We seek the absolute best-qualified employee we can find for the money we spend. Although our qualifications are too numerous to list, I do honestly believe we are color blind and race, color, or religion do not become a part of our requirements. Yours very truly, T. C. GRIFFITH AGENCY, INC., E. D. McLean, Jr."[7]

On June 14, 1973, as his eight years as mayor were coming to a close, McLean wrote a simple letter to his fellow city employees in which he apologized for not writing each of them individually. He expressed his appreciation for their support and help. He stated his belief that "during this period, our community made progress, and credit for this should be given to each employee of our city government, regardless of the position held." He felt remiss in not having expressed his gratitude as much as he should have for what many of the letter's recipients did to make his job easier.

He went on to say, "As I leave office, I do so with great pride in our city government and its employees. I will continue to be interested in our community and your welfare." Finally, he added: "The memories of these years and their associations, I shall long cherish. The good Lord willing, I trust our paths shall cross often in the future. To each of you my best. Sincerely, E. D. McLean, Jr., Mayor."[8]

This second term was marred with personal losses that profoundly affected Buddy for the rest of his life. On September 19, 1970, his father, E. D. McLean, Sr., died. The Rev. C. Ed DeWeese, Jr., pastor of the First United Methodist Church, officiated at the funeral, assisted by the Rev. August Schmidt, pastor of the Westminster Presbyterian Church, Gulfport. Danny McLean served as one of the pallbearers. Interment was in Woodlawn Cemetery in Columbia.[9]

Fifty-three days later, on November 11, Buddy's son Danny was a passenger in a car involved in a two-car collision on U.S. 98, six miles west of Hattiesburg. Danny was killed instantly. The driver of the car he was in was seriously injured, but the two young men in the other car were killed. All four were students at the University of Southern Mississippi. The Rev. Gus Schmidt officiated at the funeral, assisted by Dr. Howard Aultman, pastor of the First Baptist Church. I was returning to Richmond from a business trip in Texas and diverted to Columbia for the service, where I sat with Buddy and Tina and offered one of the prayers. Interment was in Woodlawn Cemetery.

After his second term as mayor was over, Buddy continued as a partner in the T. C. Griffith Agency, Inc. until his retirement in 1995. The McLeans divided their time between Columbia and residences they maintained in Destin, Florida and in the mountains of Colorado. Buddy died of heart failure on December 29, 2001, twenty-five days short of his seventy-seventh birthday. A memorial service was held at Walker Camp in Marion County, with interment in Woodlawn Cemetery.[10]

My wife and I had kept up with Buddy and Tina through the years. We invited them to come to Lexington one spring during the thoroughbred-racing meet at Keeneland Race Course. We visited them in Destin and Columbia. We went to Snowmass, Colorado, where I conducted young Tina's wedding. The only time I was ever back in the Columbia church—until I walked through the building when it was being renovated in August 2001—was for Danny's funeral.

All these years I have carried around in my being memories of what took place in Columbia during my brief stay there in the mid-1960s. From my perspective, what happened there was unique among the experiences of southern towns at the time. Others may dispute this observation. If there were other towns in Mississippi that achieved similar accomplishments at the time, those stories need to be told, too. If what happened in Columbia is unique, in my judgment this was due in great measure to the fact that the city had a unique person as its mayor. Buddy McLean showed great courage and imagination in the way he led the community. As we have seen, extremely powerfully conflicting forces were at play, demanding an exceptional leader to meet the challenges of the day.

One thing that stands out in my mind when I remember Buddy was his demeanor when you came in contact with him. I recognized his compelling affect the first time I met him. It was there the last time I saw him standing in the driveway as we drove away from the McLeans' place in Destin. He had a big smile and always extended a warm welcome. He was a good listener and had a unique way of acknowledging what he heard you say. I can still hear him responding to things I said to him on more than one occasion. It frequently was, "That's right, that's right, that's right," said in rapid-fire succession. This expression was more than an indication of agreement; it was a sign of mutual respect, the greatest compliment one human being can give to another. Buddy was an extraordinary person

One morning in September 2002 when I was visiting Buddy's widow, we drove along Branton Avenue beside the Columbia high school on our way to a little restaurant on Broad Street to have some breakfast. The band was getting in some early morning marching practice. I had no idea how far the quality of education had progressed or about the condition of race relations. But one thing I could see when I looked at that band: I saw about as many African Americans as whites marching together in step to a lively tune. I could not help but smile. Tina turned and asked me, "Why did you come to Columbia?" I thought about it for a moment and replied, "I guess I was simply called to be Buddy's and your pastor."

Somewhere deep in the back of Buddy's race relations file was a Christmas card from Janet Everts, assumed to be one of the summer civil rights workers. Dated 12/14/65, it reads: "Dear Sir, I still think often of Columbia, and perhaps it is naïve of me, but I feel that it is unique among southern towns. I hope that much moral and material wealth come to you and Columbia during the coming year. Sincerely, /s/ J Everts."[11]

There was another Christmas card in the file from Richard Atlee, dated 12/21/65 and posted at Turtle Creek, Pennsylvania. Atlee was one of the civil rights workers arrested picketing at the Sunflower Food Store. The long, handwritten note reads: "I hope for the sake of this country things are going well enough in Columbia to warrant some hope for a good new year for most of the people concerned. In addition to wishing you a very happy Christmas, as to all other good people, I think it's a good time of year to mention my respect and to a certain extent admiration for the way you and those who supported you acted as leaders (at least up until the time I left Columbia), even if it did pose problems for those of us who followed the 'other' side. And I should offer thanks for my opportunity to experience this new year, since there is little doubt that I and several other people owe our lives to the attitude taken by you and other Columbia leaders in favor of what rights our country is based on. Good luck in continuing . . . . /s/ Richard Atlee. P. S. give my regards to Mr. Johnson [the police chief]. I hope he gained something constructive from the summer (at least more than he appeared to)."[12]

On Atlee's card were printed the first and last verses from Robert Frost's poem, "The Road Not Taken."[13] We have no clue as to whether, when faced with two diverging roads, Buddy McLean was sorry he could not travel both. But I can say without the least hesitation, it is completely appropriate to say of Buddy, in Frost's words: "Two roads diverged in a yellow wood, and [Buddy] took the one less traveled by, and that has made all the difference."

The closest we come to having a capsule summary of the man was Buddy's tribute to John F. Kennedy, where he vowed to meet the challenge of his own words by running for mayor. With firm yet unassuming ways he dared to differ by leading the community in learning to live together in turbulent times, "where they have enjoyed the right to do so, . . . free to accomplish their wildest dreams," where to differ was not wrong, but a sign of mutual respect. Thank you, Mr. Mayor, for taking the road less traveled and making all the difference.

CHAPTER 12

In Search of Truth and Understanding

Recently, I read the document that listed property related to the 1850 census at the history center of the local Church of Jesus Christ of Latter-day Saints. Under the name of my great-grandfather, William McAtee, was listed "24 properties," aged forty-four years down to a few months old. I had known in my head that he had opened up that Choctaw land in Beat Four, Attala County, by owning and working slaves, but this was the first time the reality of my ancestor's slaveholding status came home to me with such emotional impact. There it was in black and white in classic cursive handwriting. I was so stunned that I could not eat lunch when I went home, but spent the rest of the day in shock, visualizing the horror and pain that my namesake's "arrangement" had caused those "24 properties." Moreover, trying to comprehend the full impact that this had on the slaves' descendants was more than I could deal with in that moment.

Not too many years ago, I visited an African American friend who lived in Kosciusko, county seat of Attala County. I had met her when we served together on a regional church committee. She was an elder in the Alexander Memorial Presbyterian Church, a small African American congregation with a long history in the community. It was one of the few African American Presbyterian Churches in Mississippi. She knew I came to town from time to time to check on the Old Place and she was interested in our family. We talked about how my family came to Attala County and the way in which the plantation was started. She knew all about it and wanted to know if I would like to meet some of the people who were probably descendants of the slaves from that era. She said there were some whose ancestors came from Beat Four who had changed their names from McAtee to McAfee and were probably connected in some way with my family's slaves. One of them worked in the local school system, and she would be willing to take me to meet this person if I wanted to. I lamely begged off, saying that it was too late that night but I would like to do it on a later trip. She said she understood. To my regret I never got back to see her again to make that connection.

At the outset I said that the primary reason for writing this book was to give me an opportunity to record and elaborate on my memory of those days when leadership segments of Columbia, both black and white, came together over a relatively short period of time (1964–66) to face the daunting challenges of preventing the community from being destroyed by violence and division, and to find a way to work together to make it a better place. The second reason was to give a more thoughtful answer to these questions: How did being a fourth generation Mississippian shape who I became as an individual? And how did this legacy, along with the pursuit of my call to ministry, contribute to what I did during this brief period of my life? The answers were not found simply in examining my feelings of being overwhelmed by the reality that my great-grandfather owned slaves, or by coming to terms with my hesitancy in meeting face-to-face with their possible descendents—although these were certainly important factors. More must be said before the answer is complete, if completion is ever possible.

I have already gone to great lengths to answer the question, "Hey, boy, where you from anyway?" One wonders if there is anything left to say about life as a McAtee. However, if it is true that cultural legacies were created by the life experiences of earlier generations and handed down to succeeding generations to inform a particular moment in the future, have I examined all the cultural legacies emanating from the life experiences of the McAtee generations before me that formed my identity?

Recently I was asked explicitly how my perspective on race evolved over time and how it influenced my current understanding of past events. The paramount cultural legacy for any native Mississippian inevitably involves race. For whites, this issue was often masked by idyllic days of privilege and denial. For blacks, it was immersed in psychological intimidation, institutional insults, and physical violence. How did this cultural legacy play itself out in the way the McAtee generations associated with or related to blacks? Were there some relational threads that wove their way across the generations that were worth tracing?

I let myself wander through the fragments of my memory of what I had heard concerning my Mississippi McAtee family and my own experience growing up there, searching for meaningful threads. Though I was not completely oblivious to the differences in the separate but unequal culture, how did all these differences seep into my subconscious, causing me to blink at some later date?

Assuming there is some truth in Gladwell's assertion that going back several generations for a look into the roots of family heritage can give clues to what shapes one's identity, I could not help but wonder what cultural legacies were created and handed down to me from that pre-McAtee generation of my great-great-grandparents. Was there something in the calling of those two Methodist "bishops," one to serve Native Americans and the other to serve African Americans, that might have been passed down to succeeding generations through their daughters? Could there have been a glimmer of compassion for the plight for those their fathers served? There is no way of knowing, but speculation about the influence of these men and women on subsequent generations of McAtees piqued my interest.

At one point in a later generation, Aunt Doris was diagnosed with tuberculosis. She was told to get out and ride her horse as often as she could. She would ride to visit all the neighbors, both black and white, every morning. They all said that they did not know what they would do if she ever left the community. She said they had a cook that lived in the house on the Old Place that was vacated after the death of Doris's older brother, Bunk. This cook made the best biscuits, and many a time Doris went to her house to eat those biscuits with molasses. The cook said she did not like to work for anyone but the McAtees, because "our black folks were treated like people." Did Aunt Doris, in her quiet way, pass this fair treatment of blacks on to me?

My daddy, William III, served as a supply sergeant in an all-black Corps of Engineers unit that built railroads in France. I have a picture of him marching in review before General "Black Jack" Pershing. My father was in the front line right and easy to spot, the only white soldier in the unit. In the fall of 1957, Joe Byrd, a member of the Brookhaven church, was working in the oil industry in Houma, Louisiana, where he helped my daddy locate one of the black army buddies who had served with him in France. Daddy told me he wanted me to go with him to Houma the next summer to visit this man, but that was not to be. Daddy died in March before we could make the trip. We never made contact with his friend. But was there something in my daddy's experience, both tolerance and compassion, that crept into my being by osmosis?

My experience as a very small child growing up in the Mississippi Delta was like that of so many other white children of privilege, meager though that was by ordinary material standards. In spite of difficult times during the Depression, my mother did have someone come in to help with the cooking and to look after the children. My sister Jane had many warm memories of Lucy, our black cook, but sadly we cannot recall her last name. Jane said Lucy would bring her own sassafras to make tea when she came to work. Lucy never used the toilet in the house, but always made her way to the backside of the garden for those purposes. Lucy played games with us and read to us when the adults in the household had gone somewhere in the evening.

Jane remembered that sometimes Lucy would pause in her reading and let Jane put little broom straws in the holes in her pierced ears. She kept these straws there when she did not have her earrings in. Sometimes Lucy went to the front yard, got a twig off a sweet gum tree and trimmed the bark at one end, splaying it like a brush. She then dabbed it with soda and clean her teeth. Jane also remembered Lucy's indirect way of getting her to do things that she should be doing. Lucy made her point by telling stories of how "other children she had kept" did not do what she had told them, but "you would not do that." She let the point just hang in the air for emphasis. Jane admired "Lucy's tact and patience as good examples to have known and felt."

About all I can remember about Lucy is her sitting behind the swinging door that went into the kitchen, where she sang and churned the butter. I do have a general impression of her kindness and care. I recall a happy reunion with her years later, when Jane and I were in Shaw on a short visit. We posed for a picture with Lucy in front of the bedroom window of the room in the house where I was born. We then went by Lucy's house and met her impressive son and her little grandchildren, who were visiting from New York.

Lucy played an important role in our formative years, just as Janie Jones did for my wife Millye when she was growing up in Jonesboro, Arkansas. A deep affection between Janie and the Bunn family lasted for years. She was always welcome to sit at the table and eat with the family. Her love was expressed when, in later years, she shipped a box of her best homegrown sweet potatoes to us at Amory as her gift to Neal when he was born. Was there something in those relationships, though glaringly unequal, that softened our sense of differentness, that instilled affection in our hearts for black people?

We moved to Senatobia, where I started school, in the fall of 1940, and I don't recall much contact with blacks during the short time we lived there. I remember seeing a few men working at the downtown mule barn I passed on the way to school. By the time we moved to Brookhaven in the spring of 1943, World War II was in full swing and gas was rationed. Cotton wagons pulled by mules and filled with rural tenant farmers, both black and white, parked in front of our house on Saturdays when they came to town to do their weekly shopping. I had a wide variety of casual contacts with the black janitors at the church next door and the elementary school down the block where I did my time.

I made the acquaintance of the bootleggers in the joints in the quarters where we bought our first taste of a fifty-cent jug of Sweetheart muscatel wine. On Saturday night we slipped into our high school stadium, where we watched rough and tumble football games between Alexander High and its black opponents. As graduation approached, we engaged The Re-Bops, a well-known Mississippi black band, to play for dances at our white country club. In *North Toward Home*, Willie Morris refers to "a perambulating Negro band called the 'Red-Tops' playing music for the Memphis shuffle." The Red Tops spawned "a ritualized social routine" in high school and college students who would follow the group across the state to wherever it was playing on a Saturday night.[1] I was never sure what the connection was between the Re-Bops and the Red Tops, but I felt they must be somehow related.[2] Later, in my sophomore year in college, I rented a car and drove down that long straight and flat Highway 61 into the night to introduce my wife-to-be to this Mississippi social spectacle in an auditorium in Clarksdale.

When I got my haircut in a white barbershop, I got to know "Red," the bootblack, to whom I later sold my trombone for his son. I remember years later how, with tears streaming down his face, "Red" offered me his heartfelt condolences over the death of my dad, "Brother Mac," as he was known by all in Brookhaven. Did I learn something about expressing genuine admiration and concern even from casual acquaintances, regardless of their stations in life?

In high school, my experience with race was one of benign denial shrouded in a cloak of silence. I was almost numb to what was actually going on around me. My experience was akin to the pervasive belief that "this is just the way it is, so leave it alone." I graduated from the all-white Brookhaven High School in the early 1950s, while others graduated from the all-black Alexander High. We never had a chance to know each other. I did not give it much thought until the time the Alexander High graduates were not even invited to the fortieth or fiftieth reunions for those who graduated in 1952 at what was by then the one successor public high school in Brookhaven. I asked where they were but only received a blank stare in response. I never got to know the other class of '52 graduates, even decades later. Graduates from the all-black Jefferson High School in Columbia never had a chance to know my friends, Dick Wolfe and Carolyn Pope, who graduated from the all-white Columbia High School about the same time I graduated. What lost opportunities!

I said I was almost numb to what was actually going on around me in my high school years. But I was aware of a more corrosive dynamic lurking in the shadows, a different kind of denial. It was a virulent denial that translated into the brutality of misplaced anger. I never participated in any of the violent acts that some other white adolescents did, such as riding around under cover of darkness in cars, armed with baseball bats and abusing hapless blacks just for laughs as they walked along the roadside. My encounters with blacks were much more benign. But did being aware of these cowardly acts give me my first experience with being repulsed by physical violence and by psychological intimidation and insults. Did it introduce me to the cowardice of silence in the face of such offenses?

The first job I had during my Brookhaven school days was to deliver packages on my bicycle for a fancy lady's shop to the homes in Ward Four, where well-to-do white patrons lived. Later I tried collecting overdue bills for Kings Daughter's Hospital in the "quarters." This short-lived employment ended abruptly one day. I stepped up on the porch of a rickety shotgun house and knocked on the door. When it swung slowly open, I saw a small black toddler standing there not saying a word in response to my asking if her mother were home. After a long silence, I casually glanced through the crack between the hinges and the door jam and saw someone holding a very large butcher knife! Finally catching my breath, I backed gingerly off the porch and mumbled something about coming back another time. But I decided at that point I was not cut out for the job. What did this teach me about the broken trust between the races?

I had fun and formed a productive relationship when I worked the summer of 1952 between high school and college, and later after my freshman year in college, as a deliveryman for the furniture store behind our house. P. J. Pittman, the furniture store's black repairman, was a very skilled person who taught me a great deal about installing and repairing appliances. He showed me how to install fifty-foot TV antennas that were essential to getting better reception than that afforded by the shorter ones, with their ghostly flickering images. He also regaled me with his experiences in the South Pacific during World War II. I suspected some of his tales were a bit exaggerated, but this did not matter. We became quite close as we crisscrossed the city delivering expensive furniture to elegant homes, as well as much cheaper items we delivered out in the county from the company's second-hand store across the tracks.

One thing we both hated was the repossessing part of the job. Many of the poorer people could not keep up the weekly payments on their $49.95 furniture suites. The furniture was cheap, not just inexpensive, and would often not outlast the payment schedule. We approached the houses where we needed to repossess items with great care. If the families were white, I drove the unmarked truck first, followed a ways back by P. J. in the marked van. This gave me time to park and go around to the back door to prevent any hasty retreat by the occupants, while P. J. came roaring up to the front door to cover that exit. If the families were black, we would switch vehicles and switch the process.

Late one Saturday afternoon, we were sent way down in the southwest corner of Lincoln County near the Amite County line to do a "repo." P. J. was in the lead unmarked truck, and I followed in the van. After we executed our plan with lightning efficiency, we discovered the only furniture in the house was the suites we had come to pick up. Repossessing them would leave the people with nothing. P. J. and I both looked at that poor, petrified black family and then at each other, giving our heads a slight shake from side to side, indicating we could not go through with the repo. When we got back to the store around closing time, we simply said, "Nobody was home." What do I owe P. J. for what he taught me about empathy and fairness?

Another person I learned a great deal from and loved like family was Cecil Stewart, the black man who worked for my Aunt Hallie and Uncle Troy Funchess at Glancy (Center Point) on "Rosy Dawn" farm, out in the country west of Hazlehurst. Cecil worked the fields, plowed the garden, and looked after the farm animals on the place. He helped Aunt Hallie clean up after wonderful country meals. When I spent time there in summer, he would take my cousin, McAtee "Mac" Funchess, and me hunting and fishing. We rode horses all over the county. Best of all, we would sit on the screened side porch in the heat of the afternoon and listen to the old folks tell stories. Cecil could tell stories with the best of them.

Cecil had a big family and was an active leader in his church. Over the years, my family pitched in and supported his children's education, as well as fund drives in his church. One of my favorite pictures in our album was taken in June 1968, when we came back to Mississippi on vacation. Cecil was holding the bridle while I stood by Bill with Walt in my arms and Neal up in the saddle. Bill was the horse I raised from a colt and eventually saddle-broke back in the summer of 1952. It was some wild ride out in the pasture behind Cecil's house, with Cecil and his kids looking on. Cecil plowed all the neighbor's gardens with Bill for 25 years.

I recently heard from my cousin McAtee Funchess, who still lives at "Rosy Dawn." He told me he visited with some of Cecil's kids, who still live in the area. He got a big hug from one of the children that Cecil named after Mac's aunt, who owned the land where Cecil's house was located. She brought Mac up to date about the rest of the family. Several became teachers and now are retired. One son earned a doctoral degree in chemistry and is a successful professor at Alcorn State University. He built a big house on the site of his parents' home, behind which his siblings watched me break ole Bill so many years ago. Were seeds of mutual respect sown in this uneven social ground?

My experience of race relations during my college years was in some ways but an extension of what I grew up with. There were no black students at Southwestern during the time I was there in the 1950s. The limited contact I did have with blacks on campus occurred when I worked on the maintenance crew with them. We became friends by the time we spent the summer painting Voorhies Hall. One evening they invited the white guys to one of their houses for a weekend party that turned out to be considerably wilder than I expected, but was nonetheless cordial. Were these early attempts at inclusiveness, no matter that they were ill conceived and unequal?

I mentioned earlier some transforming experiences I had at Louisville Seminary that expanded my horizons with regard to race. One incident that occurred in 1957 during my first year shook me out of my complacency with regard to race. It came courtesy of a high school boy in the Methodist youth group where I was doing my fieldwork. While there I heard a church member proudly proclaim that Salem did not have a race problem. Salem, Indiana, was in Washington County, where there were no black residents. One night after a youth group meeting I was told a story about one occasion when a black doctor from Chicago had been injured in an automobile accident within the county. The hospital did not admit blacks, so he was put in the county jail, where he received medical treatment until he was well enough to continue on home.

When I heard that story, I became a bit testy about the Salem church member's lack of racial sensitivity. Resorting to that old southern standby so frequently used by the champions of lost causes—knowing that the best defensiveness is always blind frontal offensiveness—I jumped at the chance to attack the speck in the Yankee's eye, while summarily ignoring the stick in my own. In the midst of passing judgment, without the least hesitancy in my Mississippi diction, I let the "N word" slide glibly off my tongue. A young high schooler, gently but firmly, took me to task, and I was sorely humiliated by my own behavior. Did this incident give me a glimpse of my own racial insensitivity?

As I lived through my almost idyllic days of privilege long ago, I did not think much about the lives of blacks that were approximately the same age as me. Our lives were lived in stark contrast to one another, reflecting the segregated times in which we grew up. Our stations in life were defined by the color of our skin and reinforced by the cruel legacy of racial prejudice. I could never know from experience what life was like for the *other*. Black children were taught early on to know their place and be vigilant every day in order to avoid situations that threatened their lives, something foreign to my experience. They could not walk through the front door of many restaurants in town and be served, but I could. They could not sit downstairs at the movie theater to watch a movie, but I could. They lived in a world of hand-me-down clothes and used textbooks, but not I. They, upon graduating from Jefferson or Alexander High, could not attend Ole Miss, or Mississippi State, or Mississippi State College for Women (MSCW), or Mississippi Southern, or Millsaps, or Belhaven, or Mississippi College—but I could. They could not get a good paying job in a bank or as a cashier in a department store, but I could. They could not serve on a jury of their peers, but I could.

However, in the face of this damnable reality, many blacks learned something else early on from their families and churches: pride and perseverance. Though the only door open to them for further education was at an all-black college, many made the most of the opportunities afforded them there so that, when the barriers they had confronted most of their life began to fall, they were able to take advantage of what came their way. But these opportunities were too few and too far between, and many times the clock had run out by the time they arrived.

So what have all these memories, experiences, and relationships meant for me as I have lived my life? Have I grown in insight and understanding in my views on race and racism? In summary, I would say they instilled in me many things: a deep sense of compassion for the plight of those one serves; fair treatment of blacks as people; tolerance for those with whom one works, regardless of race; a softened sense of "differentness," instilled by love and affection received from the *other*; genuine admiration and concern for the *other*, even casual acquaintances and regardless of station in life; revulsion at physical violence, psychological intimidation, and insults; sadness brought on by broken trust between races; empathy, fairness, and mutual respect sown on uneven social ground; inclusiveness no matter how conceived and how unequal the situation; and finally, culpability brought on by one's racial insensitivity.

All these values I hold are a reflection of having grown up in a society where racial differences were a given. In that separate and unequal society one had the experience of deep intimacy and affection for the other, and at the same time a sense of profound alienation from black people. As I have grown in understanding, my views on race have evolved, but still have often been overshadowed by a nagging sense of culpability born of moments when my racial insensitivity surprised me and caught me up short.

There are many symbols of our progression towards awareness and sensitivity with regard to race. There is no better illustration of this progress than changes in the words to identify the race descended from former slaves. As I look back over the years, I acknowledge that I followed this progression as I grew in my own sensitivity to the complexity of race relations. My perception of the progression is that it began with the "N word," the most denigrating designation, ineffectively disguised at times as "colored," as publicly displayed on humiliatingly labeled water fountain, restroom, waiting room signs, and no telling what else. As sensitivity to race grew, some progressive folk used the term "nigra." While this change might have been, to their minds, an improvement, those it referenced remained unconvinced. Then great lengths were taken to enunciate Negro as "knee-grow," to announce to all in one's hearing, "We got it." "Black" came into popular usage with progressives in the 1960s as a result of the Black Power movement. In addition, "Afro-American," then "African American," and "people of color" began to be widely used as politically correct terms in the latter part of the twentieth century.

I had a long and arduous struggle to overcome my deeply ingrained prejudices and behavior. The struggle continued for some time, and I admit that I backslide in certain circumstances into old patterns of thought and language I assumed I had long since abandoned. Considering how my ingrained views on race were formed growing up in that separate but unequal culture, I must confess I am a recovering racist. What does being a recovering racist mean? In spite of all my positive relational experiences with blacks, my muscles and mind had to overcome my racial prejudices and reactions. That is the way it was, but all began to change with more face-to-face encounters. One such encounter happened while I was pastor in Amory.

In 1962 we had a black woman coming to the manse to do our ironing who would also baby sit our son after he was born the next summer. I would drive over to the other side of town beyond the Frisco railroad tracks to pick her up and take her home. In the course of these rides I found out that her daughter was about to graduate from the black high school in town and wanted to go away to college. I was interested in supporting Stillman College, one of our black Presbyterian schools, and I thought I might be able to raise money for a scholarship that would help her daughter go there. It never crossed my mind to think about helping her to go to Belhaven College, our Presbyterian school for whites in Jackson.

Some time that summer we drove the woman and her daughter to Tuscaloosa, Alabama, to visit Stillman College to see if she might be accepted as a student. She and her daughter sat in the back seat; Millye and I sat in the front. It was 1962, and we still were living in a very separate but unequal world, even though racial tensions were heating up. I was a bit fearful of traveling in mixed company, even though what we were doing would have brought no special attention ten years earlier. I kept an eye out for strange cars tailing us but saw none. Millye and I felt uncomfortable when we gave our passengers lunch money and dropped them off at "their" café to have lunch because they could not eat with us at "ours." I don't recall much else about the trip except my relief when we got back to Amory, but we did experience new feelings. In a very small way, we had shared the apprehension and fear that came with confronting cultural barriers. This feeling for them was forever present, but not for us. It went away when we got back to our side of town.

And even as I grew closer to Six in Columbia, my muscles and mind had constantly to overcome my racial prejudices and reactions. It became clear that even though we experienced a certain mutual comfort in those relations, I had no inkling of what their levels of discomfort might have been. I did not stop to ask them or myself that question at the time. There was no time to do so then, and frankly speaking, it did not occur to me to do so until now.

My residual racism was there when I saw the civil rights workers picketing the Sunflower Store and marching in the streets to city hall to present their just grievances. Subconsciously I seemed to buy into the common perception that these people were anarchists. It was not until I listened to Ira Grupper decades later that I came to realize that my residual racism had misled me with regard to the true nature of their grievances. He convinced me the protesters took to the streets on behalf of the poorest of the poor, the disenfranchised, the undereducated—to say enough is enough, not to create disorder just for the sake of creating it. They firmly believed what they did was a nonviolent exercise of their constitutional rights of free speech and assembly. Picketing was their way to protest the egregious injustices brought on by unjust laws and customs of the dominant power culture. My new understanding was a witness to being a recovering racist.

George Edwards, my seminary professor of New Testament Greek, taught us to pay attention to the ingressive aorist verb tense. When the word "become" was in this form, he said it meant "becoming." The subject of the verb is never a finished product, but always a work in progress. One may be transformed in a particular moment of insight, but something else comes along that expands that understanding, so that one is always being transformed. Such is my view on race. It is always becoming, never finally settled. I know I have come a long way over the course of my life, but as a recovering racist I still am a work in progress.

Back when I got old enough to sit still and pay attention to what was being taught in Sunday school, I noticed something curious. The teacher would spend most of the time telling us the details of the scripture lesson for the day, and then time would run out. Just before the closing prayer, he would say, "I am sorry we didn't get to the application to life, but we will do that next Sunday." But the pattern rarely changed. Next Sunday it was, "same song, second verse; could be better, but gonna be worse." This pattern made me wonder if scriptures could apply to life, but I decided they must. So I spent many years in pursuit of answers. This search was particularly relevant to the pragmatic aspect of my views on race. Reflecting on my experiences as recounted in this narrative, I remember holding on to three things—two from the Bible and one from the U.S. Constitution—I tried to live out in everyday practice as a way of maintaining my sanity and navigating those turbulent times: "Love thy neighbor as thyself," even your enemies; "do justly, love mercy, and walk humbly with thy God;" and, "all men are created equal . . . with liberty and justice for all."

I was brought up in a loving family that showed compassion and respect for those who shared our separate but unequal culture. I learned by example to exhibit acts of kindness in tangible ways. But there is more to loving one's neighbor than that. We Southern Presbyterians over the years were good at sending "missionaries to the ends of the earth to convert the heathen" as a gesture of loving our neighbors at a distance, but we had some blind spots when it came to how we expressed that love for neighbors at home. Both relationships became tangled when the notion of justice got introduced to our evangelistic efforts. During the 1960s Bob Walkup, my mentor and dear friend, taught me new ways of living out love of neighbor, meaning all persons created in the image of God—with emphasis on all. But now doing justice in a world dominated by unjust laws and institutions was no weak-kneed application of last Sunday's Bible lesson. Doing justice meant renouncing all so-called biblical arguments for the superiority of one race over the other and all the faux scientific evidence purporting to support those interpretations. Both provided the arguments upon which unjust laws and institutions were founded. Often these arguments put me in direct opposition to the views of those I was called to serve and love.

Add to this theological mix the phrase in the Constitution about "all men" being created equal. Some plead to no avail that constitutional rights did not apply equally to all, because when the Bill of Rights was ratified, it applied to only a small percentage of the population, largely male landholders. Others maintained, even though the Bill of Rights did not explicitly say so, that these rights applied to men of lesser means, to women, to Native Americans, and to slaves. The founding documents' silence on the subject did not negate the principle that "unalienable Rights . . . to Life, Liberty and the pursuit of Happiness" apply equally to all people under the law.

But it was taking too long for the latter view to become self-evident. In the 1960s "all men" was beginning to be interpreted more explicitly to mean "all women," too. This change did not make it any easier for some of us to make practical application of our convictions. I was confronted with the most profound theological issue I ever had to face: applying my beliefs to my life. The same song, second verse routine was no longer sufficient. In the midst of all my other efforts at replicating church and pastor in my calls in Amory and Columbia, this pragmatic aspect of my views on race was at the core of what my life was about.

Our short stay in Columbia for Millye was exhaustingly filled primarily with caring for two small boys while I was out and about. Her memory of that time was never quite like "home in Arkansas" to her, but she knew I would never be happy until I served a church in south Mississippi. Even though I experienced adrenalin rushes from engagement in high stakes activities, it took a toll on our family as well as on me. The time came to give serious care and attention to my commitment to family and to myself, both of these aspects of my call. At one point my mother remarked, "He's left the ministry," but she really knew better. Considering the call to the Board of Christian Education for me was not a matter of leaving the ministry. It represented a vital step in self-care and understanding, not one taken lightly, but one whereby a new form of ministry could be performed. This was the first major decision, vocational or otherwise, I took solely on my own which broke the patterns associated with being a native Mississippian. I had gone to grammar school down the block, then walked across town to junior high and senior high. I rode up the Illinois Central Railroad to Southwestern, then on to Louisville Seminary, then back to my first pastorate in Mississippi, then the second one—all following a seemingly predetermined path. Now what?

My own intense internal struggle with the decision to break with the expectations of my culture was not unique. Mine was the experience for so many Mississippians, black and white. Do I stay or go, and what will my decision cost? Mississippi expatriates have carried this internal struggle with them to the ends of the earth, while those who stayed behind also got mired in it. Both were like stuck in the black alluvial gumbo mud in the flood plain of a Mississippi Delta bayou in the cold winter days of December wondering how they got in this mess; wondering how their understanding of the culture had changed; wondering if they made the right decisions. I have been there both literally and figuratively.

Breaking the expectations attached to being a fourth-generation Mississippian was but one important factor at work when I made the decision to leave Mississippi. It was not the only one. As best I can tell, my decision probably came down to something akin to Will Campbell's observation about himself and cousin Jerry, "I have absolutely no idea how it happened." It may have just had something to do with providence. What made us who we are and made us do what we do is nothing but a mystery to us at times.

That's the story of my experience with race relations in my early life, what I did as a result during the brief period 1964–66, and who I was becoming. And then I moved on.

CHAPTER 13

So What?

Being a native Mississippian, I had a great deal invested in what was taking place in the 1960s during my search for truth and understanding. I was proud of some of my heritage, and I made no apology to anyone for that part of it. But I was not blind to the manifold injustices in Mississippi, both past and present, and I repudiated them. Apologies and repudiations are tricky and sometimes difficult to separate, but separated they must be. So after all was said and done, I still had to ask, "So what?"

As I contemplated an answer to that question, I recalled the afternoon I was in shock after seeing my great-grandfather's "properties" listed on that computer screen. For years, I had not openly discussed the fact that I was a descendant of a slaveholder, for I knew that some would want to hold me accountable, and I was not sure how I would respond. My silence was troubling to me, and I struggled to figure out whether I was accountable, and if so, whether I needed to make an apology. As I have often done, I turned to the dictionary for guidance.

The first definition listed for "apology" was: "Something said or written in defense or justification of what appears to be wrong, or what may be liable to disapprobation." That was not the answer I was seeking, for I certainly did not intend to defend or justify the institution of slavery. The second definition was more helpful: "An acknowledgment intended as a reparation, or expressive of regret, for some improper, injurious, or discourteous remark or act."[1]

From this second definition it became clear to me that an apology implied that one had said or done something that was improper or injurious or humiliating, and was required to acknowledge the error or make an expression of regret. It appeared to me that there was one sense in which I could not apologize for the fact that my great-grandfather owned slaves. That was for him to do, not me, and he was long gone. However, it was proper for me not to condone what he had done, only condemn it as unacceptable human behavior. I could say how despicable and wrong slave-holding was, but since I was not an actual perpetrator of that "improper, injurious act," I could not make a legitimate primary apology for it. So I let go of any idea that I should or could be held accountable for making that type of prima facie apology. I did not feel a sense of pride for that part of my heritage, but I grew to believe I must repudiate the injustice that followed in its aftermath, now in my own time and, in my own way, give a personal accounting of myself

I am not proud of those long years of human, economic, and social injustices meted out in the multi-tier social structure of my heritage that I had embraced in acquiescent silence. My silence was my doing, something I could apologize for and behavior for which I must be held accountable. But doing so was a complex undertaking. Contemplating this task created the same ambivalence and uncertainty within me that came when I tried to figure out if I should apologize for my great-grandfather having owned slaves. I was caught in the web of institutional deceit and injustices that characterized a separate but unequal social, economic, and political system. But this time, compounding the perplexities of my dilemma, I was a participant in those injustices because of the silent acquiescence of my youth and young adulthood. What was my apology to be?

Looking back on my experience in Columbia, I concluded it constituted, in part, a form of apology, even though I do not recall thinking of it in those terms at the time. My involvement there was a personal turning point in my attempt to repudiate my past acquiescence, although I had begun to find my voice even earlier. Breaking my silence was more than simply a personal matter, for it took on a tangible corporate dimension. I was involved with a part of the primarily male-dominated power structure, and I was making an effort to begin to repudiate some institutional vestiges of past human, social, economic and political injustices. Leadership in this effort also required breaking the corporate silence. Motivation to do so came from a blend of deep religious convictions, civic commitments, and political pragmatism. Some said we went as far as we could, considering the times. Others contended we did not go far enough. Nonetheless, could it be that the series of firsts, of compliance with the Civil Rights and Voting Rights Acts was more than an apology? Could this compliance be the precursor to some primitive form of corporate reparation—another first—or was that a stretch?

There was more in that definition of apology than breaking silence and acknowledging our common failures. Saying or writing one's regrets was not enough. Some tangible response was required. The word "reparation" was part of that second dictionary definition of "apology." I had not given reparation serious consideration or comprehended its meaning in my struggle as the great-grandson of a slaveholder. In fact, I shied away from the thought, for fear it might require something of me I might not be willing to give.

Again the dictionary was helpful. One definition of "reparation" gave a tangible dimension to apology. It read, "Act of making amends for a wrong, injury, etc.; also, the amends; compensation."[2] Previously I had gotten the impression, without delving in too deeply, that some sort of financial payoff to victims was involved. I thought descendants of those who had committed various egregious acts could somehow compensate for the sins of the perpetrators and their own latent guilt. I was baffled trying to figure out the logistics of paying off multitudes of individual descendants of African American slaves—if it could be determined who they might be. And furthermore, how would it be decided which individuals should pay?

The dictionary definition of reparation went on to say: "Specif. (usually in the pl.) compensation payable by the Central Powers; esp. Germany, to various Allied countries in accordance with World War treaties as war indemnity for economic damage done by them."[3] This explanation began to help me understand that reparations were indeed a corporate response, not an individual one. It was also important to recognize that authentic reparations were predicated on authentic apologies.

I found Roy L. Brooks instructive in determining my understanding of apologies and reparations. Writing about both in *Atonement and Forgiveness: A New Model for Black Reparations*, Brooks confirmed the seriousness of these social behaviors and clearly described how they played out in reality. He cautioned: "A tender of apology is no trivial matter, particularly when made by state officials on behalf of their governments. It is an act fraught with deep meaning and important consequences." He went on to point out that, "Apology, most importantly is an *acknowledgment* of guilt rather than a punishment for guilt." He suggested several conditions that must be met when a government apologizes for an atrocity it has committed: confess the deed; admit the deed was an injustice; repent; and ask for forgiveness. All are essential steps in assuming responsibility. But apology alone was not enough for Brooks. He contended as much as possible must be done to make certain the atrocity never happens again. One final condition was required to make the apology complete: "The perpetrator must change its behavior toward the victim," a condition possible only after the atrocity had stopped.[4]

Brooks's directive seemed a tricky proposition for me, as in the case of slavery perpetrators and victims were no longer alive to participate directly in an act of reconciliation and healing, even though the descendants of both were still enmeshed in the consequences of past wrongdoing. Brooks maintains that when meaningful reparation is completed in some tangible way, the conditions of the apology function as a memorial honoring the lives of the dead victims. The question becomes whether or not there is a statute of limitations on how long descendants of dead perpetrators are morally obligated to apologize to dead victims, providing a form of reconciliation and healing in the present. Brooks contends that regardless of whether the victims are dead or alive, "Because we are dealing with a matter of morality rather than a question of legality, the duty to apologize remains until the requisite apology is made."[5]

In my search I discovered meaningful reparations took many forms for proponents of the slavery redress movement. I relied on Brooks to help me understand a couple of models and their significance. The primary means of redress, he noted, has been through what has been called the "tort model," which sometimes takes legislative form. He said this form follows a litigation model that operates on these premises: "compensation and, for some proponents, punishment or even white guilt." Proponents of this form of reparations might be satisfied if the "government or some private beneficiary of slavery were simply to write a check for X amount of dollars to every slave descendant."[6]

Though Brooks saw litigation as a useful tool in some situations, he opposed the tort model as the primary way to obtain redress because it "is too contentious, too confrontational to provide the kind of racial reconciliation and accord that is needed for future race relations." He went on to say, most importantly, "the tort model, whether in the form of litigation or legislation, is incapable of generating the one ingredient that I believe is or should be the *sine qua non* of slave redress—namely atonement and ultimately, racial reconciliation." The tort model is, to him, void of moral character.[7]

Brooks developed the "atonement model" to fill that void. In his model, he contends, the "perpetrator's duty to atone [apologize] for a past atrocity is a moral imperative . . . if substantial, reparations will make the apology believable. Then, and only then, does the atonement impose a civic obligation on the victim to forgive." The formula for his model is:

"atonement—apology and reparation—plus forgiveness leads to racial reconciliation." When this formula is followed, slave redress benefits the victim, the perpetrator, and society as a whole.[8]

My understanding of reparations was enhanced by more contemporary examples. Much has been written about the financial reparations paid out by Germany and, in this country, to Japanese Americans interned during World War II. Also, much has been written about acts of reparation after the end of apartheid in South Africa[9] and other countries, as well as responses by corporations that profited from the continuation of separate but unequal in the twenty-first century. Although there are few cases in which reparations have been paid by government and corporate entities in the United States, a number of states have taken formal first steps to apologize to blacks for wrongs committed under slavery. In early June 2009, Connecticut became the seventh state to make such a formal apology, joining Alabama, Florida, Maryland, New Jersey, North Carolina, and Virginia.[10]

Later in June 2009, California State Assemblyman Paul Fong, whose grandfather experienced immigration restrictions, introduced a resolution in the assembly citing "the contributions made by the Chinese." It also expressed California's deep regret for the discrimination the Chinese were subjected to in 1882, when "they were targets of the Chinese Exclusion Act, the nation's first law limiting immigration based on race or nationality." Fong's proposal included seeking an apology from the federal government, plus some form of reparation, "such as a contribution to maintain the Angel Island Immigration Station in San Francisco Bay, which housed Chinese immigrants between 1910 and 1940 as they tried to prove they were eligible to enter the United States."[11]

At the same time Fong was taking action in California, the U.S. Senate passed on a voice vote a resolution "calling on the United States to apologize officially for the enslavement and segregation of millions of African-Americans and to acknowledge 'the fundamental injustice, brutality, and inhumanity of slavery and Jim Crow laws.'" As the measure moved to the House for further consideration, the Congressional Black Caucus (CBC) expressed its opposition and concerns about a disclaimer stating that "nothing in this resolution authorizes or supports any claims against the United States; or serves as a settlement of any claims against the United States." The CBC saw this language as an attempt to negate future reparation claims on the part of descendants of slaves. Not all African Americans were so skeptical. Some "hailed the Senate vote as a monumental achievement."[12] A certain level of comfort with this type of apology seems to be developing, but the same cannot be said about reparations. The debate over reparations—tort, legislative, atonement, or some other form—is far from over.

In my search of truth and understanding I also discovered the meaning of the concept of impunity in Genevieve Jacques's book, *Beyond Impunity*. I had not given it much attention until now. As I began reading about impunity—itself a legal concept—I began to see in greater depth the importance of reparations. The importance of impunity caught the attention of the international community in the years following widespread violations of human rights by military dictatorships throughout South and Central America in the 1970s and 1980s. Violations were perpetrated in the name of the doctrine of national security.[13] In a nutshell, impunity arises from an event where individuals, groups, or officials, acting on behalf of the state, commit illegal or criminal human rights acts and are never punished for them. These are serious infractions, including "war crimes, crimes against humanity, genocide, torture . . . and 'gross and systematic violations' of civil and political rights and economic, social and cultural rights." Three components are involved in impunity: the act, the perpetrator, and some tangible satisfaction that justice has been rendered. It is the absence of the last that gives the concept its name, derived from the Latin *impunitas*, meaning "absence of punishment." What makes such a concept necessary is a legal system where absence of punishment became normal. Some people living under such a system begin to consider themselves above the law and above morality, and act in ways that disregard accountability to anyone, no matter how egregious their behavior.[14] When it gets to this stage, talk of reparations—tangible expression that justice has been rendered—becomes little more than academic.

Finally I began to connect the dots between the concept of impunity with what took place in Mississippi and across the South during the long run-up to the turbulence and upheaval of the 1960s. The conventional wisdom of history avoided a question that Douglas A. Blackmon raised in his recent book, *Slavery by Another Name*: "If not racial inferiority, what explained the inexplicably labored advance of African Americans in U.S. society in the century between the Civil War and the civil rights movement of the 1960s?" He claims that all the "amorphous rhetoric of the struggle against segregation, the thin cinematic imagery of Ku Klux Klan bogeymen, even the horrifying still visuals of lynching, had never been a sufficient answer . . . . How had so large a population of Americans disappeared into a largely unrecorded oblivion of poverty and obscurity?"[15]

What Blackmon discovered in doing research for his book was that the "South's practice of leasing convicts was an abhorrent abuse of African Americans, was also viewed by many as an aside in the larger sweep of events in the racial evolution of the South." He was stymied by the silence he met while searching for the few records that existed in county courthouses of arrests and imprisonment and of contracts under which black men were bought and sold. The very people that had contrived the system and reaped the most profits from it, southern whites, controlled these archives. The tragedy here is that this well-guarded secret "overlooked many of the most significant dimensions of the new forced labor." At the very center of this illicit activity was "the web of restrictions put in place to suppress black citizenship, in its concomitant relationship to debt peonage and the worst forms of sharecropping." The damning result was that the most informal and tainted local courts forced an inordinately large number of African Americans into positions of involuntary servitude.[16]

The connection between involuntary servitude and officialdom went on and on, and cleverly devised schemes of deception were used to snare "recruits" for this "employment service." With the anonymity surrounding this "abhorrent abuse," impunity ran unchecked. "A world in which the seizure and sale of a black man—even a black child—was viewed as neither criminal nor extraordinary had emerged. Millions of blacks lived in that shadow—as forced laborers or their family members, or African Americans in terror of the system's caprice." This did not diminish until the eve of World War II.[17]

This neo-slavery "poured the equivalent of tens of millions of dollars in the treasuries of Alabama, Mississippi, Louisiana, Georgia, Florida, Texas, North Carolina, and South Carolina—where more than 75 percent of the black population in the United States lived."[18] The federal government acquiesced in silence for four generations, as American blacks were terrorized in this manner. I began to wonder if this unchecked impunity might have had a more direct impact on the magnitude of racism still present in the twenty-first century than the original slavery, because so many firsthand witnesses to the former are still alive.

This whole history was completely foreign to my experience, along with the idea that "hundreds of millions of us spring from or benefit as a result of lines of descent that abided those crimes and benefited from them."[19] When I read about it, I suddenly realized I had run into a form of that practice in Mississippi among people I knew and loved and detailed in the story I retold that day around the lunch table at presbytery in 1962! The chill I experienced then ran much deeper than I realized. Did my breaking the silence in that moment constitute a sufficient apology, or was it merely a flimsy expression of personal anger at being so deceived?

Writing in the introduction to Jacques' *Beyond Impunity*, Dwain Epps said, "[M]any victims of past atrocities have become convinced that among the causes of present-day atrocities is the fact that many of the perpetrators of past crimes have not been held to account for their acts, and the truth about their crimes often remains hidden." Epps maintains, "Unless the truth is told, unless the criminals are held accountable, or unless those directly responsible and their accomplices confess their guilt, ask for forgiveness and give concrete signs of repentance, there can be no justice and therefore no healing of society."[20]

The hate crime murders of civil rights workers that were perpetrated in Mississippi during the 1950s and 1960s pale in comparison with what took place during those decades when the South's practice of leasing convicts was an everyday occurrence. That offense, however, does not diminish latter day atrocities. Impunity was at work, because it was common knowledge that in some instances the legal power structure was complicit in those acts—or at best turned a blind eye to them. The FBI launched its "Civil Rights–era Cold Case Initiative" in February 2006, a joint effort by federal, state, and local law enforcement agencies, along with community leaders and civic organizations. According to a recent report, the "FBI is currently investigating more than 100 unsolved civil rights murders that occurred prior to 1969." Twenty-five persons named on that partial list were murdered in Mississippi, some close to Columbia in neighboring towns, but none in Marion County.[21] If, by reopening these cold case hate crimes so many years after they were perpetuated can shed some light on the truth in the way Epps maintains, and even a few of the criminals are held accountable, then justice may be served and some healing of society can begin to take place in Mississippi.

But questions still remain about impunity and the proper response to it on the part of those of us who were at least tangentially involved in its creation. How does one deal with the long-term social consequences of crimes and injustice, and the barriers they pose to social healing even decades later for those who were not directly involved? I believe my story is one many have experienced. We were the vast middle of the bell shaped curve between arch segregationists on one end, and those on the other end violently oppressed by the actions of the former.[22] The sin of those in the middle was one of silence.

There was no question about it. The complicity of silence was a sin, for we "missed the mark," to use a theological way of defining that reality. At the heart of this silence was implicit denial that any injustice had been perpetrated. Furthermore—and even more damning—the implicit discounting of the other's personhood and experience is, in my judgment, the ultimate sin against the Holy Spirit.

The perception by some was that this sin of silence was the epitome of total depravity, so nothing could be done about it. In the words of the old prayer of confession in the Presbyterian *Book of Common Worship*, "And there is no health in us."[23] No meant none. Others were blasé and indifferent to it all, disclaiming any responsibility. Then some in their contrition broke the silence, but got no credit or recognition for having done so, receiving the same kind of discounting they had heaped on black people. Yet in the breaking lies hope.

These good people in the middle of the bell shaped curve, in turning from their sin of silence, soon found themselves subject to attention from the extremes. The rabid right said, "You do-gooders have gone too far." The radical left said, "You no-gooders have not gone far enough." But those in the middle often felt totally discredited as human beings, with "no good in them"—even though they knew better. In quiet and small ways they had made a difference in not yielding to the extremes. They knew they had value. In breaking their silence when it needed to be broken, they discovered a clue to individual health and the healing of society.

So what? What does all this discussion of impunity and reparations have to do with me personally? As the whole business began to come somewhat clear to me—as one who was "complicit by my silence" to those historical egregious acts—I had to face the question: "Do the concepts of impunity and reparations apply to me?" "But they are corporate concepts, not individual ones," I responded. "How can they possibly apply to me?"

One has to remember that the majority of people in the middle part of the bell curve were not necessarily "direct victims" of past atrocities or present injustices, but were nonetheless profoundly affected by them. I reserve the term "victim" for those who were actually direct recipients of atrocities or injustice, just as I regard the term "apology" narrowly as the obligation of the one administering the atrocity. Therefore, I did not feel that "victim," direct or indirect, accurately described who I was. I thought of myself in terms of being not a victim, but a "legatee." I am a legatee by virtue of the fact that my great-grandfather committed injustices as a slaveholder, and that I grew up in a separate but unequal society where others perpetrated acts of atrocity.

As a legatee within this framework, I felt some response on my part other than an apology was necessary, such as public lament, outrage, or condemnation. Also, I had an opportunity, if I desired to express my concern socially, to join others in legitimate efforts to encourage acts of reparations by government or private corporate entities, ensuring that some tangible satisfaction of justice had been rendered. If I remained silent or failed to acknowledge the need to express this particular obligation, then an apology or some other act of contrition on my part might be in order. Important as raising my voice in support of public apologies was, this did not fully absolve me of my personal moral responsibility. One of the most tangible ways of atoning for one's past sin of silence is to fulfill one's personal moral obligations in the present.

More importantly, on a personal level as a legatee, I felt I had an obligation to make a commitment to see that injustices perpetuated by society were not replicated in my own experience, in kind or in deed, and that I not engage in overt violation of someone's personhood through "some improper, injurious or discourteous remarks or acts." If such occurred, then some apology and reconciling engagement with the victim was a required moral response. This must include some substantial evidence that made the apology and act of contrition believable. Then and only then would genuine forgiveness and reconciliation become a reality.

I understand the definitions of impunity and reparations and their impact on systems as previously described. These concepts have great meaning and significance for their intended purposes. However, as currently applied, they are not helpful to those of us considered legatees of violent injustices and recipients of gratuitous impunity for our silence. These constructs were not helpful to me in understanding personal involvement and my moral responsibility.

I reached this insight in coming to terms with my own past experience as a fourth-generation Mississippian, though our Columbia experience, and in the context of dealing with racism even as the first decade of the twenty-first century winds down. I felt this breakthrough was extremely important, for I am convinced that there are countless persons who read books such as Genevieve Jacques' *Beyond Impunity* and Charles Harper's *Impunity: An Ethical Perspective* and, although they may treat these works as legitimate analytical exercises of very real atrocities, have no personal identification with the atrocities detailed or prescriptive solutions for justice called for.

Here was the "so what" I was trying to figure out. Were there other constructs derived from or collateral to the prime concepts of impunity and reparations that would be more comprehensible and instructive to those of us, not direct victims but legatees, that were more personal rather than corporate in nature? This question led me to conceive new concepts framed as "collateral impunity" and "equivalent reparation." These new concepts mirrored the inhumanities at the heart of the original concept of impunity and the substantial evidence that made apologies and repentance believable in the original concept of reparation. Both new concepts were more directly related to my personal experience.

The model for these new concepts contained three components, like the original concepts: the act, the perpetrator, and some tangible satisfaction that justice had been rendered. In the case of collateral impunity, the act was the sin of silence; the perpetrators were those in the vast middle of the bell shaped curve; the tangible satisfaction would be some act of contrition or apology to those who had been offended. The equivalent reparation would come in the form of personal investment in active pursuit of reconciliation to restoration of broken relationships. But how does an individual implement these concepts?

The phrases immediately prior to the "And there is no health in us" part of the old prayer of confession provided an important starting point. "We have left undone those things which we ought to have done; And we have done those things which we ought not to have done."[24] This confession precisely defines our past sin of silence and helps us come to terms with it. In no way can we go back and correct our omissions or commissions. We can only confess them and move on. What we now must do is not replicate the silence that denies current injustices, or because of prejudice actively discount the *other* we encounter as we live our lives.

In order to reconcile brokenness we must leave our silent separation and seek out opportunities to engage with the *other* in order to tear down the walls between us. Such opportunities abound. One may not be able to right the corporate wrongs of society, but one can certainly engage in personal forms of reconciliation. Confession is the starting point that eventually may lead to restoration.

Although I have not yet fully developed the details of the concepts of collateral impunity and its requisite response of equivalent reparation, I have concluded that they have a significant part to play in anyone's search for truth and understanding. I caught glimpses of these concepts in action in one unexpected consequence of reconstructing this narrative. Such glimpses were present in the previously described encounter between Mr. Lindsey Walker and Dr. Russell Bush. They were present in the way Mayor McLean dealt with his various constituents. They were present in the relationship that developed between Ira Grupper and me.

Ira and I started out approaching each other with fear and trepidation based on assumptions of each other. Each of us had had experiences that led us to believe our fear of the other was real, not the "unreal fear of the paranoid." As we cautiously began to disclose our "very different perceptions of the same events," we discovered in time that our original trepidation regarding each other was actually based on the "fear of the unknown." But that changed with the disclosure of the known. As Ira said after several hours of sharing experiences, "You have given me insight in ways I was not cognizant of before." These feelings of understanding were mutual.

Though the walls between us began to come down when we began telling our stories, we still maintained a healthy respect for each other's experiences and differences of opinion. Investment of time and energy; reaching out to each other in spite of our fears; sharing experiences; clearing up misconceptions; pleas to the other to accept the truth of what one said—all were simple acts of equivalent reparations, the stuff out of which reconciliation is created. The common ground we held was actually the "fear of the untruth," for both of us were searching for the truth. Something in this exchange had the feel of genuine reconciliation taking place and of collateral impunity being overcome. The transformation that happened to us is illustrative of what can happen to others.

In brief, equivalent reparation is to collateral impunity (personal) as reparation is to impunity (corporate). Both lead to reconciliation. In our encounters, we discover the meaning of ". . . first be reconciled with your brother and sister . . ." (Matthew 5:24b, NRSV). And what happens to us in the process is closely akin to St. Paul's injunction: "Do not be conformed to this world, but be transformed by the renewing of your minds, so that you may discern what is the will of God—what is good and acceptable and perfect." (Romans 12:2, NRSV). Sadly, at times we fear the middle way of compromise and reconciliation. We fearfully cling to either/or because our pain or our prejudice is too deep, and does not allow us to embrace both/and, a position considered traitorous or cowardly by some. Fear is the culprit—fear of the unreal, fear of the unknown, and fear of about almost everything under the sun and the moon, but most commonly, the fear of the *other*. In hanging on to our fear, we ignore the most dynamic ingredient of reconciliation, the reality that "Perfect love casts out fear" (I John 4:18b, NRSV).

Somehow the healing of society begins by facing and overcoming our fear of the *other* with acts of perfect love. Healing begins one-to-one, in quiet and small ways: opening oneself to the other, expecting to bring out the best in each other, making a difference. But this healing will not happen until one decides to leave one's silent separation and seek face-to-face encounters with the *other*. When these opportunities are present, one is required to look deep into the eyes of the *other* with compassion, telling the truth and searching for understanding. Here is where, I believe, those in the silent middle of the bell shaped curve who dare to break the silence have a great deal to offer to help heal society in turbulent times. This challenge becomes even more urgent when the world is as radically polarized as it is in the twenty-first century. Some *one* has to start by reaching out to the *other*.

Recently Dwain Epps responded to my "sense of overwhelming sadness" at the "attitude of mutual historical distrust" that still lingers to this day and its accompanying reluctance to tell one's story. He said, "Until it all comes out, in a spirit of humility, acknowledgment of complicity, and respect for others who were as caught up in contradiction as we were, how are we to build the ground for that better future?" He mentioned he had learned a lot from working on the healing of memories project in the World Council of Churches, which might be instructive in understanding "an attitude of mutual historical distrust" and its attendant behaviors. He shared the story the WCC got when they sent an investigative delegation to the former Yugoslavia to give advice on how to approach the terrible ethnic cleansing and battle between Bosnia-Herzegovina and the Serbs.

He said a friend of his who was in the delegation, himself the child of exiles from Nazi occupation of Yugoslavia during World War II, interviewed a young fighter in the hills and asked him why he was shelling a village down below. "Was what you are doing being done in the name of nation, ideology, ethnic purity?" The answer was straightforward. The young man said, "[S]ee that farm down there, that used to belong to my family; those bastards stole it from us and we're getting it back!" Epps's friend asked when that had happened and the answer came quickly: "In the 15th century!" Epps concluded, "Violence has a long memory, and unless it is healed, people in Columbia [and elsewhere] will still be fighting three centuries from now, I fear."[25]

Yes, violence has a long memory, and this is why people are wary of reaching out to others and telling their stories.[26] The people in Mississippi and elsewhere who inflicted pain over the decades are not all dead, and neither are those on whom it was inflicted. But there are elements in our heritage, much like those I experienced, that offer great hope. The battle for racial reconciliation is far from over.[27] Questions need to be asked, such as: What can we, who call ourselves "good people," do today to prevent perpetuating the pain? How can we work with others to bring about real change? Do we just pretend in our silence that the problem is solved, or can we find ways to break that silence? How will our children dare to differ, live out their heritage, and shape the lives of our grandchildren so they can learn to live together with others in turbulent times?

These are tough questions. Not everyone is willing to repudiate racism. It is hard to be proud of family lineage and cultural heritage, yet recognize the evil that at times lurks within them. Repentance is an important landmark on the way to reconciliation and forgiveness. Each generation must come to terms with its own "so what" transforming moments in tangible and concrete ways in search of truth and understanding.

As a fourth generation Mississippian, I discovered in the course of this narrative journey a bit more about myself and how I may have become the individual I became in pursuing my call to ministry. What my friend, Ira Grupper, said about himself, is also true for me: We were minor players in the drama that played itself out in those days on the streets of Columbia in the mid-1960s. But nonetheless, having been there and done what we did, our lives were profoundly changed forever, no matter what road we traveled down thereafter.

Epilogue

The magnitude of nationwide and regional events grabbing the headlines throughout the decade of the 1960s made the confluence of people and events at this time in Columbia seem almost obscure by contrast. But those involved deemed what transpired far from obscure and, for the most part, life changing. Even the smallest details and routine decisions at times took on epic proportions with far-reaching, unexpected implications. Determined, ordinary individuals, sometimes privately and sometimes publicly, acted in concert for the welfare of the city and county. Their actions made a difference, and this was their story. It was a time of baby steps for a community complying with the provisions of the Civil Rights Act of 1964 and the Voting Rights Act of 1965.

But to what end? What were the lasting consequences of those initiatives? It is beyond the scope of this work to explore in-depth answers to these questions. This narrative portrays only limited perspectives of what took place. Others had different experiences than those described here. To tell the complete story, they must be heard. So the telling of my own story constitutes an invitation, perhaps even a challenge to them to step forward and tell their own stories. Until others do, can an adequate foundation be laid to comprehend today the lasting significance of what transpired in the past?

The provisions of the Civil Rights Act brought about dramatic changes in society with regard to racial discrimination. The same was true of the Voting Rights Act, which "opened elections to millions of blacks and other minorities." In the spring of 2009, debate began in the Supreme Court about whether one of the key provisions of the Voting Rights Act—Section 5, the "main enforcement tool against discriminatory changes in voting since the law was enacted in 1965"—was constitutional or even necessary today. Originally, the idea behind the provision was "to prevent discriminatory measures from being put in place." At issue now recently was whether "all or parts of 16 states, mainly in the South with a history of discrimination in voting" still needed to get approval in advance of making changes in the way elections are conducted.[1]

Section 5 was the "deepest and most dramatic federal intrusion into state and local governing affairs since Reconstruction." Originally Congress made the law temporary, but it was later extended in time to cover other minorities. Though great strides had been made in the South, old patterns of voting inequities still existed in some places. Some civil rights advocates were afraid that if this section were removed, it would open the door to "discriminatory redistricting plans or changes in voting rules." Also, there was concern that "it would make local election changes harder to challenge."[2]

In June 2009, the Supreme Court did not address the issue of the constitutionality of section 5—much to the relief of some civil rights advocates—although a majority could have voted to do so. Instead, the Court simply voted 8–1 that a municipal utility district in Texas "could apply to opt out of the advance approval provision, reversing a lower federal court that ruled it could not." Clarence Thomas, who felt the provision should be struck down as unconstitutional, cast the one dissenting vote. Although the larger constitutional issue was not addressed this time, critics of the law warned "the court made clear that it might not take such a restrained approach the next time a voting rights challenge comes its way."[3] All this is by way of saying how issues have changed since 1965—and also how the struggle to combat the consequences of racism continues in the public sector.

What is true in the public sector today is also true in the arena of personal prejudices and attitudes. For some, great changes have occurred, but for others not much has changed. Anthony Walton, born in Aurora, Illinois, in 1960 to African American parents who had "escaped" Mississippi, one day found himself faced with the damning force of racism. He grew up in a middle-class neighborhood and studied at Notre Dame and Brown, all the time believing that the world his parents fled to find freedom was somewhere in the past. As he struggled with his own self-understanding, he felt compelled to return in the early 1990s to the roots of his heritage in Mississippi. For several years he traveled the state from the high loess bluff overlooking the river in Natchez, to the quiet shade of "the Grove" on the Ole Miss campus in Oxford, talking with people, seeking to comprehend the full meaning of the state's rich and tragic history.

What Walton learned about his own family's history, as well as about the intricate racial dynamics of the 1990s, profoundly changed his view of himself and the world in which he lived. What he learned about the social realities of Mississippi was that although much had changed in the legal realm and in polite social exchanges, "Blacks in Mississippi had simply continued the society my parents had grown up in, and that society was separate, if somewhat more equal than it had been before."[4] One suspects that some whites had also simply perpetuated the society their parents had grown up in.

Walton was yet more specific in his observations: "Contemporary Mississippians refuse . . . to 'recognize' each other, to acknowledge their commonality. The state's tragic history is testimony to what this refusal has wrought. And it is now likely that the members of the two racial groups are permanent strangers, doomed to gape and stare but not see, blind to each other as siblings, humans, Americans."[5] How true his conclusions will be about the relations between blacks and whites in Mississippi twenty years from now remains to be seen. Nonetheless, these conclusions represent a significant part of the picture that must be considered today. If what Walton observed is true—that two cultures exist today in Mississippi, "mutually suspicious, if not hostile and, on a good day, indifferent"—then having meaningful and open discussions about our differences presents a great challenge for those who dare to reach out to the *other* in search of truth and understanding. But great challenges have never been in short supply for Mississippians!

❖   ❖   ❖

One question remains for consideration: Other than Buddy McLean, what happened after 1966 to the principals and others featured in this narrative?

Amos Payton continued as pastor of the Owen Chapel Baptist Church in Columbia. He was active in various civic and religious organizations. He died on April 3, 1969, with interment in Pleasant Valley Cemetery. His wife, four sons, and four daughters survived Payton. The program for his memorial service included the following quote from W. C. Bryant. "Lives of great men all remind us, We can make our lives sublime; / And departing, leave behind us, Footprints on the sands of time."[6] Payton's footsteps left great impressions in Columbia. I never saw Amos after I moved away.

Isaac Pittman continued to serve as director of the Mississippi Rural Center until he retired at its annual conference in 1974. He had served the center as its first director since it was founded in 1949. During this time, the center housed one of the first Head Start programs in the county. In August of 1967, I received a letter from Mamie Heinz, an early childhood consultant connected with the Presbyterian Church U.S. She had made a trip to Columbia and knew of my continuing interest in the town. In

passing she wrote, "The trip to Columbia, Miss[issippi] was most exciting
and thrilling. The director of Head Start, there since last January, is most
efficient and is doing a marvelous job. They have a strong administrative
group. Much is being accomplished."[7] Pittman was part of this administration group. After his first wife—who had served as the first secretary of
the original bi-racial committee—died, Pittman remarried. Pittman died
on November 21, 1991. Interment was in Resthaven at Sandy Hook. The
inscription on his stone reads: "Our lives are left with an empty void that
can never be filled. We will miss him, our dearest loved one."[8] I missed
Isaac, and never saw him again after I moved from Columbia.

L. Z. Blankinship became one of the outstanding leaders in the community action arena, both locally in Columbia and in the region and state.
He served as deputy director and then executive director of Pearl River
Valley Opportunity, Inc., which served Marion, Lamar, and Pearl River
Counties. L. Z. and I corresponded after I left Columbia. In one letter,
dated August 24, 1967, he gave me a report on how things were going in
the area. He noted that the "flare-ups" in Mississippi that summer had
been "on a very small scale." He spoke of the role the Neighborhood Youth
Corps was playing for those young people going back to school: "This was a
'BIG' help to the race problem because it gave these children something to
do. With nothing to do they could have been 'troublemakers.'" He went on
to say, "Through the Bi-Racial Committee, we were able to have Negroes
at all of the voting precincts but one. We feel we have made some progress
but not as much as we hoped to. Of course we are well aware of the fact
that it takes time." He closed by noting, "Rev. Payton is fair," indicating
early signs of his decline.[9]

Blankinship sent me the March 1969 issue of *Progress Report*, the
monthly newsletter for PRVO. In it was a lengthy report of the exchange
that took place between Blankinship and President Nixon's special assistant for minority affairs, Robert J. Brown, at the NACD national conference held in Washington March 9–12. Their discussion had to do with
Vice President Agnew's statement about "the involvement of the poor in
the community action programs and in Head Start [that Brown said] was
made in ignorance." The details of the exchange are not as important as
the fact that Blankinship represented effectively the position that in Mississippi, "community action agencies have had greater success in getting
local participation because of the impact Head Start made locally." His
point was that "Head Start made some of the Power Structure concerned
enough to get community action agencies into those communities."[10] The

whole exchange illustrated the scope of Blankinship's leadership skills, which he exercised on behalf of and beyond Mississippi.

Over the years, I was able to visit with L. Z. a couple of times when I visited Columbia. I talked with him over the phone for the last time when I was there in 2002. His health was beginning to fail him. He died at home on July 3, 2004. His interment was in Christian Hill Cemetery, Foxworth.

After N. A. Dickson served the Methodist Church in Yazoo City for a year, he was appointed a district superintendent in the Methodist Church in Mississippi. He also served as capital funds coordinator and program council director for the conference, as well as a trustee of Millsaps College. In his "retirement," he returned to make his home in Columbia, but he could not stay uninvolved. He participated in the life of the Chapel of the Cross United Methodist Church. His fifty years of service in the United Methodist Church included serving as pastor in twenty-six churches; he built and renovated four. I visited him in Brookhaven when he was superintendent in that district and again in Columbia after his retirement. N. A. died in the Marion General Hospital on April 8, 2000. His interment was in Woodlawn Cemetery.[11]

Dwain Epps left Camden, Alabama, in 1965 for Germany, where he spent the following academic year studying with the faculty of the department of Protestant theology at the University of Tuebingen. Following his ordination in the United Presbyterian Church, USA, in 1967, Epps and his new wife, Kathy, left for three years in Buenos Aires, Argentina, where they acted as ecumenical interns with ISAL (Iglesia y Sociedad en America Latina/Church and Society in Latin America). From there he traveled to Geneva, Switzerland, where in 1971 he joined the staff of the Commission of the Churches on International Affairs of the World Council of Churches (CCIA/WCC) as executive secretary. In 1978, he returned to the United States as director of WCC's UN headquarters' liaison office in New York and its representative at the United Nations. He joined the National Council of Churches of Christ in the USA as assistant general secretary for international affairs in New York in 1982.

After ten years at the Interchurch Center at 175 Riverside Drive in New York, Epps returned to his previous post at the CCIA/WCC UN headquarters liaison office in New York. When he was elected director of the CCIA/WCC in 1993, he and his family returned to Geneva. He retired in 2002 to the mountain village of Montbovon in the Canton of Fribourg, where he spends his time "puttering in the garden," and writing and organizing the

WCC's international affairs archives in Geneva.[12] Epps came to Lexington several years ago to renew old acquaintances. We keep up with each other via e-mail and Skype. He returned to Lexington in September 2009 to join us in celebration of my seventy-fifth birthday. Ira Grupper was also in attendance, and on that occasion met Epps for the first time.

Frank Brooks served the Board of Christian Education in Richmond for five years before returning to the local pastorate. He was pastor of First Presbyterian Church, Batesville, Arkansas, for many years. He then moved to Ripley, Mississippi, to be pastor of the Presbyterian church there. His last active pastorate was at the Presbyterian church in Leland, Mississippi. The Brookses retired to Corinth, Mississippi, to live in the Biggers' family home. Frank continues to be active as mentor to seminary students supplying the small country Presbyterian church in nearby Biggersville. He was the only one of the five of us who had come to Mississippi after graduation from Louisville Seminary in 1959–60 and then left to later return to Mississippi in active service as a pastor in a local congregation. We talk on the telephone every couple of weeks and get together occasionally to visit.

Russell Bush retired from his practice of dentistry and at age sixty-six became pastor of the Main Street Baptist Church in Hattiesburg for fifteen years, though he retained his residency in Columbia. Bush actively engaged in public speaking engagements on a variety of subjects, such as serving as principal speaker at a big anti-drinking rally in the fall of 1966, as advertised in a full page ad of the *Columbian-Progress*.[13] He maintained contact with several of the blacks that served with him on the bi-racial committee, such as Lindsey Walker. He spoke to civic clubs and other gatherings about his service with them. Bush retired again at eighty years of age in 2000 and joined his wife in operating the Berean Bookstore in Columbia.[14] They live in the same home they lived in for years out on Broad Street.

Lindsey Walker served a regular term as chairman on the bi-racial committee. His term got extended by three months because he completed Bill Walker's term when Bill moved to Jackson. The Wolfe Construction Company employed Walker and several members of his family as bricklayers and stonemasons working on a variety of projects, including many at Camp Shelby, south of Hattiesburg. Walker told me he personally laid all the stonework in the new Presbyterian church building when it was built back in the late 1950s. Walker left the employ of the Wolfe Company to form Walker Brothers Construction Company, one of the few African American building contractors in the county. Lindsey Walker served as owner and manager of this successful business that did "mostly big jobs,

such as church construction or other large buildings."[15] Walker is retired
and continues to live in Columbia.

Not long after Ira Grupper left Columbia in the fall of 1966, he ended
up in Louisville, Kentucky, working with Carl and Anne Braden on the
staff of the Southern Conference Educational Fund (SCEF). Ira's was
among the first group of disabled persons in the United States to win an
employment discrimination case under the Rehabilitation Act of 1973, the
predecessor to the Americans With Disabilities Act (ADA). He worked for
twenty-four years on the assembly line of a cigarette processing plant in
Louisville, where he was involved as union shop steward, leader of a union
rank-and-file caucus, and union delegate to the Greater Louisville Central
Labor Council.

Grupper's activism for social justice was not limited to the unions.
He once served as national co-chair of the New Jewish Agenda (NJA) and
as vice-chair of the Louisville & Jefferson County (KY) Human Relations
Commission. He is active in the Kentucky Alliance Against Racism and
Political Repression, Metro (Louisville) Disabilities Coalition, and the
Committees of Correspondence for Democracy and Socialism. His inter-
est was not just domestic, but international. He has been to the Middle
East four times, once for six months, when he was based in Jerusalem and
spent time in the West Bank, the Gaza Strip, and Amman, Jordan.[16]

In January 2009 he visited Vietnam with a group of international
socialists. In January 2010, Grupper joined more than 1,400 committed
internationalist protestors from forty-three countries in Egypt for the
Gaza Freedom March to demand that Israel (and, in effect, Egypt) lift the
siege on the Palestinian people in Gaza. He currently writes a monthly
column, *Labor Paeans*, for FORsyth, the newspaper of the Louisville, Kentucky, chapter of FOR, the Fellowship of Reconciliation. As an adjunct faculty member at Bellarmine University in Louisville, Kentucky, he teaches
courses on the civil rights movement and Israeli-Palestinian Issues.

Grupper summed up what his life's experiences have meant to him
when he wrote: "The Civil Rights Movement enabled me to meet, and learn
from some of the most dedicated freedom fighters, helped me understand
the nature of racism, its relation to class oppression, and the international
aspects of capital accumulation. It provided purpose to life, the building
of the 'beloved community.' For this I will always be grateful."[17] We have
gotten together several times since we discovered each other. I participated on several occasions in the civil rights movement class he teaches at
Bellarmine.

Curtis Styles moved to Philadelphia, Pennsylvania, when Grupper went to New York City and then Louisville. Curt earned a master's degree in social work and got a job in a minimum-security prison. According to Grupper in *Labor Paeans*, Curt's "charges, mostly young African American first-time offenders, were motivated by Curt to learn to read or improve their reading, using Malcolm X's and other writings he gave them. Curt established a strong rapport with these boys; he was fired for not following established principles of social work." Curtis vowed never to return to social work, and instead drove a truck until he retired at age fifty-four due to a medical condition. He died sometime around 1996 and was buried outside Philadelphia. He was fifty-nine years old. Grupper had the honor of saying a few words of eulogy at his funeral.[18]

W. J. McClenton remained in Columbia, his hometown, and continued to be active in the civil rights movement after Curtis Styles and Ira Grupper left. His name showed up as a representative of Marion County on a list of the committee appointed by SCLC to present demands of this group to Governor John Bell Williams on June 23, 1969.[19] Writing in *Labor Paeans*, Ira Grupper said of W. J.: "a third-grade drop out . . . at best, functionally illiterate . . . not only did he become proficient with the English language, but he helped people who had been denied, for example, disability claims, write appeals. He remained, to be sure, rough-hewn, often bawdy, but always an advocate for his people, and, indeed, for all poor and working class people."

W. J. died on January 23, 2002. He lived to be seventy-three years old. Grupper said, "He was a good person. He was my friend. He was my brother." Grupper had the honor of eulogizing W. J. at his funeral, held at Friendship Missionary Baptist Church just outside Columbia. The funeral program stated; "W. J. was a Civil Rights leader . . . who . . . never started a job he didn't finish. He knew no boundaries when it came to helping someone, no matter the race, origin or gender. He will always be remembered as a strong devoted African American who stood with Dr. Martin Luther King . . . . If there was nothing in the world he could do to help you, there would have been nothing in the world he would do to hurt you." Of both Curtis and W. J. Ira Grupper said: "They were local people who gave their all self-effacingly."[20]

Now for what happened to William McAtee IV after Columbia. The five years on the staff of the Presbyterian Board of Christian Education in Richmond opened new opportunities of service for me in ministry. With the domestic upheavals of the latter half of the 1960s, I was faced with very different challenges in race relations and social justice, though none as immediate and tangible as what I experienced in Columbia.

One event that reconnected me to Columbia happened on the morning of April 5, 1968. I now rode the bus to work in downtown Richmond. That morning, as the bus passed through a somewhat rundown business section of town, I looked out the window and saw an accident involving an eighteen-wheeler and an automobile that had pulled out of a parking spot at the curb and was stuck under the trailer. I noticed a sullen and somewhat agitated crowd of white working people gathered around the scene. In an instant I saw the writing on the side of the trailer: Stringer Moving Van, Columbia, Mississippi!

And then I saw my black friend, the driver who had moved my family twice, standing alone by the cab. I jumped off the bus and ran back and stood with him until the police came to make their inquiry and report. It became apparent that the driver of the automobile was at fault, but the air was filled with hostility toward my friend. The matter was soon cleared up and he was free to leave. He thanked me for stopping, we shook hands, he drove on, and I caught the next bus to work. I still was puzzled at the mood surrounding the accident. Only when I got to work did I discover that Martin Luther King, Jr., had been assassinated in Memphis the night before. The country had moved to a new level of turbulence and racial tension.

In 1971, we moved to Lexington, Kentucky, where I served Transylvania Presbytery in central and eastern Kentucky for ten years as associate executive presbyter, then for sixteen years as executive presbyter. I was honorably retired from active ministry in March of 1997 and was granted executive presbyter emeritus status on September 11, 2001, at the fall stated meeting of presbytery—the very moment the world changed forever in the calamity in lower Manhattan.

To give purpose to my retirement years, I continued my life-long educational commitment to "discovery learning." As adjunct faculty, I taught a course on "Managing Time/Energy and Effectiveness," based on my doctoral work there, in McCormick Seminary's doctor of ministry program; taught courses in Presbyterian studies at Lexington Seminary (Disciples); and co-taught a course on small church ministry with Marcia C. Myers at Louisville Seminary. I was commissioned by the Presbyterian Church (USA) as an international volunteer in mission and took twelve travel study seminars to Cuba. Along with Lewis L. Wilkins, my longtime friend and associate, I developed the concept of "Story as Theological Reflection" and led a series of workshops on that subject.

The Presbyterian Church was my life, making my heart ache when the Columbia Presbyterian Church left our mainline Presbyterian denomination and joined a denomination that split off from it. This schism caused an upheaval in the congregation, and several families left. I knew personally what that loss meant, because half of the congregations my dad served and half of the congregations I served left our denomination. That was a burden that was slow to ease over time.

In August 2001, I took son Walt on a sentimental trip around Mississippi to see the place where he was born and to visit all the places where I had lived. My time spent in Mississippi after I left Columbia consisted mainly of visiting occasionally with friends and the few members of our family still living there, preaching a week of services in Brookhaven and at the one hundredth anniversary of the church in Amory, attending several high school class reunions, and making periodic visits to look after the Old Place. Lone Hill Farm is at the approximate geographic center of the Magnolia State, a fact I have often said makes me steward of that center and keeper of its heart.

About all that is left of Lone Hill Farm now is the land, with its covering of Loblolly pine, some hardwoods, briars, and bramble. Wild turkeys, deer, and an assortment of smaller wildlife have the run of the place where sugar cane and cotton fields used to produce their meager yield. The dwellings, barn, and out buildings are all but gone. One fading remnant of the main house fights time and undergrowth and heat and rain thanks to its heart pine skeleton and a good tin roof over its head.

The marble-topped McAtee sideboard and parlor table with telltale hatchet marks, reminders of where family and tenants once pounded tough meat for edible consumption in harder days, presided over the proceedings in my sister's dining room in Memphis for years. The McAtee clothes chest sits quietly in the guest room in our house in Lexington, awaiting occasional visits of sixth generation McAtee grandchildren. The wool combs and shoe last rest now from their labors a century and a half ago in my shop behind the garage, a long way from their first home at Seneasha Plantation in Beat Four, Attala County, Mississippi. These five items, plus a mission style desk I last saw in the possession of a cousin in Kosciusko, are about all the tangible evidence of that heritage that is left. Oh, if they could talk!

But there is the land, passed down from the U.S. government to Gordon Boyd and Sylvester Pear, land agents, in 1836; to George Pope then to James Meek in 1852; to Junious McAtee, William I's brother, and Sarah

Meek McAtee, his widow in 1884; to William II in 1889; to his surviving children in 1936; to William III, who bought them out in the 1940s; to his widow, Queen Graeber McAtee, in 1958; to his daughter, Emma Jane, and his son, William IV, in 1998. I bought my sister out the following year. My wife and I are currently co-trustees of the McAtee family trust and current stewards of the Old Place, beat Four, Attala County, Mississippi. Our sons, William Neal (V) and Walter Bunn, are co-successor trustees and one day will assume the family stewardship.

When my mother died in 1998, we had to sell some timber to pay estate taxes. It was an emotional experience to cut the trees. Some I had planted in the 1970s when I was looking after the place for her. Others had been there for years. One pine tree was so big I could only reach halfway around it. I almost cried to see it cut, but red heart rot was setting in, and it was beginning to die. It stood beside the old main road into the place, which no longer exists. From the timber man's estimate of its age when he read the rings, I figured that it was a sapling standing there when my daddy came walking up that road to home after serving in France during World War I.

Over the years I would make a long day's drive down from Kentucky just to walk the place and draw on the spirit of my ancestors. Other times I took the family there to camp. I knew enough to show them where the cane, cotton, and cornfields were. No telling how my grandpa would feel knowing that I planted trees in those fields that he wrested clear of brush and bramble so he could plant his marginal crops! I pointed to where the sugar cane mill stood. I remember seeing it operating for the last time, worked by a cousin, close to where Uncle Bunk's and Aunt Una's houses once were. Many of our extended family that are still living have a deep emotional connection with the Old Place, even though it has changed dramatically from our memories of it and what it stood for. But the place triggers memories of my heritage and my growing up in Mississippi.

I left turbulent times in Mississippi more than forty years ago and ended up in Kentucky, traveling a full circle that took this William McAtee back to where the first William launched out from his Washington County home on a wild water-way adventure some 170 years ago down to Mississippi. I am back in Kentucky now; what's past is past. And I am at peace with it.

Now we live in very different, very turbulent times and places, calling for new ways to dare to differ so we can learn to live together in peace and harmony. We dare not linger in the past, only relish and celebrate most of that heritage and repudiate the rest. It does matter where one came from, because our lives are shaped and inextricably entwined with countless folk in "discriminating slices" and "shard-like artifacts" of that heritage. But, thank God, we are not bound by it.

◆ ◆ ◆

When Chris Watts first approached me in November 2008, asking me to recall events in the 1960s related to the civil rights movement in Columbia, he indicated he wanted those in the African American community to feel the Marion County Museum and Archives was "their museum and 'have a pride in our shared history,' especially the school children that came in with their class to visit." He recently reported in an e-mail to me that he had had a church group of all African American children come to the museum, and he gave them the "school-child" tour. Before leaving, one young girl politely tugged at his sleeve, looked up at him and said: "Mr. Watts, my Momma told me that used to, back in sixties, whites and blacks fought all the time, but now we are all friends." Those simple words from a child were very meaningful to Chris and caught him off guard. Then Watts closed his e-mail by saying, "For me, she was able to put a profound excla-mation point at the end of all the sentences that you have written since you began last November [2008]. I could not help but think not only of you, but Styles, McClenton, Grupper, McLean, and all of Six, and how much things have truly changed over the past forty-three years, maybe not huge changes, but there has been change."[21]

Yes, thank God, we are not bound by the past. The challenge of the present and the hope for the future are enough to say grace over now, and maybe a little child will show the rest of us the way. So be it and let it be . . .

Acknowledgments

I owe a simple debt of gratitude to a special group of people who helped me make the sharing of this narrative possible. To the following persons for the contributions they made, I offer a simple thank you.

Chris Watts was appalled to discover there was little or no information about the civil rights movement in the mid-1960s in the records of the Marion County Museum and Archives when he became its curator. He never dreamed that his request would provide me the motivation to write a book. Neither did I. He volunteered countless hours of his own time researching primary and secondary resources on the Internet, in the archives at the University of Southern Mississippi, and in all the issues of the *Columbian-Progress* during these years. His uncanny knack for on time delivery of data from Mayor McLean's files and other sources provided me with indispensable material at the very moment I needed it. Sharing his own and family stories made him part of the ongoing narrative, giving it a contemporary context and helping me reconnect with Columbia. We both have an abiding commitment to passing on to future generations lessons we have learned from the history we have experienced, especially to those of McAtee and Watts lineage. Whether or not learnings drawn from this story are well received as being valid for another generation, only time will judge.

My sister, our family historian and archivist Emma Jane McAtee Patterson, provided her perspective on many aspects of our early life together growing up in Mississippi. Her files and unpublished stories of our family history provided me with details that enriched my memory. Hardly a week passes without my receiving in the mail from her—my own personal clipping service—news of Mississippi from the Memphis *Commercial Appeal*, both past and present. Together our exchanges make us better keepers of family memory.

Dwain Epps was very much part of the story from the beginning. In a very real sense, this is partly his story. He was there briefly during the initial summer of 1964, and he followed the journey from a distance over the years through the letters and e-mails we shared. He provided me with a broader perspective about injustices perpetuated with impunity in many locations around the world, and the devastating impact the lack of proper resolution had on future generations. He was my sounding board for my reflections on the learnings I drew from the narrative and generously supplied me with penetrating responses. He was extremely helpful in critiquing various drafts of the manuscript.

Frank Brooks, with whom I share the longest and closest friendship, was instrumental in suggesting my name for consideration as pastor, an event that got me to Columbia in the first place. We shared many experiences as the story unfolded. He read the manuscript through the eyes of a native Mississippian, who experienced many of the same things I did growing up there, and serving together as pastors in later years. This shared past gave his responses to the manuscript a special quality. He provided accuracy to the recounting of many details, such as the numbers and names of the trains we rode!

What a rare privilege it was to have our two sons participate in perfecting the presentation of this story, which in fact began at the beginning of their lives. Son Neal, in anticipation of what I would write based on bits and pieces of the story he had heard over the years, volunteered his understanding of the power of derogatory slurs: "[W]ords do not kill. But words represent ideas. And when the ideas they represent are born of prejudice, resentment and ignorance, they kill——they kill people, they kill hope." In doing so, he captured the essence of a major point of the narrative. Later, he read the manuscript through the eyes of his generation, one that did not have the perspective of firsthand experience of what took place during the 1960s in Mississippi. From this perspective he made helpful suggestions as to how better to describe what he had not experienced, thereby making it more meaningful to his generation.

Son Walt saw immediately that telling this story was very important to me and wanted to help me present it in the most compelling way. Relying on his literary training and background, he pushed me for clarity of thought in the sentences I wrote and in the structure and style through which they were presented in the first draft. He made candid suggestions as to ways the material could be organized to improve its flow. He suggested I give more concrete examples at some points of what was happening during events I described. He provided a contemporary sensitivity check on the way I wrote about diversity issues, past and present. How blessed I am to have this in-house literary critic.

Governor William F. Winter, a friend of long standing through our connections in the Presbyterian Church, receives my special thanks. He was very enthusiastic about the project from the outset when I first shared my proposal with him. He was a friend of Buddy McLean through their connections in the political arena and knew of Buddy's accomplishments as mayor of Columbia. As he began to read the manuscript, he commented to me that this "ought to be a well received book." He generously agreed to write the foreword, for which I am deeply grateful.

Craig Gill, editor-in-chief of the University Press of Mississippi, provided the skillful guidance I needed to see me through the submission and final production processes. In our initial visit after he received the first draft, I said to him by way of introduction, "You know four hundred pages about me, but I know nothing about you." His gracious response gave me the kind of assurance that this was the beginning of a rewarding venture. That has turned out to be the case, especially when freelance copyeditor Lisa Paddock applied her creative editorial attention to detail to the manuscript. Thanks to Anne Stascavage, managing editor, Shane Gong Stewart, senior production editor, and all the staff of the Press, who took care of the myriad of production tasks involved in making this book a reality.

A special thanks to Monica King of Lynn Imaging's Monster Color in Lexington for preparing the photographs for publication.

Finally, my wife Millye, even though she spent her days caring for our two young sons as the story originally unfolded, was keenly aware of the significance of what I was involved in with the mayor and others. Knowing how important this time was in our lives, she encouraged me in many ways as I climbed the stairs to spend long hours at the computer writing the manuscript. She is indeed an integral part of the story.

Notes

Preface

1. The information about Watts was gleaned from our exchange of e-mails. Watts grew up in the Improve Community in Marion County and graduated from East Marion High School in 1993. He received a B.A. degree in European History from the University of Southern Mississippi in 1997. He never taught school; instead he went to work for the Mississippi Highway Patrol for a while in a civilian position. His love of history led him to accept the position as the first curator of the Marion County Museum and Archives, which had been operated up to that point by volunteers.

Watts wanted to create interest and pride in the history of the area, so he decided to write a series of newspaper columns "from the museum" based on fresh stories that no one had ever heard. His first column was one such story he stumbled on. It was about an expedition of Yankee raiders that moved up from Baton Rouge through Columbia and on to Leakesville to cut the Mobile and Ohio railroad, which was Gen. John B. Hood's supply line in central Tennessee.

He spent years researching his family's violent history, much of it appearing in "The Cox, Morris, and Pace Feud of Marion County, Mississippi, 1872–1876," published in the *Journal of Mississippi History* in the fall of 2007. It seems that "Big Bill Morris" was his great-great-grandfather, who was killed in that feud on August 22, 1875. Watts has in his possession the Sunday clothes Big Bill was wearing on the way to church the day he was killed. He also has a handwritten bill of sale confirming Big Bill sold his slave, which reads: "a negro boy named 'Isah' aged twenty five years, I further warrant said boy in every respect given under my hand and seal this 22 day of December, 1861." Watts still lives on Big Bill's farm with his wife Monica and their young sons, Luke and C. J., who are the sixth generation to live on the same forty acres.

2. Showing no disrespect, further reference to Mayor McLean or the mayor in this work at times may be either as Buddy McLean, Mr. Buddy, as some affectionately referred to him, or simply Buddy.

3. For years I used "fourth generation Mississippian" in this line because I was counting the four generations of William McAtees who lived here. Actually a generation of my family existed in Mississippi before the name McAtee entered my generational story. I had two sets of great-great-grandparents who migrated to Mississippi in the 1800s from Alabama: Rev. James W., a circuit-riding Methodist missionary to the Choctaw Indians, and Mary (Polly) Wyche Meek (1833), and Rev. Humphrey, a circuit-riding Methodist minister who served many appointments in Mississippi, including appointments to "colored mission points," and Rebecca Thompson Williamson (1845). On the basis of these facts, I qualify as fifth generation

Mississippian. But because during the time detailed in this narrative I used the fourth generation reference, I use it in this book.

4. See Tex Sample, *Ministry in an Oral Culture: Living with Will Rogers, Uncle Remus, & Minnie Pearl* (Louisville, KY: Westminster/John Knox Press, 1994), p. 3. Sample described the world he came from as "not one of discourse, systematic coherence, the consistent use of clear definitions, and the writing of discursive prose that could withstand the whipsaws of academic critique [literate culture]. Rather, it was a world made sense of through proverbs, stories, and relationships [oral culture]." This is the world I grew up in too. The first time I met Tex I was in the third grade and he was in the second grade in Brookhaven, Mississippi! As we moved through subsequent grades to high school, we were exposed to excellent teachers of literate culture that introduced us to this other world we adopted as ministers and authors, though we never abandoned our original culture.

5. William G. McAtee, *Dreams, Where Have You Gone?: Clues for Unity and Hope* (Louisville, KY: Witherspoon Press, 2006), p. x.

Chapter One: Columbia Comes Calling

1. See Barbara R. Thompson, *Just Plain Bill* (Decatur, GA: Pathway Communications Group, 1996), pp. 69–73, 76. Bill Walker was faced with the challenge of a cultural transition in the 1960s. The Walker Chain Stores, dry goods and variety stores, he was operating in equal partnership with his mother Minnie J and sister Tina, experienced declining profits. Seeking a way to serve the shopping needs of rural consumers in small towns, he opened his first dollar store at the corner of Main and Church Streets in Columbia in 1961. The concept was simple: stock "opportunity buys" of merchandise bought in large quantities when available for low prices, usually with only 1 to 3 percent markups. By 1962, his sixty-five stores in Mississippi, Louisiana, and Alabama had a sales volume of $7,500,000. By 1967, there were 154 stores employing over eight hundred people; by 1972, there were 245 stores with sales close to $49 million. The demographic profile for his customer base was 90 percent female, 65 percent black, and 60 percent dependent on government financial assistance. Seventy-five percent of their households had income of less than $15,000 per year. Bill felt his ministry was to give working people the best value for their dollar. He also wanted to provide job opportunities for those seeking to better themselves.

2. "Healthy Beginnings," in McAtee Collection.

3. Thompson, *Just Plain Bill*, p.22.

4. Ibid., p. 24.

5. "I'll Remember April," No. 469, Psalm 34; Philippians 3:1–16, First Presbyterian Church, Amory, Mississippi, April 26, 1964.

6. Frank Sinatra (artist), Patricia Johnston, Patricia and Don Raye (lyricists), Gene De Paul (composer), "I'll Remember April," *Complete Capitol Singles Collection*, Capitol, 1996. I learned from Bob Walkup, my colleague and mentor, the practice of writing some sermons based on current popular songs of the day. "I'll Remember April" is an old jazz standard that dates back to the 1940s and has been recorded by

numerous artists. I got my inspiration for this sermon from listening to Erroll Garner's and Frank Sinatra's renditions.

7. Here is why cars appear in this narrative. "One cultural mark by which many of us growing up in Mississippi remembered important occasions in our lives related to the vehicles we rode in or drove at the time. Cars we chose identified much about us—our personal tastes or traits as well as our position in society. The big three auto companies provided an impressive selection reflecting the socio-economic status of their customers—Chevies to Cadillacs, Fords to Lincolns, Plymouths to Chryslers. Domestic automakers beyond the big three were becoming extinct; 'foreign' cars were suspect though Volkswagens began to appear in showrooms and on roadways. We considered a German made Opel before we bought the Rambler because it was somehow connected with GM, but stayed with American Motors. Even those with whom we bought or sold our cars were important expressions of relationships." Excerpt from William G. McAtee, "*SEER*, 'Me and Cars'" (Unpublished manuscript of short stories, essays, eulogies, and reflections), in McAtee Collection.

8. "The Priority of God," No. 72, Genesis 1:1–19, Columbia Presbyterian Church, Columbia, Mississippi, May 3, 1964.

9. Members of the presbytery commission: Rev. Adrian DeYoung, First Presbyterian Church, Hazlehurst, to preside and propound the constitutional questions (my mother's pastor at the time); Rev. Jim Johnson, First Presbyterian Church, Laurel, to preach; Frank A. Brooks, Jr., Westminster Presbyterian Church, Gulfport, to charge the pastor; Elder Mike Carr, First Presbyterian Church, Brookhaven, to charge the congregation; other members: Rev. David Laverty, Trinity Presbyterian Church, Laurel; Elder Orrick Metcalf, First Presbyterian Church, Natchez; Elder Watson Wood, Ocean Springs, and stated clerk of South Mississippi Presbytery.

10. "When It Rains, It Pours," No. 173, Mark 9:42–50, First United Methodist Church, Columbia, Mississippi, May 31, 1964.

11. Robert H. Walkup, Letter to Margo Reitz Cochran, his former director of Christian education at Starkville, November 3, 1964, p. 3, in McAtee collection.

12. "Forbid Them Not," No. 91, Genesis 17:1–17, Columbia Presbyterian Church, Columbia, Mississippi, June 14, 1964.

13. "Pigs and Pearls," No. 222, Matthew 7:1–12, Columbia Presbyterian Church, Columbia, Mississippi, June 14, 1964.

14. Malcolm Gladwell, *Outliers: The Story of Success* (New York, NY: Little, Brown and Company, 2008), p. 170.

15. "Territory of Mississippi, 1798–1817," available online, http://www.tngenweb .org/maps/ms-terr.html.

16. "Treaty of Mount Dexter," available online, http://www.rootsweb.ancestry .com/~msalhn/NativeAmerican/treatymountdexter1805.htm and http://www.choctaw .org/History/Treaties/treaty5.html.

17. The only real evidence to prove that Native Americans ever lived in the area of Marion County and Columbia was their weapons and a few shards of flint and pottery. The only artifacts of any quantity are the spear points and arrowheads on display in the Tom Ford Collection at the Marion County Museum and Archives in Columbia.

According to Curator Watts, those pieces were picked up in the southern part of the county years and years ago.

18. "The Great Migration to the Mississippi Territory," by Charles Lowery, available online, http://mshistory.k12.ms.us/articles/169/the-great-migration-to -the-mississippi-territory-1798–1819.

19. *Statistics on slave transfers from 1790 to 1850.* Included are: number of slaves in the United States in original and added areas,1790–1860; number of slaveholding families; number of white persons directly or indirectly connected with slaveholding; ratio of slaves to whites; value of slaves. Samples from Table 67: In 1790 only 9.3 percent of the white population in the Southwest Territory (Tennessee, Alabama, Mississippi) were related to slaveholding, while SC had 34.3 percent, and the U.S. overall had 17.8 percent. Table 68: By 1850, 44.6 percent of the MS population related to slaveholding; SC had 58.1 percent; and the U.S. had 10.1 percent. Table 70: The number of slaves for every one hundred whites in 1850 in MS was 105; in SC was 140; in all slaveholding states was 51. For every 100 whites, the number of Negroes in 1900 in MS was 142; in SC was 140; on all slaveholding states was 43. Available online, http://www2.census.gov/prod2/decennial/documents/00165897ch14.pdf.

20. "Voices of Slavery in Marion County," by Chris Watts, Museum and Archives, *Columbian-Progress*, February 20, 2010. Watts included in this article various surviving accounts from slaves who toiled in Marion County. He told of a modern Methuselah who died in Marion County in October 1971 at 130 years of age. This man was buried in Pleasant Valley Cemetery in Marion County. Sylvester Magee was born in North Carolina on May 29, 1841, and sold at Enterprise, Mississippi. He was present at the final siege of Vicksburg and pressed into service in the Union army as a gravedigger. Though some have disputed the contention that he was the last living slave of the millions held in the bondage for so long in the United States, Magee may have been the last living human being that possessed any firsthand memory of the Civil War or institutionalized slavery. Before he died he was feted by presidents, governors, talk show hosts, and even an insurance company as being the oldest living citizen of the United States at the time. Efforts are underway at present to erect a proper gravestone and historical marker at his grave.

21. See James Mellon, *Bullwhip Days: The Slaves Remember: An Oral History* (New York, NY: Grove Press, 2002). Online review: "In the 1930s, the Works Progress Administration commissioned an oral history of the remaining former slaves. *Bullwhip Days* is a remarkable compendium of selections from these extraordinary interviews, providing an unflinching portrait of the world of government-sanctioned slavery of Africans in America. Here are twenty-nine full narrations, as well as nine sections of excerpts related to particular aspects of slave life, from religion to plantation life to the Reconstruction era. Skillfully edited, these chronicles bear eloquent witness to the trials of slaves in America, reveal the wide range of conditions of human bondage, and provide sobering insight into the roots of racism in today's society." Available online, http://books.google.com/books?id=JL 4iDpT7acwC&pg=PA178&lpg=PA178&dq=Charley+Moses,+Mississippi&source= bl&ots=yZQFVhrGwp&sig=66w2XlpT-vY4slk7TYtqmwthbT8&hl=en&ei=igQuS qekMMOK_Qbb69DDCg&sa=X&oi=book_result&ct=result&resnum=1.

See also Alan Lomax, *The Land Where the Blues Began* (New York, NY: Dell, 1993). This book not only provides an extensive compilation of the contributions of Mississippi black men and women singers to the blues in African American culture and an account of its connection to African Culture, but also opens to the world the way African Americans coped through their music with the harsh realities of the life they endured.

See also "A History of Blacks Contributing to the Progress of Marion County," complied by Gennett Daniels, C.D.M., Columbia, MS 39429, unpublished paper, in the Marion County Museum and Archives.

See also Donald W. Shriver, *Honest Patriots: Loving a Country Enough to Remember Its Misdeeds.* Chapter 3, "Old Unpaid Debt To African Americans," and Chapter 4, "Unreflected Absences, Native Americans," (New York, NY: Oxford University Press, 2005).

22. "Some Historic Homes in Mississippi" by Mrs. N. D. Deupree, p. 335. Available online, http://books.google.com/books?id=AkkTAAAAYAAJ&pg=PA334&l pg=PA334&dq=Ford+House+Marion+County+Mississippi&source=bl&ots=m2wK69 W7Cu&sig=IUu1RStVg3d679jeXHrzEZxoSXU&hl=en&ei=p8EaSsXcCMrJtgea8cjhDA &sa=X&oi=book_result&ct=result&resnum=2#PPA335,M1.

23. "Marion County History," Available online, http://www.mcdp.info/area/ history.html.

24. "Some Historic Homes in Mississippi" by Mrs. N. D. Deupree, p. 335.

25. "Marion County History." See also "Early Settlements," Available online, http://www.msgw.org/lamar/WPA/marion/MAR7.htm.

26. For one detailed account of these issues, see Jon Meacham, *American Lion: Andrew Jackson in the White House* (New York, NY: Random House, 2008).

27. "Balancing Agriculture with Industry: Capital, Labor, and the Public Good in Mississippi's Home-Grown New Deal," by Connie L. Lester, *Journal of Mississippi History*, Volume LXX, No. 3 Fall 2008, pp. 244–46.

28. Ibid, pp. 255, 262.

29. "The Mississippi Rural Center," in *History of Marion County, MS*, 1976.

30. Ibid.

31. *Fiftieth Anniversary of the Columbia Presbyterian Church* booklet, designed and compiled by Mary Wolfe, 1960.

32. Ibid.

33. Ibid.

34. The *Ministerial Directory* of the Presbyterian Church U.S., 1945, 1951, 1967, 1975, 1983. All render the spelling of his name as Marsh M. Callaway. (See, for example, 1983, p. 106). The *Fiftieth Anniversary of the Columbia Presbyterian Church* booklet spells it as Calloway.

35. *Fiftieth Anniversary of the Columbia Presbyterian Church*, booklet.

36. Ibid.

37. Ibid.

38. Ibid.

39. "A Christian View on Segregation," Rev. G. T. Gillespie, D. D., President Emeritus of Belhaven College, made before the Synod of Mississippi of the

Presbyterian Church in the U.S., November 4, 1954, Reprint by Citizens' Council, 254 East Griffith Street, Jackson, Mississippi 39202. In McAtee collection.

40 See McAtee, *Dreams*, pp. 80-82, for a description of the evidence for this contention.

41. Ibid., pp. 78–79.

Chapter Two: Where You From?

1. Will D. Campbell, *Brother to a Dragon Fly* (New York, NY: Seabury Press, 1977), pp. 80–81.

2. Will D. Campbell, *Providence* (Atlanta, GA: Longstreet Press, 1992), pp. 11–12.

3. Ibid., see pp. 12–13 for a more detailed description.

4. Ibid., see chapters 14 and 15 for a fuller account of the final disposition of Providence Farm.

5. Ruth Joyce Keppler, great-granddaughter of William J. Fatheree, on October 2, 1984, compiled a list of appointments of Rev. Humphrey Williamson taken from the Mississippi Conference of the Methodist Church. Those included: Yazoo, Sharon District (1845); Middleton, Yazoo District (1846–47); Holmes, Yazoo District (1848–49); Attala, Sharon District (1850); Superannuated (retired) (1851); Honey Island Colored Mission, Yazoo District (1952–53). The following appointments were all in the Yazoo District. Holmes (1854); Black Hawk (1855); Honey Island Mission (1856); Carrolton (1857); Yazoo Circuit and Colored Mission (1858–59); Honey Island Colored Mission (1860); Ebenezer (1861–62); presiding elder of the Yazoo District (1863–64); Yazoo Circuit and colored charge (1865); No record of conference proceedings (1866); Superannuated (1867); No record (1868–69). North Mississippi Conference now established. Greenville, Yazoo District (1870); Superannuated (1871–74); Honey Island, Friar's Point District (1875); Superannuated (1876); Tallahatchie, Grenada District (1877); Superannuated (1878–82); Died February 2, 1883 at 80 years of age. In McAtee collection.

6. My sister and I donated this letter to the Mississippi Department of Archives and History in the fall of 2007.

7. Orval W. Baylor, *Early Times in Washington County Kentucky*, chapter nine, "Early Commerce in Washington County," (Cynthiana, KY: Hobson Press, 1942), pp. 68–73.

8. Remembrances of these early generations of family were taken in part from "McAtee Family History and Letters, Lone Hill Farm, 'The Old Place,'" compiled by Emma Jane McAtee Patterson, May 1995, unpublished paper, in the collection of William G. McAtee.

9. After a successful career as pitcher for the Boston Red Sox, my childhood baseball hero, Dave "Boo" Ferriss, returned to his hometown of Shaw, Mississippi, and bought the town dentist's house next door to the manse where I was born. At one point he also bought my birthplace. One bright October afternoon in 1946, I came home from my day in the seventh grade at Brookhaven Junior High to find a brand new light blue Lincoln Continental sedan parked in front of our house. I went inside and found "Boo" sitting there talking to my daddy, his former pastor and Boy Scout

master. The city of Boston had given "Boo" the car for his performance as pitcher, winning the third game win against the St. Louis Cardinals in the 1946 World Series. He pitched in the decisive losing game against the Cardinals for no record. That day in Brookhaven he gave me a miniature autographed bat and "high kick" picture of him signed, "To my friend, 'Sonny' McAtee, Dave 'Boo' Ferriss." I still have these two prized possessions among my mementos. "Boo" went on to be a successful baseball coach at Delta State in Cleveland, Mississippi. I called "Boo" shortly after he returned from attending the Red Sox's World Series win over the St. Louis Cardinals in 2004, the closer on an eighty-six-year wait to end the longest world championship drought in baseball history: the "Curse of the Bambino." "Boo" was ecstatic!

10. Miss Nutt's was no ordinary discipline. On one occasion she kept Bobby Day Sartin, Bruce Brady (younger son of Judge Tom "Black Monday" Brady) and me after school for no identified reason other than that I had that day brought a toy pistol, which I waved around in my role as a safety patrol crossing guard. We sat silently in her presence for a couple of hours, broken only by "Wee Brucie" and Sartin alternately swatting aimlessly at an errant fly. Then she finally let us go without a word, only a stern look that presumably indicated, "You now know what I expect of you in the future." On the way out she gave me back my toy pistol. As best I recall, we all left mystified, not only at the larger offense, but also by the punishment and its results.

11. Riding and watching passenger trains provided another cultural experience for my generation. They defined our lives experientially in a manner similar to the way cars figured in our existences. For this reason a few illustrations of this dimension of life appear in this book.

Chapter Three: First Call

1. "Korean War Timeline." Available online, http://www.rt66.com/~korteng/SmallArms/TimeLine.htm.

2. Ibid.

3. Future Governor Paul B. Johnson's daughter, Trish, was a camper in the private camp run by Mrs. Paul Watson at Camp Hopewell. Her husband was a colleague of my dad and pastor at Marks, Mississippi, for a long time. At the time of the camp, she was one of the housemothers in the women's dorm at Southwestern.

4. The title was a knockoff of a sermon I heard my daddy preach numerous times. Our family used to keep count of the number of times we heard it and could almost repeat it verbatim! The content of my sermon was significantly different.

5. "Living Monuments," No. 13, II Corinthians 3:1–6; I John 4:10–24, College Hill Presbyterian Church, Oxford, Mississippi, March 11, 1956.

6. Campbell, *Providence*, pp. 15–16.

7. Ibid.

8. Ibid.

9. Bill of sale from Jordan Auto Co. to W. G. McAtee, 1956 Chevrolet, May 10, 1956, in McAtee Collection. It listed for $1,785, with automatic transmission, heater, and radio as extras.

10. Edwards lived to be ninety years old. I sat with Ira Grupper at his memorial service on June 15, 2010, in Caldwell Chapel on the campus of Louisville Presbyterian Seminary. This was one more surreal experience the two of us shared after our providential meeting.

11. Anne Braden, *The Wall Between* (New York, NY: Monthly Review Press, 1958), pp. xi–xii.

12. "Plessy v. Ferguson." Available online, http://www.bgsu.edu/departments/acs/1890s/plessy/plessy.html.

13. Erle Johnston, *I Rolled With Ross: A Political Portrait* (Baton Rouge, LA: Moran Publishing, 1980), p. 23.

14. Ibid., preface.

15. Erle Johnston, *Mississippi's Defiant Years: 1953–1973* (Forest, MS: Lake Harbor Publishers, 1990), p. 97.

16. Ibid., pp. 23–24.

17. "Invasion at Bay of Pigs." Available online, http://www.historyof cuba.com/history/baypigs/pigs3.htm.

18. Bill of sale from George Ruff Buick Co. to W. G. McAtee, 1962, Rambler station wagon, January 22, 1962, in McAtee Collection. It had 6 cylinders, listed for $2,380, with $241 worth of extra accessories, including individual front seats with reclining backs, heater, radio, and heavy shocks.

19. "Pilgrimage of the Soul," No. 322, Psalm 46; Exodus 3:1–17, First Presbyterian Church, Amory, Mississippi, September 2, 1962.

20. Not all elected officials in Mississippi responded to this crisis as did Barnett and Johnson. State Representative Karl Wiesenburg of Pascagoula, a well-known legal scholar, traced the court actions that preceded Meredith's entrance into Ole Miss in a series of articles in his hometown newspaper, the *Chronicle*. He warned that continued defiance "will lead to even a bloodier tragedy in months to come." Ira Harkey, editor and publisher, called these articles "a major contribution to the welfare of Mississippi [that] form[s] a reasoned viewpoint around which may rally all Mississippians who are appalled at what is happening in their state. It can be the foundation for their credo." See Rep. Karl Wiesenburg, *The Oxford Disaster . . . Price of Defiance*, reprint (December 31, 1962) of articles appearing in the *Chronicle*, Pascagoula, MS (December 17–21, 1962), in McAtee Collection.

21. Callicott served in the Mississippi House of Representatives from 1960 to 1976. He later served as mayor of Senatobia for three terms. He retired as owner of the Callicott Insurance Company, a business his grandfather began in 1915. He was a veteran of World War II and the Korean conflict and later retired as a general of the Mississippi National Guard. He died on July 25, 2010, at the age of 86. See the *Commercial Appeal*, July 27, 2010.

22. William Doyle, *An American Insurrection: The Battle of Oxford, Mississippi, 1962* (New York: Doubleday, 2001), pp. 240–41. Scenes and quotes of Callicott: Doyle Interview, William Callicott, August 30, 1999.

23. Ibid., pp. 241–242.

24. Ibid., p. 170.

25. See Charles W. Eagles, "'The Fight for Men's Minds'": The Aftermath of the Ole Miss Riot of 1962," *Journal of Mississippi History*, Volume LXXI, No. 1 (Spring

2009), pp. 30–36, for an account of what happened when Walker was stopped by soldiers leaving Oxford's downtown square on Monday morning, October 1, and his subsequent arrest and legal proceeding through the courts. This article gives a vivid picture of the emotional and political climate that existed in Mississippi in the aftermath of the Ole Miss Riot, as well as an accounting of the public relations and legal battles over many months between federal and local entities attempting to portray their version of what took place at Ole Miss and where blame for the violence should be placed.

26. Copy of St. Andrew Resolution in McAtee Collection.

27. "An Overview of the Crisis." Available online, http://www.library.thinkquest.org/11046/days/index/html.

28. Leah H. Gass, reference archivist, Department of History, PC (USA), e-mail to William G. McAtee, May 18, 2009, in McAtee Collection.

29. "Paul Burney Johnson, Jr.: Fifty-fourth Governor of Mississippi: 1964–1968." Available online, http://mshistory.k12.ms.us/index.php?s=extra&id=151.

30. "Collision Course," No. 410, Psalm 111; Hosea 8:1–14, First Presbyterian Church, Amory, Mississippi, September 1, 1963.

31. "On the Death of the President," No. 430, Psalm 127; Matthew 5:17–26, First Presbyterian Church, Amory, Mississippi, November 24, 1963.

32. Donald W. Shriver, Jr., *The Unsilent South: Prophetic Preaching in Racial Crises* (Richmond, VA: John Knox Press, 1965). See "Not Race but Grace," three sermons preached by Robert H. Walkup at First Presbyterian Church, Starkville, Mississippi, September 30–October 7, 1962, pp. 58–71; also, "Love Disqualified," sermon preached by Charles L. Stanford, Jr., Jones Memorial Presbyterian Church, Meridian, Mississippi, October 7, 1962, pp. 72–76.

33. Walkup, Letter to Margo Reitz Cochran, p. 1.

34. Ibid., p. 2.

35. Frank Brooks and I would transfer our membership from South Mississippi Presbytery, one of the most conservative presbyteries in the General Assembly, to Potomac Presbytery, probably the most liberal presbytery, after we left Mississippi and moved to Richmond, Virginia, in 1966.

36. Minutes of the One Hundred-Fourth General Assembly (PCUS), Montreat, NC, April 23–28, 1964, pp. 80–81.

Chapter Four: Freedom Summer

1. William G. McAtee, "A Study of the Impact of Existential Theology on the Campus Ministry," master's thesis, Louisville Presbyterian Theological Seminary, May 1965.

2. This and the following references to what I observed and did were taken from notes I had made of my time at Oxford. In McAtee Collection.

3. Robert E. Juckett, Jr., "Annie Devine: A Mother in and of the Civil Rights Movement," *Journal of Mississippi History*, Vol. LXX, No. 3 (Fall 2008), p. 273.

4. "Negro Voting Teacher Returns to His Classes," *Clarion-Ledger*, August 19, 1961; "118 Negroes In McComb Face Trial," *Jackson Daily News*, October 5, 1961. Both mention Moses's activities in Liberty and McComb.

5. "Annie Devine," *Journal of Mississippi History*, p. 273.

6. Doug McAdam, *Freedom Summer* (New York, NY: Oxford University Press, 1988), p. 78. This book provides from one perspective a comprehensive account of the Freedom Summer activities in Mississippi. According to its dust jacket it was "the first book to gauge the impact of Freedom Summer on the project volunteers and the period we now call 'the turbulent '60s.'" I am aware that many other books have been written that may give different perspectives and take exception to McAdams's conclusions. But reading this one over two decades later jarred me out of my late 1980s lethargy and propelled me back to that day in 1964 in Oxford. I had not taken pictures that day, but those in the book, along with what McAdams wrote, made it all come alive for me again—but in a different way as I reassessed my experience and got partial answers to my unanswered questions.

7. Ibid.

8. Ibid., p. 83.

9. The "1964 Freedom School Curriculum Packet" has remained intact in the order in which it was received. In McAtee Collection.

10. "Civil Rights Act of 1964." Available online, http://www.spartacus.schoolnet .co.uk/USAcivil64.htm.

11. Jim Haskins, *I Have a Dream: The Life and Words of Martin Luther King, Jr.* (Brookfield, CT: Millbrook Press, 1992), p. 76.

12. "The Mississippi State Sovereignty Commission: An Agency History." Available online, http://mshistory.k12.ms.us/articles/243/mississippi-sovereignty-commission-an-agency-history. The commission had twelve appointed and legislatively elected members. The governor, the lieutenant governor, the speaker of the house, and the attorney general were *ex officio* members. The governor served as chair.

13. Ibid.

14. SCRID# 2-31-0-11-1-1-1: Mississippi Sovereignty Commission, "Marion County-Columbia," January 12, 1961, Series 2515, Mississippi State Sovereignty Commission Records, 1994–2006, MDAH, January 9, 2009.

15. David R. Davies, ed., *The Press and Race* (Jackson, MS: University Press of Mississippi, 2001). These nine essays present the broad spectrum of the writings of print journalism regarding the civil rights movement.

16. P. D. East, *The Magnolia Jungle: The Life, Times and Education of A Southern Editor* (New York, NY: Simon and Schuster, 1960), p. 194.

17. "Freedom Writers Office Now Open on Second Street," *Columbian-Progress*, April 23, 1964.

18. "To The Citizens of the 5th District," *Columbian-Progress*, May 28, 1964.

19. Curtis Wilkie, *The Fall of the House of Zeus: The Rise and Ruin of America's Most Powerful Trial Lawyers* (New York, NY: Crown, 2010), pp. 8–10. Curtis Wilkie's stepfather, J. Leighton Stuart, Jr., was the Presbyterian pastor at Summit, MS, and served as counselor at the presbytery youth conferences I attended at Percy Quinn State Park. Stuart was born in Hangchow, China, to Presbyterian missionaries. His father was the American ambassador to China in the 1940s.

20. "City Pools Set to Open June 7; Courses Offered," *Columbian-Progress*, May 28, 1964.

21. Dwain C. Epps, e-mail to Chris Watts, with copy to William McAtee, written November 14, 2008. All following quotations and descriptions regarding Epps's activities taken from this e-mail, unless otherwise noted.

22. "Civil Rights Act of 1964." Available online, http://www.spartacus.schoolnet .co.uk/USAcivil64.htm.

23. Daniel L. Migliore, *Faith Seeking Understanding* (Grand Rapids, MI: William B. Eerdmans, 1991), p. 44.

24. Joel L. Alvis, Jr., (Tuscaloosa, AL: University of Alabama Press, 1994), p. 143.

25. "A Christian View on Segregation," Rev. G. T. Gillespie, D.D., pp. 8–13.

26. Ibid., p. 13.

27. "On the Historicity of Adam," *The Presbyterian Outlook*, July 26, 1965, p. 4.

28. "No Precedent for State Invasion," *Columbian-Progress*, July 9, 1964.

29. "North and South Need Better Understanding," *Columbian-Progress*, August 6, 1964.

30. McAdam, *Freedom Summer*, pp. 96–97 and appendix D, which contains the twenty-six pages of "hostile incidents."

31. Ibid., pp.122–23.

32. Ibid., p. 126.

33. "Pilgrimage of the Soul," No. 322 Revised, Exodus 3:1–17; Acts 14:8–18, Columbia Presbyterian Church, Columbia, Mississippi, September 6, 1964.

34. Bill of Sale from David A. Laverty to William G. McAtee, 1961 VW Bug, September 24, 1964. In McAtee Collection.

35. "Bigger Plans Next Year Despite 'Sea of Hate,' Speaker Says," *San Rafael Independent Journal*, October 29, 1964.

36. Details in the following paragraphs found in brochure, "Beauty for Ashes," in McAtee Collection.

37. A copy of the memo to student advisors on Mississippi campuses. In McAtee Collection.

38. Ralph McGill, "Mississippi Shows 2 Faces," *Atlanta Constitution*, September 17, 1964.

39. Ibid.

40. "Lions Speaker Notes Changes in State," *Columbian-Progress*, October 22, 1964.

41. "CRS and NCC Duties Explained," *Columbian-Progress*, October 29, 1964.

42. Ibid.

43. McAdam, *Freedom Summer*, appendix D.

44. "Citizens for Progress," *McComb Enterprise Journal*, November 17, 1964.

45. Ibid.

46. A copy of this resolution may be in the session minute book. My handwritten copy on a slip of paper was in the *Book Of Church Order*, the constitution of the Presbyterian Church U.S., that I used during that time. In McAtee Collection.

Chapter Five: Moments of Truth in the Making

1. "One Man Can Try," No. 180, Ezekiel 36:22–32, Columbia Presbyterian Church, Columbia, Mississippi, November 8, 1964.

2. "5 Grains of Corn," No. 182, Hebrews 6:1–12, Columbia Presbyterian Church, Columbia, Mississippi, November 22, 1964.

3. SCRID# 2-31-0-18-1-1-1: Mississippi Sovereignty Commission, "NAACP And COFO Activity in Lawrence, Walthall, and Marion Counties," November 23, 24, 1964, Series 2515: Mississippi State Sovereignty Commission Records, 1994–2006, MDAH, January 9, 2009.

4. "City Schools Begin Re-Evaluation Study," *Columbian-Progress*, December 17, 1964.

5. "Pilgrimage to Advent," No. 264, Psalm 119:161–176; Job 23:1–17, Columbia Presbyterian Church, Columbia, Mississippi, November 19, 1964.

6. "So You Want Freedom," No. 473, John 8:31–37; Romans 6:12–23, Columbia Presbyterian Church, Columbia, Mississippi, January 10, 1965.

7. "Important Notice: Poll Taxes Must Be Paid By Feb. 1st," *Columbian-Progress*, January 14, 1965.

8. "The 24th Amendment Ended the Poll Tax January 23, 1964." Available online, http://www.americaslibrary.gov/jb/modern/jb_modern_polltax_1.html.

9. "School Boards Face Momentous Decision," *Columbian-Progress*, January 21, 1965.

10. "Federal Government Sacrificing States' Rights Barnett Reports," *Columbian-Progress*, January 28, 1965.

11. Ibid.

12. "Civil Rights Act Employment Provisions Discussed," *Times-Picayune*, February 4, 1965.

13. A copy of this letter and enclosures were sent to: Rev. Lee Tucker, Rev. Horace Vilee [*sic*], Rev. Paul Crouch, Rev. William Stanway, Rev. Ed Jussely, Rev. Newton Cox, Dr. William Davis. In the McAtee Collection.

14. "Happy Are the Slave-Drivers," No. 131, Psalm 118:1–14; John 16:25–33, Columbia Presbyterian Church, Columbia, Mississippi, February 14, 1965.

15. "Sunflower Stores Open Here Monday," *Columbian-Progress*, February 18, 1965.

16. "Happy Are The Troublemakers," No. 134, Jeremiah 8:4–15; John 16:25–33, Columbia Presbyterian Church, Columbia, Mississippi, February 21, 1965.

17. "Happy Are the Wise-Guys," No. 132, Psalm 24; I Timothy 1:3–17, Columbia Presbyterian Church, Columbia, Mississippi, February 28, 1965.

18. "Dr. Gilbert R. Mason, Sr. (1929–2006), As remembered by Ira Grupper." Available online, http://www.crmvet.org/mem/masong.htm. Also, Ira Grupper, taped oral history interview conducted by William G. McAtee, Louisville, Kentucky, January 19, 2009. Several Oral History Interviews, conducted and tape-recorded by me, with several individuals in conjunction with the writing of this book are referenced throughout these notes. I was authorized by the interviewees in their oral history program release forms to execute a deed of gift on our behalf to the University of Southern Mississippi for these tape-recorded interviews as an unrestricted gift, and to transfer legal title and all property rights, including copyright, for scholarly and educational uses in its civil rights movement collection. This gift did not preclude any use that the interviewer and interviewees wished to make of the information in the recordings and/or subsequent transcripts of such.

19. Grupper (Ira) and Beech (Bob) Civil Rights Collection, unprocessed manuscript collection. Available online, http://www.lib.usm.edu/legacy/archives/grupper.htm

20. "A Costly Ministry," *Presbyterian Life*, March 1, 1965, p. 9.

21. Grupper (Ira) and Beech (Bob) Civil Rights Collection.

22. "No Time for Street Protests," *Columbian-Progress*, March 4, 1965.

23. "City and County School Boards Take No Action On CR Pledge," *Columbian-Progress*, March 4, 1965.

24. Ibid.

25. On August 31, 2010, I participated in a phone interview with Joseph T. Reiff, associate professor of religion at Emory & Henry College, Emory, Virginia, as part of his research on the "Born of Conviction" statement published in the *Mississippi Methodist Advocate* on January 2, 1963. Reiff is interviewing the surviving signers and other persons with knowledge pertinent to understanding the story of the statement's creation, signing, and publication, as well as the reactions and responses to it in the larger context of the Mississippi Methodist Church's role in the complex story of the civil rights movement in Mississippi during the 1960s. I was interviewed because of my relationship and work with N .A. Dickson. Dwain Epps participated in the interview via a Skype and speaker phone hookup because of his relationship with Dickson during the summer of 1964 while a seminary intern at the Columbia Presbyterian Church. Reiff is writing a book based on his extensive research.

26. In some places L. Z.'s name is spelled Blankinship, such as in the program of the forty-ninth annual session of the South Mississippi Baptist State Convention, November 10–12, 1965; in his August 24, 1967, letter to me; and in his 2004 obituary in the *Columbian-Progress*. In other places his name is spelled Blankenship, such as in PRVO's *Progress Report*, March 1969. Based on his personal use, I have chosen to use the Blankinship spelling in this book.

27. "E. D. McLean, Jr. Announces for Mayor," *Columbian-Progress*, March 11, 1965.

28. "3 Choices Face School Board Under CR Law," *Columbian-Progress*, March 18, 1965.

29. Ibid.

30. Ibid.

31. "Schools Have Five Years to Meet New Standards," *Columbian-Progress*, April 1, 1965.

32. Ibid.

33. "A. E. 'Buck' Webb Announces for Mayor," *Columbian-Progress*, April 15, 1965.

34. "Boycott: A Step Toward Anarchy," *Columbian-Progress*, April 15, 1965.

35. Ibid.

36. "The Day Far Spent," No. 137, Luke 24:13–35, Columbia Presbyterian Church, Columbia, Mississippi, April 18, 1965.

37. Minutes of the One Hundred-Fifth General Assembly (PCUS). Montreat, N. C., April 21–26, 1965, p. 94.

38. William G. McAtee, letter to Columbia Presbyterian Church, Earl D. McLean, treasurer, written May 1, 1965. Copy in the personal collection of William G. McAtee.

39. Dwain Epps, letter to William G. McAtee written "Saturday" (May 1), 1965. In McAtee Collection.

40. "ASC Committee Employs Negro Field Workers," *Columbian-Progress*, May 6, 1965.

41. "First Primary Tuesday For Mayor, Alderman," *Columbian-Progress*, May 6, 1965.

42. "Ward 4 Changes Alderman; McLean Elected New Mayor." *Columbian-Progress*. May 13, 1965.

43. "City General Election Officials Announced," *Columbian-Progress*, May 27, 1965.

44. "Fiddle-Dee-Dee," No. 145, Psalm 121, I Timothy 6:2b–16, Columbia High School Baccalaureate, Columbia, Mississippi, May 30, 1965.

45. "City Officials Sworn In; Changes Revealed," *Columbian-Progress*, July 8, 1965.

46. Memo, Subjects: Sam Gross, Curtis Styles, Ann Marsh, Richard Atlee, Shana Shumer, July 1, 1965. In McLean File.

Chapter Six: A Confluence of Perspectives

1. "Annie Devine: A Mother in and of the Civil Rights Movement," by Robert E. Juckett, Jr., *Journal of Mississippi History*, Vol. LXX, No. 3 (Fall 2008), pp. 279–80.

2. Ibid.

3. Ibid., pp. 282–83.

4. "Profile of Marion County," SNCC Research, June 30, 1965. Available online, http://digilib.usm.edu/cdm4/document.php?CISOROOT=/manu& CISOPTR=4462&REC=10. According to their profile, 66 percent (15,390) of the population of Marion County in 1965 was white and 34 percent (7,903) was black. The total school population for whites was 3,848, and for blacks 2,682. Enrollment in high school for whites was 1,040, and for blacks 533. The median number of school years completed by whites was 9.3 years, and for blacks 6.6 years.

There were 3,977 white men in the labor force, and 1,317 black men. There were 664 white women in the labor force, and 1,727 black women. Forty-nine percent (322) of black women were domestic workers. Twenty-two percent (295) of black men were farmers; 10 percent (129) of black men worked as farm laborers; 19 percent (307) of black men were listed as laborers; and 29 percent (327) of black men were factory workers.

The number of whites with family income of $0–1000 was 490, and the number for blacks was 584; $2000–3,000: whites 638, and blacks 267; $4,000–5,000: whites 413, and blacks 60; $6,000–$7,000: whites 211, and blacks 15; $8,000–9,000: whites 121, and blacks 4; and $10,000 and over: whites 218, and blacks, 8. The median family income was $3,750 for whites and $1,394 for blacks.

There were 10,123 eligible white voters, of which 8,997 were registered. There were 3,530 eligible black voters, of which 383 were registered. Votes cast in the 1960 presidential election: Democrats, 1,082, Republicans, 698, Independents, 1,265; in the 1964 presidential election: Democrats, 531, Republicans, 5,460, Independents, 0; in the 1965 mayoral Democratic primary: McLean, 1,081, Webb, 454.

5. All of the original drafts of the three documents are in the McAtee Collection.

6. Copies in the McAtee Collection and in the McLean File.

7. "Almost Dead, and Don't Know It," No. 484, Revelation 3:1–6, Columbia Presbyterian Church, Columbia, Mississippi, July 18, 1965.

8. "Blaze Damages Home on Nathan," *Columbian-Progress*, August 5, 1965.

9. Telegrams Regarding Bombing of Freedom House: 2 received, August 4, 1965; 1 reply, August 5, 1965. Copies of texts and names of recipients of telegrams in the McLean File.

10. "Marion Organizes for Anti-Poverty Program, *Columbian-Progress*, August 5, 1965.

11. Ibid.

12. Ibid.

13. Ibid.

14. "Evening Circle Meeting Monday in Church Hall," *Columbian-Progress*, August 5, 1965.

15. Notes of meeting with restaurant owners and operators, August 3, 1965. In the McLean File.

16. "Health Officer Orders Swimming Pool Closed," *Columbian-Progress*, August 12, 1965.

17. "The Voting Rights Act of 1965. Available online, http://www.ourdocuments .gov/doc.php?doc=100.

18. Memo, list of private citizen observers in the area of the movie theater and Ja-Gees, August 11, 1965. In the McLean File.

19. "Support Of Lawlessness Helped Bring On Riots," *Columbian-Progress*, August 19, 1965.

20. "A Time For Leadership," *Columbian-Progress*, August 19, 1965.

21. Ibid.

22. "Statement of Beliefs," *Columbian-Progress*, August 19, 1965.

23. W. E. Walker, Jr., letter to Bud Sowell written August 23, 1965. In the McLean File.

24. Memos, call to Mac Seacrest, August 25 and 26, 1965. In the McLean File.

25. Notes of Meeting with Jim Draper of Community Relations Service, August 27, 1965. In the McLean File.

26. Ibid.

27. Resolution of the board of trustees of Columbia Municipal Separate School District, Columbia, Mississippi, including the Annual Letter to Parents, Exhibit "B", August 27, 1965. In the McLean File.

28. Ibid.

29. "Other State Schools May Begin Squirming," *Hattiesburg American*, August 28, 1965.

30. Ibid.

31. Notes of Meeting at City Hall, August 28, 1965. In the McLean File.

32. "Who Is A Minister?," No. 486, Luke 11:29–36; Colossians 4:7–17, Columbia Presbyterian Church, Columbia, Mississippi, August 29, 1965.

33. Note with trial oath, undated. In the McLean File.

34. Notes concerning picketing of Sunflower Store, August 31, 1965. In the McLean File.

35. All of the original drafts of Miss Mary's lists are in the McAtee Collection.

36. William G. McAtee, "Tiredly Bill" to "All," written September 2, 1965. In the McAtee Collection and in the McLean File.

Chapter Seven: Broken Silence

1. Lewis L. Wilkins and I created the mythical W & M Associates in the 1970s as our self-directed form of continuing education. Based on our observations of the world about us and the learnings we drew from them, we developed educational and communication concepts and tested them in a series of workshops. One of the communication theories we created was "Gesture, Response and Common Understanding."

2. Simon, Paul (composer/lyricist/artist) and Art Garfunkle (artist), "The Sounds of Silence," *Sounds of Silence*, Columbia, 1965.

3. Ira Grupper recently confirmed the different perceptions of these pastors held by some in the community. Grupper also mentioned to me that several children of Rev. Amos Payton were involved in some of the protests and marches conducted by the MFDP. A person, who identified herself as a member of Friendship Baptist Church, where Rev. L.Z Blankinship preached, took issue with Blankinship's leadership in a letter printed in the Mississippi Newsletter of the Freedom Information Service on April 5, 1968. Grupper later told me, "[S]he and her family were deeply involved in the MFDP in Columbia." In her letter she noted that Blankinship held a position to help poor people with jobs. "but instead he tells his member about get together with the big man, which is white. I wonder if it any way he can be put the presser on so when he meet his board with white people he will hafter put pressour on them about the anti-poverty program." She went on to say she was in financial need and would like to work on any of these programs. She implied she had contacted them, pointing out she had "volunteered on the job of TCCA . . . and once work under headstart in Marion County . . . but they did not call me back." She closed her letter by asking, "Please if anything you can help me to get a job, Thank you." SCRID# 2-163-0-19-4-1-1, Mississippi Sovereignty Commission, "Letters," Freedom Information Service Mississippi Newsletter, Number Fifty-Three, Box 120, Tougaloo, MS 39174, April 5, 1969, pages 4–5, Series 2515: Mississippi State Sovereignty Commission Records, 1994–2006, MDAH, January 9, 2009.

4. Copies in the McAtee Collection and in the McLean File.

5. Copies in the McAtee Collection and in the McLean File.

6. Resolution of the board of trustees of Columbia Municipal Separate School District, August 27, 1965.

7. Black citizens: Mr. Charles Henry Otis, Mrs. I. C. Pittman, Mr. Lindsey Walker, Rev. Carl Bias, Jr., Mr. W. C. Collins, Mr. Cleophus Smith, Mr. W. T. Maynard, Mr. Roosevelt Otis,* Mr. William J. Rice, Mr. Wilton James, Rev. Amos Payton, Rev. Claude Lumsey, Rev. C. F. Jackson. White citizens: Mr. Sedgie Griffith, Mr. Will Cooper, Mr. Ben McCraw, Dr. Russell Bush, Jr., Mr. Thomas Watts, Mr. W. E. Walker, Jr., Mr. Richard Foxworth,* Rev. N. A. Dickson, Mr. H. H. Wolfe, Mr. Charles Rogers, Mr. R. L. Barnes, Miss Helen McDaniel, Dr. C. C. Thompson. Note: There are twenty-six names here because two of the members moved away or were unable to serve after their

original appointment and election to membership. (* Replacements to fill vacancies.) In the McLean File.

8. Memo, Committee of Concerned (watchdog), undated. In the McLean File.

9. "Committee Is Organized To Explore Problems," *Columbian-Progress*, September 30, 1965.

10. Ibid.

11. Ibid.

12. "Bi-Racial Unit Is Formed," *Times-Picayune*, October 2, 1965.

13. Ibid.

14. "The American Dream Comes Home," No. 488, John 8:31–38; Galatians 5:1–12, Columbia Presbyterian Church, Columbia, Mississippi, September 12, 1965.

15. "The Challenge of Change," No. 491, Mississippi District YWCA Fall Conference of Area V, Tay's Restaurant, Columbia, Mississippi, October 16, 1965.

16. Details about these two meetings were taken from notes of the meetings of October 21 and 23, 1965, on note cards McAtee used during the meetings. In the McAtee Collection. A summary of these two meetings also appeared in the December 9 edition of the *Columbian-Progress* in, "Committee of Concern Reports on Discussions."

17. Ibid.

18. Dr. Russell Bush, taped phone oral history interview conducted by William G. McAtee, February 19, 2009.

19. "Best Fight In War on Poverty Begins At Home; REA's Cited," *Columbian-Progress*, September 30, 1965.

20. SCRID# 2-31-0-19-1-1-1: Mississippi Sovereignty Commission, "Investigation of a report that the Freedom Democratic Party would have a meeting on the night of Thursday, October 7, 1965," date of report, October 8, 1965, Series 2515: Mississippi State Sovereignty Commission Records, 1994–2006, MDAH, January 9, 2009. The following details describing what took place are taken from this report.

21. Copy of complete text in the mayor's file.

22. Forty-ninth Annual Session of the South Mississippi Baptist State Convention, Dr. R. W. Woullard, president. Owens Chapel Baptist Church, 1223 Marion Avenue, Columbia, Mississippi, November 10–12, 1965. In the McAtee Collection.

23. A copy of the complete text of my introduction is in the McAtee Collection.

24. Notes of meeting with Louis Ashley from SNCC, November 15, 1965. In the McLean File.

25. Notes of meeting with Grupper et al., November 16, 1965 outlining parade route for December 17–18, 1965. In the McLean File.

26. Notes regarding phone call from man in Bogalusa, November 23, 1965. In the McLean File.

27. "Negroes Picket Bogalusa Stores," *Times-Picayune*, November 30, 1965.

28. "Basic Title 1 Grant Allotment Said '317,665 For Local Schools,'" *Columbian-Progress*, November 25, 1965.

29. Copy of complete text in the McLean File.

30. Copy of complete text in the McLean File.

31. "Owens Street Area In Line for Improvements," *Columbian-Progress*, December 9, 1965.

32. "COFO Civil Rights Group No Longer Exists in State," *Times-Picayune*, December 12, 1965. According to Ira Grupper (April 7, 2009 interview) Jan Hillegas, who came to Jackson, Mississippi, from upstate New York during this time and still lives there, kept all the files for the Freedom Information Service. They are now musty and yellow, and Grupper is not sure will happen to them. Hillegas archived records of many groups: local autonomous groups, Delta Ministry, NCC, SNCC, COFO, MFDP.

33. Minutes of the meeting of the Marion County Community Relations Committee, December 16, 1965. In the McLean File.

34. "Breakfast Special, Ja-Gee's Restaurant," *Columbian-Progress*, December 17, 1965.

35. Copies of some of the parade permits issued by the mayor are in the McLean File. Not all permits are recorded here.

36. Notes regarding conduct of parade and picketing, December 17, 1965. In the McLean File.

Chapter Eight: Crossing the Line

1. "Negro Student Enrolls [in] Formerly All-White School," *Columbian-Progress*, January 6, 1966.

2. "Marion Ministers Hold Meeting," *Hattiesburg AMERICAN*, January 5, 1966.

3. "Mayor McLean Speaks to County Ministerial Group," *Columbian-Progress*, January 6, 1966.

4. Descriptions of this and related events were taken from the "Answer of Respondent, City of Columbia, to Petition For Removal," filed in the United States District Court for the Southern District of Mississippi, Hattiesburg Division, Criminal Action No. 1394, February 5, 1966. Copy provided McAtee by Grupper.

5. "Respondent's Motion To Remand," filed in the United States District Court for the Southern District of Mississippi, Hattiesburg Division, Criminal Action No. 1393, February 5, 1966. Copy provided McAtee by Grupper.

6. "Closing Notice: The Banks of Columbia," *Columbian-Progress*, January 13, 1966.

7. "Important Notice: Poll Taxes Must Be Paid by Feb. 1st," *Columbian-Progress*, January 13, 1966.

8. "Outlook on Mississippi Politics, Economy," *Columbian-Progress*, January 13, 1966.

9. Rev. A. G. Payton, letter to Rev. W. G. McAtee, January 18, 1966. In the McAtee Collection. Ira Grupper recently asked me if Sandra participated in a competition for this scholarship, or if Payton had approached me asking for it. Grupper told me that there were those in the community who believed the granting of this scholarship was a "payoff" for Payton's involvement in the bi-racial committee and support for the mayor. Nothing could be further from the truth. What I did to secure the scholarship was purely on my own initiative and based on my perception of the need.

10. Details presented here are from McAtee's notes of the meeting of the committee (CRC) on January 20, 1966. In the McAtee Collection.

11. "Complaints End Courtesy Feeding Meters by Police," *Columbian-Progress*, March 24, 1966.

12. Memo of "Observations" presented by McAtee at meeting of CRC on January 20, 1966. In the McAtee Collection.

13. Bill of Sale from Steadman Motor Company to W. G. McAtee, 1966 VW Squareback, January 26, 1966. In the McAtee Collection.

14. "$61,674 Title I Grant to Aid Marion Central," *Columbian-Progress*, January 27, 1966.

15. "Directors Named for City, County Title One Projects," *Columbian-Progress*, February 3, 1966.

16. "Marion Ministers Hold Meeting," *Hattiesburg AMERICAN*, January 5, 1966.

17. "Respondent's Motion To Remand," Criminal Action No. 1393, February 5, 1966.

18. See memorandum brief of U.S. Supreme Court decision of 20 June 1966, in *City of Greenwood, Miss. V. Peacock, et al.* In the McLean File.

19. Ira Grupper, taped oral history interview conducted by William G. McAtee, Louisville, Kentucky, April 7, 2009.

20. "Mayor's Report Shows City Making Progress," *Columbian-Progress*, February 17, 1966.

21. "Mayor Announces New City School Board Member," *Columbian-Progress*, February 17, 1966.

22. "Paving, Water Lines and Sewer Proposed," *Columbian-Progress*, March 3, 1966.

23. "Colmer Says Attacks on State Communist-Inspired Conspiracy," *Columbian-Progress*, February 24, 1966.

24. Mrs. Seaborn Hasson, president of Columbia Education Association to club members, written on March 3, 1966. In the McLean File.

25. Edward E. Ellis, Lawyer's Committee for Civil Rights Under Law, letter to E. D. McLean, Jr., T. C. Griffith Insurance Agency, Inc., January 25, 1966. In the McLean File.

26. E. D. McLean, Jr., T. C. Griffith Insurance Agency, Inc., letter to Fred Garraway, F. W. Williams State Agency, February 9, 1966, in McLean File.

27. E. D. McLean, Jr., T. C. Griffith Insurance Agency, Inc., letter to Edward E. Ellis, Lawyer's Committee for Civil Rights Under Law. In the McLean File.

28. Memo, Mrs. Weary—Threats to blow her house up, March 16, 1967. In the McLean File.

29. William G. McAtee Letter to C. H. Lipsey, March 14, 1966. In the McAtee Collection.

30. Crawford Lipsey letter to William McAtee, March 21, 1966. In the McAtee Collection.

31. "Vocational Training Program Plans Are Announced," *Columbian-Progress*, March 17, 1966.

32. "State First In South To Have Food Program In All Counties," *Columbian-Progress*, March 24, 1966.

33. "Watching the Poverty Warriors," *Columbian-Progress*, March 31, 1966.

34. "Quality Leadership Must Live," *Columbian-Progress*, April 7, 1966.

35. Grupper interview, April 7, 2009.

36. Details about the event with the college students, April 8, 1966, from McAtee notes. In the McAtee Collection.

37. The Wolfe family was one of several dynamic and influential families, in the Presbyterian Church and in the community, who were very supportive of my involvement in the community and expected me to be so. Hessie and Doc Wolfe formed a construction company after service in World War II, dedicated to improving the economic plight of the Negro citizens of the community and paying salaries comparable to those paid whites. On one occasion, Hessie told me he received a call from a car company salesman, concerning the salary figures one of his Negro employees had put on a loan application for a new Cadillac, which seemed too high by local standards. Wolfe confirmed the figure and said, "Sell him the car!" Karl Wolfe, an artist, designed the stained glass window in the new sanctuary of the Presbyterian church building. As has been noted, Wiley Wolfe ran the Wolfe Lumber Yard and served on the Columbia City School Board during this period. According to records of the board of aldermen, dated July 21, 1968, Wiley resigned from the school board and was replaced by Ben Rawls. Mary Wolfe provided invaluable service as my "unofficial pastor's aide."

38. Marilyn Dickson Foxworth, daughter of N. A. Dickson, taped oral history phone interview conducted by William G. McAtee, February 16, 2009.

39. Memo, "Resist Arrest," April 13, 1966. In the McLean File.

40. Chris Watts, e-mail to William G. McAtee, April 16, 2009. In the McAtee Collection.

41. "Choice of School Forms Must Be Returned Soon," *Columbian-Progress*, April 28, 1966.

42. Chauncey and my brother-in-law, Ronald Bunn, were Southwestern at Memphis college mates and traveled together to Europe one summer.

43. Minutes of the 106th General Assembly (PCUS), Montreat, NC, April 21–26, 1966, pp. 105, 107, 117.

44. "Three Counties Get Anti-Poverty Grant," *Columbian-Progress*, May 19, 1966.

45. "City School Bond Issue Passes 427-93," *Columbian-Progress*, May 19, 1966.

46. "3 Head Start Centers Open This Summer," *Columbian-Progress*, May 26, 1966.

47. "Jefferson First City School to Graduate," *Columbian-Progress*, June 2, 1966.

48. "1966 Columbia High School Senior Class Given Guidelines for Successful Living," *Columbian-Progress*, June 2, 1966.

Chapter Nine: Dwindling Days

1. During my rounds of delivering meals-on-wheels in 2007, I discovered one of our clients, Mr. William "Bill" Cornish, was a ground support refueler in the 1901st Quartermaster Truck Company, a part of the 332nd Fighter Group. In March 2007, I helped secure a replica of the Congressional Gold Medal awarded to the original Tuskegee Airmen, and had it presented to him in a special ceremony on Memorial

Day, 2007. I became a charter member of the local B/Gen Noel F. Parrish Chapter of the Tuskegee Airmen, Inc., and currently am serving as its chaplain. Parrish, a resident of Versailles, Kentucky, was the white general instrumental in getting the Tuskegee Airmen operational during World War II. His wife of later years, Dr. Florence Parrish-St. John, visited with the chapter in November 2008. In an earlier life, when her name was Flo Tucker, she served as organist at the Westminster Presbyterian Church in Gulfport and played the organ on the day its sanctuary was dedicated on October 31, 1965. She grew up in Greenville, Mississippi.

2. "Rev. Dickson Family Moved to Yazoo City," "New Methodist Pastor Assumes Duties Sunday," *Columbian-Progress*, June 23, 1966.

3. "City Schools Face Loss Federal Funds," *Columbian-Progress*, June 23, 1966.

4. Ibid.

5. Harold Howe II letter to Congressman William Colmer, October 1966. In the Wiley Wolfe Papers, Marion County Museum and Archives, hereafter referred to as the Wiley Wolfe Papers. This letter contains the most complete summary of "information concerning the compliance review conducted in Columbia, Mississippi," by the U.S. Department of Health, Education, and Welfare, Office of Education. This letter is the source for information regarding that review and action subsequent to it used in this chapter.

6. Policies and Guidelines for School Desegregation: Hearings—Committee on Rules, House of Representatives, Eighty-ninth Congress, second session of HR Res. 826: A Resolution to Establish a Select Committee to Investigate the Guidelines and Policies of the Commissioner of Education on School Desegregation, September 29 and 30, 196. In the Wiley Wolfe Papers.

7. Howe letter to Colmer, October 1966. In the Wiley Wolfe Papers.

8. "Over 200 Students In Summer School at Marion Central," *Columbian-Progress*, June 23, 1966.

9. "Welcome to Columbia," flyer and notes on parade, July 6, 1966. In the McLean File.

10. Notes of conversation with University of Wisconsin law student, July 8, 1966. In the McLean File.

11. "Funeral Services For Prof. Bowles Set at Lampton," *Columbian-Progress*, July 14, 1966.

12. Chris Watts, e-mail to William G. McAtee, January 16, 2009. In the McAtee Collection.

13. "Funeral Services For Prof. Bowles . . . ," *Columbian-Progress*, July 14, 1966.

14. "An Appeal to the Christian Conscience of the White Citizenship of my Home County, Marion," *Jackson Advocate*, May 28, 1960.

15. "A Fatal Demand," No. 393, Luke 15:11–32, Columbia Presbyterian Church, July 10, 1966.

16. Howe letter to Colmer, October 1966. In the Wiley Wolfe Papers.

17. Dr. Charles L. King, letter to Rev. James V. Johnson, July 1, 1966. In the McAtee Collection.

18. Rev. James V. Johnson, Jr., letter to Dr. Charles L. King, July 14, 1966. In the McAtee Collection.

19. "Pickets March At Furniture Factory," *Columbian-Progress*, July 21, 1966.

20. Copies of parade permits issued by the mayor for July 26, 27, and 29 (none in file for July 25 and 28). In the McLean File.

21. Notes of meeting at city hall between Willis McClenton and the mayor, July 25, 1966; copies of demands, flyer, and notes regarding parade. In the McLean File.

22. Ibid.

23. Ibid.

24. "Columbia mayor discusses problems with Negro leader," reprint from yesterday's final edition, newspaper unknown, July 26, 1966. In the McLean File.

25. Memo, route for second parade, July 26, 1966. In the McLean File.

26. Notes outlining events of second parade, July 26, 1966. In the McLean File.

27. This synod commission had the responsibility of adjudicating all the subsequent complaints and counter-complaints arising from the re-examination of Rev. Mac Hart at a called meeting of the Presbytery of Central Mississippi at Pearl Presbyterian Church, July 9, 1964. William F. Winter served as Chairman of the Commission. Copy of minutes in the McAtee Collection.

28. Notes of steering committee meeting of "loyal ministers," First Presbyterian Church, Starkville, MS, July 26, 1966. Those key "loyal ministers" no longer in the synod: Richard T. Harbison, Robert Lawrence, Spencer C. Murray, Sam B. Laine, Charles L. Stanford, J. Eade Anderson, Murphy C. Wilds, Robert H. Walkup, J. Whitner Kennedy, William S. Blanton, and Russell Nunan. J. Moody McDill and James A. Nisbet had calls outside the synod, but they remained members of presbyteries within it. In the McAtee Collection.

29. Notes regarding third parade, July 27, 1966. In the McLean File.

30. Notes regarding fourth parade, July 28, 1966. In the McLean File.

31. "Both City Pools Closed to Avoid Possible Strife," *Columbian-Progress*, July 28, 1966.

32. William G. McAtee, Letter to Dr. Charles L. King, July 29, 1966. Copy in the McAtee Collection.

33. Notes regarding fifth parade, July 29, 1966. In the McLean File.

34. Notes regarding picketing on Main Street in two groups, August 1–2, 1966. In the McLean File.

35. "Anti-Poverty Projects to Cost $1,000,000 in Tri-County Area," *Columbian-Progress*, August 4, 1966.

36. "Civil Order Is Nation's Right," *Columbian-Progress*, August 4, 1966.

37. Howe letter to Colmer, October 1966. In the Wiley Wolfe Papers.

38. Notes regarding picketing on Main Street, August 6, 1966. In the McLean File.

39. SCRID# 2-31-0-20-1-1-1: Mississippi Sovereignty Commission, "Memorandum from Erle Johnston, Jr., Director, Sovereignty Commission to File, Subject: Ira Grupper," Series 2515: Mississippi State Sovereignty Commission Records, 1994–2006, MDAH, January 9, 2009.

40. Ira Grupper, taped oral history interview conducted by William G. McAtee, Louisville, Kentucky, February 10, 2009.

41. Ira Grupper, taped oral history interview conducted by William G. McAtee, Louisville, Kentucky, April 7, 2009.

42. Agenda for the Community Relations Committee meeting, August 18, 1966. In the McLean File.

43. Howe letter to Colmer, October 1966. In the Wiley Wolfe Papers.

44. "7 Poverty Programs Under Study," *Columbian-Progress*, September 1, 1966.

45. "Improve Baptist Church Ad, Vote Dry," *Columbian-Progress*, August 25, 1966.

46. "An Open Letter to Negro Voters," *Columbian-Progress*, September 1, 1966.

47. "Wanted Experienced Sales Ladies," *Columbian-Progress*, September 1, 1966.

48. "Food Stamp Program Expansion Announced," *Columbian-Progress*, September 15, 1966.

49. "Workers in Food Stamp Program Needed Here," *Columbian-Progress*, September 29, 1966.

50. Purchase contract through Harrison & Bates Residential Sales, Inc., signed September 16, 1966, and accepted September 21, 1966. Copy in the McAtee File.

51. Frank Sinatra (artist), Maxwell Anderson (lyricist) and Kurt Weill (composer), "September Song," *September of My Years*, Concord, 1965.

52. William B. Kennedy and Harmon B. Ramsey, call letter to William G. McAtee, September 22, 1966. In the McAtee Collection.

53. "Rainey Assumes Duties as Chief of City Police," *Columbian-Progress*, October 6, 1966.

54. "Voluntary Compliance or Court Order Makes Little Difference," *Columbian-Progress*, October 20, 1966.

55. Notice of school desegregation plan under Title VI of the Civil Rights Act of 1964, February 14, 1967. In the Wiley Wolfe Papers.

56. B. F. Duncan, superintendent, Letter to Parents, February 14, 1967. In the Wiley Wolfe Papers.

57. Copy of details of the plan in the Wiley Wolfe Papers.

58. SCRID# 2-31-0-22-1-1-1: Mississippi Sovereignty Commission, "Letter from Erle Johnston, Jr., to B. F. Duncan, Superintendent, March 7, 1967," Series 2515: Mississippi State Sovereignty Commission Records, 1994–2006, MDAH, January 9, 2009.

59. "I Believe in the Forgiveness of Sins," No. 371, Matthew 18:15–35; I Corinthians 4:1–13, Columbia Presbyterian Church, Columbia, Mississippi, October 16, 1966: "C'est Finè [*sic*]!"

60. Sinatra, "September Song."

Chapter Ten: Another Reality

1. "Veterans of the Civil Rights Movement—Ira Grupper," April 22, 2008. Available online, http://www.crmvet.org/vet/grupper.htm.

2. Most of what I relate in this chapter comes from this series of oral history interviews I conducted with Ira Grupper on January 19, 2009, February 10, 2009, and April 4, 2009. I also conducted a fourth phone interview with Grupper and Chris Watts on February 28, 2009. Other sources are noted as they occur.

3. "W.J. and Curt" by Ira Grupper, *Labor Paeans*, March 2002, published by FORsyth, newspaper of Louisville, KY, chapter of FOR, the Fellowship of Reconciliation.

4. "Mary Spencer" by Ira Grupper, *Labor Paeans*, November 2008, published by FORsyth, newspaper of Louisville, KY, chapter of FOR, the Fellowship of Reconciliation.

5. "Two Counties, Marion County, Mississippi," by Ira Grupper, ca. February 1966. In the personal collection of Ira Grupper and reprinted by permission in the McAtee Collection.

6. "Discrimination and the Civil Rights Movement by Lillie Lowe-Reid," *Labor Paeans*, in Ira Grupper's column, February 2009, published by FORsyth, newspaper of Louisville, KY, chapter of FOR, the Fellowship of Reconciliation. Lillie Lowe-Reid (Ira knew her as Elaine) notes in the article that she went to college at the University of Southern Mississippi and obtained a bachelors degree in social and rehabilitation services. She began working for a community action agency, assisting the economically disadvantaged and disabled students to obtain work experience, employability skills, and their GEDs. She went back to college in 1998 and completed a degree in the field of education and psychology with a masters in counseling psychology. Since then, she has "worked exclusively with the disabled population, first with Helen Keller Services for the Blind, then the Epilepsy Foundation of America, The Center for Education Advancement, and finally with New Jersey Protection and Advocacy, now Disability Rights New Jersey," where she works today. In this article she said, "Working with these agencies, I still see the need for mainstream America to open up and make room for the talents of hard-working people with disabilities, and not categorize and stereotype those with disabilities." She also said, "One thing that I have learned through all my experiences, is that you can change laws, and laws can change behaviors—but not minds and attitudes. Experiencing the things I did in life made me want to help others who society was not so eager to reach out to."

7. "A Hattiesburg Diary (transcript)," February 9–15, 1964, Civil Rights in Mississippi digital archive, The University of Southern Mississippi, McCain Library and Archives. Available on line, http://anna.lib.usm.edu/~spcol/crda/zeman/zz091 .html.

8. Dwain Epps, e-mail to William G. McAtee, May 9, 2009. In the McAtee Collection.

9. Ira Grupper, taped oral history interview conducted by William G. McAtee, Louisville, Kentucky, February 10, 2009.

Chapter Eleven: Thank You, Mr. Mayor

1. C. David Heymann, *RFK: A Candid Biography of Robert F. Kennedy* (New York: Dutton, 1998), p. 509.

2. Gladwell, *Outliers*, p. 167.

3. Gladwell, *Outliers*, p. 19.

4. See William A. Gamson, *Power and Discontent*. (Homewood, IL: Dorsey Press, 1968), for comprehensive treatment of the concepts of "power" and "influence" and how they function in the context of discontent.

5. "Mayor's Report Shows City Making Progress," *Columbian-Progress*, February 17, 1966.

6. Charles H. Otis, memorandum to all contractors and sub-contractors, early July 1971. In the McLean File.

7. E. D. McLean, Jr., T. C. Griffith Agency, Inc., letter to Mr. Charles H. Otis, Pearl River Valley Opportunity, Inc., July 8, 1971. In the McLean File.

8. E. D. McLean, Jr., Mayor to city employees. In the McLean File.

9. "Earle McLean, Sr. Funeral Services Held Saturday," *Columbian-Progress*, September 24, 1970.

10. "Earl D. 'Buddy' McLean," Obituary, *Columbian-Progress*, January 3, 2002.

11. Christmas card to Buddy McLean from Janet S. Everts, Royal Oak, Michigan, written 12-14-65. In the McLean File.

12. Lengthy handwritten Christmas card to Buddy McLean from Richard Atlee, written 12-21-65. In the McLean File.

13. Robert Frost, "The Road Not Taken," *Mountain Interval* (New York: Henry Holt, 1920), p. 11.

Chapter Twelve: In Search of Truth and Understanding

1. Willie Morris, *North Toward Home* (Oxford, MS: Yoknapatawpha Press, 1982), pp. 127–28.

2. Quote from, "The Red Tops: The Orchestra that Covered the Delta," by Ben E. Bailey, JSTOR: The Black Perspective in Music, Vol. 16, No. 2 (Autumn, 1988), pp. 177–90. Available online, http://www.jstor.org/pss/1214807. "Vicksburg, Mississippi, was a music town before the Civil War, and in the period between the end of the war and the beginning of the twentieth century it became even more important as a musical center . . . . Black bandsmen were an essential part of the tradition . . . . The Red Tops, who became the most popular and innovative dance band in Mississippi during the 1950s, came out of this rich band tradition. Actually, the genesis of the Red Tops was an earlier group, called the Re-Bops, which was organized during WW II. The Re-Bops played mainly on Morrisey's Showboat, which was docked across from Vicksburg on the Louisiana side of the Mississippi River where liquor and gambling were legal. Young whites slipped across the river to indulge in the forbidden pleasures and to listen to the Re-Bops."

Chapter Thirteen: So What?

1. Webster's Collegiate Dictionary, Fifth edition, 1948, p. 50.

2. Ibid., p. 843.

3. Ibid.

4. Roy L. Brooks, *Atonement and Forgiveness: A New Model for Black Reparations* (Berkeley, CA: University of California Press, 2004), p. 144. This work presents a thorough exploration of the slavery redress issue, the dominant models for apologies and reparations, the constitutionality of and opposing arguments regarding reparations, and ways of dealing with the residual effects of prior acts of discrimination.

5. Ibid., pp. 144–45.

6. Ibid., pp. 142–43.

7. Ibid.

8. Ibid., p.143.

9. See Donald W. Shriver, *Honest Patriots*, Chapter 2, "South Africa In the Wake of Remembered Evil."

10. "Calif. Legislator Seeks Apology for Treatment of Chinese Immigrants," *Lexington Herald-Leader*, June 18, 2009.

11. Ibid.

12. "Senate Asks U.S. to Apologize for Slavery," *Lexington Herald-Leader*, June 19, 2009.

13. Genevieve Jacques, *Beyond Impunity* (Geneva, Switzerland: WCC Publications, 2000), p. 1.

14. Ibid., pp. 1–3.

15. Douglas A. Blackmon, *Slavery by Another Name* (New York: Doubleday, 2008), pp. 4–5.

16. Ibid., pp. 5–6.

17. Ibid., p. 9.

18. Ibid., p. 8.

19. Ibid., p. 396.

20. Jacques, *Beyond Impunity*, p. xiii.

21. "Civil Rights-Era Cold Case Initiative: FBI Investigates Unsolved Pre-1969 Murders," by Charles Montaldo, About.com. Available online, http://www.ask.com/bar?q=civil+rights+cold+cases&page=1&qsrc=2417&ab=4&u=http%3A%2F%2Fcrime.about.com%2Fb%2F2009%2F03%2F04%2Fcivil-rights-cold-cases-re-opened.htm.

22. "What is Normal Distribution?" Available on line, http://www.children's-mercy.org/stats/definitions/normal_dist.htm. The "bell shaped curve mathematical theory" states that the greater the concentration of a value expressed in the center (median) of the curve, the lesser probability that unusually extreme expressions of that value will be produced in either direction from the center. Conversely, the lesser concentrated at the center, the greater probability of unusually extreme expressions at both ends of the spectrum. In both cases the probability of distribution is comparable and symmetrical in both directions.

23. *The Book of Common Worship*, Second Order of Morning Worship, (Philadelphia, PA: Board of Christian Education of the Presbyterian Church in the United States, 1946), p. 21.

24. Ibid.

25. Dwain Epps, e-mail to William G. McAtee, February 9, 2009. In the McAtee Collection.

26. In the course of conducting oral history interviews for this project, on two occasions persons in the African American community I talked with in Columbia who had lived through the 1960s would not give me permission to quote them directly. Neither would they sign interview release forms so that I could give the tapes to the University of Southern Mississippi's archives.

27. The writing of this book began shortly after this country elected its first African American president in 2008. It was submitted to the publisher shortly after the 2010 mid-term election that many said was a referendum on the president.

Whether that sentiment had to with his policies or the color of his skin, one can only speculate. What was clear, however, was that blatant racism shook its ugly head unchecked in many campaign incidents, raising the stakes for future battles for racial reconciliation.

Epilogue

1. "Justices Attack Voting Rights Act," *Lexington Herald-Leader*, April 30, 2009.

2. "Voting Rights Act Needs Update for Changing Times," *Lexington Herald-Leader*, May 5, 2009.

3. "Voting Right Act Loosened," *Lexington Herald-Leader*, June 23, 2009.

4. Anthony Walton, *Mississippi: An American Journey* (New York, NY: Alfred A. Knopf, 1996), p. 162.

5. Ibid., p. 163.

6. *Obsequiers of Rev. A. G. Payton, 1906–1969*. In the McAtee Collection.

7. Mamie Heinz, letter to Rev. William G. McAtee, August 5, 1967. In the McAtee File in the Marion County Museum and Archives.

8. Chris Watts, e-mail to William G. McAtee, February 9, 2009. In the McAtee Collection.

9. L. Z. Blankinship, letter to William G. McAtee, August 24, 1967. In the McAtee File in Marion County Museum and Archives.

10. "Nixon Assistant Meets With Blankenship, Says Agnew Spoke in Ignorance," *Progress Report*, March 1969. In the McAtee File in the Marion County Museum and Archives.

11. "Rev. N. A. Dickson," *Columbian-Progress*, April 13, 2000.

12. Dwain C. Epps, e-mail to William G. McAtee, July 4, 2009. In the McAtee Collection.

13. Chris Watts, e-mail to William G. McAtee, February 2, 2009. In the McAtee Collection.

14. Dr. Russell Bush, Jr., letter to William G. McAtee, February 12, 2009. In the McAtee Collection. Also, Bush taped phone oral history interview, February 19, 2009.

15. "Business," *History of Marion County, MS*. Marion County Historical Society, 1976, p. 96.

16. "Veterans of the Civil Rights Movement—Ira Grupper," April 22, 2008. Available online, http://www.crmvet.org/vet/grupper.htm.

17. Ibid.

18. Ira Grupper, "W.J. and Curt," *Labor Paeans*, March 2002. Published by FORsyth, newspaper of Louisville, KY, chapter of FOR, the Fellowship of Reconciliation.

19. SCRID# 1-102-16-2-1-1: Mississippi Sovereignty Commission, "List of Committee Appointed by SCLC to Present Demands to Governor John Bell Williamson June 23, 1969," Series 2515: Mississippi State Sovereignty Commission Records, 1994–2006, MDAH, January 9, 2009.

20. Ira Grupper, "W. J. and Curt," *Labor Paeans*, March 2002.

21. Chris Watts, e-mail to William G. McAtee, July 7, 2009. In the McAtee Collection.

Bibliography

A. Books

Alvis, Joel L., Jr. *Religion and Race: Southern Presbyterians, 1946–1983.* Tuscaloosa, AL: University of Alabama Press, 1994.

Baylor, Orval W. "Early Commerce in Washington County," Chap. 9 in *Early Times in Washington County Kentucky,* Cynthiana, KY: Hobson Press, 1942.

Blackmon, Douglas A. *Slavery by Another Name.* New York, NY: Doubleday, 2008.

Braden, Anne. *The Wall Between.* New York, NY: Monthly Review Press, 1958.

Brooks, Roy L. *Atonement and Forgiveness: A New Model for Black Reparations.* Berkeley: University of California Press, 2004.

Campbell, Will D. *Brother to a Dragon Fly.* New York, NY: Seabury Press, 1977.

———. *Providence.* Atlanta, GA: Longstreet Press, 1992.

Davies, David R., ed. *The Press and Race.* Jackson, MS: University Press of Mississippi, 2001.

Doyle, William. *An American Insurrection: The Battle of Oxford, Mississippi, 1962.* New York, NY: Doubleday, 2001.

East, P. D. *The Magnolia Jungle: The Life, times and Education of a Southern Editor.* New York, NY: Simon and Schuster, 1960.

Frost, Robert. "The Road Not Taken," *Mountain Interval.* New York, NY: Henry Holt, 1920.

Gamson, William A. *Power and Discontent.* Homewood, IL: Dorsey Press, 1968.

Gladwell, Malcolm. *Outliers: The Story of Success.* New York, NY: Little, Brown and Company, 2008.

Harper, Charles, ed. *Impunity: An Ethical Perspective.* Geneva, Switzerland: WCC Publications, 1996.

Haskins, Jim. *I Have a Dream: The Life and Words of Martin Luther King, Jr.* Brookfield, CT: Millbrook Press, 1992.

Heymann, C. David. *RFK: A Candid Biography of Robert F. Kennedy.* New York, NY: Dutton, 1998.

History of Marion County, MS. The Mississippi Rural Center. Marion County Historical Society, 1976.

Huey, Gary. *Rebel With A Cause: P. D. East, Southern Liberalism, and the Civil Rights Movement 1953–1971.* Wilmington, DE: Scholarly Resources, 1985.

Jacques, Genevieve. *Beyond Impunity.* Geneva, Switzerland: WCC Publications, 2000.

———. *Resisting the Intolerable: Guided by a Human Rights Compass.* Trans. Nathan Lechler. Geneva, Switzerland: WCC Publications, 2007.

Johnston, Erle. *I Rolled With Ross: A Political Portrait*. Baton Rouge, LA: Moran Publishing, 1980.

——. *Mississippi's Defiant Years: 1953–1973*. Forest, MS: Lake Harbor Publishers, 1990.

——. *Politics: Mississippi Style, Book One 1911–1979*. Forest, MS: Lake Harbor Publishers, 1993.

Lomax, Alan. *The Land Where the Blues Began*. New York, NY: Dell, 1993.

McAdam, Doug. *Freedom Summer*. New York, NY: Oxford University Press, 1988.

McAtee, William G. *Dreams, Where Have You Gone? Clues for Unity and Hope*. Louisville, KY: Witherspoon Press, 2006.

Meacham, Jon. *American Lion: Andrew Jackson in the White House*. New York, NY: Random House, 2008.

Mellon, James. *Bullwhip Days: The Slaves Remember: An Oral History*. New York, NY: Grove Press, 2002.

Mullins, Andrew P., Jr., ed. *The Measure of Our Days: Writings of William F. Winter*. Jackson, MS: William Winter Institute for Racial Reconciliation, University of Mississippi, Distributed by University Press of Mississippi, 2006.

Sample, Tex. *Ministry in an Oral Culture: Living with Will Rogers, Uncle Remus, & Minnie Pearl*. Louisville, KY: Westminster/John Knox Press, 1994.

Shriver, Donald W. *Honest Patriots: Loving a Country Enough to Remember Its Misdeeds*. New York, NY: Oxford University Press, 2005.

——, ed. *The Unsilent South: Prophetic Preaching in Racial Crises*. Richmond, VA: John Knox Press, 1965.

Strauss, William, and Neil Howe, *Generations: The History of America's Future, 1584–2069*. New York, NY: William Morrow, 1991.

The Book of Common Worship, Second Order of Morning Worship. Philadelphia, PA: Board of Christian Education of the Presbyterian Church in the United States, 1946.

Thompson, Barbara R. *Just Plain Bill*. Decatur, GA: Pathway Communications Group, 1996.

Walton, Anthony. *Mississippi: An American Journey*. New York, NY: Alfred A. Knopf, 1996.

Webster's Collegiate Dictionary, Fifth edition. Springfield, ME: C & G Merriam Co., 1948.

Webster's New World Dictionary, College edition. Cleveland, OH, and New York, NY: World Publishing, 1959.

Wilkie, Curtis. *The Fall of the House of Zeus: The Rise and Ruin of America's Most Powerful Trial Lawyer*. New York, NY: Crown, 2010.

B. Court Documents

"Answer of Respondent, City of Columbia, to Petition For Removal." Filed In the United States District Court for the Southern District of Mississippi, Hattiesburg Division. Criminal Action No. 1394. February 5, 1966.

"Respondent's Motion To Remand." Filed In the United States District Court for the Southern District of Mississippi, Hattiesburg Division. Criminal Action No. 1393. February 5, 1966.

C. Electronic Resources

"The 24th Amendment Ended the Poll Tax January 23, 1964." Available online, http://
www.americaslibrary.gov/jb/modern/jb_modern_polltax_1.html.

"A Hattiesburg Diary (transcript)," February 9–15, 1964. Civil Rights in Mississippi
Digital Archive, University of Southern Mississippi, McCain Library and Archives.
Available on line, http://anna.lib.usm.edu/~spcol/crda/zeman/zz091.html.

"An Overview of the Crisis." Available online, http://www.library.thinkquest.org/
11046/days/index/html.

Bullwhip Days: The Slaves Remember: An Oral History. Review available online,
http//books.google.com/books?id=JL4iDpT7acwC&pg=PA178&dq=Charley+
Moses,+Mississippi&source=bl&ots=yZQFVhrGwp&sig=66w2XlpT-vY4slk7
TYtqmwthbT8&hl=en&ei=igQuSqekMMOK_Qbb69DDCg&sa=X&oi=book_
result&ct=result&resnum=1.

"Civil Rights Act of 1964." Available online, http://www.spartacus.schoolnet.co.uk/
USAcivil64.htm.

"Civil Rights-Era Cold Case Initiative: FBI Investigates Unsolved Pre-1969 Murders,"
by Charles Montaldo, About.com. Available online, http://www.ask.com/bar?q=civ
il+rights+cold+cases&page=1&qsrc=2417&ab=4&u=http%3A%2F%2Fcrime.about
.com%2Fb%2F2009%2F03%2F04%2Fcivil-rights-cold-cases-re-opened.htm.

"Dr. Gilbert R. Mason, Sr. (1929–2006), As remembered by Ira Grupper." Available
online, http://www.crmvet.org/mem/masong.htm.

"Early Settlements." Available online, http://www.msgw.org/lamar/WPA/marion/
MAR7.htm.

"The Great Migration to the Mississippi Territory," by Charles Lowery, Available
online, http://mshistory.k12.ms.us/articles/169/the-great-migration-to-the
-mississippi-territory-1798-1819.

Grupper (Ira) and Beech (Bob) civil rights collection. Unprocessed manuscript
collection. Available online, http://www.lib.usm.edu/legacy/archives/grupper.htm.

"Invasion at Bay of Pigs." Available online, http://www.historyof cuba.com/history/
baypigs/pigs3.htm.

"Korean War Timeline." Available online, http://www.rt66.com/~korteng/SmallArms/
TimeLine.htm.

"Marion County History." Available online, http://www.mcdp.info/area/history.html.

"The Mississippi State Sovereignty Commission: An Agency History." Available online,
http://mshistory.k12.ms.us/articles/243/mississippi-sovereignty-commission-an
-agency-history.

"Paul Burney Johnson, Jr.: Fifty-fourth Governor of Mississippi: 1964–1968." Available
online, http://mshistory.k12.ms.us/index.php?s=extra&id=151.

Plessy v. Ferguson. Available online, http://www.bgsu.edu/departments/acs/1890s/
plessy/plessy.html.

"Profile of Marion County," SNCC Research, June 30, 1965. Available
online, http://digilib.usm.edu/cdm4/document.php?CISOROOT=/
manu&CISOPTR=4462&REC=10.

"The Red Tops: The Orchestra that Covered the Delta," by Ben E. Bailey. JSTOR: The
Black Perspective in Music, Vol. 16, No. 2 (Autumn, 1988). Available online: http://
www.jstor.org/pss/1214807.

"Some Historic Homes in Mississippi," Mrs. N. D. Deupree. Publications of the Mississippi Historical Society. Published by the Society, 1903. Available online, http://books.google.com/books?id=AkkTAAAAYAAJ&pg=PA334&lpg=PA334&dq =Ford+House+Marion+County+Mississippi&source=bl&ots=m2wK69W7Cu&sig= IUu1RStVg3d679jeXHrzEZxoSXU&hl=en&ei=p8EaSsXcCMrJtgea8cjhDA&sa=X&o i=book_result&ct=result&resnum=2#PPA335,M1.

Statistics on slave transfers from 1790 to 1850. Available online, http://www2.census .gov/prod2/decennial/documents/00165897ch14.pdf.

"Territory of Mississippi, 1798–1817." Available online, http://www.tngenweb.org/ maps/ms-terr.html.

"Treaty of Mount Dexter." Available online, http://www.rootsweb.ancestry.com /~msalhn/NativeAmerican/treatymountdexter1805.htm, and http://www .choctaw.org/History/Treaties/treaty5.html.

"Veterans of the Civil Rights Movement—Ira Grupper." April 22, 2008. Available online, http://www.crmvet.org/vet/grupper.htm.

"The Voting Rights Act of 1965." Available online, http://www.ourdocuments.gov/doc .php?doc=100.

D. Files, Papers, Collections

E. D. McLean, Jr. "Race Relations," file in Marion County Museum and Archives. Agendas, cards, letters, memoranda, meeting notes, resolutions, and telegrams.

Wiley Wolfe Papers, in Marion County Museum and Archives. Letters, notices, policies, and guidelines for school desegregation.

William G. McAtee, personal collection. E-mails, letters, meeting notes, reports, theses, unpublished manuscripts, and miscellaneous items.

E. Minutes

Minutes of the One-Hundred-Fourth General Assembly (PCUS). Montreat, NC, April 23–28, 1964.

Minutes of the One-Hundred-Fifth General Assembly (PCUS). Montreat, NC, April 21–26, 1965.

Minutes of the One-Hundred-Sixth General Assembly (PCUS). Montreat, NC, April 21–26, 1966.

Minutes of the Synod of Mississippi Special Judicial Commission, August 10, 1965, September 7, 1965, and September 14, 1965.

F. Mississippi State Sovereignty Commission

(Courtesy of Mississippi Department of Archives and History)

SCRID# 1-102-16-2-1-1: Mississippi Sovereignty Commission, "List of Committee Appointed by SCLC to Present Demands to Governor John Bell Williamson June 23,

1969," Series 2515: Mississippi State Sovereignty Commission Records, 1994–2006, Mississippi Department of Archives and History, January 9, 2009.

SCRID# 2-31-0-11-1-1-1: Mississippi Sovereignty Commission, "Marion County-Columbia," January 12, 1961, Series 2515: Mississippi State Sovereignty Commission Records, 1994–2006, Mississippi Department of Archives and History, January 9, 2009.

SCRID# 2-31-0-18-1-1-1: Mississippi Sovereignty Commission, "NAACP And COFO Activity in Lawrence, Walthall, and Marion Counties," November 23, 24, 1964, Series 2515: Mississippi State Sovereignty Commission Records, 1994–2006, Mississippi Department of Archives and History, January 9, 2009.

SCRID# 2-31-0-19-1-1-1: Mississippi Sovereignty Commission, "Investigation of a report that the Freedom Democratic Party would have a meeting on the night of Thursday, October 7, 1965," Date of Report, October 8, 1965, Series 2515: Mississippi State Sovereignty Commission Records, 1994–2006, Mississippi Department of Archives and History, January 9, 2009.

SCRID# 2-31-0-20-1-1-1: Mississippi Sovereignty Commission, "Memorandum from Erle Johnston, Jr., Director, Sovereignty Commission to File, Subject: Ira Grupper," Series 2515: Mississippi State Sovereignty Commission Records, 1994–2006, Mississippi Department of Archives and History, January 9, 2009.

SCRID# 2-31-0-22-1-1-1: Mississippi Sovereignty Commission, "Letter from Erle Johnston, Jr., to B. F. Duncan, Superintendent, March 7, 1967," Series 2515: Mississippi State Sovereignty Commission Records, 1994–2006, Mississippi Department of Archives and History, January 9, 2009.

SCRID# 2-150-1-49-1-1-1: Mississippi Sovereignty Commission, "Two Counties: Marion County Mississippi, by Ira Grupper, (c. February 1966)," Series 2515: Mississippi State Sovereignty Commission Records, 1994–2006, Mississippi Department of Archives and History, January 9, 2009.

SCRID# 2-163-0-19-4-1-1: Mississippi Sovereignty Commission, "Letters," Freedom Information Service Mississippi Newsletter, Number Fifty-Three, Box 120, Tougaloo, MS 39174, April 5, 1969, pages four-five," Series 2515: Mississippi State Sovereignty Commission Records, 1994–2006, Mississippi Department of Archives and History, January 9, 2009.

G. Periodicals and Newspapers

Atlanta Constitution. Atlanta, GA.
Clarion-Ledger. Jackson, MS.
Columbian-Progress. Columbia, MS.
Commercial Appeal. Memphis, TN.
Jackson Advocate. Jackson, MS.
Jackson Daily News. Jackson, MS.
Journal of Mississippi History. Mississippi Department of Archives and History. Jackson, MS.
Hattiesburg American. Hattiesburg, MS.

Labor Paeans. Published by FORsyth, newspaper of Louisville, KY, chapter of FOR, the Fellowship of Reconciliation.

Lexington Herald Leader. Lexington, KY.

McComb Enterprise Journal. McComb, MS.

Presbyterian Life. New York, NY.

Presbyterian Outlook. Richmond, VA.

Progress Report. Columbia, MS.

San Rafael Independent Journal. San Rafael, CA.

Times-Picayune. New Orleans, LA.

H. Programs, Booklets, Speeches

"A Christian View on Segregation." Rev. G. T. Gillespie, D. D., president emeritus of Belhaven College. Made before the Synod of Mississippi of the Presbyterian Church in the U.S. November 4, 1954. Reprint by Citizens' Council, 254 East Griffith Street, Jackson, MS 39202.

Forty-ninth Annual Session of the South Mississippi Baptist State Convention. Dr. R. W. Woullard, president. Owens Chapel Baptist Church, 1223 Marion Avenue, Columbia, MS. November 10–12, 1965.

An [sic] Historical Sketch of the Columbia Presbyterian Church. Fiftieth Anniversary. Columbia Presbyterian Church, Columbia, MS, 1910–1960. Designed and Compiled by Mary Wolfe, 1960.

John F. Kennedy Memorial, E. D. McLean, Jr. Columbia Presbyterian Church, Columbia, MS. November 23, 1963.

Obsequiers of Rev. A. G. Payton, 1906–1969. In the personal collection of William G. McAtee.

The Oxford Disaster . . . Price of Defiance. Rep. Karl Wiesenburg. Reprint (December 31, 1962) of articles appearing in the *Chronicle*, Pascagoula, MS, December 17–21, 1962.

Separation—Only Permanent Solution of the Race Question. Speeches of Senator Theodore G. Bilbo of Mississippi in the Senate of the United States, June 27, 28, July 3, 6, 24, and 28, 1945. United States Government Printing Office, Washington, DC, 1945. Not printed at government expense.

The War; Constitutional Government; and the Race Issue—America's Greatest Unsolved Domestic Problem. Address by Senator Bilbo Before a Joint Session of the Mississippi Legislature, March 22, 1944. Extension of Remarks of Hon. Theodore G. Bilbo of Mississippi in the Senate of the United States, April 17, 1944. United States Government Printing Office, Washington, DC, 1945. Not printed at government expense.

I. Recorded Albums

Simon, Paul (composer/lyricist/artist) and Art Garfunkle (artist). "The Sounds of Silence," *Sounds of Silence.* Columbia, 1965.

Sinatra, Frank (artist), Maxwell Anderson (lyricist) and Kurt Weill (composer). "September Song," *September of My Years*. Concord, 1965.

Sinatra, Frank (artist), Patricia Johnston, Patricia and Don Raye (lyricists), Gene De Paul (composer), "I'll Remember April," *Complete Capitol Singles Collection*. Capitol, 1996.

J. Taped Oral History Interviews

Bush, Dr. Russell, Jr. Taped phone oral history interview conducted by William G. McAtee. Columbia, MS. February 19, 2009.

Foxworth, Marilyn Dickson. Taped phone oral history interview conducted by William G. McAtee. February 16, 2009.

Grupper, Ira. Taped oral history interview conducted by William G. McAtee. Louisville, KY. January 19, 2009.

———. Taped oral history interview conducted by William G. McAtee. Louisville, KY. February 10, 2009.

———. Taped oral history interview conducted by William G. McAtee. Louisville, KY. April 7, 2009.

Grupper, Ira, and Chris Watts. Taped oral history interview conducted by William G. McAtee. February 28, 2009.

K. Unpublished Papers

Daniels, Gennett, C. D. M. "A History of Blacks Contributing to the Progress of Marion County." Complied by Gennett. Columbia, MS. Unpublished paper. In the Marion County Museum and Archives.

Index